SINGAPORE

12TH EDITION

Where to Stay and Eat
for All Budgets

Must-See Sights
and Local Secrets

Ratings You Can Trust

Fodor's Travel Publications   New York, Toronto, London, Sydney, Auckland
www.fodors.com

B&T   6/05
mw

FODOR'S SINGAPORE
Editor: Pamela Lee

Editorial Production: Jacinta O'Halloran
Editorial Contributors: Candice Foo, Tracey Furniss, Satu Hummasti, Ilsa Sharp, Josie Taylor
Maps: David Lindroth, *cartographer;* Bob Blake and Rebecca Baer, *map editors*
Design: Fabrizio La Rocca, *creative director;* Guido Caroti, *art director;* Moon Sun Kim, *cover designer;* Melanie Marin, *senior photo editor*
Production/Manufacturing: Colleen Ziemba
Cover Photo: R. Ian Lloyd/Masterfile

SPECIAL SALES
This book is available for special discounts for bulk purchases for sales promotions or premiums. Special editions, including personalized covers, excerpts of existing books, and corporate imprints, can be created in large quantities for special needs. For more information, write to Special Markets/Premium Sales, 1745 Broadway, MD 6-2, New York, New York 10019, or e-mail specialmarkets@ randomhouse.com.

AN IMPORTANT TIP & AN INVITATION
Although all prices, opening times, and other details in this book are based on information supplied to us at press time, changes occur all the time in the travel world, and Fodor's cannot accept responsibility for facts that become outdated or for inadvertent errors or omissions. So **always confirm information when it matters,** especially if you're making a detour to visit a specific place. Your experiences—positive and negative—matter to us. If we have missed or misstated something, **please write to us.** We follow up on all suggestions. Contact the Singapore editor at editors@fodors.com or c/o Fodor's at 1745 Broadway, New York, New York 10019.

PRINTED IN THE UNITED STATES OF AMERICA

10 9 8 7 6 5 4 3 2 1

DESTINATION
SINGAPORE

With myriad ethnic groups crammed into its 263 square miles, Singapore is a city of many faces. All in the same day, you can tour Chinese shophouses offering everything from ginseng to frog porridge, eat fiery South Indian curry, sit down at a sushi bar or pizzeria, listen to a bit of Bach by a Western-style orchestra, or shop for Gucci handbags and skin-tight jeans in chrome-and-glass malls as a Malay muezzin beckons Muslim faithful to prayer in the distance. With so many different voices and languages, and such diversity of religion and culture, Singapore is understandably a city of contradictions: a multicultural, ever-changing metropolis that still nods to its colonial beginnings; a bastion of capitalism sustained by an energetic (sometimes frenetic) people, an orderly city that champions the indulgence of simple pleasures, while simultaneously creating safety valves for those who like to walk on the wilder side.

Tim Jarrell, Publisher

CONTENTS

Maps

CloseUps

ABOUT THIS BOOK

The best source for travel advice is a like-minded friend who's just been where you're headed. But with or without that friend, you'll be in great shape to find your way around your destination once you learn to find your way around your Fodor's guide.

SELECTION

Our goal is to cover the best properties, sights, and activities in their category, as well as the most interesting communities to visit. We make a point of including local food-lovers' hot spots as well as neighborhood options, and we avoid all that's touristy unless it's really worth your time. You can go on the assumption that everything in this book is recommended wholeheartedly by our writers and editors. Flip to On the Road with Fodor's to learn more about who they are. It goes without saying that no property pays to be included.

RATINGS

Orange stars ★ denote sights and properties that our editors and writers consider the very best in the area covered by the entire book. These, the best of the best, are listed in the Fodor's Choice section in the front of the book. Black stars ★ highlight the sights and properties we deem Highly Recommended, the don't-miss sights within any region. In cities, sights pinpointed with numbered map bullets ❶ in the margins tend to be more important than those without bullets.

SPECIAL SPOTS

Pleasures & Pastimes and text on chapter title pages focus on experiences that reveal the spirit of the destination. Also watch for Off the Beaten Path sights. Some are out of the way, some are quirky, and all are worthwhile. When the munchies hit, look for Need a Break? suggestions.

TIME IT RIGHT

Check On the Calendar up front and chapters' Timing sections for weather and crowd overviews and best days and times to visit.

SEE IT ALL

Use Fodor's exclusive Great Itineraries as a model for your trip. Either follow those that begin the book, or mix regional itineraries from several chapters. In cities, Good Walks guide you to important sights in each neighborhood; ⌐ indicates the starting points of walks and itineraries in the text and on the map.

BUDGET WELL

Hotel and restaurant price categories from ¢ to $$$$ are defined in the opening pages of each chapter—expect to find a balanced selection for every budget. For attractions, we always give standard adult admission fees; reductions are usually available for children, students, and senior citizens. Look in Discounts & Deals in Smart Travel Tips for information on destination-wide ticket schemes. Want to pay with plastic? AE, D, DC, MC, V following restaurant and hotel listings indicate whether American Express, Discover, Diners Club, MasterCard, or Visa are accepted.

BASIC INFO

Smart Travel Tips lists travel essentials for the entire area covered by the book; city- and region-specific basics end each chapter. To find the best way to get around, see the transportation section; see individual modes of travel ("Car Travel," "Train Travel") for details.

ON THE MAPS	Maps throughout the book show you what's where and help you find your way around. Black and orange numbered bullets ❶ ❶ in the text correlate to bullets on maps.
BACKGROUND	We give background information within the chapters in the course of explaining sights as well as in CloseUp boxes and in Understanding Singapore at the end of the book.
FIND IT FAST	Within the Exploring Singapore chapter, sights are grouped by neighborhood, and neighborhoods are arranged in a roughly clockwise direction starting with Colonial Singapore in the eastern part of the city. The Side Trips from Singapore section is included in this chapter. Where to Eat and Where to Stay are also organized by neighborhood—Where to Eat is further divided by cuisine type. The Nightlife & the Arts and Sports & the Outdoors chapters are arranged alphabetically by entertainment type. Within Shopping, a description of the city's main shopping districts is followed by a list of specialty shops grouped according to their focus. The Side Trips from Singapore section, covered in Exploring, explores the East and West coasts, nature spots, and offshore islands like Sentosa.
DON'T FORGET	Restaurants are open for lunch and dinner daily unless we state otherwise; we mention dress only when there's a specific requirement and reservations only when they're essential or not accepted—it's always best to book ahead. Hotels have private baths, phones, TVs, and air-conditioning and operate on the European Plan (a.k.a. EP, meaning without meals). We always list facilities but not whether you'll be charged extra to use them, so when pricing accommodations, find out what's included.
SYMBOLS	

Many Listings
- ★ Fodor's Choice
- ★ Highly recommended
- ⊠ Physical address
- ✚ Directions
- ⌖ Mailing address
- ☎ Telephone
- 🖷 Fax
- ⊕ On the Web
- ✉ E-mail
- 🖼 Admission fee
- ☉ Open/closed times
- ► Start of walk/itinerary
- Ⓜ Metro stations
- ▭ Credit cards

Outdoors
- ⚑ Golf
- ⚑ Camping

Hotels & Restaurants
- 🏨 Hotel
- 🛏 Number of rooms
- ⚘ Facilities
- ⑩ Meal plans
- ✕ Restaurant
- ⚘ Reservations
- 🏛 Dress code
- ⚲ Smoking
- ⚲ BYOB
- ✕🏨 Hotel with restaurant that warrants a visit

Other
- ℃ Family-friendly
- 🔒 Contact information
- ⇨ See also
- ⊠ Branch address
- ☞ Take note

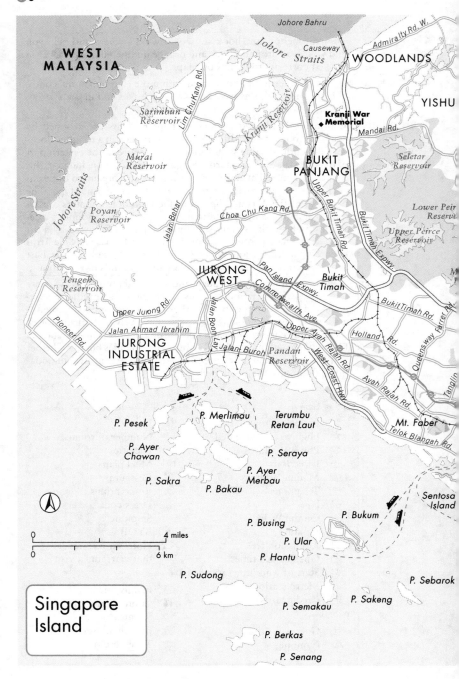

Singapore Island

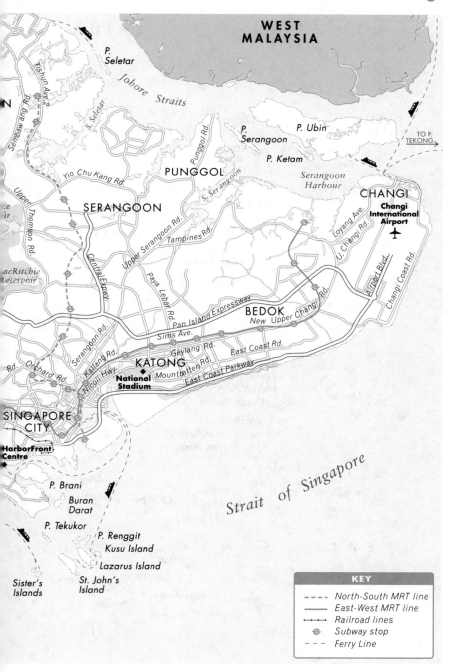

KEY

---- North-South MRT line
—— East-West MRT line
+---+ Railroad lines
⊖ Subway stop
--- Ferry Line

Southeast
Asia

Taipei

TAIWAN

PACIFIC

LUZON

Quezon City

Manila

PHILIPPINES

MINDORO

PALAU

PANAY Iloilo

SAMAR

Bacolod

Cebu

NEGROS

MINDANAO

Sulu Sea

Davao

OCEAN

Celebes Sea

HALMAHERA

PAPUA-
NEW GUINEA

Makassar Strait

SULUWESI
(The Celebes)

T
H
E

BURU   *SERAM*

IRIAN JAYA

Ujung
Pandang

Banda Sea

*KEPULAUAN
ARU*

Flores Sea

SER SUNDA ISLANDS

*KEPULAUAN
TANIMBAR*

FLORES

EAST TIMOR

SUMBA

TIMOR

Timor Sea

AUSTRALIA

ON THE ROAD WITH FODOR'S

Our success in showing you every corner of the Singapore area is a credit to our extraordinary writers. Although there's no substitute for travel advice from a good friend who knows your style, our contributors are the next best thing—the kind of people you would poll for travel advice if you knew them.

Candice Foo, who updated the Exploring chapter, is a passionate globetrotter who calls faithful Singapore home. Her expert knowledge of Singapore comes from her desire to probe every nook and cranny of her home base. A perennial tour guide to friends in transit, Candice is a freelance writer and photographer who has worked for several magazines.

Tracey Furniss, who updated Where to Stay, has lived in Southeast Asia for most of her life, mainly in Hong Kong with spells in Malaysia and Singapore. She started out writing for various magazines in Hong Kong, then went on to work in radio and television, including six years at CNN. She now presides as editor of *The Parents' Journal* in Hong Kong and writes for the *South China Morning Post.* Tracey freelances for various publications in the United Kingdom and the United States, and has worked on *Fodor's Hong Kong.*

Ilsa Sharp is a freelance writer and Chinese Studies graduate formerly based in Singapore from 1968 to '98 who now commutes regularly to the region from her base in Western Australia. She is the author of several books on the history, culture, and wildlife of Singapore and the Asia-Pacific region.

For more than a decade Josie Taylor, who updated Where to Eat, Shopping, and Smart Travel Tips, has been on a epicurean Singapore adventure; from its hawker stalls to its five star culinary pleasures. When not feasting, she can be found boosting the national economy through some indulgent retail therapy across the island. Josie recovers from her road to excess at one of her bases in either Hong Kong or Bali.

The diamond-shape island of the Republic of Singapore, lying offshore but connected by a causeway to peninsular Malaysia, is only 267 square mi (692.7 square km), including its 63 smaller satellite islands, and yet it has nature reserves, a thriving metropolis, ethnic enclaves, industrial parks, beaches, and entertainment parks. Slightly more than 4 million people now live in Singapore, of which just over 3 million are citizens. The ancestors of most Singaporeans arrived from all points of the compass within the past 200 years. They brought cultural diversity, which shaped Singapore's evolution into today's vibrant ethnic mix.

By adroitly manipulating rivalries within the local Malay sultanate, Sir Thomas Stamford Raffles realized his goal of developing Singapore into a trading center for the East India Company. The island's commanding position on the Straits of Malacca and its safe anchorage in the southwestern harbor at the mouth of the Singapore River made it an ideal vantage point for this British commercial emporium. Singapore was to be a cauldron of sweat and toil. Paramount to maintaining a smooth trading operation was the prevention of racial strife. From Raffles's perspective, racial harmony was best achieved by geographical segregation: the resident Malays, the Europeans attracted to Singapore by his vision, and the Chinese and Indian workers imported to turn his dream into reality, were each allotted separate domains in the new settlement. The vestiges of these racial divisions are still apparent.

Colonial Singapore

Since the most desirable land lay to the east of the river and overlooking the waterfront, Raffles designated it as the domain of the British and their administration. Here, in Colonial Singapore, is what's left of the work of the Irish architect George Coleman, who with Raffles created one of the major entrepôts in Asia. Coleman's Palladian-style buildings now serve as a buffer zone between the glitz of Orchard Road and the old ethnic quarter of Chinatown.

Central Business District

Designed by contemporary planners as the new downtown, the Central Business District (CBD) runs along the waterfront in the Marina/Raffles Boulevard area. You can see some exciting, if somewhat coldly contemporary, architecture here. I. M. Pei designed Raffles City as well as the Oversea-Chinese Banking Corporation Centre in Raffles Place. The striking prickled domes of the Esplanade–Theatres on the Bay are here, as well as several refurbished colonial structures. There's the magnificent, riverfront Fullerton Hotel and Cavenagh Bridge. Still, the romance of the colonial waterfront once haunted by old sea-dogs like Joseph Conrad has largely been supplanted by modern buildings, though it lingers in pockets like "Change Alley" (Clifford Quay), once lined by sidewalk money changers.

Chinatown

The Chinese, on whose backs Singapore's trade depended, were allotted the area south of the Singapore River. Arriving with no money and in debt to the boat captains who brought them, these immigrants sought shelter with those who came from the same region, forming concentrations in specific areas of Chinatown (e.g., the Cantonese in Telok Ayer). Rows of shophouses (bilevel buildings with a store or a factory at ground level and living space upstairs); streets specializing in such particularities as herbal medicines; elaborate temples to the gods of the old country; and wet markets maintain the flavor of Raffles's day.

Little India

Land to the east and north of Colonial Singapore beginning at Sungei Road was allotted to the Indian community. While many Indians came as convict labor and later taught crafts, others came to work as traders, clerks, teachers, and moneylenders. Many of them shared the Hindu religion, and here, in what is known as Little India, you'll find several ornate temples. The whole area, especially the streets branching off Serangoon Road, is perfumed with smells of spices and curries, colored by women wearing saris, and crammed with stores selling goods from the Indian subcontinent.

Arab District

Slightly to the east of Little India, bordered by Beach and North Bridge roads, is the Arab District, also known by its older name Kampong Glam. Though Malays lived in *kampongs* (small village-style communities) throughout the island, this area was assigned to Malays (and Muslim traders) who wanted to be close to the action or to the sultan's Istana residence. Streets named Bussorah and Kandahar not only evoke images of the Muslim world, but also provide excellent shopping for imported batiks, Indonesian crafts, chili sambals, and coconut-milk curries.

Orchard Road

Modern, fashion-conscious Singapore is north and slightly west of Colonial Singapore. Orchard Road, its main street, is like New York's Fifth Avenue or London's Regent Street. There are countless glittering shopping plazas and hotels in what long ago was an agricultural area of experimental spice farms and gardens.

Side Trips

The East and West Coasts. Out of the central city, the East Coast Parkway runs toward Changi Airport and the infamous Changi Prison. This area encompasses such significant ethnic areas as Geylang, Katong, and Joo Chiat, as well as the iconic National Stadium. Along this coast are the best, albeit limited, beach areas with facilities for water sports. Along the West Coast Highway are several theme parks like the Jurong Bird Park, gardens, village-style neighborhoods like Pasir Panjang, and nature spots.

The Garden Isle. Less than 5% of the island remains forested. However, there's more to Singapore than its concrete buildings and glass skyscrapers. It's not too much of a stretch to call at least the interior the Garden Isle. Going north and inland from downtown, you come upon the beautiful Botanic Gardens. Farther north and slightly to the west is the Bukit Timah Nature Reserve, where trails wind their way through a rain forest, and the attractive little Bukit Batok Town Park, formerly a quarry. The Singapore Zoological Gardens, Night Safari, Mandai Orchid Gardens, and Sungei Buloh Nature Park are all here.

Pulau Ubin. This 2,471-acre mangrove-fringed island off Singapore's northeastern coast is a must-see living museum of 1960s rural life. In the main village are Singapore's last fixed *wayang* (opera) stage, small holder farms, coconut plantations, fish ponds, and simple restaurants that serve chili crab and other local delicacies.

Sentosa and the Southern Islands. Some 63 small islands lie off Singapore's southern coast within sight of Indonesia. The largest is Sentosa, linked by a causeway and a cable car, which is a full-blown entertainment island with hotels, restaurants, museums, aquariums, and nature parks.

Batam and Bintan. These Indonesian resort islands in the Singapore Strait are easily reached by ferry. Besides fancy resorts, most run by Singaporean investors, there's rich history and culture here.

Singapore in 5 Days

Keep in mind that Singapore's hot-and-humid climate takes no prisoners: stay hydrated (tap water is safe), take frequent breaks, and carry an umbrella against the sun. Plan walking tours in half-day segments so that you can retreat to your hotel and get refreshed. With an EZ-Link farecard, you'll have access to convenient and fully air-conditioned public transportation. *Consult the festivals calendar so that you know when and where things might be closed, or simply more exciting.*

DAY 1: Take the MRT to City Hall. Get a sense of 19th-century Singapore by treading the historic pathways around the famed Raffles Hotel and the Singapore Cricket Club on the Padang, where you'll also find the venerable Singapore Recreation Club, the Supreme Court, and City Hall. From Raffles Hotel, digress up Bras Basah Road to Chijmes, a former convent, before looping up to the erstwhile St. Joseph's Institution, now the Singapore Art Museum. Head for the Cathedral of the Good Shepherd (Singapore's first permanent Catholic church) on Queen Street where it intersects Bras Basah, then pass by the Singapore History Museum building on Stamford Road. (Those with the energy should climb up beautifully landscaped Ft. Canning Hill park behind the museum.) Stroll down Armenian Street to take in one building of the Asian Civilisations Museum, then turn left onto Coleman Street to see the Armenian Church. Walk along Coleman to see St. Andrew's Cathedral (there's another City Hall MRT entrance here) before turning right down St. Andrew's Road. Once you pass the Padang you'll see a "wedding cake cluster" of buildings, which includes Victoria Theatre, the old Parliament House (in Singapore's oldest private house), and Empress Place Building where there's an imposing bronze statue of Sir Stamford Raffles. A marble replica of this statue is on the riverbank marking Raffles's first landfall in Singapore.

From the river, take a bumboat to Boat Quay for an evening meal and stroll. There are also eateries in the Asian Civilisations Museum, in the nearby Fullerton Hotel, or in Raffles City. Several small and affordable restaurants are tucked behind Raffles Hotel on Seah and Purvis streets.

DAY 2: Time for a break with nature. Go for an early morning walk in the Singapore Botanic Gardens. Start as early as possible (the gardens open at 5 AM), as it'll be much cooler. You can pick up a guide brochure from the visitor center, but you'll be fine wandering on your own. On the premises are the National Orchid Garden (retreat to the Coolhouse for high-altitude orchids if it gets too hot outside) and the Ginger Garden. You can break for lunch at swanky Au Jardin (you'll need reservations) or at the more casual Halia Restaurant.

After visiting the gardens you can either walk to urban Holland Village's shops and cafés, head to Mandai Orchid Garden, or spend the afternoon in the Singapore Zoological Gardens (via the Ang Mo Kio or Choa Chu Kang MRT). Tour the zoo's 148-acre barrier-free grounds on a tram (you can hop on and off) or a guided buggy; there are countless air-conditioned shelters and food stops. The animal shows, including Fragile

Forest, Polar Bear Underwater, and Primate Kingdom, are all worth seeing. When the zoo closes at 6, cross the road to grab dinner before entering the Night Safari park, which opens at 7:30. Take a tram tour to see a remarkable display of nocturnal animals in their natural surroundings. Afterwards, select from the special Walking Trails for close-up views of other animals such as the Fishing Cats and the Civet Cats (a.k.a. Musang).

Don't go on a weekend or half of Singapore may be there with you.

DAY 3: Ready yourself for the city fray and head to Little India, which is served by an MRT station of the same name. This enclave, near Orchard Road and the CBD, centers around Serangoon Road. Its side streets are crammed with the pungent smells and the vivid sights, sounds, and colors of India. Courteous bargaining is normal at Tekka Market, on the corner of Buffalo Road, which has sundry Asian products. Mustafa's, on Syed Alwi Road, is a well-known bargain emporium, which sells pretty much everything. Many Hindu temples line Serangoon; you're welcome to tour them provided that you remove your shoes, cover up, and behave respectfully. If you're hungry, you can opt for the torrid meat curries available on Race Course Road, parallel to Serangoon, or the vegetarian eats on Serangoon and side streets such as Upper Dickson.

After lunch, move on to Kampong Glam, a Malay-Arab district around Victoria Street, which is parallel to Serangoon Road. The nearest MRT station is Bugis. Focus on the region around the golden minarets of the Sultan Mosque: Sultan Gate, Kandahar, Bussorah, and Arab streets. Muezzins at the mosque sing the call to prayer five times daily. Istana Kampong Glam, formerly the sultan's palace, is sandwiched between Victoria Street and Beach Road. This is an area rich with the culture and ornate textiles of India, Indonesia, and the Middle East. Order yourself a *teh halia* (ginger tea) at one of the many Malay cafés and stalls. Note that people tend to take their dinner early here; all the food may be gone if you try to eat after 7. Remember: this is a Muslim area, so dress respectfully.

Avoid the Serangoon area on Sunday when laborers on vacation pack it to bursting; don't bother with Kampong Glam during Ramadan (October/November), except to visit the post-sunset markets around Bussorah Street and the Sultan Mosque. Little India is particularly exciting just before the Hindu festival of Deepavali (late October/early November).

DAY 4: Take a trip to Chinatown, which is served by several MRT stations (Chinatown, Outram Park, Tanjong Pagar, and Raffles Place). Start by taking the train to Tanjong Pagar; walk up Telok Ayer Street to see the iconic Thian Hock Keng Temple. Stop for a snack at Maxwell Road Hawker Centre, at the junction where South Bridge meets Tanjong Pagar, before proceeding up South Bridge to Sri Mariamman Hindu temple. If you walk past the temple along Temple Street, towards New Bridge Road and Eu Tong Sen Street, you'll arrive at the People's Park shopping complex (the Chinatown MRT is here). As you approach this area, notice the attractive pre-World War II architecture, and duck into the herbal medicine and grocery shops along the way. Both New Bridge and Eu Tong Sen are lined with several large shopping malls, including Chinatown Complex and Yue Hwa. For refreshment, you can try a Chinese herbal tea or a freshly steamed white rice-flour dumpling ("pau") stuffed with sweet beans or shredded pork.

This area is at its peak just before Chinese New Year (late January/early February); it's good to visit at night.

DAY 5: Join the shoppers lugging thousands of dollars in purchases, celebrities in disguise, and fashionable wannabes as they stroll Orchard Road's shopping and entertainment strip, which is centered around the intersection of Scotts and Orchard roads. Take the MRT to Orchard. Start at Tanglin Shopping Centre (on Orchard where it intersects Tanglin) and browse its stores for antiques, crafts, and books. Walking down Orchard you'll pass malls on both sides. Any time you get tired of shopping, you can step on a bus (any one that's going to Marina or Shenton Way is safe to board, as these travel the length of Orchard Road). Eateries line the route; keep your eyes peeled for the more hidden local food centers, which are usually in the basement. Take a brief detour down historic Emerald Hill Road on your left just before Centrepoint. Continue down Orchard Road to Cuppage Terrace and Orchard Point (left), where more bargains can be found. If you hang around long enough, the handful of foodstalls in the parking lot next to the Specialists' Centre will start serving yummy local dinners. Otherwise, cross the Central Expressway junction, pass the gateway to the President's official residence (the Istana), and move on to Plaza Singapura next door (left), after which you can board the MRT at Dhoby Ghaut.

Pedestrian crossing points for trafficky Orchard Road are few and far between. Don't risk crossing except at crosswalks or underground walkways. Note that the main strip is dangerously slippery on rainy days.

If You Have More Time
Sentosa Island, off Singapore's southern coast, has been unfairly maligned as a tacky resort. It actually has an impressive variety of activities for the whole family, such as World War II sites, cultural museums, aquariums, nature trails, and gardens, not to mention outdoor sports galore and countless food offerings. It would be a shame to miss the Jurong BirdPark, a fascinating zoo with intriguing bird shows and walk-in aviaries granting visitors close contact with rare tropical birds.

If You Have Only 3 Days
For the first two days follow the plan for Day 3, and then for Day 2. For the third day, pack the historical tour (Day 1) into a half-day, then proceed to Chinatown (Day 4) for the other half. If shopping is more your thing, substitute Day 5 for either of the half-day itineraries.

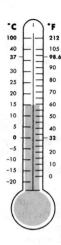

Climatic considerations shouldn't figure much when you're planning a visit to Singapore. There's very little year-round variation in weather patterns, though it does get rainier between November and January. The trees and flowers look their best at pretty much any time of the year. It's the social climate that waxes and wanes rather than the natural environment or the weather.

Shoppers thirsty for freebies, bargains, and promotions should come for the Great Singapore Sale from late May through early June. Those seeking some culture should time a visit with one of Singapore's annual arts festivals including the annual international Singapore Arts Festival in June, August's WOMAD in Ft. Canning Park, and the Singapore Film Festival in April. For dedicated foodies, there's the Singapore Food Festival in July.

Climate

With the equator only 129 km (80 mi) to the south, Singapore is typically either hot or very hot. The average daily temperature is 80°F (26.6°C); it usually reaches 87°F (30.7°C) in the afternoon and drops to a cool 75°F (23.8°C) just before dawn. The months from November through January, during the northeast monsoon, are generally the coolest. The average daily relative humidity is 84.5%, although it drops to 65%–70% on dry afternoons.

Rain falls year-round, but the wettest months are November through January. February is usually the sunniest month; December, the most inclement.

F Forecasts **Automated Weather Information Service Helpline** ☎ 6542-7788 ⊕ www. nea.gov.sg/metsin.

AVERAGE TEMPERATURES

Jan.	86F	30C	May	89F	32C	Sept.	88F	31C
	74	23		75	24		75	24
Feb.	88F	31C	June	88F	31C	Oct.	88F	31C
	74	23		75	24		74	23
Mar.	88F	31C	July	88F	31C	Nov.	88F	31C
	75	24		75	24		74	23
Apr.	88F	31C	Aug.	88F	31C	Dec.	88F	31C
	75	24		75	24		74	23

Singapore's festivals are drawn from the world's great religions and some truly exotic and ancient folk events (Thaipusam, Festival of the Nine Emperor Gods). Some festival dates and seasons vary from year to year according to the lunar calendar.

WINTER

Dec. 25	As a multicultural society, Singapore has taken Christmas to heart. A lighting ceremony takes place on Orchard Road sometime during the last 10 days of November.
Jan.–Feb.	Hari Raya Haji is a Muslim holy day set by the Islamic calendar, which commemorates the Haj (pilgrimage) to Mecca.
Mid-Jan.–Feb.	During Pongal, the four-day harvest festival, Tamil Indians from South India give thanks to the Hindu gods. You can view the rites at the Perumal Temple on Serangoon Road. Thaipusam celebrates the victory of the Hindu god Subramaniam over the demon Idumban. Penitents pierce their flesh with steel rods and fishhooks, which radiate from a huge metal contraption (the "kavadi"). The 2.5-mi (4-km) procession travels from the Sri Srinivasa Perumal Temple on Serangoon Road to the Chettiars Sri Thandayuthapani Temple on Tank Road. Thaipusam is banned in its homeland, India, and isn't for the squeamish. Chinese New Year is a Lunar New Year celebration that lasts for 15 days; most shops and businesses close for a week. The night-time Chingay Procession marks the end of Chinese New Year. Lion dancers, accompanied by clashing gongs and beating drums, lead stilt-walkers, swordsmen, warriors, acrobats, and mythological figures up Orchard Road.

SPRING

Mar.–Apr.	On the Birthday of the Saint of the Poor, the image of Guang Ze Zun Wang is carried from White Cloud Temple on Ganges Avenue and paraded through streets thronged with devotees.
Late Mar.–early Apr.	St. Joseph's Catholic Church on Victoria Street holds a candlelight procession on Good Friday.
Early Apr.	During Qing Ming (a.k.a. All Soul's Day) families honor their ancestors by visiting graves, cleaning cemeteries, and making offerings.
Apr. 18	Songkran is a Thai water festival that marks the start of the year's solar cycle. The liveliest (and wettest) celebrations are at the Ananda Metyrama Thai temple on Jalan Bukit Merah, and the Sattha Puchaniyaram Temple on Bukit Batok West Avenue 8. Visitors are welcome.

May–June	**Vesak Day** is the most sacred Buddhist holiday. It commemorates the Buddha's birth, enlightenment, and death. Many temples offer vegetarian feasts and special exhibitions. Kong Meng San Phor Kark See on Bright Hill Drive and the Temple of 1,000 Lights on Race Course Road are particularly recommended. The **Great Singapore Sale** is an eight-week extravaganza where just about all shopping centers and boutiques extend considerable discounts (up to 80%).

SUMMER

June	The **Singapore International Dragon Boat Festival** commemorates the martyrdom of Qu Yuan, a Chinese poet and minister of state during the Chou Dynasty (4th century BC). Crews from all over the world race 38-foot-long (11.6-meter-long) boats—each manned by up to 24 rowers and a drummer—in the sea off East Coast Park.
July	During the **National Songbird Competition**, owners of tuneful cage-birds hold competitions to see whose chirps best.
Aug. 9	**National Day**, the anniversary of Singapore's independence, is marked by fireworks, folk and dragon dances, and national pride. National Stadium holds a mega-party.
Aug.–Sept.	For a month each year, during the **Chinese Festival of the Hungry Ghosts**, the Gates of Hell are opened and ghosts wander the earth freely. Street-opera performances begin in the late afternoon and continue until late evening.

FALL

Sept.	The **Mooncake Festival** (a.k.a. the Mid-Autumn or Lantern Festival) is held on the night of the year when the full moon is at its brightest and is named for the legendary mini cakes. **The Birthday of the Monkey God** celebrates a Chinese character who's believed to cure illness and absolve sin. Events are held at temples along Eng Hoon and Cumming streets.
Oct.	During the nine-day **Navarathri Festival**, Hindus extol three goddesses: Parvati, Laskshmi, and Sarawathi. You can catch classical Indian music, dance, and drama nightly 7–10 at most Hindu temples (such as Sri Srinivasa Perumal and Sri Veeramakaliamman on Serangoon Road). The most colorful event is at the Chettiar Sri Thandayutha-pani Temple on Tank Road. The popular deities celebrated in the **Festival of the Nine Emperor Gods** are honored in Chinese temples on the ninth day of the ninth lunar month; the most spectacular celebrations are in Kiu Ong Yiah Temple on Upper Serangoon Road.
Oct.–Nov.	During the **Pilgrimage to Kusu Island**, over 100,000 Taoist believers travel to the Tua Pekong temple dedicated to Tua Pek Kong, the god of prosperity. If you want to join in, take one of the many ferries that leave from Clifford Pier.

Mid-Oct.– mid-Nov.	Ramadan is the Muslim month of daytime fasting. Stalls in Bussorah Street and around the Sultan Mosque sell Malay rice cakes in banana leaves, fragrant puddings, and mutton cubes with roasted coconut; drop by between 5 and 7:30 PM. Hari Raya Puasa is a major feast marking Ramadan's end. Geylang Serai has a bustling and festive night market.
Nov.	In the Thimithi Festival, Indian Hindus honor the goddess Draupadi, who tread barefoot over flaming coals to prove her chastity. Watch the fire-walkers beginning at 3 PM at the Sri Mariamman Temple on South Bridge Road. Deepavali celebrates the triumph of light over dark, of the blue-faced love-god Krishna over the demon king Narakasura. Indian homes and temples are decorated with oil lamps and garlands for the Hindu festival, which marks a time for cleaning house and wearing new clothes.

PLEASURES & PASTIMES

Let's Makan! Singaporeans sure do love eating (a.k.a. *makan* in Singlish). The island's three major cultures—Chinese, Malay, and Indian—keep citizens plenty stuffed with such regional eats as Nonya and Malay-Chinese fusion food. Eurasian chefs combine Portuguese, Dutch, and British influences with Asian flavors. Spices, which aren't necessarily hot, figure strongly in the cuisines of Singapore. Flavors can be mellow, as in rich, thick coconut gravies; pungent, as in Indian curries; tart, as with sour and hot tamarind-, vinegar-, and lime-based gravies; or sweet and fragrant, as in Indian desserts and beverages. Food is the common language of Singapore. Pick up the free 72-page food guide published by the Singapore Tourism Board, which is distributed at Changi Airport, visitor centers, various sights, and hotels.

Gardens & Parks Downtown may leave you with the impression that everything's concrete and glass in Singapore. However, the country is dubbed the Garden Isle for good reason. Naturally lush tropical vegetation, abundant parkland, and 7,017 acres of wild nature reserve make Singapore much more of an environmental haven than most people realize. You can escape to Mandai Orchid Garden or to the wonderfully kept Singapore Botanic Gardens. At the Chinese Garden MRT station, near Jurong, there's an elegant Chinese Garden alongside a serene Japanese Garden; each is a 32-acre island of tranquility amidst an industrial and residential zone. You can hike the trails of Bukit Timah Nature Reserve—the tigers have long gone, but the sounds and smells of the jungle are still here. If you really want to see a tiger, head for the Singapore Zoological Gardens. The nocturnal animals are nearby, at Night Safari, where rhinos wake at dusk to feed.

Boating & Islands Though they live in an island nation, Singaporeans spend surprisingly little time in the water. It's a shame because boat trips are an ideal way to escape the city's hurly-burly and see the place from a different perspective. You can take a bumboat across the Singapore River from quay to quay. From Changi Point, it's a short ferry ride to Pulau Island, and from HarbourFront Centre, you can take a ferry to Sentosa Island. You can tour Singapore harbor aboard a Chinese junk. You can cross international waters (remember your passport) and head for the Indonesian islands of Batam (a 30-minute trip) or Bintan (75 minutes). If you can authenticate your certified sailing ability, you can hire boats from the Royal Singapore Yacht Club on the southwest coast, and sail the southern islands area by yourself.

Shelter Although Singapore isn't the same indulgent retreat it once was, it's hard to match the standard of comfort, efficiency of staff, and level of services that Singapore hotels offer. The luxury establishments cater to every whim—and so they should at more than S$300 a night—but you can find good service, freshly decorated rooms, cleanliness, and modern facilities for around S$200. For less money, there are simple, clean hotels (often more personal than the larger ones), with rooms for about S$90. Increasingly, these are small "boutique" hotels in downtown locations.

Browser's Paradise

Once upon a time Singapore, a duty-free republic, was a haven for shoppers. Although shopping is still the major pastime, nowadays the shoppers tend to be rich and sassy. Except for lucky finds in antiques stores, bargains are hard to come by—they're more likely in the less central areas, and in ethnic quarters, particularly Little India, Kampong Glam/Arab Street, Chinatown, and Geylang/Katong. Still, the quantity of the products you'll find in Singapore's stores is nothing short of astounding. Browsing is as much fun as shopping.

Theme Parks

Few countries of Singapore's size have put as much effort into creating attractions for citizens and tourists. Overzealous planners and visionaries may have spent millions destroying historical buildings and erecting sleeker structures in their place, but fortunes have also been spent recreating old theme parks, usually intended to educate and entertain. Haw Par Villa on the west coast emphasizes Chinese mythology, and the Tang Dynasty Village in Jurong, also in the west, reveals life as it was in ancient China. Sentosa Island's excellent "Images of Singapore" series uses high-tech effects to present a moving, talking 3-D reconstruction of the country's history and culture, including a well-documented section on the Japanese occupation during World War II.

War Games

Those eager for a history lesson can view relics from World War II and the Japanese occupation of Singapore from 1942 to 1945. Sentosa has several museums and remnants of World War II fortifications. Some contend (perhaps unjustifiably) that the guns at Labrador Park were facing the wrong way when the Japanese, as legend has it, crossed the Causeway from Malaysia on bikes. Changi, where the great prison was, now has the large Kranji War Memorial and military cemetery. You can't turn around without hitting some site of historical interest: the Ford Factory in Bukit Timah where the British surrendered to the Japanese; Alexandra Hospital, the site of an infamous Japanese massacre; the YMCA Orchard, once the dreaded Kempeitai military police HQ; a derelict war-time Japanese Shinto shrine deep in the jungle off the MacRitchie Reservoir lake; and in the Esplanade park is the pagoda-style monument to Chinese hero Lim Bo Seng, who led the resistance against the Japanese until he was captured and tortured to death, together with the Indian National Army monument to Subhas Chandra Bose, who supported the Japanese in hopes of accelerating India's independence from Britain. There are many more such sites; for guidance, contact the Singapore Tourism Board.

Temples, Mosques & Churches

It would take an ice age to visit all of Singapore's places of worship. Temples, mosques, churches, and synagogues—they're the tangible representation of Singapore's multicultural landscape. For Christian churches, head to the central colonial district around Bras Basah and Stamford roads; Buddhist and Hindu temples and a synagogue line Waterloo Street, just off Bras Basah. The glorious Sultan Mosque is on Beach Road, near Raffles Hotel. You can catch colorful rituals at the smaller Malabari Mosque and the Hajjah Fatimah Mosque. Chinatown is a rich hunting ground for southern Chinese Buddhist temples. Watch for places you need to remove your shoes, cover your head, keep your voice down, and your manner respectful. If you extend this concept to old graveyards you're guaranteed a fascinating walk around the Chinese cemetery at Bukit Brown, which is full of botanical and bird life, off Sime and Kheam Hock roads, or in Choa Chu Kang's cemetery in the far west. Both of these cemeteries, however, require a bit of perseverance to get to, since they're pretty far off the beaten path.

FODOR'S CHOICE

The sights, restaurants, hotels, and other travel experiences on these pages are our editors' top picks—our Fodor's Choices. They're the best of their type in the area covered by the book—not to be missed and always worth your time. In the destination chapters that follow, you will find all the details.

RESTAURANTS

$$$$	**Jade,** CDB. Fundamentally Chinese dishes get a new lease on life at this stunning restaurant in the Fullerton Hotel.
$$$$	**Les Amis,** Orchard. Hobnob with Singaporean tycoons, celebrities, and wannabe celebrities at this swanky French restaurant.
$$$	**Nude,** Orchard. Sashay over a transparent catwalk, above running water, toward a colossal aquarium. Welcome to Nude. All the food is prepared free of preserved, stored, or artificial additives.
$$$	**Doc Cheng's,** Colonial Singapore. How novel: an Asian fusion restaurant that actually works.
$$–$$$	**Blood Café,** Orchard. Hidden in the rear of an avant garde boutique, the casual café is less experimental and serves some of the island's best salads, sandwiches, and cakes.
$$–$$$	**Blue Ginger,** Tanjong Pagar. The popular restaurant serves the closest thing to Singaporean cuisine. Perhaps only the brave should dare order the dessert made from the infamous durian.
$$–$$$	**mezza9,** Orchard. Indecisive diners will appreciate mezza9's "modest" nine kitchens distributed throughout a minimalist dining area.
$$–$$$	**Thanying,** Tanjong Pagar. This Thai food is royally good. Make sure you save room for the dessert buffet.

BUDGET RESTAURANTS

$	**Banana Leaf Apolo,** Little India. "Spicy" is the operative word at this South Indian restaurant, which specializes in robust curries.
$	**Samy's Restaurant,** Holland Village. The simple banana-leaf eats at this no-frills Indian curry house are delivered by a parade of shuffling waiters, and come with sundry condiments.

LODGING

$$$$	**The Oriental, Singapore,** Marina Square. Extraordinarily remarkable service is the thing at this elegant pyramid-shape hotel.
$$$$	**Raffles Hotel,** Colonial Singapore. Opened in 1887 and visited by such writers as Rudyard Kipling and Somerset Maugham, noble Raffles Hotel continues to ooze tradition and gentility today.

$$$$ The Ritz-Carlton, Millenia Singapore, Marina Square. The most dramatic luxury hotel in Marina Bay has 32 floors of unobstructed harbor and city views, and uncommonly large rooms.

$$$ Berjaya Hotel, Tanjong Pagar. The nation's first boutique hotel offers an intimate whiff of Singapore's character before it sold out to steel girders and glass.

BUDGET LODGING

$ RELC International Hotel, Nassim Hill. The guest rooms at this conference center–"hostel" are pretty comfortable; they even throw in breakfast.

$ Sha Villa, Orchard. Housed in what was once a ballet academy, this Peranakan-style hotel is welcoming and economical—and minutes away from Orchard Street.

EXPLORING

Carlsberg Sky Tower. Ascend to the top of this 361-foot (110-meter) tower on Sentosa Island for a breathtaking view of Singapore.

Empress Place, CBD. This is the best place for a crash course on the fascinating Peranakan culture.

Old Parliament House, Colonial. Originally designed by George Coleman, the building is considered Singapore's oldest government building.

Singapore Botanic Gardens. It's at once an escape from the city and a peerless education in tropical flora, with black swans and awe-inspiring fan palms on the main grounds. The massive National Orchid Garden is also here.

Night Safari. Taken by tram, this safari has two major advantages over the usual zoo experience: the cover of night coaxes even the shyest animals out of hiding, and the open, natural setting means that no bars block your view.

Singapore Science Centre. A little learning never hurt anyone: aviation, nuclear science, robotics, astronomy, space, and the Internet are seldom as fascinatingly explored as they are at this center's 750 exhibits.

Sri Srinivasa Perumal Temple, Little India. Intricate sculptures depicting Vishnu in his nine forms cover this lively temple, a starting point for many important Hindu festivals.

Sultan Mosque, Arab District. An imposing structure with a gold dome, minarets, and vast green-and-gold-accented prayer hall, this is the central place of worship for Singapore's Muslims.

Thian Hock Keng Temple, Chinatown. Built in 1839, this is Singapore's oldest Chinese temple.

SPORTS & THE OUTDOORS

Pulau Ubin Recreation Area. Experience steaming chili crab, mangrove swamps, rare birds, and rural life on this attractive island off the northeast coast.

Bukit Timah Nature Reserve. Not your typical urban park, this small rainforest has well-marked trails and abundant wildlife.

Singapore Polo Club. The sport of kings is showcased at this historic clubhouse off Thomson Road. Indeed, Malaysian royals occasionally play on the greens.

Singapore Cricket Club. Take a walk around the green Padang and admire this structure's sensational colonial architecture.

Singapore Turf Club. Come on a live racing day to experience the pulse of Singaporean gamblers.

East Coast Sailing Centre, East Coast Parkway. At this sailing center you can wind-surf and then linger past sunset at the outdoor Pasta Fresca Italian restaurant.

SHOPPING

The Camera Workshop, Colonial. Enthusiastic photographers educate, rather than force sales on inexperienced shoppers.

Chinatown Complex Wet Market, Chinatown. Spy and smell virtually every edible animal, seafood, and plant that makes its way onto a Singapore table. Colorful, hectic, entertaining, and wet.

Club 21, Orchard. All the best fashion designers are concentrated in this underground store linked to the Hilton Hotel.

Evolution Prehistoric Art Gallery, Colonial Singapore. If you've ever wanted to own a fossilized dinosaur footprint, this is the place for you.

Jamal Kazura Aromatics, Arab District. Have your own signature scent created and select a one-of-a-kind handblown glass bottle from Persia to store it in.

Jewel Ashley Gallery, River Valley/Clarke Quay. It's the place for elegantly displayed mod, Asian furnishings.

Ngee Ann City, Orchard. Anchored by Takashimaya, this complex sucks you in with more than 100 specialty stores and the largest bookstore in Southeast Asia.

projectshopBloodbros, Orchard. This local line is so hip, they don't even have a sign outside their store. It's streetwear for the rebels with credit cards.

Sim Lim Square, Colonial. More than a hundred stores with everything and anything that can be plugged in.

Asian Civilizations Museum, CBD. The museum's two locations—one on Armenian Street and the other at Empress Place—showcase pan-Asian culture.

Anywhere, Orchard Road. This crowded, smoky club is home base for Tania, a local band, as well as for Malay rock tunes.

Chinese Theatre Circle, Chinatown. The troupe is a leader in the move to make Chinese opera more accessible to all, including non-Chinese speakers.

Crazy Elephant, Clarke Quay. Come here for a scorching blues jam any weeknight.

Harry's Quayside Cafe, Boat Quay. A jazz bastion and staple of the lively Boat Quay scene, this casual hangout also has stunning river views.

Ice Cold Beer, Orchard. This expat favorite is a beer-drinker's paradise and a great spot to rendezvous with friends—or make some new ones.

New Asia Bar, CBD. This upscale bar sits atop Singapore's highest building.

NUS Museums, West Coast. At any one time NUS displays some 1,000 objets d'art from a collection of 10,000 pieces.

Tan Swie Hian Museum, East Coast. Singapore's first private art museum has a serious collection by this Singaporean artist.

Zouk, Velvet Underground, Phuture, Robertson Quay. The hip and beautiful gather at these world-class dance clubs, where varying music styles and age groups mix effortlessly.

Learning about Singapore before you leave home means you won't squander time organizing everyday minutiae once you've arrived. You'll be more streetwise when you hit the ground as well, better prepared to explore the aspects of Singapore that drew you here in the first place. The organizations in this section can provide information to supplement this guide; contact them for up-to-the-minute details. Happy landings!

ADDRESSES

People rarely refer to street numbers when citing an address. Almost all buildings (except houses) have names—use them to quickly find a location. A common address includes the name of the building followed by the floor and unit number. The floor and unit number is usually represented by a hex symbol followed by two digits that designate the floor, a dash and then two digits that refer to the unit number. So, "#02–01" means it's on the second floor and in office, store, or apartment number 1.

AIR TRAVEL

BOOKING

When you book, look for nonstop flights and remember that "direct" flights stop at least once. Try to avoid connecting flights, which require a change of plane. Two airlines may operate a connecting flight jointly, so ask whether your airline operates every segment of the trip; you may find that the carrier you prefer flies you only part of the way. To find more booking tips and to check prices and make online flight reservations, log on to www.fodors.com.

CARRIERS

Singapore Airlines, the national carrier, offers direct, non-stop flights to Singapore from New York, Los Angeles (the world's longest non-stop commercial flight), London, and New Zealand. United Airlines has direct, one-stop flights from Los Angeles, San Francisco, and Seattle, and connecting flights (one stop, with a change in Tokyo) from Chicago, New York, and

Washington, D.C. One-stop flights from the North American west coast usually stop at either Seoul, Taipei, Tokyo, or Hong Kong; departures from the east coast stop in one of the European capitals, Delhi, or Dubai. Asian budget airlines such as Tiger Airways and ValueAir also operate out of Singapore. Other major airlines that serve Singapore are listed below.

🔁 To & From Singapore **Air France** ☎ 800/237-2747 ⊕ www.airfrance.com. **Air New Zealand** ☎ 800/262-1234 ⊕ www.airnz.co.nz. **American Airlines** ☎ 800/433-7300 ⊕ www.aa.com. **British Airways** ☎ 800/247-9297 ⊕ www.britishairways.com. **Cathay Pacific** ☎ 800/233-2742 ⊕ www.cathaypacific.com. **China Airlines** ☎ 800/227-5118 ⊕ www.china-airlines.com. **Korean Air** ☎ 800/438-5000 ⊕ www.koreanair.com. **Malaysia Airlines** ☎ 800/552-9264 ⊕ www.malaysiaairlines.com. **Northwest Airlines** ☎ 800/225-2525 ⊕ www.nwa.com. **Qantas** ☎ 800/227-4500 ⊕ www.qantas.com. **Singapore Airlines** ☎ 6223-8888 ⊕ www.singaporeair.com. **Thai Airways International** ☎ 800/388-8888 ⊕ www.thaiair.com. **United Airlines** ☎ 800/864-8331 ⊕ www.ual.com.

🔁 Within Singapore **Garuda Indonesia** ☎ 6250-5666 ⊕ www.garuda-indonesia.com. **Japan Airlines** ☎ 6542-5908 ⊕ www.jal.com. **Tiger Airways** ☎ 1800/388-8888 ⊕ www.tigerairways.com. **Value Air** ☎ 6229-8338 ⊕ www.valuair.com.sg.

CHECK-IN & BOARDING

Always **find out your carrier's check-in policy.** Plan to arrive at the airport about two hours before your scheduled departure time for domestic flights and 2½ to 3 hours before international flights. You may need to arrive earlier if you're flying from one of the busier airports or during peak air-traffic times. Arrive at least two hours before a flight out of Changi Airport, unless you're catching a shuttle flight to Malaysia for which you'll need to arrive one hour beforehand. To expedite the process, many carriers encourage passengers to check in on-line or over the phone between 48 and 2 hours prior to their departure. Passengers with check-in baggage who use these services should be at the designated check-in counters at least 45 minutes before the scheduled departure.

Check with your carrier. If you're traveling in the days leading up to a multiday public holiday, such as Chinese New Year, check in another 30 minutes earlier.

Airlines routinely overbook planes. After volunteers, the first passengers to get bumped are those who check in late and those flying on discounted tickets, so **get to the gate and check in as early as possible,** especially during peak periods. Always **bring your passport** to the airport. You won't be able to enter or leave Singapore without it.

CUTTING COSTS

A new breed of budget airlines has started servicing Singapore; Tiger Airways (flights to and from Thailand) and ValuAir (to and from Bangkok, Hong Kong, and Jakarta) among them. The least expensive airfares to Singapore are priced for round-trip travel and must be purchased in advance. Airlines generally allow you to change your return date for a fee; most low-fare tickets, however, are nonrefundable. **Call a number of airlines and check the Internet;** when you're quoted a good price, **book it on the spot**—the same fare may not be available the next day, or even the next hour. Tickets during the off season between September and the end of November are cheaper. It's most expensive to fly anytime between January and the end of May. Always **check different routings** and look into using alternate airports. Also, price off-peak flights, which may be significantly less expensive than others. Travel agents, especially low-fare specialists (⇨ Discounts & Deals), can be helpful.

Consolidators are another good source. They buy tickets for scheduled flights at reduced rates from the airlines, then sell them at prices that beat the best fare available directly from the airlines. (Many also offer reduced car-rental and hotel rates.) Sometimes you can even get your money back if you need to return the ticket. Carefully read the fine print detailing penalties for changes and cancellations, purchase the ticket with a credit card, and confirm your consolidator reservation with the airline.

Many airlines, singly or in collaboration, offer **discount air passes** that allow foreigners to travel economically in a particular country or region. These visitor passes must be reserved and purchased before you leave home. Information about passes can be found on most airline Web pages; try searching for "pass" within the carrier's site. Some require that all sectors have to be confirmed at time of ticketing. Others are more flexible and as long as the routing remains the same, reservations can be changed at any time.

If you plan to travel a lot within Asia, consider purchasing an air pass. The Star Alliance Asian Airpass (www.staralliance. com) includes 3 to 6 coupons that cost $59 to $270 each. It's valid on Asiana, Singapore, Thai, and United airlines. Contact participating airlines or tour operators and travel agents who specialize in Southeast Asian travel for information and purchase.

🚩 Consolidators **AirlineConsolidator.com** ☎ 888/ 468-5385 ⊕ www.airlineconsolidator.com; for international tickets. **Best Fares** ☎ 800/880-1234 or 800/576-8255 ⊕ www.bestfares.com; $59.90 annual membership. **Cheap Tickets** ☎ 800/377-1000 or 800/652-4327 ⊕ www.cheaptickets.com. **Expedia** ☎ 800/397-3342 or 404/728-8787 ⊕ www.expedia. com. **Hotwire** ☎ 866/468-9473 or 920/330-9418 ⊕ www.hotwire.com. **Now Voyager Travel** ✉ 1717 Avenue M, Brooklyn, NY 11230 ☎ 212/459-1616 🖷 718/504-4762 ⊕ www.nowvoyagertravel.com. **Onetravel.com** ⊕ www.onetravel.com. **Orbitz** ☎ 888/656-4546 ⊕ www.orbitz.com. **Priceline. com** ⊕ www.priceline.com. **Travelocity** ☎ 888/ 709-5983, 877/282-2925 in Canada, 0870/876-3876 in the U.K. ⊕ www.travelocity.com.

ENJOYING THE FLIGHT

State your seat preference when purchasing your ticket, and then repeat it when you confirm and when you check in. For more legroom, you can request one of the few emergency-aisle seats at check-in, if you're capable lifting at least 50 pounds—a Federal Aviation Administration requirement of passengers in these seats. Seats behind a bulkhead also offer more legroom, but they don't have under-seat storage. Don't sit in the row in front of the emergency aisle or in

front of a bulkhead, where seats may not recline.

Ask the airline whether a snack or meal is served on the flight. If you have dietary concerns, request special meals when booking. On long flights, try to maintain a normal routine, to help fight jet lag. At night, get some sleep. By day, eat light meals, drink water (not alcohol), and **move around the cabin** to stretch your legs. For additional jet-lag tips consult *Fodor's FYI: Travel Fit & Healthy* (available at bookstores everywhere). Smoking is prohibited on flights in and out of Singapore.

FLYING TIMES

From Los Angeles and Vancouver, flights to Singapore are 18½ hours. From New Zealand, flights are 10½ hours; from Sydney, 8 hours. The flying time from New York is 21 hours, and from London it's 13 hours to Singapore. Bali and Bangkok are 2½ hours away, and Hong Kong is 3½ hours away.

HOW TO COMPLAIN

If your baggage goes astray or your flight goes awry, complain right away. Most carriers require that you **file a claim immediately.** The Aviation Consumer Protection Division of the Department of Transportation publishes *Fly-Rights*, which discusses airlines and consumer issues and is available online. You can also find articles and information on mytravelrights.com, the Web site of the nonprofit Consumer Travel Rights Center.

🚩 Airline Complaints **Aviation Consumer Protection Division** ✉ U.S. Department of Transportation, Office of Aviation Enforcement and Proceedings, C-75, Room 4107, 400 7th St. SW, Washington, DC 20590 ☎ 202/366-2220 ⊕ airconsumer.ost.dot.gov. **Federal Aviation Administration Consumer Hotline** ✉ for inquiries: FAA, 800 Independence Ave. SW, Washington, DC 20591 ☎ 800/322-7873 ⊕ www.faa.gov.

🚩 Lost & Found **Changi International Airport** ☎ 1800/542-9727 in Terminal 1, 1800/542-9702 in Terminal 2.

RECONFIRMING

Always confirm international flights at least 72 hours ahead of the scheduled departure time. Check the status of your flight before you leave for the airport. You can do this on your carrier's Web site or by calling your carrier or travel agent.

AIRPORTS

Changi International Airport, the major gateway to Singapore, is on the island's eastern end and is a 20-minute drive from downtown. It has two terminals with a third one under construction. Most airlines are based in Terminal 1. The terminals are connected by a free, two-minute ride on the Skytrain monorail, which operates daily 6 AM–midnight. Take the travelators to move between terminals during non-operating hours.

Changi's facilities are second to none. Each terminal is served by the Ambassador Transit Hotel (⇨ Where to Stay), where you can shower or rent a room for six-hour periods. You take shorter naps at Terminal 2's Shower, Fitness and Lifestyle Centre. Terminal 2 also has a rooftop swimming pool and jacuzzi, a movie theater, a supermarket, medical facilities, smoking rooms, and outdoor rest areas among other things. All local calls from the phones in the Departure/Transit areas are free. There are Free Internet Corners throughout the airport. You can fax documents from Terminal 2's Singapore Telecom & Singapore Post, which is open from 6 AM–midnight. If you have at least five hours to kill at Changi, register for a 2-hour sightseeing tour of Singapore at one of the clearly marked tour counters.

⚡ Airport Information **Changi International Airport** ☎ 6542-1122 for airport information, 1800/542-4422 for flight information ⊕ www.changiairport.com.sg.

AIRPORT TRANSFERS

From Terminal 2, you can take an MRT to downtown for S$2; these trains run every 12 minutes from 5:31 AM–11:18 PM. The trip takes about 30 minutes, but you'll need to switch trains twice to get to most hotels. A taxi ride downtown takes about 20 to 30 minutes. Each terminal has two clearly marked taxi stands; look for signs once you exit from baggage claim's clear glass doors. Cab fares range from S$13 to S$15, plus an airport

surcharge (S$5 Friday–Sunday before 5 PM, S$3 all other times) that only applies if you're coming *from,* not going to, the airport. Other surcharges apply between midnight and 6 AM or when baggage is stored in the trunk. Limo taxis usually provide cold water and newspapers. They charge a flat fee of $35 to any destination, which is a good value if you have lots of luggage. There's also a six-seat Airport Shuttle that runs to and from all the major hotels—except in Sentosa and Changi. These shuttles run every 30 minutes from 6 AM–6 PM, and every 15 minutes at other times. Bus terminals are in the basement of Terminals 1 and 2. Take Bus 36 to get downtown; it costs S$2 in exact change.

⚡ Taxis & Shuttles **Airport Shuttle** ☎ 6542-1721. **CityCab** ☎ 6552-2222. **Comfort Cablink** ☎ 6552-1111. **Premier Cabs** ☎ 6552-2828. **TIBS Taxis** ☎ 6555-8888.

DUTY-FREE SHOPPING

There are over 100 stores at Changi. You can be fairly confident that you'll get better prices here than on the island. The "Double the Difference" guarantee means that if an item you purchased at an airport outlet is cheaper at a downtown outlet or major department store, you'll get a refund that's double the difference in pricing. You can pre-order items online from www.changiairport.com.sg, and pick up your purchases when you arrive.

When you depart Singapore you can get a 5% Goods & Services Tax (GST) refund on your purchases. Look for the Global Refund Tax Free Shopping sign and ask for a Global Refund Shopping Check when you make your purchase. You must spend at least S$300 total to qualify. When leaving Singapore you'll need to show these checks with the purchases, receipts, and your passport. If you're packing the goods in your luggage, go to the GST Refund Inspection Counter in the departure hall of either terminal before check-in. If your items are carry on, head to the counter that's after immigration. Either way, your checks will be stamped, and at the counter next to customs you'll get a cash refund, Changi Airport Shopping Vouchers, credit to your credit card, or have a bank check sent to you.

BIKE TRAVEL

Even die hard cyclists should steer clear of riding on Singapore's roads. Nonexistent bike lanes, a lack of shade, and aggressive drivers combine with blazing heat and energy-zapping humidity to make bikes a hazardous mode of transportation. Nevertheless, they are an excellent way to rub shoulders with locals and explore Singapore's parks at your own pace. The East Coast Parkway, Sentosa Island, Bishan Park, and Pasir Ris Park, close to Changi airport, have special tarred lanes (that you'll share with roller bladers), which are ideal for leisurely rides. If you want something more challenging try mountain biking at Bukit Timah Nature Reserve or the tiny island of Pulau Ubin. Bike trail maps are available at visitor centers.

You can rent bikes and protective gear, along with baby baskets, at park kiosks. These usually open 8–8 on weekends and public holidays, and 9–6 at other times. Prices vary, but generally bikes can be rented for S$7 per hour. Stay on the designated tracks and keep to the left but pass on the right. In all parks there's a speed limit of 15 km/h, which is 9 mph. These parks are among the few areas where Singaporeans can master bike riding, so be patient with unsteady learners.

🚲 Bike Rental **Comfort Bicycle Rental** ⊠ 18 Pulau Ubin 🕾 6545-3232. **Leisure @ East Coast Pte. Ltd. (Beach Cabana)** ⊠ Car Park C3, East Coast Park (Next to McDonald's) 🕾 6448-7120. **Our Family Corner** ⊠ Car Park E2, East Coast Park 🕾 6443-3489. **Parks Resort Enterprises** ⊠ Bishan Park, next to skating rink (section between Bishan and Marymount roads) 🕾 6451-5905. **Pasir Ris Beach Resort** ⊠ Pasir Ris Park 🕾 6583-4723. **SDK Recreation** ⊠ Siloso Beach, Sentosa Island 🕾 6272-8738.

BIKES IN FLIGHT

Most airlines accommodate bikes as luggage, provided they are dismantled and boxed; check with individual airlines about packing requirements. Some airlines sell bike boxes, which are often free at bike shops, for about $20 (bike bags can be considerably more expensive).

International travelers often can substitute a bike for a piece of checked luggage at no charge; otherwise, the cost is about $100. Most U.S. and Canadian airlines charge $40–$80 each way.

TRISHAWS

Bicycle-rickshaws, known as trishaws, number a few dozen. They're favored only by tourists, and were last used as bona fide local transport in the 1960s. You can find them near Raffles Hotel, on Stamford Road in front of the Singapore History Museum, and at Bugis Junction. Bargain for the fare; you shouldn't pay more than S$25 for a 45-minute ride. The best time to take a rickshaw ride is 7 PM or later, after the rush hour.

BUS TRAVEL TO & FROM SINGAPORE

The cheapest way to get to Singapore's nearest Malaysian city, Johor Bahru, is to catch Singapore Bus Service (SBS) bus number 170 to Larkin Ter in JB. It's a two-hour ride that leaves from Queens Street bus station every 9–12 minutes and costs S$1.60 one-way. The bus will drop you at the Singapore checkpoint, but it will not wait, so bring all your belongings through immigration. Keep your bus ticket and hop on the next one that comes along.

Air-conditioned private buses between Singapore and Malaysia are quite comfortable. The Singapore–Johor Bahru Express runs daily every 15 minutes 6:30 AM–midnight from the Queens Street bus station; the one-way cost is S$2.40. The Malacca–Singapore Express takes about 4½ hours, costs S$11 one-way, and leaves from the Lavender Street bus station seven times daily. The direct Kuala Lumpur–Singapore Express leaves from the Lavender Street station eight times daily. Several more expensive (S$30–S$47 one-way) and more comfortable express coaches travel between Singapore and Kuala Lumpur. Aeroline departs from the Hotel Asia on Scotts Road four times daily, Nice Bus departs from the Copthorne Orchid hotel on Dunearn Road almost hourly, and Gunung Raya leaves from the Golden Mile Complex along Beach Road three times daily. You may need to pay a small fee to book your seat. Book at least a day in advance for coaches to Kuala Lumpur. Most operators only accept cash.

⊞ Bus Information Aeroline Bus ☎ 6341-9338 ⊕ www.aeroline.com.sg. **Gunung Raya Travel** ☎ 6294-7911 ⊕ www.gunungraya.com. **Kuala Lumpur-Singapore Express** ☎ 6292-8254. **Malacca-Singapore Express** ☎ 6293-5915. **Nice Bus Services** ☎ 6256-5755. **Singapore-Johor Bahru Express** ☎ 6292-8149.

BUS TRAVEL WITHIN SINGAPORE

More than 2,500 buses run some 190 routes covering Singapore's major sites and entertainment areas between 5:30 AM and midnight every day. Unlike the underground trains, buses are an excellent way to see Singapore. The two main operators are Singapore Bus Services (SBS) and Trans-Island Bus Services (TIBS). Within the city, reserved bus lanes along the main roads and frequent service—usually every 5–10 minutes—make buses quick transportation options. The excellent *TransitLink Guide,* available for S$2 at any bookstore or subway (MRT) station, pinpoints major stops. Fares range from S$0.60 to S$1.20 for buses without air-conditioning and from S$0.75 to S$1.75 for those with it. If you'll be making multiple trips on buses and trains, save money by purchasing an EZ-Link stored value card from any MRT station for S$15. Alternatively, deposit exact change and collect your ticket each time you board. Most buses run 6 AM–midnight daily.

To reach Sentosa Island, catch a Special E bus, which runs down Orchard Road, or take a regular bus—number 65 or 143—to the HarbourFront Centre before transferring onto a shuttle across the causeway. Shuttles operate weekdays 7 AM–10:30 PM and weekends until 12:30 AM; the S$7 round-trip fare includes admission to the island.

The vividly colored SIA Hop-On bus is a good way to explore Orchard Road, Bugis Junction, Suntec City, the Civic District, Boat Quay, Chinatown, Little India, and the Singapore Botanic Gardens. As the name suggests, you can get on and off the route as you please. Singapore Airlines or SilkAir passengers who show their air ticket or boarding pass pay S$3 for a day pass. Otherwise, tickets are S$6 and can be purchased from most hotels, downtown SIA ticket offices, or from the driver.

The red Singapore Explorer bus connects the Orchard Road shopping belt, the colonial district, the Singapore River, Chinatown, Raffles Hotel, Clarke Quay, Marina, and Suntec City. It makes 22 stops and your ticket (S$9) is good for a day of unlimited travel, as well as a riverboat tour. You can buy it (you'll need exact change) when you board or from your hotel concierge.

The S$10 MRT tourist day ticket allows you to take up to 12 rides a day, regardless of distance traveled, on all trains and public buses. Inform the ticketing officer of the exact date you wish to use it as it's printed on the card and valid for that day only.

For more information on bus travel within Singapore, contact SBS, TIBS, or the TransLink Hotline.

⊞ Bus Information SIA Hop-On Bus ☎ 6734-9923. **Singapore Bus Services (SBS)** ☎ 1800/287-2727. **Singapore Explorer** ☎ 6339-6833. **Trans-Island Bus Services (TIBS)** ☎ 1800/482-5433 ⊕ www.tibs.com. sg. **TransLink Hotline** ☎ 1800/779-9366 ⊕ www. transitlink.com.sg.

BUSINESS HOURS

BANKS & OFFICES

Businesses are generally open weekdays 9 or 9:30 to 5 or 5:30; a few are also open on Saturday morning. In general, banks open weekdays 9:30–3, Saturday 9:30–noon. Branches of the Post Office Savings Bank (POSB), however, in the Orchard area open Monday through Thursday 11–7; some branches of the Development Bank of Singapore (DBS) open until 3 on Saturday. The DBS bank at Changi Airport is open whenever there are flights. Post offices are usually open weekdays 8:30–5, Saturday 8:30–1. The Killiney Road branch, just off Orchard Road, facing the Orchard Point shopping center, is open Sunday and in the evenings.

GAS STATIONS

Called petrol or service stations in Singapore, gas stations open daily 7 AM–midnight.

MUSEUMS & SIGHTS

Many museums close on Monday; otherwise, they're generally open from 9 to 4:30 or 5:30, and often until 9 PM on Wednesday.

PHARMACIES

Pharmacies throughout the country generally open daily 9–6, though some pharmacies in the major shopping centers open until 10 PM.

SHOPS

Shop hours vary in Singapore. Department stores and most shops in the big shopping centers, such as those on Orchard Road, generally open daily 10–9, sometimes later on weekends; smaller stores tend to close on Sunday.

CABLE CAR TRAVEL

You can catch a cable car to Sentosa Island from one of two terminals on the Singapore side: the Cable Car Towers, next to the HarbourFront Centre, and the Mt. Faber Cable Car Station. The longer, 13-minute trip from Mt. Faber has better views, but there's no bus to the station and it's a long walk up the hill; a taxi is your best bet. The Cable Car Towers station is accessible by bus: from Orchard Road take bus 65 or 143; from Clifford Pier, bus 10, 30, 65, 80, 93, 97, 100, 125, or 131; from Chinatown, Bus 61, 84, 143, 145, or 166. The closest MRT station is HarbourFront. Cable cars run regularly daily 8:30 AM–9 PM; fares are S$7.50 one-way and S$8.90 round-trip.

⑦ Cable Car Information Singapore Cable Cars ☎ 6270-8855 ⊕ www.cablecar.com.sg.

CAMERAS & PHOTOGRAPHY

Always ask permission before taking pictures of most locals. Don't hesitate to ask a passerby to take shots of you at a hawker center, in front of the Merlion, with a Raffles Hotel doorman, or on the Singapore River. Military facilities are among the few areas where taking photographs is prohibited. The *Kodak Guide*

to *Shooting Great Travel Pictures* (available at bookstores everywhere) is loaded with tips.

⑦ Photo Help Kodak Information Center ☎ 800/242-2424 ⊕ www.kodak.com.

EQUIPMENT PRECAUTIONS

Singapore's humidity can wreak havoc on lenses. Before your trip, clean them thoroughly. Once in Singapore, let them breathe; keeping them wrapped in plastic may cause them to mold. Singapore's daylight can be very strong, so carry a UV filter. Bring a dry bag to protect your equipment from rain.

Don't pack film or equipment in checked luggage, where it's much more susceptible to damage. X-ray machines are extremely powerful and therefore likely to ruin your film. Try to ask for hand inspection of film, which becomes clouded after repeated exposure to airport X-ray machines, and keep videotapes and computer disks away from metal detectors. Always keep film, tape, and computer disks out of the sun. Carry an extra supply of batteries, and be prepared to turn on your camera, camcorder, or laptop to prove to airport security personnel that the device is real.

FILM & DEVELOPING

Internationally recognized brands and formats of film are readily available throughout Singapore. Expect to pay S$12 for a three pack of 36-exposure color print film. Most film developers charge S$10 for a 36-exposure roll. They can also burn your print images onto a CD for under S$10. Same-day service is common. For the best quality prints, head to the camera stores in Peninsula Plaza.

VIDEOS & DVDS

You can purchase videotapes in packs of three for about S$8. If you purchase videos that aren't blank, note that the system used in Singapore is PAL, whereas it's NTSC in the U.S. Blank CDs and DVDs usually cost about S$1.

CAR RENTAL

It's not advisable to rent a car in Singapore. There's really no reason to rent a car in here, unless you'd like to drive into

Malaysia. Driving can be a harrowing experience thanks to road congestion, particularly during rush hour and on weekends and holidays. Highway names, tariffs, and all licensing schemes are abbreviated, causing great confusion. Thankfully, the island is relatively small and its public transportation system is excellent. Taxis are safe, clean, cheap, and can cater to travelers with specific needs and large groups. Renting a car will cost up to S$800 per day, plus insurance and payment for compulsory safety seats if you're traveling with children. Additionally, you'll need to pay for fuel, parking, and a stored value CashCard (from a convenience store or post office), from which tolls are automatically deducted.

Local Agencies **Avis National** ✉ Changi Airport, Terminal 2, Arrival Hall ☎ 6542-8855 ⊕ www.avis. com ✉ #07-01 Grand Copthorne Waterfront Plaza Hotel, 392 Havelock Rd., Havelock ☎ 6737-1668. **CityLimo** ✉ #01-41 Specialists' Shopping Centre, 277 Orchard Rd., Orchard ☎ 6737-8282 ⊕ www. citylimo.com.sg. **Hertz** ✉ Changi Airport, Terminals 1 & 2, Arrival Hall ☎ 6542-5300 ⊕ www.hertz.com. **Sans Tours** ✉ 100 Kim Seng Plaza, River Valley ☎ 6734-9922 ⊕ www.asiatours.com.sg.

CUTTING COSTS

If you're set on renting a car, book through a travel agent who will shop around for you. Compact or moderate-size cars are ideal. Rent from local companies to save up to 40% on the daily rental rate. Late returns are charged at a hefty rate—often one-fifth of the daily rate—so try to return it on time to avoid late charges.

An alternative is to hire a car and driver to free you from the angst of driving in Singapore. Most car rental agencies also have a "chauffer service." A 9-seater minivan can be hired for S$120 per three-hour block and a luxury car costs S$450 for three hours. It's significantly cheaper to hire a taxi and driver for the day, usually at hourly rates.

Renting a car in Malaysia and driving it over the border is another potentially money saving alternative. Rental fees are about 30% less than they are in Singapore. There's often, however, a minimum four-day rental period. Also, Malaysian-registered vehicles must have a valid Vehicle Entry Permit (VEP). At border crossings in Tuas or Woodlands you'll have to purchase a VEP for S$30 per day (they're free on weekends, holidays, and between 7 PM and 2 AM weekdays). You also need to pay a toll (S$3.20 at Tuas, S$1.20 at Woodlands) each time you enter or leave Singapore. Use a stored value CashCard on the Singapore side to avoid paying the S$10 fee on cash transactions. Border crossings and charges are managed by the Land Transport Authority. Their hotline (1800/225–5582) and Web site (www.lta.gov.sg) are good information sources. The Immigration and Checkpoints Authority (ICA) also has a hotline (6863–0117) and a Web site (www.ica. gov.sg) that you can check for traffic conditions at Woodlands and Tuas.

INSURANCE

When driving a rented car you are generally responsible for any damage to or loss of the vehicle. You also may be liable for any property damage or personal injury that you may cause while driving. Most insurance charges are included in the rental price. Before you rent, see what coverage you already have under the terms of your personal auto-insurance policy and credit cards. If you don't have personal accident insurance as part of your travel insurance, opt for the up to S$100,000 coverage, which costs S$5 daily.

REQUIREMENTS & RESTRICTIONS

Although Singaporeans can get their licenses at 18, most agencies only rent cars to drivers who are at least 21. Some companies even charge an extra fee (up to S$30 daily) for drivers under 25. On paper, many profess an upper age limit of 60, but healthy seniors are rarely prevented from renting. Most companies will accept a valid home country license as long as it's in English. Children under 8 are required to have child safety seats, so inform the rental company upon booking and they'll provide you with them for less than S$10 per week. Bring your own devices for infants under six months.

SURCHARGES

Rental cars are hired for use within Singapore only. An additional surcharge of between S$25 and S$40 will be levied for driving your rental into Malaysia. You can get your car delivered to your hotel or another location for a fee, usually S$20. Most companies have offices at Changi Airport and downtown; there's no fee for dropping your car at either of these locations. To avoid a hefty refueling fee, fill the tank just before you turn in the car, but be aware that gas stations near the rental outlet may overcharge.

CAR TRAVEL

At the time of rental, you'll need to present a driver's license, which has been valid for at least one year and is in English. The license may not be recognized if it's in another language. Universally recognized International Driving Permits (IDPs) are available from the American or Canadian automobile association, and in the U.K., from the Automobile Association or Royal Automobile Club. These are only valid in conjunction with your regular license; having one may save you from problems with the authorities.

Electronic Road Pricing (ERP) is a system of road pricing based on a pay-as-you-use principle. You car will be fitted with an In-vehicle Unit (IU) into which you slide a stored value CashCard. The minimum value is $20. You'll be charged up to S$2.50 per entry. Electronic readers deduct ERP charges from CashCards—you'll hear a beep. Make sure you use a CashCard and it has sufficient funds, otherwise you'll be fined S$70 for each unpaid entry.

🚗 **ERP Hotline** ☎ 1800/553-5226. **NETs (for CashCard information)** ☎ 6272-0533 ⊕ www.nets.com.sg.

EMERGENCY SERVICES

Closed-circuit cameras routinely scan the expressways for accidents and, as a result, the police tend to arrive promptly on accident scenes. The Automobile Association of Singapore (AAS) has 24-hour emergency road service. Most car rental companies will also provide you with an emergency number for breakdowns.

🚗 **Automobile Association of Singapore (AAS)** ☎ 6748-9911 ⊕ www.aas.com.sg. **Police** ☎ 999. **Ambulance or Fire** ☎ 995.

GASOLINE

Unleaded gas starts at S$1.60 per liter (S$6 per gallon) in Singapore. Cars driving into Malaysia must not leave Singapore with gas tanks less than three-quarters full. The government imposes fines for breaking this law, which is intended to discourage Singaporeans from driving into Malaysia for cheap gas, a previous practice that hurt Singapore's revenues.

PARKING

The most common way to park is with parking coupons, which should be displayed on the dashboard. Denominations of parking coupons are S$0.50, S$1, S$1.80, and S$2 (for overnight parking). Generally, parking rates are S$0.50 per half hour outside the CBD and S$1 per half hour within it. Parking coupons are available from gas stations, post offices, shopping centers, and some shops.

The two other ways of parking—paid parking and stored value CashCards—are practiced at shopping centers and office buildings. You pay for the amount of time your car is parked. Some shopping centers offer a rebate on your parking charges, as do some hotels. Avoid parking in lots marked with red, which belong to office tenants or apartment block residents.

ROAD CONDITIONS

For the most part road conditions are quite good, especially on the expressways. Some streets have fairly deep ditches for drainage and may not be well lit in the evenings. Watch for speed humps, especially in residential streets.

ROAD MAPS

The SBS Transit Guide and an official Singapore map are free at Changi Airport, hotels, and tourist centers. They include the main streets, expressways, border routes, hotels, shopping complexes, and major attractions. Either one will be adequate for driving to the main sites. If you plan on exploring back streets or would feel more confident with a street directory, invest in the street maps available at news kiosks and bookstores. The exhaustive ⊕ www.streetdirectory.com.sg allows you to search for locations via street address or building name.

RULES OF THE ROAD

Driving is on the left-hand side of the road in both Singapore and Malaysia. Parking coupons (⇨ Parking, *above*) should be displayed on the dashboard. Seat belts and child seats are mandatory. Head lights must be on between 7 PM and 7 AM. Drunk-driving laws are strict. The legal limit is 80 mg of alcohol per 100 ml of blood.

There are some common road markings that you should be aware of. Yield to oncoming traffic when you see parallel white lines in front of you. Parallel white lines down the center of the road prohibit parking or passing; a single white line prohibits parking at any time on either side. A yellow line by the roadside means no parking 7 AM–7 PM on that side. Parallel yellow lines prohibit parking at all times on that side of the road. Zigzag lines by the side of the road indicate a pedestrian crossing ahead. Painted triangles indicate that you must give way to traffic on a major road ahead.

The speed limit is 50 kph (31 mph) in residential areas and 80 kph (50 mph) on expressways. Speed cameras are installed throughout the island. Fines, which are comparable to those in, say, New York City or Toronto, are electronically issued immediately and delivered by courier. Bus lanes or extreme-left lanes marked by unbroken yellow lines should not be used by cars during the following hours: weekdays 7:30 AM–9:30 AM and 4:30 PM–7 PM, Saturday 7:30 AM–9:30 AM and 11:30 AM–2 PM.

CHILDREN IN SINGAPORE

Bringing yours along may be your ticket to meeting locals. Family is very important to Singaporeans. While older relatives are treated with upmost respect, children are the jewels in the crown. Most places are extremely child-friendly.

Singaporeans bring their children to more places, and later at night, than most Westerners would. Nonetheless, the physical streets of Singapore aren't particularly stroller-friendly. For walking with babies, a baby-sling is probably the most practical option. Singaporeans usually carry their infants around in their arms rather than wheeling them. Many pavements are uneven and there are a lot of stairs, including very steeply angled pedestrian bridges over highways with no ramp alternatives to cross very busy roads. Keep a close eye on toddlers as traffic can be fairly frenetic. If you're renting a car, don't forget to arrange for a car seat when you reserve.

You won't need to leave your children behind often as they're welcome almost everywhere in Singapore. Still, if you do need a babysitter, your hotel is likely to have contacts with dependable babysitters; they're most likely local student teachers or nurses. For general advice about traveling with children, consult *Fodor's FYI: Travel with Your Baby* (available in bookstores everywhere).

FLYING

If your children are two or older, ask about children's airfares. As a general rule, infants under two not occupying a seat fly at greatly reduced fares or even for free. But if you want to guarantee a seat for an infant, you have to pay full fare. Consider flying during off-peak days and times; most airlines will grant an infant a seat without a ticket if there are available seats. When booking, confirm carry-on allowances if you're traveling with infants. In general, for babies charged 10% to 50% of the adult fare you are allowed one carry-on bag and a collapsible stroller; if the flight is full, the stroller may have to be checked or you may be limited to less.

Experts agree that it's a good idea to use safety seats aloft for children weighing less than 40 pounds. Airlines set their own policies: if you use a safety seat, U.S. carriers usually require that the child be ticketed, even if he or she is young enough to ride free, because the seats must be strapped into regular seats. And even if you pay the full adult fare for the seat, it may be worth it, especially on longer trips. Do **check your airline's policy about using safety seats during takeoff and landing.** Safety seats are not allowed everywhere in the plane, so get your seat assignments as early as possible.

When reserving, request children's meals or a freestanding bassinet (not available at all airlines) if you need them. But note that bulkhead seats, where you must sit to use the bassinet, may lack an overhead bin or storage space on the floor.

Singapore Airlines' frequent flyer program, KrisFlyer, has a *Young Explorer Club* for kids between two and 12. They can earn and redeem miles for free travel awards just like adult KrisFlyer members, plus they get their own magazine.

PRECAUTIONS

Singapore is largely safe for kids with the proviso that you should watch them carefully in areas with dense traffic as motorists are typically impatient and speedy. Singaporeans express their affection for children openly, so on the whole you shouldn't misinterpret such displays by strangers of either sex as signalling something more sinister. Although mosquitoes are well under control in Singapore, they may bother young children, especially when trying to sleep at night. **Ask a pharmacist or doctor's advice on which brands of mosquito repellent are best for children.** Prickly heat rashes can also be a problem; try dousing your children in talcum powder as a preventative measure. Children should wear light shoes on the beach and when paddling. It's not a good idea to pick up interesting-looking shells on the seashore, as tropical waters may have a few nasty surprises.

You may also need to watch out for the effects of spicy local food. Carry a couple of rubber bands with you to tie the ends of chopsticks together; it makes them much easier to use. Most importantly make sure your children keep hydrated, and wear hats and sunscreen when out in the open. If your child becomes unusually tired, headachy, or grumpy, or if their urine turns orange, it may be due to lack of liquids.

SIGHTS & ATTRACTIONS

The Singapore Zoological Gardens has elephant and pony rides (S$2), daily feedings, and entertaining animal shows. The whole family can even camp out and "sleep with the beasts" here. The Jurong Bird Park has educational programs for kids of all ages. Seeing animals in the dark at Night Safari can be a very exciting experience for children. All the exhibits at the Singapore Science Centre are hands on and designed to pique children's curiosity about how things work. Many of Sentosa Island's attractions—such as Fantasy Island's water slides, the Lost Civilisation and Ruined City gardens, and the multicolored Musical Fountain—are geared for kids.

Places that are especially appealing to children are indicated by a rubber-duckie icon (🐤) in the margin.

SUPPLIES & EQUIPMENT

Most department stores, supermarkets, and pharmacies, particularly in the Orchard Road area, stock basic child-rearing supplies such as disposable diapers (locally known as "nappies"), baby talcum powder, bottles, etc. A wide variety of milk formula and milk-powder brands is available; **check the milk-tin labels to ensure they're meant for babies,** as it's common to use milk powder for ordinary home and adult use in Singapore and not all of these brands are suitable for babies. If you need fresh milk, you may find the Australian imported brands have a more familiar taste than some of the local brands. Local department stores, especially Takashimaya, all have well-stocked children's sections.

TRANSPORTATION

Taxis can legally carry up to four children if they're accompanied by one adult. Fares on trains and buses are partly determined by height. Children up to 3 feet (0.9 m) tall and accompanied by a fare-paying adult may travel free. If they're taller, but under 8 years old, they're eligible for a S$6 stored value card. Individual fares then cost around S$0.50 per ride.

COMPUTERS ON THE ROAD

Most hotels have computers available in their business centers or have rental laptops. Wireless internet is widely available in hotels, cafés, and public buildings. If you plan to bring your own laptop it's wise to **travel with international adaptors and multiple-headed socket adapters** as well as an extra-long modem cable with phone jacks at either end, for those hotels or other facilities that don't have a lot of phone sockets in the room or have them inconveniently located, away from desks, out of the best light, etc. The electricity supply is 220V–240V. A word of warning, retail outlets aren't overly helpful with computer problems if they don't see a sale of new equipment in the deal.

CONSUMER PROTECTION

Whether you're shopping for gifts or purchasing travel services, **pay with a major credit card** whenever possible, so you can cancel payment or get reimbursed if there's a problem (and you can provide documentation). If you're doing business with a particular company for the first time, contact your local Better Business Bureau and the attorney general's offices in your state and (for U.S. businesses) the company's home state as well. Have any complaints been filed? Finally, if you're buying a package or tour, always consider travel insurance that includes default coverage (⇨ Insurance).

Look for the CASE TRUST logo in retailer windows, which indicates that the merchant has been distinguished for excellent service and fair pricing by the Consumers Association of Singapore and the Singapore Tourism Board (STB). Lodge complaints with the tourist board.

Be sure to ask for receipts, both for your own protection and for customs. Though shopkeepers are often amenable to stating false values on receipts, customs officials are wary and knowledgeable.

🔢 **BBBs Council of Better Business Bureaus** ✉ 4200 Wilson Blvd., Suite 800, Arlington, VA 22203 ☎ 703/276-0100 🖷 703/525-8277 ⊕ www.bbb.org.

🔢 **Complaints STB Complaints Hotline** ☎ 800/736-3366 ⊕ www.visitsingapore.com.

CRUISE TRAVEL

More than 14 million people a year pass through the Singapore Cruise Centre's passenger terminals on their way to and from equatorial adventures throughout Asia. Many of the international lines, including Crystal Cruises of Los Angeles, Cunardine of New York, Holland America Line of Seattle, and Seabourn Cruise Line of San Francisco, have a Singapore stopover as part of their multi-week cruise itineraries.

Star Cruises, Singapore's most popular cruise company, covers the immediate region, Malaysia, Thailand, Indonesia, and Vietnam in particular, as well as longer-distance (usually fly-cruise) to Hong Kong, China, and Japan. The larger ships are fully equipped with karaoke, swimming pools, gyms, libraries, cinemas, discos, and restaurants (as well as casino facilities). In the simplest package, the overnight "Cruise to Nowhere," the ship heads into the open sea and starts up its gambling tables and duty-free bars, which close as soon as it reenters Singapore's waters. Depending on how far you go, for how long and in what class, you're looking at costs ranging between S$450 and S$1,400 per person, or even up to S$2,510, but this does include great comfort and an abundance of food. To get the best deal on a cruise, **consult a cruise-only travel agency** or look for special deals in *Straits Times'* classified section.

To learn how to plan, choose, and book a cruise-ship voyage, consult *Fodor's FYI: Plan & Enjoy Your Cruise* (available in bookstores everywhere).

🔢 Cruise Information **Singapore Cruise Centre** ☎ 6321-2803. **Star Cruises** ✉ #11–08 Park Mall, 9 Penang Rd., Orchard ☎ 800/327-9020 Ext. 1105 in the U.S., 6223-0002 in Singapore.

CUSTOMS & DUTIES

When shopping abroad, keep receipts for all purchases. Upon reentering the country, **be ready to show customs officials what you've bought.** Pack purchases together in an easily accessible place. If you think a duty is incorrect, appeal the assessment. If you object to the way your clearance was handled, note the inspector's badge number. In either case, first ask to see a supervisor. If the problem isn't resolved, write to the appropriate authorities, beginning with the port director at your point of entry.

ON ARRIVAL IN SINGAPORE

Visitors over 18 arriving from countries other than Malaysia and who've spent no less than 48 hours outside of Singapore are allowed to bring in up to one liter of spirits, wine, or beer; all personal effects; and less than S$50 in foodstuffs such as chocolates, biscuits, and cakes. **The following imports are prohibited:** drugs; pornography (including such publications as *Playboy* and *Playgirl*); seditious and treasonable materials (e.g., banned books/tapes); toy Singapore coins and currency notes; cigarette lighters in pistol/revolver shapes; duty-free cigarettes; or reproductions of copyrighted publications, videotapes, records, or cassettes. Chewing gum in amounts deemed large enough for resale, chewing tobacco and imitation tobacco products, and endangered species of wildlife and their by-products are also prohibited. Special import permits are required for animals, live plants, meats, arms, and controlled drugs. **Penalties for drug abuse are very severe in Singapore and are rigidly enforced.** The death penalty is mandatory for trafficking certain amounts of drugs (for example, 15g of heroin, 30g of cocaine, 500g of cannibis). Customs is also extremely strict regarding the import of any form of arms, including such items as ceremonial daggers purchased as souvenirs in other countries. These are held in bond and returned to you on your departure. There are no import (or export) restrictions or limitations on the amount of cash, foreign currencies, checks, and drafts.

ON DEPARTURE FROM SINGAPORE

Export permits are required for arms, ammunition, explosives, animals, gold, platinum, precious stones and jewelry, poisons, and medicinal drugs. The export of narcotics is punishable by death under Singapore law.

🇸🇬 **Singapore Customs** ✉ Duty Office Singapore Changi Airport ☎ 6542-7058 or 6545-9122 in Terminal 1, 6543-0755/0754 in Terminal 2.

IN AUSTRALIA

Australian residents who are 18 or older may bring home A$900 worth of souvenirs and gifts (including jewelry), 250 cigarettes or 250 grams of cigars or other tobacco products, and 2.25 liters of alcohol (including wine, beer, and spirits). Residents under 18 may bring back A$400 worth of goods. Members of the same family traveling together may pool their allowances. Prohibited items include meat products. Seeds, plants, and fruits need to be declared upon arrival.

🇦🇺 **Australian Customs Service** ✪ Locked Bag 3000, Sydney International Airport, Sydney, NSW 2020 ☎ 02/6275-6666 or 1300/363263, 02/9364-7222 or 1800/020-504 quarantine-inquiry line 🖷 02/8339-6714 ⊕ www.customs.gov.au.

IN CANADA

Canadian residents who have been out of Canada for at least seven days may bring in C$750 worth of goods duty-free. If you've been away fewer than seven days but more than 48 hours, the duty-free allowance drops to C$200. If your trip lasts 24 to 48 hours, the allowance is C$50. You may not pool allowances with family members. Goods claimed under the C$750 exemption may follow you by mail; those claimed under the lesser exemptions must accompany you. Alcohol and tobacco products may be included in the seven-day and 48-hour exemptions but not in the 24-hour exemption. If you meet the age requirements of the province or territory through which you reenter Canada, you may bring in, duty-free, 1.5 liters of wine *or* 1.14 liters (40 imperial ounces) of liquor *or* 24 12-ounce cans or bottles of beer or ale. Also, if you meet the local age requirement for tobacco products, you may bring in, duty-free, 200 cigarettes and 50 cigars. Check ahead of time with the Canada Border Services Agency or the Department of Agriculture for policies regarding meat products, seeds, plants, and fruits.

You may send an unlimited number of gifts (only one gift per recipient, however) worth up to C$60 each duty-free to Canada. Label the package UNSOLICITED

GIFT—VALUE UNDER $60. Alcohol and tobacco are excluded.

⚐ Canada Border Services Agency ⊠ 2265 St. Laurent Blvd., Ottawa, Ontario K1G 4K3 ☎ 800/461-9999 in Canada, 204/983-3500, 506/636-5064 ⊕ www.ccra.gc.ca.

IN NEW ZEALAND

All homeward-bound residents may bring back NZ$700 worth of souvenirs and gifts; passengers may not pool their allowances, and children can claim only the concession on goods intended for their own use. For those 17 or older, the duty-free allowance also includes 4.5 liters of wine or beer; one 1,125-ml bottle of spirits; and either 200 cigarettes, 250 grams of tobacco, 50 cigars, *or* a combination of the three up to 250 grams. Meat products, seeds, plants, and fruits must be declared upon arrival to the Agricultural Services Department.

⚐ New Zealand Customs ⊠ Head office: The Customhouse, 17-21 Whitmore St., Box 2218, Wellington ☎ 09/300-5399 or 0800/428-786 ⊕ www.customs.govt.nz.

IN THE U.K.

From countries outside the European Union, including Singapore, you may bring home, duty-free, 200 cigarettes, 50 cigars, 100 cigarillos, or 250 grams of tobacco; 1 liter of spirits or 2 liters of fortified or sparkling wine or liqueurs; 2 liters of still table wine; 60 ml of perfume; 250 ml of toilet water; plus £145 worth of other goods, including gifts and souvenirs. Prohibited items include meat and dairy products, seeds, plants, and fruits.

⚐ HM Customs and Excise ⊠ Portcullis House, 21 Cowbridge Rd. E, Cardiff CF11 9SS ☎ 0845/010-9000 or 0208/929-0152 advice service, 0208/929-6731 or 0208/910-3602 complaints ⊕ www.hmce.gov.uk.

IN THE U.S.

U.S. residents who have been out of the country for at least 48 hours may bring home, for personal use, $800 worth of foreign goods duty-free, as long as they haven't used the $800 allowance or any part of it in the past 30 days. This exemption may include 1 liter of alcohol (for travelers 21 and older), 200 cigarettes, and 100 non-Cuban cigars. Family members from the same household who are traveling together may pool their $800 personal exemptions. For fewer than 48 hours, the duty-free allowance drops to $200, which may include 50 cigarettes, 10 non-Cuban cigars, and 150 ml of alcohol (or 150 ml of perfume containing alcohol). The $200 allowance cannot be combined with other individuals' exemptions, and if you exceed it, the full value of all the goods will be taxed. Antiques, which U.S. Customs and Border Protection defines as objects more than 100 years old, enter duty-free, as do original works of art done entirely by hand, including paintings, drawings, and sculptures. This doesn't apply to folk art or handicrafts, which are in general dutiable.

You may also send packages home duty-free, with a limit of one parcel per addressee per day (except alcohol or tobacco products or perfume worth more than $5). You can mail up to $200 worth of goods for personal use; label the package PERSONAL USE and attach a list of its contents and their retail value. If the package contains your used personal belongings, mark it AMERICAN GOODS RETURNED to avoid paying duties. You may send up to $100 worth of goods as a gift; mark the package UNSOLICITED GIFT. Mailed items do not affect your duty-free allowance on your return.

To avoid paying duty on foreign-made high-ticket items you already own and will take on your trip, register them with Customs before you leave the country. Consider filing a Certificate of Registration for laptops, cameras, watches, and other digital devices identified with serial numbers or other permanent markings; you can keep the certificate for other trips. Otherwise, bring a sales receipt or insurance form to show that you owned the item before you left the U.S.

For more about duties, restricted items, and other information about international travel, check out U.S. Customs and Border Protection's online brochure, *Know Before You Go.*

⚐ U.S. Customs and Border Protection ⊠ for inquiries and complaints, 1300 Pennsylvania Ave. NW,

Washington, DC 20229 ⊕ www.cbp.gov ☎ 877/227–5551, 202/354–1000.

DISABILITIES & ACCESSIBILITY

Singapore eclipses the rest of Southeast Asia in meeting the needs of visitors with disabilities, but this doesn't say much. The proliferation of grand stairways, steeply stepped, unramped pedestrian bridges over major roads, and similar descents into the MRT underground rail system, translate into a nightmare for people in wheelchairs. Nevertheless, most major hotels, office buildings, shopping complexes, and tourist attractions do have wheelchair access and grab bars in public toilets. Traffic lights (mostly within the city) make a chirping sound when the signal turns to WALK and screens count down the seconds until the light changes. **Be aware that Singaporeans still haven't integrated people with disabilities into mainstream society** and may act awkward around them; they may hang back from helping out of embarrassment or not knowing what to do.

For more information, contact the Disabled People's Association of Singapore or the National Council of Social Services, which publishes guides on touring Singapore. Contact these organizations at least three weeks before you plan to visit Singapore. If the guides aren't available online, they'll happily send any printed materials to you via airmail.

◪ Local Resources **Disabled People's Association of Singapore** ✉ #02-00 Day Care, 150A Pandan Gardens Centre ☎ 6899–1220 ⊕ www.dpa.org.sg. **National Council of Social Services** ✉ 11 Penang La. ☎ 6210–2500.

LODGING

More than 20 (mostly upscale) hotels claim to have special services for travelers with disabilities. There isn't any watchdog organization, however, that verifies this information, so check with properties directly. Local hotels aren't used to accommodating travelers with disabilities.

RESERVATIONS

When discussing accessibility with an operator or reservations agent, ask hard questions. Are there any stairs, inside or

out? Are there grab bars next to the toilet *and* in the shower/tub? How wide is the doorway to the room? To the bathroom? For the most extensive facilities meeting the latest legal specifications, opt for newer accommodations. If you reserve through a toll-free number, consider also calling the hotel's local number to confirm the information from the central reservations office. Get confirmation in writing when you can.

SIGHTS & ATTRACTIONS

Tourist attractions friendly to visitors in wheelchairs include the Singapore Zoological Gardens, Night Safari, and Jurong Bird Park—all have good paths and ramps. With its undulating terrain and its attractions dispersed over a wide area, Sentosa Island isn't as accessible. Major shopping areas like Orchard Road have smooth modern mall surfaces, but older parts of town are characterized by arcaded sidewalks linked by ubiquitous steps, occasional open drains, and heavy car traffic, so street level sightseeing in such ethnic quarters as Chinatown or Little India can present serious challenges to those with disabilities.

TRANSPORTATION

The MRT underground railway is inaccessible to people in wheelchairs; entry to most stations begins with an extremely steep flight of descending stairs, following by escalators. The bus system is also unfriendly to passengers with disabilities—seats are hard to come by, the buses are often packed, and it's hard to maintain your balance with the way bus drivers hit their brakes. To board a local bus you must first hike a couple of steps set quite high up.

The Disabled People's Association of Singapore recommends CityCab to get around the island. The Handicaps Welfare Association also has vans fitted with hydraulic lifts—book in advance—and manual wheelchairs for rental.

The airport is well organized for travelers with disabilities, although arrivals should note that the ramp down to the baggage collection area is somewhat steep and Immigration counters are high. Both terminals have ground handling agents from Changi International Airport Services (CIAS) and Singapore Airport Terminal Services (SATS) who assist with clearing passengers in wheelchairs through Immigration and Customs checkpoints. Wheelchair rental is possible 24 hours, for S$10 plus a refundable deposit of S$20.

⁊ Transportation Resources Raffles Medical Group (Airport Wheelchair Rental) ☎ 6543-1118 ⊕ www.rafflesmedical.com.sg. **CityCab** ☎ 6553-1170 ⊕ www.citycab.com.sg. **Handicaps Welfare Association** ✉ 16 Whampoa Dr. (behind Block 102) ☎ 6254-3006 ⊕ www.hwa.org.sg.

⁊ Complaints Aviation Consumer Protection Division (⇨ Air Travel) for airline-related problems. **Departmental Office of Civil Rights** ✉ for general inquiries, U.S. Department of Transportation, S-30, 400 7th St. SW, Room 10215, Washington, DC 20590 ☎ 202/366-4648 🖷 202/366-9371 ⊕ www.dot.gov/ost/docr/index.htm. **Disability Rights Section** ✉ NYAV, U.S. Department of Justice, Civil Rights Division, 950 Pennsylvania Ave. NW, Washington, DC 20530 ☎ ADA information line 202/514-0301, 800/514-0301, 202/514-0383 TTY, 800/514-0383 TTY ⊕ www.ada.gov. **U.S. Department of Transportation Hotline** 🖷 for disability-related air-travel problems, 800/778-4838 or 800/455-9880 TTY.

TRAVEL AGENCIES

In the U.S., the Americans with Disabilities Act requires that travel firms serve the needs of all travelers. Some agencies specialize in working with people with disabilities.

⁊ Travelers with Mobility Problems Access Adventures/B. Roberts Travel ✉ 206 Chestnut Ridge Rd., Scottsville, NY 14624 ☎ 585/889-9096 ⊕ www.brobertstravel.com ✍ dltravel@prodigy.net, run by a former physical-rehabilitation counselor. **Flying Wheels Travel** ✉ 143 W. Bridge St., Box 382, Owatonna, MN 55060 ☎ 507/451-5005 🖷 507/451-1685 ⊕ www.flyingwheelstravel.com.

DISCOUNTS & DEALS

Be a smart shopper and compare all your options before making decisions. A plane ticket bought with a promotional coupon from travel clubs, coupon books, and direct-mail offers or purchased on the Internet may not be cheaper than the least expensive fare from a discount ticket agency. And always keep in mind that what you get is just as important as what you save.

DISCOUNT RESERVATIONS

To save money, look into discount reservations services with Web sites and toll-free numbers, which use their buying power to get a better price on hotels, airline tickets (⇨ Air Travel), even car rentals. When booking a room, always **call the hotel's local toll-free number** (if one is available) rather than the central reservations number—you'll often get a better price. Always ask about special packages or corporate rates.

When shopping for the best deal on hotels and car rentals, look for guaranteed exchange rates, which protect you against a falling dollar. With your rate locked in, you won't pay more, even if the price goes up in the local currency.

⁊ Airline Tickets Air 4 Less ☎ 800/AIR4LESS; low-fare specialist.

⁊ Hotel Rooms Accommodations Express ☎ 800/444-7666 or 800/277-1064 ⊕ www.acex.net. **Hotels.com** ☎ 800/246-8357 ⊕ www.hotels.com. **Steigenberger Reservation Service** ☎ 800/223-5652 ⊕ www.srs-worldhotels.com. **Turbotrip.com** ☎ 800/473-7829 ⊕ www.turbotrip.com. **Vacation-Land** ☎ 800/245-0050 ⊕ www.vacation-land.com.

PACKAGE DEALS

Don't confuse packages and guided tours. When you buy a package, you travel on your own, just as though you had planned the trip yourself. Fly/drive packages, which combine airfare and car rental, are often a good deal. In cities, ask the local visitor's bureau about hotel and local transportation packages that include tickets to major museum exhibits or other special events.

ELECTRICITY

To use electric-powered equipment purchased in the U.S. or Canada, **bring a converter and adapter.** If your appliances are dual-voltage, you'll only need an adapter. Don't use 110-volt outlets marked FOR SHAVERS ONLY for high-wattage appliances such as blow-dryers. Most laptops operate equally well on 110 and 220 volts and so require only an adapter. The electrical current in Singapore is 220–240 volts, 50 cycles alternating current (AC), as in Australia and the U.K. Wall outlets take plugs with three square-tipped prongs. Most hotels lend their guests adapters and converters.

EMBASSIES

Most countries maintain a diplomatic mission in Singapore. Call ahead to confirm hours; most are closed Saturday. If you hope to obtain visas for neighboring countries, be aware that the visa-application process at Singapore consular offices may take several days.

🇦🇺 Australia **Australian High Commission** ⊠ 25 Napier Rd., Napier ☎ 6836–4100 🖷 6737–7465 ⊕ www.australia.org.sg.

🇨🇦 Canada **Canadian High Commission** ⊠ 80 Anson Rd., Tanjong Pagar ☎ 6325–3200 🖷 6325–3296 ⊕ www.dfait-maeci.gc.ca/singapore.

🇳🇿 New Zealand **New Zealand High Commission** ⊠ #15/06–10 Ngee Ann City, Tower A, 391A Orchard Rd., Orchard ☎ 6235–9966 🖷 6733–9924 ⊕ www.nzembassy.com/singapore.

🇬🇧 United Kingdom **British High Commission** ⊠ 100 Tanglin Rd., Tanglin ☎ 6424–4200 🖷 6424–4264 ⊕ www.britain.org.sg.

🇺🇸 United States **U.S. Embassy** ⊠ 27 Napier Rd., Napier ☎ 6476–9100 🖷 6476–9340 ⊕ www.usembassysingapore.org.sg.

EMERGENCIES

Most train station employees are trained in first aid. Large department stores and hotel have doctors on call. The Singaporean police are well trained.

🔳 Doctors & Dentists **Alpha Dental Group** ⊠ #01–13 Temasek Tower, 8 Shenton Way, CBD ☎ 6224–8003. **Atria-City Dental Group** ⊠ #08–09 Ngee Ann City, Tower B, 391B Orchard Rd., Orchard ☎ 6737–2777 ☎ 6535–8833 for after-hours emergencies. **Raffles Medical Group** ⊠ Level 1, 585 North Bridge Rd., Chinatown ☎ 6311–2360. **Yip Dental Surgery** ⊠ #04–01, 3 Mt. Elizabeth, Orchard ☎ 6535–8833.

🔳 Emergency Services **Ambulance and fire** ☎ 995. **Police** ☎ 999.

🔳 Hospitals **Gleneagles Hospital** ⊠ 6A Napier Rd., Tanglin ☎ 6473–7222. **Mt. Alvernia Hospital** ⊠ 820 Thomson Rd., Thomson ☎ 6347–6688. **Mt. Elizabeth Hospital** ⊠ 3 Mt. Elizabeth, Orchard ☎ 6737–2666. **Raffles Medical Group** ⊠ Level 1,

585 North Bridge Rd., Kreta Ayer ☎ 6311–1555 for 24-hour emergency center. **Singapore General Hospital** ⊠ Outram Rd., Outram ☎ 6321–4311.

🔳 Hotlines **Samaritans of Singapore** ☎ 1800/221–4444.

🔳 Pharmacies **Unity Pharmacies** Tanglin Mall ⊠ #B–13, 163 Tanglin Rd., Orchard ☎ 6732–1380; Raffles City ⊠ #03–21, 252 North Bridge Rd., Colonial Singapore ☎ 6337–1358; Tanjong Pagar Plaza ⊠ #01–01 NTUC Supermarket, Tanjong Pagar Rd., Block 5, Chinatown ☎ 6323–1281.

ENGLISH-LANGUAGE MEDIA

English is used extensively in the Singapore media, both print and broadcast, alongside the major local languages: Mandarin Chinese, Malay, and Tamil Indian. All Singapore media are constrained in their reporting and take their cue from the People's Action Party Government. International media aren't exempt: the government intermittently bans, sues, or restricts the circulation of foreign publications or journalists when they're considered to have overstepped the mark.

Singapore practices official censorship. Certain books and magazines can't be sold; it may be a blanket ban or simply a prevention of a particular issue criticizing the government. Movies are routinely edited to remove sexual references—it took more than eight years for *Sex and the City* to be broadcast in Singapore. Non-offending international newspapers and magazines are generally available in larger hotels or the roadside magazine stands on the corner of Lor Lippit and Holland Avenue in Holland Village.

BOOKS

Since English is the lingua franca, all regular bookstores carry English-language books. Borders at Wheelock Place, Kinokuniya at Ngee Ann City (Takashimaya), and Times the Bookshop at Centrepoint are all good bets.

🔳 Bookstores **Borders** ⊠ #01–00 Wheelock Place, 501 Orchard Rd., Orchard ☎ 6235–7146. **Kinokuniya** ⊠ #03–09/10/15 Ngee Ann City (in Takashimaya), 391 Orchard Rd., Orchard ☎ 6737–5021 ⊕ www.kinokuniya.com.sg. **Times the Bookshop** ⊠ #04–08/16 Centrepoint, 176 Orchard Rd., Orchard ☎ 6734–9022.

NEWSPAPERS & MAGAZINES

There are several local English-language newspapers. The leading English-language "paper of record" is the daily *Straits Times*. Read this to get a better understanding of the government's current priorities and pending policy announcements. The letters to the editor section provides great insight into some of the alternative views held by locals. The *Business Times* daily is a serious business newspaper pitching a bit higher than the Straits Times, while *The New Paper* afternoon tabloid is Singapore's punchiest and most populist paper. *Streates* is a weekday commuter freebie.

For international news with coherent regional and local coverage, seek out the *International Herald Tribune,* the *Asian Wall Street Journal,* the *Financial Times* (of London), and the *Far Eastern Economic Review*. The *Economist* weekly covers Asian and international affairs fairly well. The weekly *8 Days* and fortnightly *IS* magazine are useful guides to events in Singapore; the latter is available for free from various dining, retail, and entertainment outlets.

RADIO & TELEVISION

Singapore's television and radio services are broadcast in multiple languages. In recent years there has been a commendable focus on producing locally generated drama, sitcoms, comedy, and current affairs documentaries. Serious news and features, however, are still passed through a careful socio-political filter. *Channel NewsAsia,* a local channel, broadcasts Singaporean and Asian current affairs and business news. There's also the Media Corporation of Singapore's *Channel 5* (mostly English content with some Mandarin), *Channel 8* (predominantly Mandarin), *Suria* (Malay programs), and *Central* (children's programs). It's illegal for private homes to have satellite dishes, but hotels are exempt from this.

English-language radio stations are dominated by light and easy-listening music, such as *Class 95 FM* and *Gold 90.5 FM*. Even the self-professed hard-rock stations, *Power 98 FM* and *98.7 FM Perfect 10,* are relatively middle of the road. *Symphony*

92.4 FM broadcasts classical music. Talk radio is a great gauge of local opinions and priorities; tune into *News Radio 93.8 FM* for great banter. Some of the topics of discussion may seem tame compared to what you're used to back home, but the responses can be fascinating. All of these stations broadcast hourly news bulletins; the *BBC World Service* on 88.9 FM broadcasts uncensored news.

ETIQUETTE & BEHAVIOR

Don't use your left hand for greeting, gesturing, giving something to, or eating with a Malay, Indonesian, or Indian person—it's the hand traditionally used for toiletry purposes. Refrain from kissing or touching the opposite sex, as some communities might be offended. Note that it's common for men, particularly from the Indian subcontinent, to hold hands or interact affectionately.

If you're invited for dinner by Chinese friends or business acquaintances, **leave some food on your plate** to indicate that your host's generosity is so great, you can't eat another bite. At a formal meal, rice will often be served amongst the final dishes rather than at the same time as the meat and vegetable dishes. Don't pile your plate full of rice at the end of the meal. Your hosts may think that they didn't provide you with enough food. There's no shame in asking for a knife and fork instead of chopsticks. Hindus are often vegetarian, Muslims don't eat pork and must abide by strict food preparation guidelines, and some Chinese may be devout Buddhist vegetarians. Check on dietary preferences before dining with multicultural company in Singapore.

It's mandatory that you **remove your shoes in places of worship.** You should cover up your arms and legs in Indian temples and Muslim mosques. For women, a head covering is advisable. Use extreme caution when visiting mosques, perhaps seeking the permission of locals or the nearest person in authority to enter, and then ask where you may walk and what you may do. There may be areas where you aren't permitted to go, particularly if you're a woman.

Don't litter: it's against the law and you can be fined S$1,000. Chewing gum stuck in train doors was blamed for the shutdown of the subway system more than ten years ago, and as a result the government banned it from being sold in Singapore. You may bring it in for personal use, but be sure to dispose of it properly.

Smoking isn't permitted in public service vehicles or in most buildings. You can be fined up to S$1,000 for smoking in prohibited areas. Most restaurants and some bars have outdoor terrace areas where you can light up.

Don't publicly criticize Singapore, its politics, or its leaders, and refrain from jokes about them unless you're sure of your company—Singaporeans can joke all they want, but you're an outsider and a guest. Share your opinions only when asked and, if negative, in a gentle manner.

BUSINESS ETIQUETTE

Bring along a stash of business cards— everyone exchanges them, even vacationers. If you don't have business cards, consider having personal cards with your home contact details produced instead. Offer your business card using both hands with the card facing the recipient. Likewise, when a card is offered to you, accept it with both hands and make it a point to read the card. This shows your respect for the person's title and position. If you're dealing mainly with Chinese, it's not essential but is much appreciated if you make the effort to have a Chinese translation on the reverse side of your card.

Should business contacts visit you, whether in your hotel or the office, the first thing to do is **offer them something to drink,** either water, tea, or coffee; you can expect the same courtesy automatically when you visit their office.

You should never separate a Singaporean from his *makan* (food). Avoid scheduling meetings between noon and 2 PM; if it's lunch time, make sure there's lunch, or break to go out for lunch. Be mindful that Friday is the holy day of Islam, so practicing Muslims might require a longer break to fulfill their religious obligations.

Similarly, during the fasting month of Ramadan, Muslims aren't supposed to eat anything from sunrise to sunset. Scheduling long meetings in the afternoon during this time may be counterproductive.

Meetings can be very long and often inconclusive because the final decision makers are often considered too senior to attend, so be prepared for multiple meetings to achieve simple goals. Find out who's attending from their party and be sure to **include people that are of equal standing in your group.** Introduce the most high-ranking people to each other first and seat people of the same rank opposite one another. **Listen carefully and be subtle in your approach.** Confrontation is a no-no and Singaporeans couch discussions so that no one loses face. As a result, you'll hear polite vagaries rather than an outright "no." Group dynamics prevent any member from speaking frankly about the performance or actions of their colleagues, let alone their boss. Using language such as, "Yes, I can see your point, but I was thinking that as a group we could try another way." is highly effective. Expressing anger or frustration is considered a sign that you don't have the maturity to be trusted. Keep in mind that politeness is an important business tool.

You should accept invitations to social events, which invariably involve food. A successful business relationship may hinge on your social relationship and whether you've shown a willingness to try to understand Singapore better. Typically, spouses are neither present nor invited if business is to be discussed. The unwritten rule is that if you invite someone (and his party) to lunch or dinner, you're paying the entire bill. Singaporeans ordinarily don't split bills, rather they'll trade favors and take turns paying. You may witness a theatrical tussle between guest and host as they fight to pay the bill—this is an expected ritual—but in the end, one or the other pays the whole lot. It's an important matter of preserving face. Also, showy late-night entertaining is customary among Chinese businessmen, so **prepare for sleep deprivation.** You may have to endure not only full 10-course show-off dinners, but also rowdy nightclubs (possibly with clinging and wallet-sapping "hostesses"), where premium brandy is tippled like water, if you really want to get that contract.

For a more exhaustive cultural briefing, pick up JoAnn Meriwether Craig's *Culture Shock! Singapore* and make it your "bible."

FERRY TRAVEL

Larger commercial passenger ferries arrive at and leave from the Singapore Cruise Center (SCC) ferry terminal in HarbourFront Centre. Dino Shipping and the Penguin Fast Ferry travel to Sekupang in Batam ten times daily. There are 20 daily departures to Batu Ampar, also in Batam. If you want to go to Batam's main shopping area, hop on one of the ten daily ferries (Indo Falcon or Dino Shipping) to Waterfront City. Most ferry tickets need to be pre-booked and can be paid for with credit cards. Check in an hour before sailing time or you'll risk losing your seat. Get here by taking the MRT to the HarbourFront station, or by hopping on SBS bus 10, 30, 61, 65, 84, 93, 97, 100, 131, 143, 145, or 166. A cab ride will take about 15 minutes from the main hotels.

Ferries to Nongsapura (Batam) leave from Tanah Merah Ferry Terminal (TMFT) five times daily and take 35 minutes. TMFT is a very popular gateway to Bintan's resort islands. Bintan Resort Ferries run several times daily to Bandar Bentan Telani; the 45-minute ride costs S$45. Dino Shipping, Penguin, and Berlian ferries have ten daily departures to Tanjung Pinang. Taxis from the airport to TMFT take less than 10 minutes (15 from downtown); SBS bus 65 leaves from the Bedok Interchange every 15 minutes and take 20 minutes.

To get to Tanjong Belungkor and Desaru in eastern Johor, Malaysia, take one of the Cruise Ferries from Changi Point. The 45-minute trip costs S$22 and departs daily at 10 AM, 5 PM, and 8 PM (returning at 8:15 AM, 3:30 PM, and 6:45 PM).

To get to Singapore's Southern Islands take a ferry from Sentosa Island Ferry Terminal. Ferries loop from Sentosa to Kusu

Island, then to St John's Island, back to Kusu, and then back to Sentosa. Ferries depart from Sentosa Monday through Saturday at 10 AM and 1:30 PM, and return at 11:45 AM, 2:15 PM, and 3:15 PM. They depart on Sunday and public holidays at 9 AM, 11 AM, 1 PM, 3 PM, and 5 PM (return at 10:15 AM, 12:15 PM, 2:15 PM, 4:15 PM, and 6:15 PM).

A bumboat is a motorized, privately owned water taxi that's used for island hopping. The most popular route is from Changi Jetty to Pulau Ubin. Walk along the farthest jetty at Changi Village to the tethered craft, pay the owner S$2, and wait until he has enough passengers (or gets bored). He shuttles between the two points without a fixed schedule, so it's a good idea to ask him when he expects to make the last journey back from Pulau Ubin. To reach Sisters Island, where there's no regular ferry service, hire a larger bumboat (S$55 an hour) at Jardine Steps or Clifford Pier.

⚓ Ferry Information Auto Batam Ferries ☎ 6271-4866 (SCC), 6542-7105 (TMFT). **Berlian Ferries** ☎ 6546-8830. **Bintan Resort Ferries** ☎ 6542-4369. **Cruise Ferries** ☎ 6546-8518, 6546-0650. **Dino Shipping** ☎ 6270-2228 (SCC), 6542-6130 (TMFT). **Ferrylink** ☎ 6545-3600. **Indo Falcon** ☎ 6270-6778. **Penguin Ferry Services** ☎ 6271-4866. **Singapore Cruise Centre** ✉ HarbourFront Maritime Square ☎ 6275-1683 ⊕ www.singaporecruise.com for schedules from SCC. **Tanah Merah Ferry Terminal** ✉ 50 Tanah Merah Ferry Rd. ☎ 6540-8087.

GAY & LESBIAN TRAVEL

Singaporean attitudes towards gays and lesbians are full of contradictions. On one hand, the rights of gays and lesbians aren't as protected as they are in other parts of Southeast Asia (sex between consenting males is punishable by a two-year jail term). The state also prohibits the free association of gay organizations and the publication of gay literature. Yet, a vibrant gay scene is blooming with many gay bars and clubs opening in and around Chinatown. You can visit Web sites, such as Fridae, People Like Us, Singapore Boy, and Utopia, for more information about where to go. The government has also made encouraging remarks about gays and lesbians joining the civil service, but the general attitude is conservative and a discreet "don't ask, don't tell" convention prevails. Gay and lesbian travelers shouldn't face any problems in Singapore's hotels. The usually non-confrontational nature of Singaporean society means that harassment is close to zero and public displays of affection will largely be ignored.

⚑ Gay- & Lesbian-Friendly Travel Agencies Different Roads Travel ✉ 8383 Wilshire Blvd., Suite 520, Beverly Hills, CA 90211 ☎ 323/651-5557 or 800/429-8747 (Ext. 14 for both) 🖷 323/651-5454 ✉ lgernert@tzell.com. **Kennedy Travel** ✉ 130 W. 42nd St., Suite 401, New York, NY 10036 ☎ 212/840-8659, 800/237-7433 🖷 212/730-2269 🌐 www.kennedytravel.com. **Now, Voyager** ✉ 4406 18th St., San Francisco, CA 94114 ☎ 415/626-1169 or 800/255-6951 🖷 415/626-8626 🌐 www.nowvoyager.com. **Skylink Travel and Tour/Flying Dutchmen Travel** ✉ 1455 N. Dutton Ave., Suite A, Santa Rosa, CA 95401 ☎ 707/546-9888 or 800/225-5759 🖷 707/636-0951; serving lesbian travelers.

⚑ Web Sites Fridae 🌐 www.fridae.com. **People Like Us** 🌐 www.plu-singapore.com. **Singapore Boy** 🌐 sgboy.com. **Utopia** 🌐 www.utopia-asia.com.

HEALTH

Each year more than 200,000 people travel from neighboring countries to Singapore for top-notch medical care. First-rate doctors and well-equipped hospitals, all English-speaking, abound in Singapore.

Proof of vaccination against yellow fever is required if you're entering from an infected area (e.g., Africa or South America).

FOOD & DRINK

Tap water is safe to drink, but opt for bottled water just to be safe. Every eating establishment—from the most elegant hotel dining room to the smallest sidewalk stall—is regularly inspected by the strict health authorities. If your stomach is delicate, watch out for the powerful local *chilli sambal* (chili paste) and be prepared for some minor upsets because your body may not be used to local herbs. MSG is still used in some food stalls or cheaper restaurants to enhance flavoring; you should ask for it to be omitted as it can

lead to a headache or upset stomach. It may be wise to pack a remedy for mild stomach upsets.

OVER-THE-COUNTER REMEDIES

Quality medicines are freely available over the counter from supermarkets and pharmacies. There isn't much you can't get.

PESTS & OTHER HAZARDS

With the relentless heat in Singapore it's important to beware of dehydration and sunstroke. Pace yourself when planning outdoor activities; avoid long periods of time in direct sunlight and drink at least 50% more water than you would at home. Should you begin to develop dry mouth, headaches, lethargy, nausea, or a fever you'll need to increase your fluid intake (avoid sodas and caffeine). When swimming in the waters of Singapore's offshore islands, be aware not only of the water quality but also of the strong undercurrents. Although there's virtually no malaria risk in Singapore, there are occasional flare-ups of dengue, so protect yourself at all times from mosquitoes. If you plan to visit Bintan Island, Indonesia, you'll need to take precautions against malaria. Check with your doctor about medication before you leave home and pack plenty of bug spray. Note, however, that resorts on the island will have netting, insect repellent, and mosquito coils.

HOLIDAYS

Singapore has 11 public holidays, of which only four (New Year's, Labour Day, National Day, and Christmas) fall on fixed dates. The rest are religious holidays whose dates depend on the lunar calendar. Some dates, such as Deepavali, will only be confirmed the year before. Consult the Singapore Ministry of Manpower Web site (www.mom.gov.sg) for updates. If a holiday falls on a Sunday, the following Monday will be a public holiday. If you plan to travel to Singapore during Chinese New Year, plan your shopping around the official holiday days as most stores close. This is the only time of year when finding open restaurants outside of hotels can be tough.

PUBLIC HOLIDAYS

New Year's Day: January 1.

Hari Raya Haji: Jan. 10, 2006; Dec. 20, 2007; Dec. 9, 2008.

Chinese New Year (2 days): Jan. 29 & 30, 2006; Feb. 18 & 19, 2007; Feb. 7 & 8, 2008.

Good Friday: Apr. 14, 2006; Apr. 6, 2007; Mar. 21, 2008.

Labour Day: May 1.

Vesak Day: May 12, 2006; May 31, 2007; May 19, 2008.

National Day: Aug. 9.

Deepavali: Nov. 1, 2005; Oct. 20, 2006; Nov. 9, 2007; Oct. 27, 2008.

Hari Raya Puasa: Nov. 3, 2005; Oct. 4, 2005; Oct. 24, 2006; Oct. 13, 2007; Oct. 2, 2008.

Christmas: Dec. 25.

INSURANCE

The most useful travel-insurance plan is a comprehensive policy that includes coverage for trip cancellation and interruption, default, trip delay, and medical expenses (with a waiver for preexisting conditions).

Without insurance you'll lose all or most of your money if you cancel your trip, regardless of the reason. Default insurance covers you if your tour operator, airline, or cruise line goes out of business. Trip-delay covers expenses that arise because of bad weather or mechanical delays. Study the fine print when comparing policies.

If you're traveling internationally, a key component of travel insurance is coverage for medical bills incurred if you get sick on the road. Such expenses aren't generally covered by Medicare or private policies. U.K. residents can buy a travel-insurance policy valid for most vacations taken during the year in which it's purchased (but check preexisting-condition coverage). British and Australian citizens need extra medical coverage when traveling overseas.

Always **buy travel policies directly from the insurance company**; if you buy them from a cruise line, airline, or tour operator that goes out of business you probably won't be covered for the agency or operator's default, a major risk. Before making any purchase, review your existing health and home-owner's policies to find what they cover away from home.

⚑ Travel Insurers In the U.S.: **Access America** ✉ 2805 N. Parham Rd., Richmond, VA 23294 ☎ 800/284-8300 🖶 804/673-1469 or 800/346-9265 ⊕ www.accessamerica.com. **Travel Guard International** ✉ 1145 Clark St., Stevens Point, WI 54481 ☎ 715/345-0505 or 800/826-1300 🖶 800/955-8785 ⊕ www.travelguard.com.

⚑ In the U.K.: **Association of British Insurers** ✉ 51 Gresham St., London EC2V 7HQ ☎ 020/7600-3333 🖶 020/7696-8999 ⊕ www.abi.org.uk. In Canada: **RBC Insurance** ✉ 6880 Financial Dr., Mississauga, Ontario L5N 7Y5 ☎ 800/387-4357 or 905/816-2559, 🖶 888/298-6458 ⊕ www.rbcinsurance.com. In Australia: **Insurance Council of Australia** ✉ Insurance Enquiries and Complaints, Level 12, Box 561, Collins St. W, Melbourne, VIC 8007 ☎ 1300/780808 or 03/9629-4109 🖶 03/9621-2060 ⊕ www.iecltd.com.au. In New Zealand: **Insurance Council of New Zealand** ✉ Level 7, 111-115 Customhouse Quay, Box 474, Wellington ☎ 04/472-5230 🖶 04/473-3011 ⊕ www.icnz.org.nz.

INTERNET

Singapore has a love–hate relationship with the Internet. The government encourages citizens to use technology in business and education to improve national competitiveness. At the same time, authorities struggle to censor online content in the same way that it tries to guide newspaper, television, and film content. As a visitor, you'll benefit from the former and probably not notice the latter. If you travel with a wireless laptop, you'll be able to access e-mail and the Internet in one Singapore's many wi-fi zones, which are centered around the main tourist areas, hotels, and office buildings. Web access is available in just about all hotel rooms and business centers. The cheapest way to get online is to visit one of the Internet cafés, which usually charge around S$2 per hour.

⚑ Internet Cafés **Chills Cafe** ✉ #01-07 Stamford House, 39 Stamford Rd., Colonial Singapore ☎ 6883-1016. **Cyberarena** ✉ #01-09 Capitol Bldg., 11 Stamford Rd., Colonial Singapore ☎ 6337-0075. **Cyberia** ✉ #02-28 Far East Shopping Centre, 545 Orchard Rd., Orchard 🖶 6732-1309. **Surf@Café**

✉ #01-42 Specialists' Shopping Centre, 277 Orchard Rd., Orchard ☎ 6737-4901.

LANGUAGE

Singapore is a multiracial society with four official languages: Malay, Mandarin, Tamil, and English. Other Chinese dialects are spoken, particularly Hokkein, but the government promotes Mandarin as the official dialect in order to unify the Chinese communities through its Speak Mandarin Campaign. The national language is Malay, but English is the lingua franca. It's used in government administration, is a required course for every schoolchild, and is used in university entrance exams. Virtually all Singaporeans speak English with varying degrees of fluency. At street level, as well as in business, you'll hear "Singlish," a vibrant Singaporean version of English with its own cross-cultural vocabulary and structure. Singlish sentences often end with a "lah" sound. "Can" means yes, "can not" means no, and "can can not" means maybe. Don't be surprised if Singaporean children call you "auntie" or "uncle"—it's a sign of respect.

MAIL & SHIPPING

Most hotels provide mail services for their guests. Allow a week for letters and postcards to reach North America and the U.K. Letters to Australia and New Zealand generally take about five days. Singapore's postal services are decentralized; no focal office has sprung up since the magnificent General Post Office became part of a deluxe hotel. Two useful Singapore Post offices are the Tanglin Road Post Office, open 8–8 daily, and the Killiney Road Post Office off Orchard Road, which is open later than other post offices, until 9 PM Monday–Saturday and 9–4:30 Sunday and holidays.

When sending mail to Singapore include the six-figure postcode, which is specific to each building.

⌀ Post Offices **Singapore Post Toll Free Enquiries** ☎ 1605 ⊕ www.singpost.com.sg for the closest post office. **Killiney Road Post Office** ✉ 1 Killiney Rd., off Orchard Road ☎ 6734-7899. **Tanglin Shopping Centre** ✉ 56 Tanglin Rd., Orchard ☎ 6734-5899.

OVERNIGHT SERVICES

Singapore is serviced by key international courier companies, however, it's rare for documents or packages to reach the U.S. or Europe overnight. Expect parcels to arrive at least 48 hours after they're posted. Your hotel will be able to organize an international courier service.

⌀ Major Services **Federal Express** ☎ 1800/743-2626. **United Parcel Service (UPS)** ☎ 1800/738-3388.

POSTAL RATES

It costs S$0.23 to send a letter within Singapore. Letters from Singapore to the U.S., Canada, and Europe cost S$1, postcards are S$0.50. Letters to Australia or New Zealand cost S$0.70, postcards are also S$0.50.

RECEIVING MAIL

If you know which hotel you'll be staying at, have mail sent there marked HOLD FOR ARRIVAL. American Express cardholders or traveler's check users can have mail sent to their offices c/o American Express. Envelopes should be marked "Client Mail." Poste Restante is available at the Singapore Post Centre on Eunos, about a 10-minute taxi ride from Orchard Road, which is open weekdays 8 AM–9 PM, Saturday 8 AM–6 PM, and Sunday and holidays 10 AM–4 PM.

⌀ **American Express International** ✉ #18-01/07 The Concourse, 300 Beach Rd., 199555 ☎ 6299-8133. **Singapore Post** ✉ 10 Eunos Rd., Eunos 408600 ☎ 6841-2000 ⊕ www.singpost.com.sg Ⓜ Eunos.

SHIPPING PARCELS

All reputable furniture, curio, and antiques dealers can arrange for your goods to be shipped home. It's a good option because they can ensure that the items make it to you in one piece. Ask for written confirmation of delivery details and the contact information for the freight forwarder in your home country so that you can follow-up. Items made of wood that are sent to Australia or New Zealand will be sprayed with pesticides as per customs regulations. This won't harm the look or quality of your goods.

MONEY MATTERS

Singapore is one of the most expensive cities in Southeast Asia; its prices rank up there with other metropolises. Eating at the top restaurants and staying in the best hotels will cost you almost as much as in New York or London. It's relatively easy to keep costs down by eating at hawker food centers, using public transportation, and taking advantage of bar happy hours. Even the finest hotels have great value promotional, corporate, and weekend rates; always ask about such deals before booking.

In moderately priced restaurants expect to pay S$5 for a coffee, S$9–S$11 for a beer, S$3 for a soda, S$50 for a bottle of house wine, and S$5 for a sandwich. Transportation costs are about S$4 for a 2-km (1-mi) taxi ride and S$0.70 to take a city bus. Museum entrance is generally S$3.

Prices throughout this guide are given for adults. Substantially reduced fees are almost always available for children, students, and senior citizens. For information on taxes, *see* Taxes.

ATMS

ATMs seem to be on every corner in Singapore. They can be found at banks, on the street, in MRT stations, in convenience stores, and in shopping centers. They're reliable and usually safe to use, even at night. Most major banks are members of the Cirrus or Plus networks.

CREDIT CARDS

You can get cash advances on your credit cards at airport money changers or through most ATMs. Major cards are generally accepted in Singapore. However, some shopkeepers are reluctant to accept American Express because of the high merchant fees. If you plan to pay for a cab ride by credit card, tell the driver if you're hailing one from the street or the telephone operator when you're booking. Report lost or stolen credit cards immediately to lessen your liability for any unauthorized purchases. Throughout this guide, the following abbreviations are used: **AE,**

American Express; **DC,** Diners Club; **MC,** MasterCard; and **V,** Visa.

Reporting Lost Cards American Express ☎ 6880–1111. **Diners Club** ☎ 6416–0800. **Master-Card** ☎ 800/110–0113. **Visa** ☎ 800/448–1250.

CURRENCY

The local currency is the Singapore dollar (S$), which is divided into 100 cents. Notes in circulation are S$1, S$2, S$5, S$10, S$20, S$50, S$100, S$500, S$1,000, and S$10,000. Coins: S$0.01, S$0.05, S$0.20, S$0.50, and S$1.

CURRENCY EXCHANGE

Currency exchange facilities are available at banks and money changers throughout Singapore. In some cases, money changers give better rates than banks. At press time the exchange rate was S$1.29 to the Australian dollar, S$1.38 to the Canadian dollar, S$1.16 to the New Zealand dollar, S$1.63 to the U.S. dollar, S$3.05 to the pound sterling, and S$2.17 to the Euro. Note that the Malaysian Ringgit is a controlled currency. It's difficult to exchange in Singapore so if you're traveling from Malaysia change it before you leave.

For the most favorable rates, **change money through banks.** Although ATM transaction fees may be higher abroad than at home, ATM rates are excellent because they're based on wholesale rates offered only by major banks. You won't do as well at exchange booths in airports or rail and bus stations, in hotels, in restaurants, or in stores. To avoid lines at airport exchange booths, get a bit of local currency before you leave home. Money changers can also give you good rates, particularly since you can bargain with them.

Exchange Services International Currency Express ✉ 427 N. Camden Dr., Suite F, Beverly Hills, CA 90210 ☎ 888/278–6628 orders ☎ 310/278–6410 ⊕ www.foreignmoney.com. **Travel Ex Currency Services** ☎ 800/287–7362 orders and retail locations ⊕ www.travelex.com.

TRAVELER'S CHECKS

Traveler's checks can be easily cashed at banks and money changers in Singapore. If you're going to rural areas and small towns, go with cash; traveler's checks are best used in cities. Lost or stolen checks can usually be replaced within 24 hours. To ensure a speedy refund, buy your own traveler's checks—don't let someone else pay for them: irregularities like this can cause delays. The person who bought the checks should make the call to request a refund.

PACKING

Bring casual, loose-fitting clothes made of natural fabrics to keep cool in the heat and high humidity. Walking shorts, T-shirts, slacks, and sundresses are acceptable everywhere. It's important to bring comfortable walking shoes because there are so many sights to explore on your feet. If you plan to visit religious sites, cover your arms and legs—a sarong over shorts is a good temporary option. Wear shoes that you can slip on and off easily as you'll need to remove them for most shrines and temples. Take a sweater or jacket to counter the often arctic air-conditioning in hotels and restaurants. Evening wear is casual, but some discos and nightclubs may necessitate flashier attire. Though few restaurants require a jacket and tie, some prohibit jeans, T-shirts, and open-toed shoes: check when booking. The standard businessman's outfit in Singapore includes trousers, a dress shirt, and a tie. Businesswomen wear lightweight suits or a blouse and either skirt or trousers. Most hotels have same-day laundry and pressing services.

Wear a hat, sunglasses, and sunblock while sightseeing. Sunglasses are horrendously expensive to buy in Singapore, so don't forget to pack them before you leave. An umbrella is necessary year-round; you can pick up inexpensive ones locally. Leave the plastic or nylon raincoats at home—they're extremely uncomfortable in the high humidity. For the same reason, avoid panty hose and synthetic-fiber underwear, both of which are uncomfortable and likely to encourage fungal infections in Singapore's climate.

In your carry-on luggage, pack an extra pair of eyeglasses or contact lenses and enough of any medication you take to last

a few days longer than the entire trip. You may also ask your doctor to write a spare prescription using the drug's generic name, as brand names may vary from country to country. In luggage to be checked, **never pack prescription drugs, valuables, or undeveloped film.** And don't forget to carry with you the addresses of offices that handle refunds of lost traveler's checks. Check *Fodor's How to Pack* (available at online retailers and bookstores everywhere) for more tips.

To avoid customs and security delays, carry medications in their original packaging. Don't pack any sharp objects in your carry-on luggage, including knives of any size or material, scissors, nail clippers, and corkscrews, or anything else that might arouse suspicion.

To avoid having your checked luggage chosen for hand inspection, don't cram bags full. The U.S. Transportation Security Administration suggests packing shoes on top and placing personal items you don't want touched in clear plastic bags.

CHECKING LUGGAGE

You're allowed to carry aboard one bag and one personal article, such as a purse or a laptop computer. Make sure what you carry on fits under your seat or in the overhead bin. Get to the gate early, so you can board as soon as possible, before the overhead bins fill up.

Baggage allowances vary by carrier, destination, and ticket class. On international flights, you're usually allowed to check two bags weighing up to 70 pounds (32 kilograms) each, although a few airlines allow checked bags of up to 88 pounds (40 kilograms) in first class. Some international carriers don't allow more than 66 pounds (30 kilograms) per bag in business class and 44 pounds (20 kilograms) in economy. On domestic flights, the limit is usually 50 to 70 pounds (23 to 32 kilograms) per bag. In general, carry-on bags shouldn't exceed 40 pounds (18 kilograms). Most airlines won't accept bags that weigh more than 100 pounds (45 kilograms) on domestic or international flights. Expect to pay a fee for baggage that exceeds weight limits. Check baggage restrictions with your carrier before you pack.

Airline liability for baggage is limited to $2,500 per person on flights within the United States. On international flights it amounts to $9.07 per pound or $20 per kilogram for checked baggage (roughly $640 per 70-pound bag), with a maximum of $634.90 per piece, and $400 per passenger for unchecked baggage. You can buy additional coverage at check-in for about $10 per $1,000 of coverage, but it often excludes a rather extensive list of items, shown on your airline ticket.

Before departure, itemize your bags' contents and their worth, and label the bags with your name, address, and phone number. (If you use your home address, cover it so potential thieves can't see it readily.) Include a label inside each bag and **pack a copy of your itinerary.** At check-in, make sure each bag is correctly tagged with the destination airport's three-letter code. Because some checked bags will be opened for hand inspection, the U.S. Transportation Security Administration recommends that you leave luggage unlocked or use the plastic locks offered at check-in. TSA screeners place an inspection notice inside searched bags, which are re-sealed with a special lock.

If your bag has been searched and contents are missing or damaged, file a claim with the TSA Consumer Response Center as soon as possible. If your bags arrive damaged or fail to arrive at all, file a written report with the airline before leaving the airport.

🔁 Complaints **U.S. Transportation Security Administration Contact Center** ☎ 866/289-9673 ⊕ www.tsa.gov.

PASSPORTS & VISAS

When traveling internationally, carry your passport even if you don't need one (it's always the best form of ID) and **make two photocopies of the data page** (one for someone at home and another for you, carried separately from your passport). If you lose your passport, promptly call the nearest embassy or consulate and the local police.

U.S. passport applications for children under age 14 require consent from both parents or legal guardians; both parents must appear together to sign the application. If only one parent appears, he or she must submit a written statement from the other parent authorizing passport issuance for the child. A parent with sole authority must present evidence of it when applying; acceptable documentation includes the child's certified birth certificate listing only the applying parent, a court order specifically permitting this parent's travel with the child, or a death certificate for the nonapplying parent. Application forms and instructions are available on the Web site of the U.S. State Department's Bureau of Consular Affairs (⊕ travel.state.gov).

ENTERING SINGAPORE

U.S., Canadian, U.K., Australian, and New Zealand citizens only need a valid passport for stays up to 14 days. Your passport must be valid for the next six months or more and in good condition. You may automatically be given a 30-day Social Visit Pass upon your arrival if you come from any of these countries; apply to Singapore Immigration after you arrive if you require a longer stay. Women in an advanced stage of pregnancy (six months or more) should make prior application to the nearest Singapore overseas mission or the Singapore Immigration Department.

Check with the Indonesian foreign mission before visiting Bintan or Batam Island for visa requirements. At press time, Australian, American, New Zealand, and most European passport holders need a visa to enter Indonesia. Getting a visa in your home country may take up to five days. It cost S$25 entry for less than three days and S$41 for more than three days.

🔁 **Immigration & Checkpoints Authority (ICA)** ✉ ICA Bldg., 10 Kallang Rd., Bugis ☎ 6391-6100 ⊕ www.app.ica.gov.sg.

PASSPORT OFFICES

The best time to apply for a passport or to renew is in fall and winter. Before any trip, check your passport's expiration date, and, if necessary, renew it as soon as possible.

⨍ Australian Citizens Passports Australia Australian Department of Foreign Affairs and Trade ☎ 131-232 ⊕ www.passports.gov.au.

⨍ Canadian Citizens Passport Office ✉ to mail in applications: 200 Promenade du Portage, Hull, Québec J8X 4B7 ☎ 819/994-3500 or 800/567-6868 ⊕ www.ppt.gc.ca.

⨍ New Zealand Citizens New Zealand Passports Office ☎ 0800/22-5050 or 04/474-8100 ⊕ www. passports.govt.nz.

⨍ U.K. Citizens U.K. Passport Service ☎ 0870/ 521-0410 ⊕ www.passport.gov.uk.

⨍ U.S. Citizens National Passport Information Center ☎ 877/487-2778, 888/874-7793 TDD/TTY ⊕ travel.state.gov.

RESTROOMS

Singapore has some of the region's cleanest public restrooms. Vigilant attendants are stationed at most public facilities and the widespread installation of self-flushing toilets helps maintain cleanliness. Some public restrooms charge a small 10- or 20-cent admission fee to finance their upkeep.

Nevertheless, you may find that some public toilets have wet floors; this is usually due to the local, and particularly Muslim or Indian custom of washing with tap-water after using the toilet—you might see a little tap and bucket. Avoid putting your parcels down without checking the area first. Local preferences mean that some public restrooms may have both sit-down and squat toilets; foreigners may find squat toilets difficult or uncomfortable to use, but they tend to be more hygenic.

It's not unusual to see office girls washing up their lunch crockery in a restroom's wash basins. Generally, you'll find public toilets to be noisier and more uninhibited than you might like. For a more peaceful and genteel experience, seek out hotel restrooms.

SAFETY

Singapore has a very low crime rate; it's safe to walk around unaccompanied at night and people often leave their bags unattended. Bear in mind, however, that low crime doesn't mean no crime. Be

watchful of your handbag in busy pedestrian areas and packed trains. Don't wear a money belt or a waist pack, both of which peg you as a tourist. Distribute your cash and any valuables (including your credit cards and passport) between a deep front pocket, an inside jacket or vest pocket, and a hidden money pouch. Do not reach for the money pouch once you're in public.

Jaywalk at your own risk; Singapore drivers won't slow down or stop to let you cross.

WOMEN IN SINGAPORE

If you carry a purse, choose one with a zipper and a thick strap that you can drape across your body; adjust the length so that the purse sits in front of you at or above hip level. (Don't wear a money belt or a waist pack.) Store only enough money in the purse to cover casual spending. Distribute the rest of your cash and any valuables between deep front pockets, inside jacket or vest pockets, and a concealed money pouch.

In general, attitudes toward women are fairly liberated and relaxed. You're unlikely to be hassled. Men on the prowl generally avoid public confrontation and will retreat at the first loud reprimand.

SENIOR-CITIZEN TRAVEL

Because senior-citizens engender a high level of respect in Asian culture, Singapore is an ideal place for mature travelers to get a taste of Asia. Nearly everyone speaks English; getting around by public transit is safe, clean, and inexpensive; world-class medical facilities abound; the water is safe to drink, even from the tap (this reflects the high standard of hygiene found almost everywhere); and there are ample cultural, historical, and shopping sites. Some sites offer promotional discounts for seniors—ask when you book tickets.

To qualify for age-related discounts, mention your senior-citizen status up front when booking hotel reservations (not when checking out) and before you're seated in restaurants (not when paying the bill). Be sure to have identification on hand. When renting a car, ask about promotional car-rental discounts, which can be cheaper than senior-citizen rates.

Educational Programs **Elderhostel** ✉ 11 Ave. de Lafayette, Boston, MA 02111-1746 ☎ 877/426-8056, 978/323-4141 international callers, 877/426-2167 TTY ☎ 877/426-2166 ⊕ www.elderhostel.org.

SIGHTSEEING TOURS

A wide range of sightseeing tours covers the highlights of Singapore and are a good introduction to the island. Tours can take two hours or the whole day, and prices range from S$30 to S$90. The air-conditioned coaches are usually comfortable and the cost often includes pickup and return. Tour agencies can also arrange private-car tours with guides; these are more expensive, but you'll have a more personalized experience. There's no need to book tours in advance of your visit; they can be easily arranged through the tour desks in hotels. Also, if you're only in Singapore on a six-hour stopover, there are free city tours from Changi Airport. See the Singapore Tourist Board desk there.

Tour Operator Recommendations **East West Executive Travellers** ☎ 6238-8488 ⊕ www.ewet.com. **Holiday Tours** ☎ 6738-2622 ⊕ www.toureast.net. **Journeys** ☎ 6325-1631 ⊕ www.singaporewalks.com. **Malaysia and Singapore Travel Centre** ☎ 6737-8877. **RMG Tours** ☎ 6220-1661 ⊕ www.rmgtours.com. **SH Tours** ☎ 6734-9923 ⊕ www.asiatours.com.sg. **Singapore Trolley** ☎ 6339-6833 ⊕ www.singaporeexplorer.com.sg.

BOAT TOURS

Singapore River tours, some of them on old Chinese junks, leave from Boat Quay, Clarke Quay, and Clifford Pier; operators include Eastwind Organisation, Singapore River Boat Tours, Singapore River Cruises & Leisure, and WaterTours. The Singapore Duck is an amphibious craft that cruises around Marina Square and the Padang area; the tour includes a dive into the Singapore River and Marina Bay.

Tour Companies **Eastwind Organisation** ☎ 6533-3432 ⊕ web.singnet.com.sg/~eastwind. **Singapore Ducktours** ☎ 6333-3825 ⊕ www.ducktours.com.sg. **Singapore River Boat Tours** ☎ 6338-9205 ⊕ www.singaporeexplorer.com.sg. **Singapore River Cruises & Leisure** ☎ 6336-6111

⊕ www.rivercruise.com.sg. **WaterTours** ☎ 6533-9811 ⊕ www.watertours.com.sg.

BUS TOURS

Singapore has more than a hundred full- and half-day bus tours that suit most tastes and budgets. You can tour major attractions, ethnic enclaves, or the Singaporean heartland, as well as join a special interest tour, which centers on food history. The Singapore Tourism Board is an excellent source of information; visit the Tours & Promos section of www.visitsingapore.com for descriptions, prices, and contact information. Tours typically cost S$28 to S$44 per person. Pick ups are usually at 9:30 AM and 2:30 PM.

Tour Companies **East West Executive Travellers** ☎ 6238-8488 ⊕ www.ewet.com. **Holiday Tours** ☎ 6738-2622 ⊕ www.toureast.net. **RMG Tours** ☎ 6220-1661 ⊕ www.rmgtours.com. **SH Tours** ☎ 6734-9923 ⊕ www.asiatours.com.sg. **Siakson Coach Tours** ☎ 6336-0288.

ISLAND TOURS

Although it's easy to get around Sentosa Island on your own, Sentosa Discovery Tours offers three-hour guided trips that cover the major attractions. The tours commence every 3½ hours, beginning at 9:30; tickets cost S$46.

SH Tours offers day trips to Batam for S$85 (including a high-speed roundtrip ferry ride and lunch). Check with your embassy regarding visa requirements for entry into Indonesia. If no visa is required, please ensure that your passport is valid for at least the next six months. To facilitate immigration clearance, please provide your passport number, validity, expiration date, date of birth, and nationality at the time of booking.

Tour Companies **Sentosa Discovery Tours** ☎ 6270-8855 ⊕ www.sdtours.com.sg. **SH Tours** ☎ 6734-9923 ⊕ www.asiatours.com.sg.

PRIVATE GUIDES

In Singapore all tourist guides are required to pass a test and must be licensed by the government. For the most part, they all have a deep knowledge of Singapore, and many focus their tours around such special interests as cooking, flora, or architecture.

If in doubt about the credibility of a guide, ask to see a license. The Singapore Tourism Board (⊕ www.visitsingapore. com/guides-online) has an online service to help you find a guide.

TAXI TOURS

Singapore's most streetwise citizens can take you to sites beyond those on standard tour itineraries and share their insights on everything from local housing issues to the island's best chicken rice. You can take a set tour or develop your own itinerary with your driver. A three-hour tour usually costs S$98–S$135 per vehicle, which isn't necessarily a typical taxicab, but may be a maxicab or a Mercedes.

🚖 Tour Companies **CityCab** ☎ 6542-5831 ⊕ www. citycab.com.sg. **Comfort** ☎ 6550-8588 ⊕ www. comfort-transportation.com.sg. **SMTR** ☎ 6555-8888 ⊕ www.smrttaxis.com.sg.

WALKING TOURS

Walking tours are less popular in Singapore because of its heat and humidity. If you take such a tour carry plenty of water and be prepared to make frequent rest stops. Singapore Walks runs daily tours that stop in graveyards, "haunted houses," old red light districts, and archaeological sites. You don't need to book ahead with this group, just show up at designated meeting points. The Singapore Tourism Board publishes suggested walking itineraries at www.visitsingapore.com.

🚶 Tour Companies **Original Singapore Walks** ☎ 6325-1631 ⊕ www.singaporewalks.com.

STUDENTS IN SINGAPORE

Singapore is a popular stop for students backpacking through Asia. It isn't, however, as reasonably priced as its neighboring countries. Expect to pay a minimum of S$30 a night for a bed in a very basic guest house.

You may notice "student" rates for ferries, for example—this only refers to people ages 12 to 18. Carry your international student ID with you at all times, though, as entertainment venues may offer discounts.

To save money, **look into deals available through student-oriented travel agencies.**

To qualify you'll need a bona fide student ID card. Members of international student groups are also eligible.

🎫 IDs & Services **STA Travel** ✉ 10 Downing St., New York, NY 10014 ☎ 212/627-3111, 800/777-0112 24-hr service center 🖷 212/627-3387 ⊕ www.sta. com. **Travel Cuts** ✉ 187 College St., Toronto, Ontario M5T 1P7, Canada ☎ 800/592-2887 in the U.S., 416/979-2406 or 866/246-9762 in Canada 🖷 416/979-8167 ⊕ www.travelcuts.com.

SUBWAY TRAVEL

The superb subway system, known as the MRT (Mass Rapid Transit), consists of three color-coded lines: the red North–South Line, the green East–West Line, and the purple North–East lines. A new Circle Line is being constructed in stages and won't be complete until 2009. The East–West and North–South lines intersect at the City Hall and Raffles Place stops. The North–East line intersects with the East–West line at Outram Park, and with the North–South Line at Dhoby Ghaut. The MRT has more than 51 stations and is supplemented by a 14-station Light Rail System (LTR) in the island's far western regions. All trains and underground stations are air-conditioned, and the trains operate between 6 AM and midnight daily, at frequencies of three to eight minutes. Trains tend to be busiest during commuter hours (8–9 AM and 5:30–6:30 PM). Like everywhere else in Singapore, there are rules. Durians, the infamously smelly fruit of Singapore, aren't allowed on the trains or buses. There are signs posted at all stations listing the fines that can be levied if you're caught smoking, eating, drinking, or littering anywhere on the transit system.

One-use Standard Tickets are available from station vending machines (which give change). Fares, which include a refundable S$1 deposit, are between S$1.60 and S$3 and depend on which stations you're traveling between. Large maps showing fares between stations hang above each vending machine. **Make sure you buy the right ticket for your destination.** If you underpay you won't be able to exit the station until you pay the difference in cash to an attendant. If you plan to take public transportation more than once, you can save money by purchasing an EZ-Link stored value card for S$15 (including a S$3 refundable travel deposit). To get between Orchard Road and Raffles Place, for example, it costs S$.74 using EZ-Link and S$1 for a Standard Ticket. EZ-Link can be used on all buses and trains. You simply tap the card on the reader when you enter and exit a train station or bus and the fare is automatically deducted. Depending on your schedule, it may be cost-effective to purchase a S$45 Visitor's Card. It gives you S$10 worth of subway travel, but comes with a booklet of discount coupons for attractions, shopping, golf hotels, and restaurants.

🔝 **Subway Information** **EZ-Link** ☎ 800/767-4333 ⊕ www.ezlink.com.sg. **Singapore Bus Services** ☎ 800/287-2727 ⊕ www.sbstransit.com.sg. **Singapore MRT Ltd.** ☎ 800/336-8900 ⊕ www.smrt.com.sg. **TransitLink** ☎ 800/779-9366 ⊕ www.transitlink.com.sg.

TAXES

DEPARTURE TAX

Everyone leaving Singapore pays a departure tax, known as a Passenger Service Charge, of S$21. If it's not already included with the price of your ticket, it's payable at the airport. To save time and avoid standing in line, buy a tax voucher at your hotel or any airline office. Passengers who are in Singapore for less than 24 hours may leave the airport without paying this tax.

PLUS PLUS PLUS

You'll see "+++," a.k.a. Plus Plus Plus, on most restaurant and bar menus. These are the 10% service charge, the 5% goods and services tax, and the 1% government tax that are automatically added to your bill.

VALUE-ADDED TAX

There's a 5% sales tax, called the Goods & Services Tax (GST), the equivalent of Value-Added Tax. You can get the tax refunded at Global Refund Singapore counters in the airport as you leave the country, for purchases of more than S$300 made at a store or retail chain displaying the Tax Free Shopping sticker (you can pool individual receipts for S$100 or more). When making a purchase, **ask for a Tax Free Shopping Cheque** and find out whether the merchant gives refunds—not all stores do, nor are they required to. Have the form stamped like any customs form by customs officials when you leave Singapore. Be ready to show customs officials what you've bought. If you want to pack your purchases in your check-in luggage, head for the GST Refund Inspection Counter after you're through passport control. You can either take the form to a refund-service counter for an on-the-spot refund, mail it to the address on the form (or the envelope with it) after you arrive home, or ask for a refund to your credit card, though a surcharge may be levied for this option. Visit www.changiairport.com.sg for more information.

TAXIS

Taxis are an efficient and affordable option for getting around Singapore, which has nearly 20,000 strictly regulated, metered taxis. Most companies charge S$2.40 for the first km (0.62 mi), but thereafter may charge S$.10 for each subsequent 225 meters (738 feet) or 240 meters (787 feet). Every 30 seconds of waiting time when the taxi isn't moving carries an S$.10 charge. Drivers carry tariff cards, which you may see if you want clarification of your tab. You can **catch cabs at taxi queues or by hailing them from any curb not marked with a double yellow line.** Alternatively, you can call a taxi ahead of time; most taxi stands have ads with a destination code and phone number to call to have a taxi automatically dispatched to you. Drivers don't expect tips.

Be aware of several surcharges that may apply. For starters, at peak hours on busy roads, the additional Electronic Road Pricing (ERP) charge will be added to the metered fare, shown on the upper display of the cab's In-Vehicle Unit. An S$3.20 charge is added for taxis booked by phone (there's an additional S$2 surcharge for every booking half an hour or more in advance of a trip). Trips made between midnight and 6 AM have a 50% surcharge, and rides from, *not to,* the airport carry a S$3 surcharge

(S$5 Fri.–Sun., 5 PM–midnight). A S$1 surcharge is added for all trips in London cabs and station wagon taxis; an extra 10% of the fare is charged for payment by credit card.

🚖 Taxi Companies **CityCab** ☎ 6552-2222. **Comfort CabLink** ☎ 6552-1111. **Tibs** ☎ 6481-1211 ⊕ www. smrttaxis.com.sg.

TELEPHONES

Singapore phone numbers have eight digits. The local system is highly organized, efficient, and reliable. Although public phones requiring phone-cards predominate, a few old-style coin-operated payphones also exist and usually take 10-cent coins. It's quite easy to use your cell phone in Singapore, but if you want to keep roaming costs down, the cheapest option may be to rent a Singapore SIM-card (from S$28) and swap it into your set, thus acquiring a temporary Singapore phone number during your trip.

AREA & COUNTRY CODES

Singapore has no area codes. The country code for Indonesia is 62; the area code for Bintan is 771 and Batam is 778. Calling from Malaysia to Singapore is a separate case: you simply dial 02 and then the Singapore number. The country code is 1 for the U.S. and Canada, 61 for Australia, 64 for New Zealand, and 44 for the U.K.

DIRECTORY & OPERATOR ASSISTANCE

English directory and operator assistance is available 24 hours by dialing 100. Dial 104 for voice-activated information on country codes and international time. Citisearch, an operator-assisted yellow pages, can be reached at 1900/777–7777.

INTERNATIONAL CALLS & LONG-DISTANCE SERVICES

To call Singapore, first dial your national IDD access code, then the country code (65), then the number (Singapore has no area codes).

To make direct overseas calls dial 001 (from a Singtel telephone), 002 (from a M1 telephone), or 008 (from a Starhub telephone), then the country code (011 for the U.S.) and the number; if you'd like op-

erator assistance, dial 104. To call Malaysia dial 02 before the local number.

To save money on calls overseas, use the Home Country Direct service available from your hotel room or any public phone. This puts you in touch with an operator in your home country, who places your call, charging either your home phone or your credit card. You can also use pay phones by first depositing S$.10 and then dialing an access code to reach an operator. Note also that some public phones at the airport and many at city post offices accept Diners Club, MasterCard, and Visa.

AT&T, MCI, and Sprint access codes make calling long-distance relatively convenient, but you may find the local access number blocked in many hotel rooms. First ask the hotel operator to connect you. If the hotel operator balks, ask for an international operator, or dial the international operator yourself. One way to improve your odds of getting connected to your long-distance carrier is to travel with more than one company's calling card (a hotel may block Sprint, for example, but not MCI). If all else fails, call from a pay phone.

🚖 Access Codes **AT&T** ☎ 800/011-1111. **MCI** ☎ 800/011-2112. **Sprint** ☎ 800/017-7177.

LOCAL CALLS

There are neither any local area codes or special codes for dialing mobile telephone numbers in Singapore. Wherever you are on the island, dial the local or mobile number as printed. From a pay phone the cost is S$.10 per three minutes. You can insert a coin and dial the eight-digit number, however most new phones only take stored value cards. These come in S$2, S$5, S$10, S$20, and S$50 denominations. Phone cards (⇨ *below*) in a variety of denominations are sold at most kiosks, newsstands, and gift shops. Hotel's charge up to S$1 per minute for a local connection however virtually all the phones at Changi Airport are free.

PHONE CARDS

To avoid hefty hotel service charges, use a stored value card available from post offices, newsstands, and kiosks. Each country has a different rate. This is usually displayed on a poster at the point of purchase. Look for the card that offers the most minutes to where you intend to call most often. The price of each call is deducted from the card total.

PUBLIC PHONES

Pay-phone calls within Singapore cost S$.10; insert a coin and dial the seven-digit number. Hotels charge anywhere from S$.10 to S$.50 a call. (Note that there are free public phones at Changi Airport, just past immigration.) Many pay phones only accept cards; the coin-operated phones are smaller and frequently found in shopping malls and at information desks.

TIME

Singapore is in the same time zone as Beijing, Hong Kong, Kuala Lumpur, Manila, Perth, and Taipei. It's 2 hours behind Sydney, 8 hours ahead of London (GMT), 16 hours ahead of Los Angeles (U.S. Pacific Standard Time), 14 hours ahead of Chicago (Central Standard Time), and 13 hours ahead of New York (Eastern Standard Time). Singapore doesn't practice day-light savings, given its proximity to the equator.

TIPPING

Tipping isn't common in Singapore. It's prohibited at the airport and discouraged in hotels. Restaurants automatically levy a 10% service charge. Taxi drivers don't receive tips from Singaporeans.

TOURS & PACKAGES

Because everything is prearranged on a prepackaged tour or independent vacation, you spend less time planning—and often get it all at a good price.

BOOKING WITH AN AGENT

Travel agents are excellent resources. But it's a good idea to collect brochures from several agencies, as some agents' suggestions may be influenced by relationships with tour and package firms that reward them for volume sales. If you have a special interest, find an agent with expertise in that area; the American Society of Travel Agents (ASTA; ⇨ Travel Agencies) has a database of specialists worldwide. You can log on to the group's Web site to find an ASTA travel agent in your neighborhood.

Make sure your travel agent knows the accommodations and other services of the place being recommended. Ask about the hotel's location, room size, beds, and whether it has a pool, room service, or programs for children, if you care about these. Has your agent been there in person or sent others whom you can contact?

Do some homework on your own, too: local tourism boards can provide information about lesser-known and small-niche operators, some of which may sell only direct.

BUYER BEWARE

Each year consumers are stranded or lose their money when tour operators—even large ones with excellent reputations—go out of business. So check out the operator. Ask several travel agents about its reputation, and try to **book with a company that has a consumer-protection program.** (Look for information in the company's brochure.) In the United States, members of the United States Tour Operators Association are required to set aside funds ($1 million) to help eligible customers cover payments and travel arrangements in the event that the company defaults. It's also a good idea to choose a company that participates in the American Society of Travel Agents' Tour Operator Program; ASTA will act as mediator in any disputes between you and your tour operator.

Remember that the more your package or tour includes, the better you can predict the ultimate cost of your vacation. Make sure you know exactly what is covered, and beware of hidden costs. Are taxes, tips, and transfers included? Entertainment and excursions? These can add up.

▣ Tour-Operator Recommendations American Society of Travel Agents (⇨ Travel Agencies). **CrossSphere—The Global Association for Packaged Travel** ⊠ 546 E. Main St., Lexington, KY 40508 ☎ 859/226-4414 or 800/682-8886 🖷 859/226-4414 ⊕ www.CrossSphere.com. **United States Tour Operators Association** (USTOA) ⊠ 275 Madison Ave., Suite 2014, New York, NY 10016 ☎ 212/599-6599 🖷 212/599-6744 ⊕ www.ustoa.com.

TRAIN TRAVEL

Malaysian operated trains run regularly between Singapore and key cities in western Peninsular Malaysia, including the capital, Kuala Lumpur (called KL), and Johore Bahru (JB). There are four daily departures to JB; the trip takes about an hour and costs roughly S$20 one-way. The air-conditioned express train to KL also leaves mornings, afternoons, and nights (sleepers are comfortable). The trip takes about six hours, and the first-class one-way daytime fare is S$68, second-class S$34. Second class has comfy reclining seats; first-class has more legroom and fewer seats. Tickets for the "2 Plus" first-class cabin—which has air-conditioning, a washbasin, and two-berth compartments—on an overnight train to KL cost S$130; second-class tickets cost S$40 and are bunk-style with curtains for privacy.

E&OE Services, the company that operates the *Venice Simplon–Orient Express,* runs the deluxe *Eastern & Oriental Express;* the train travels between Singapore and Bangkok and on to Chiang Mai, Thailand, once a week, with stops in KL and in Butterworth, Malaysia, permitting an excursion to Penang. The 1,943-km (1,200-mi) journey takes 41 hours. Fares, which vary according to cabin type and include meals, start at more than S$2,500 per person one-way to Bangkok.

Most train lines accept major credit cards as well as cash. Reservations are recommended for trains to Malaysia especially on Friday and the eve of public holidays when locals head home. Call or check the Malaysian Railway's Web site to book ahead.

Train Information **E&OE Services** ☎ 6392–3500 or 6323–4390. **Keretapi Tanah Melayu Berhad (KTM) Malaysian Railway** ☎ 6222–5165 (for information) or 03/22671200 (Malaysian number for bookings) ⊕ www.ktmb.com.my.

TRANSPORTATION AROUND SINGAPORE

Singapore may be a tiny island, but it's got one of the most efficient, cost-effective, and reliable public transportation systems in the world. The Mass Rapid Transit (MRT) system covers the main stretches across the island, while buses cover other routes. All stations, carriages, and vehicles are well-maintained, well-lit, and safe. Announcements, route maps, and exit guides are in English and easy to understand. Taxis provide a faster and more comfortable ride, but at a higher price. You can hail one from the street, wait for one at taxi stands, or call one for a pick up. Exploring on foot makes the most sense around the self-contained ethnic areas of Chinatown, Little India, and Kallang as well as along the designated paths along Singapore River and the East Coast Parkway.

TRAVEL AGENCIES

A good travel agent puts your needs first. Look for an agency that has been in business at least five years, emphasizes customer service, and has someone on staff who specializes in your destination. In addition, **make sure the agency belongs to a professional trade organization.** The American Society of Travel Agents (ASTA) has more than 10,000 members in some 140 countries, enforces a strict code of ethics, and will step in to help mediate any agent-client disputes involving ASTA members if necessary. ASTA (whose motto is "Without a travel agent, you're on your own") also maintains a Web site that includes a directory of agents. (If a travel agency is also acting as your tour operator, *see* Buyer Beware *in* Tours & Packages.)

Local Agent Referrals **American Society of Travel Agents (ASTA)** ✉ 1101 King St., Suite 200, Alexandria, VA 22314 ☎ 703/739–2782 or 800/965–2782 24-hr hotline 🖷 703/684–8319 ⊕ www.astanet.com. **Association of British Travel Agents** ✉ 68–71 Newman St., London W1T 3AH ☎ 020/7637–2444 🖷 020/7637–0713 ⊕ www.abta.com. **Association of Canadian Travel Agencies** ✉ 130 Albert St., Suite 1705, Ottawa, Ontario K1P 5G4 ☎ 613/237–3657 🖷 613/237–7052 ⊕ www.acta.ca. **Australian Federation of Travel Agents** ✉ Level 3, 309 Pitt St., Sydney, NSW 2000 ☎ 02/9264–3299 or 1300/363–416 🖷 02/9264–1085 ⊕ www.afta.com.au. **Travel Agents' Association of New Zealand** ✉ Level 5, Tourism and Travel House, 79 Boulcott St., Box 1888, Wellington 6001 ☎ 04/499–0104 🖷 04/499–0786 ⊕ www.taanz.org.nz.

VISITOR INFORMATION

Learn more about foreign destinations by checking government-issued travel advisories and country information. For a broader picture, consider information from more than one country.

The Singapore Tourism Board (STB) is open daily from 8:30 to 7. Multilingual staff members can answer your questions and attend to legitimate complaints. If you're planning a trip to Batam or Bintan islands, contact the Indonesian Tourist Promotion Office for tourist, passport and visa, health, and currency information.

🛂 In Singapore **Indonesia Tourist Promotion Office** ⊠ #15-07 Ocean Bldg., 10 Collyer Quay, Singapore 049315 🖷 6534-2837 ⊕ www.budpar.go.id. **Singapore Tourism Board** ⊠ Tourism Court, 1 Orchard Spring La., Singapore 247729 🖷 6736-6622 or 800/6736-2000 ⊕ www.stb.com.sg.

🛂 STB Abroad **U.S. & Canada:** ⊠ 1156 Avenue of the Americas, Suite 706, New York, NY 10036 ☎ 212/302-4861 🖷 212/302-4801 ⊕ www.singapore-usa.com ⊠ 4929 Wilshire Blvd., Suite 510, Los Angeles, CA 90010 🖷 323/677-0808 🖷 323/677-0801.

U.K.: ⊠ 1st Floor, Carrington House, 126-130 Regent St., London W1B 5JX 🖷 0207/437-0033, 08080/656-565 🖷 0207/734-2191.

Australia: ⊠ Level 11 AWA Bldg., 47 York St. Sydney, NSW NSW 2000 🖷 02/9290-2888, 02/9290-2882 🖷 02/9290-2555.

New Zealand: ⊠ c/o Vivaldi World Ltd., 18 Ronwood Ave., Suite 10K, Manukau City, Auckland 1702 🖷 09/262-3933 🖷 09/262-3927.

🛂 Government Advisories **U.S. Department of State** ⊠ Overseas Citizens Services Office, 2100 Pennsylvania Ave. NW, 4th floor, Washington, DC 20520 🖷 202/647-5225 interactive hotline or 888/407-4747 ⊕ www.travel.state.gov. **Consular Affairs Bureau of Canada** 🖷 800/267-6788 or 613/944-6788 ⊕ www.voyage.gc.ca. **U.K. Foreign and Commonwealth Office** ⊠ Travel Advice Unit, Consular Division, Old Admiralty Bldg., London SW1A 2PA 🖷 0870/606-0290 or 020/7008-1500 ⊕ www.fco.gov.uk/travel. **Australian Department of Foreign Affairs and Trade** 🖷 300/139-281 travel advice, 02/6261-1299 Consular Travel Advice Faxback Service ⊕ www.dfat.gov.au. **New Zealand Ministry of Foreign Affairs and Trade** 🖷 04/439-8000 ⊕ www.mft.govt.nz.

WEB SITES

Do check out the World Wide Web when planning your trip. You'll find everything from weather forecasts to virtual tours of famous cities. Be sure to visit Fodors.com (⊕ www.fodors.com), a complete travel-planning site. You can research prices and book plane tickets, hotel rooms, rental cars, vacation packages, and more. In addition, you can post your pressing questions in the Travel Talk section. Other planning tools include a currency converter and weather reports, and there are loads of links to travel resources.

The tourism board's site is updated daily, has local festival listings and recommended tours, and is a good place to start planning for your trip. The Changi Airport site has information about getting into the country and getting to your hotel. Singapore's popularity as an expat destination has spurred several useful Web sites. Asia Xpat has short-term accommodation information, travel advice, currency conversion tools, personals, service listings, and a useful "Ask the Expat" forum. Expat Singapore is geared for people who are interested in settling in Singapore, and includes some discusses food, etiquette, transportation, and culture shock. Singapore Expats has bar, restaurant, and shopping reviews. The Singaporean government has an extensive and helpful site. You can find just about any place in Singapore on the Street Directory. For local news read Asia One or Channel News Asia, a homegrown version of CNN.

🛂 Web Sites **Asia Xpat** ⊕ www.asiaxpat.com.sg. **Asia One** ⊕ www.asia1.com.sg. **Catcha Singapore** ⊕ www.catcha.com.sg. **Changi Airport** ⊕ web1.asia1.com.sg/airport/main.html. **Channel NewsAsia** ⊕ www.channelnewsasia.com. **Contact Singapore** ⊕ www.contactsingapore.org.sg. **Expatriate Singapore** ⊕ www.expatsingapore.com. **Singapore Expats** ⊕ www.singaporeexpats.com. **Singapore Government** ⊕ www.gov.sg. **Singapore InfoMap** ⊕ www.sg. **Singapore Street Directory** ⊕ www.streetdirectory.com.sg. **Singapore Tourism Board** ⊕ www.visitsingapore.com.

EXPLORING SINGAPORE

1

Updated by
Candice Foo

TO ARRIVE IN SINGAPORE is to step into a world where the call to prayer competes with the bustle of capitalism; where old men play mah-jongg in the streets and white-clad bowlers send the ball flying down well-tended cricket pitches; where Chinese fortune-tellers and high-priced management consultants advise the same entrepreneur. This great diversity of lifestyles, cultures, and religions thrives within the framework of a well-ordered society. Singapore is a spotlessly clean—some say sterile—modern metropolis surrounded by green, groomed parks and populated by 4 million orderly and well-regulated people, including many foreigners.

Although the Malays, Chinese, and Indians account for 98% of Singapore's population, other ethnic groups—from Eurasians to Filipinos and Thais—contribute significantly to the cultural mix. Understandably, the heritage of the British colonial stay is profoundly felt even though Singapore became fully independent in 1965.

Modern Singapore dates its nascency from the early morning of January 29, 1819, when a representative of the British East India Company, Thomas Stamford Raffles, stepped ashore at Singa Pura (Sanskrit for "Lion City"), as the island was then called, hoping to establish a British trading settlement on the southern part of the Malay Peninsula. There's clear evidence, however, of earlier Malay settlements, and also of an early Chinese presence, such as the 14th-century city of Temasek, which had an elegant and prosperous aristocracy. At various times Singapore fell under the sway of the Javanese and Thai empires. When Raffles arrived, the two sons of its previous sultan, who had died six years earlier, were in dispute over the throne. Raffles backed the claim of the elder brother, Tunku Hussein Mohamed Shah, and proclaimed him sultan. Offering to support the new sultanate with British military strength, Raffles persuaded him to grant the British a lease allowing them to establish a trading post on the island in return for an annual rent; within a week the negotiations were concluded. (A later treaty ceded the island outright to the British.) Within three years the fishing village, surrounded by swamps and jungle and populated only by tigers, 200 or so Malays, and a scattering of Chinese, had become a boomtown of 10,000 immigrants, administered by 74 British employees of the East India Company.

As Singapore grew, the British erected splendid public buildings, churches, and hotels, often using Indian convicts for labor. The Muslim, Hindu, Taoist, and Buddhist communities—swelling rapidly from the influx of fortune-seeking settlers from Malaya (now Malaysia), India, and South China—built mosques, temples, and shrines. Magnificent houses for wealthy merchants sprang up, and the harbor was soon lined with *godowns* (warehouses) to hold all the goods passing through the port.

By the turn of the century, Singapore had become the entrepôt of the East, a mix of adventurers and "respectable middle classes." World War I hardly touched the island, although its defenses were strengthened to support the needs of the British navy, for which Singapore was an important base. When World War II broke out, the British were complacent, expecting that any attack would come from the sea and that they would be well prepared to meet it. But the Japanese landed to the north, in Malaya. The two British battleships that had been posted to Singapore were sunk, and Japanese land forces raced down the peninsula on bicycles.

In February 1942 the Japanese captured Singapore. A huge number of Allied civilians and military were sent to Changi Prison; others were marched off to prison camps in Malaysia or to work on the notorious "Death Railway," in Thailand. The three and a half years of occupation was a time of privation and fear; an estimated 100,000 people died. The Japanese surrendered August 21, 1945, and the Allied forces returned to Singapore. The security of the British Empire was, however, never again to be felt, and independence for British Southeast Asia was only a matter of time.

In 1957 the British agreed to the establishment of an elected 51-member legislative assembly in Singapore. General elections in 1959 gave an overwhelming majority—43 of 51 seats—to the People's Action Party (PAP), and a young Chinese lawyer named Lee Kuan Yew became Singapore's first prime minister. In 1963 Singapore became part of the Federation of Malaysia, along with the newly independent state of Malaysia.

Mainly due to Malays' anxiety over a possible takeover by the ethnic Chinese, the federation broke up two years later, and Singapore became an independent sovereign state. The electorate supported Lee Kuan Yew and the PAP time and again. In 1990 Lee resigned after 31 years as prime minister, though as a senior minister he maintains his strong grip. His firm leadership of the party, his social and economic legislation, *and* his suppression of criticism led to his reputation as a (usually) benevolent dictator; yet Singaporeans recognize that his firm control had much to do with the republic's economic success and high standard of living. Lee's son, Lee Hsien Loong, officially took over from Lee's hand-picked successor, Goh Chok Tong, as prime minister on August 12, 2004. His style of governing seems to reveal a determination to distance himself from his father's style of leadership.

Getting Your Bearings

The main island of Singapore is shaped like a flattened diamond, 42 km (26 mi) east to west and 23 km (14 mi) north to south. Near the northern peak is the causeway leading to peninsular Malaysia—Kuala Lumpur is less than four hours away by car. At the southern foot is Singapore city, with its gleaming office towers and working docks. Offshore are Sentosa and some 60 smaller islands—most of them uninhabited—that serve as bases for oil refining or as playgrounds or beach escapes from the city. To the east is Changi International Airport, connected to the city by a parkway lined for miles with amusement centers of one sort or another. Of the island's total land area, more than half is built up, with the balance made up of parkland, farmland, plantations, swamp areas, and forest. Well-paved roads connect all parts of the island, and Singapore city has an excellent public transportation system.

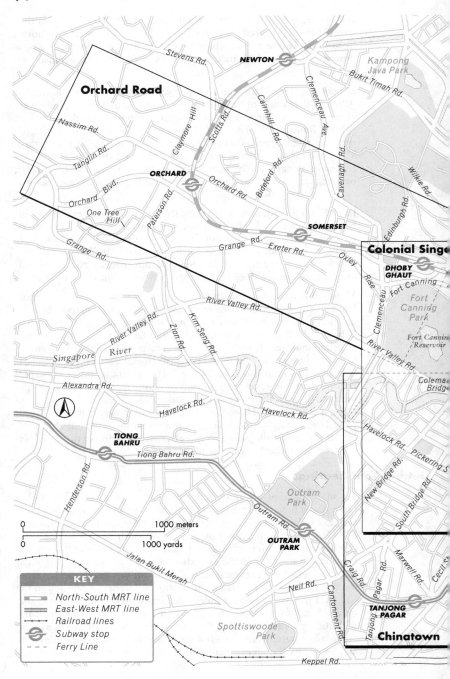

Orchard Road

Nassim Rd.

Stevens Rd.

NEWTON

Kampong Java Park

Bukit Timah Rd.

Tanglin Rd.

Claymore Hill

Scotts Rd.

Cairnhill Rd.

Clemenceau Ave.

Cavenagh Rd.

Wilkie Rd.

ORCHARD

Orchard Rd.

Bideford Rd.

Edinburgh Rd.

Orchard Blvd.

Paterson Rd.

One Tree Hill

SOMERSET

Colonial Sing

Grange Rd.

Grange Rd.

Exeter Rd.

Oxley

Rise

Clemenceau

Fort Canning

DHOBY GHAUT

Fort Canning Park

River Valley Rd.

Fort Canning Reservoir

Singapore River

River Valley Rd.

Zion Rd.

Kim Seng Rd.

River Valley Rd.

Colema Bridg

Alexandra Rd.

Havelock Rd.

Havelock Rd.

Havelock Rd.

Pickering S

TIONG BAHRU

Tiong Bahru Rd.

New Bridge Rd.

South Bridge Rd.

Henderson Rd.

Outram Park

| 0 | 1000 meters |
| 0 | 1000 yards |

OUTRAM PARK

Outram Rd.

Craig Rd.

Pagar Rd.

Maxwell Rd.

Cecil S

Jalan Bukit Merah

Neil Rd.

Cantonment Rd.

Tanjong Pagar

TANJONG PAGAR

Spottiswoode Park

Chinatown

Keppel Rd.

KEY

▬▬ North-South MRT line
▬▬ East-West MRT line
+—+ Railroad lines
Ⓢ Subway stop
--- Ferry Line

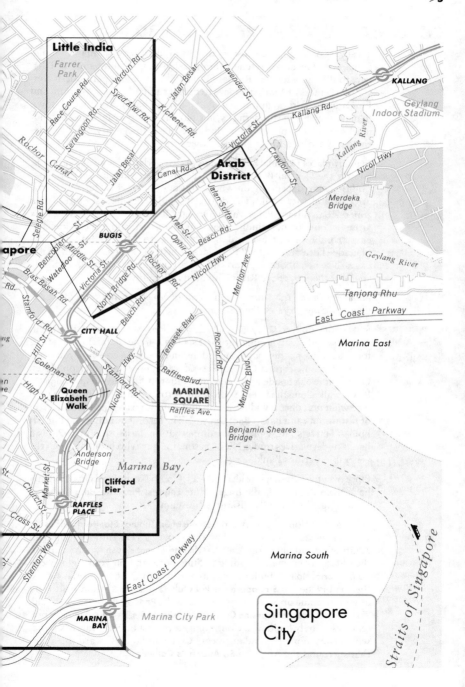

Singapore
City

COLONIAL SINGAPORE & THE CBD

The heart of Singapore's history and its modern wealth are in Colonial Singapore. The area stretches from the skyscrapers in the financial district to the 19th-century Raffles Hotel and from the supermodern convention centers of Marina Square to the Singapore History Museum and Ft. Canning. Although most of old Singapore has been knocked down to make way for the modern city, in Colonial Singapore most major landmarks have been preserved, including early-19th-century buildings designed by Irish architect George Coleman.

In many places Colonial Singapore seems to overlap other neighborhoods, namely the Central Business District (CBD), a relatively new designation that can, depending on whom you talk to, reach as high up as the area around City Hall. (The district broadly encompasses three main zones: Zone A is the River Valley/Orchard Road area; Zone B is the area around Chinatown, including the financial district; and Zone C stretches east from Bugis Street and Beach Road to Marina Square.) Esplanade–Theatres on the Bay is one of the CBD's most recognized anchors. The neighborhood starts inland around Empress Place, continues south of the Singapore River, and abuts Chinatown.

Numbers in the text correspond to numbers in the margin and on the Colonial Singapore & the CBD map.

a good walk

Start from **Collyer Quay** ❶ and Clifford Pier, where most European colonists and Asian immigrants first set foot on the island. Leaving Clifford Pier, walk up the quay—toward the Singapore River—until you come to the imposing former **General Post Office** ❷, now the Fullerton Hotel. On the hotel's left side is the gracious, old iron-link **Cavenagh Bridge** ❸. If you walk along the river's south bank before crossing the bridge, you'll find what was once a wide towpath and is now a paved pedestrian street of restaurants and bars—**Boat Quay** ❹. The second building on your left houses Harry's Bar, which gained international attention in 1995 as a haunt of derivatives trader Nick Leeson, the guy who brought down the venerable Barings Bank.

Once over the Cavenagh Bridge, take a left onto North Boat Quay. Slightly back from the river is the huge, white **Empress Place Building** ❺, home of the flagship Asian Civilisations Museum.

A bit farther along the quay is the **statue of Sir Thomas Stamford Raffles** ❻, who is believed to have landed on this spot in 1819. Turn right onto St. Andrew's Road until you come to **Old Parliament House** ❼, on your left, the oldest government building in Singapore, and on your right, **Victoria Memorial Hall** ❽, built in 1905 as a tribute to Queen Victoria. Across the road is the old **Singapore Cricket Club** ❾. Just past it, on your right as you continue up St. Andrew's Road, is the **Padang** ❿, or playing field. To your left are the **Supreme Court** ⓫ and **City Hall** ⓬, two splendidly pretentious, stately buildings. Continuing northeast on St. Andrew's Road, which runs along the Padang, cross Coleman Street toward the lawns that surround the Anglican **St. Andrew's Cathedral** ⓭.

Northeast of the cathedral is the huge **Raffles City** ⓮ complex, easily recognized by the towers of two hotels—Swissôtel The Stamford and Raffles The Plaza. Cross Stamford Road and walk through Raffles City to Bras Basah Road. Across the street is the renowned **Raffles Hotel** ⓯. After touring the hotel, continue up Bras Basah Road to Queen Street and make a right to the **Singapore Art Museum** ⓰. Across Bras Basah Road and down Victoria Street, you'll no doubt find a place to rest and people-watch at the **Chijmes** ⓱ complex. Continue southwest on Victoria Street (it becomes Hill Street after Stamford Road); the **Armenian Church** ⓲ will be on your right just before Coleman Street. From here stamp collectors should turn left onto Coleman and visit the **Singapore Philatelic Museum** ⓳; alternatively, turn right on Coleman, then right again onto Armenian Street, and you'll be at the **Asian Civilisations Museum, Armenian Street** ⓴. To see the **Singapore History Museum** ㉑ instead, return to Stamford Road and make a left. You may wish to conclude your tour with a stroll through **Ft. Canning Park** ㉒, pausing at the European Cemetery and the Tomb of Iskander Shah, or visit Singapore's biggest underground military operations quarters (used during World War II) at the Battle Box. South of the park is **Clarke Quay** ㉓, where you can eat and shop.

TIMING   With time factored in to wander through the Raffles Hotel and view the exhibits at one or more of the area's four museums, this walk should take a full day. Allow an hour for the Raffles, including time out for a Singapore Sling in the Long Bar. It should take at least an hour to view the museum exhibits. Avoid the Boat Quay area from noon–2 PM, when the lunchtime crowd takes over. Remember to buy water wherever you can; it's easy to get dehydrated in Singapore's heat.

What to See

⓲ **Armenian Church.** Also known as the Church of St. Gregory the Illuminator, this is one of Singapore's most elegant buildings. Built in 1835, this is the republic's oldest surviving church. The Armenians were but one of many minority groups that came to Singapore in search of better lives. A dozen wealthy Armenian families (and several non-Christian merchants) donated the funds for renowned colonial architect George Coleman to design this church. The main internal circular structure is imposed on a square plan with four projecting porticoes. In the churchyard is the weathered tombstone of Agnes Joaquim, who bred the orchid hybrid that has become Singapore's national flower. The pink-and-white orchid, with a deeper purplish pink center, was discovered in her garden in 1893 and still carries her name: Vanda Miss Joaquim. ✉ *60 Hill St., Colonial Singapore* ☎ *6334–0141* Ⓜ *City Hall.*

★ ⓴ **Asian Civilisations Museum, Armenian Street.** Formerly the Tao Nan School, built in 1910, this grand colonial building is now the first phase of the Asian Civilisations Museum (Phase II is at the **Empress Place Building**). With a mandate to provide an Asia-wide insight into the legacies of the past and the cultural traditions of the peoples who live in the region, the museum is a fascinating blend of permanent and changing themed exhibitions. The pride of the second floor is a striking Peranakan-culture display from the museum's permanent collection—this fascinating culture is the unique product of blended Chinese and Malay/Southeast

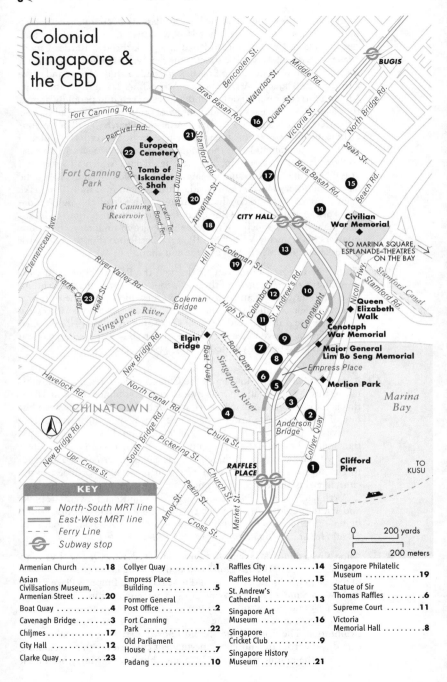

Colonial Singapore & the CBD

BUGIS

Fort Canning Rd.

Percival Rd.

European Cemetery 22

Fort Canning Park

Tomb of Iskander Shah

Fort Canning Reservoir

CITY HALL

Civilian War Memorial

TO MARINA SQUARE, ESPLANADE–THEATRES ON THE BAY

Coleman Bridge

Queen Elizabeth Walk

Cenotaph War Memorial

Elgin Bridge

Major General Lim Bo Seng Memorial

Empress Place

Merlion Park

Singapore River

CHINATOWN

Marina Bay

Anderson Bridge

RAFFLES PLACE

Clifford Pier

TO KUSU

KEY

- North-South MRT line
- East-West MRT line
- Ferry Line
- Subway stop

0   200 yards
0   200 meters

Asian influences in art, cuisine, costume, decor, language, and lifestyles. ✉ *39 Armenian St., Colonial Singapore* ☎ *6332–3015* ⊕ *www.nhb. gov.sg* 🖭 *S$3* ⏱ *Mon. 1–6, Tues.–Thurs. and weekends 9–7, and Fri. 9–9* Ⓜ *City Hall.*

❹ Boat Quay. Local entrepreneurs have created a mélange of eateries and nightclubs to satisfy diverse tastes at this popular entertainment hub along the Singapore River. Between 7 PM and midnight the area swells with people strolling along the pleasant quay. At the end of Boat Quay and named after Lord Elgin, a British governor-general of India, **Elgin Bridge** links Chinatown to the colonial quarter. The original rickety wooden structure was replaced in 1863 with an iron bridge imported from Calcutta; the current ferroconcrete bridge was installed in 1926. Ⓜ *Raffles Place.*

❸ Cavenagh Bridge. This gracious steel bridge, the oldest surviving bridge across the Singapore River, is named after Major General Orfeur Cavenagh, governor of the Straits Settlements from 1859 to 1867. Built in 1868 with girders imported from Glasgow, Scotland, it was the main route across the river until 1909; now Anderson Bridge bears the brunt of the traffic. From the bridge you get a spectacular view of the Fullerton Hotel. On the riverbank are whimsical sculptures of boys in half-dive over the water, which make for great pictures. ✉ *N. Bridge Rd., CBD* Ⓜ *City Hall.*

⓱ Chijmes. The oldest building in this walled complex is the Coleman-designed Caldwell House, a private mansion built in 1840. This, together with other buildings, became in 1852 the Convent of the Holy Infant Jesus, where nuns housed and schooled abandoned children. A church was added between 1901 and 1903. After World War II both the convent and the church fell into disrepair. The buildings received a S$100 million renovation in 1996 and were reopened as a shopping and entertainment complex. Today the lovingly restored church is rented out for private functions, and the grounds are used for free concerts and jazz festivals. The name Chijmes (pronounced "chimes") is an acronym of the convent's name. ✉ *30 Victoria St., Colonial Singapore* ☎ *6337–7810* Ⓜ *City Hall.*

⓬ City Hall. Popular as a backdrop for wedding photos, this pompous government building was completed in 1929. It was here that the British surrendered in 1942, followed by the Japanese surrender in 1945. The Padang field in front was the site of independence rallies in the 1950s. Each year on August 9, the building's steps serve as a viewing stand for the National Day Parade, celebrating Singapore's 1959 independence from Great Britain and the birth of the republic in 1965. Visitors can't enter City Hall, which has active government offices, but can relax on the steps or take photos with the Padang in the background. ✉ *St. Andrew's Rd., Colonial Singapore* Ⓜ *City Hall.*

⟳ ㉓ Clarke Quay. This festival village, which was for Sir Andrew Clarke, the second governor of Singapore, has entertainment, restaurants, and shops. Here you can observe a tinsmith demonstrating his skill, groove to a blues band in the central square's small gazebo, watch stilt-walkers wobble down pedestrians-only streets, or scout for bargain antiques. The river along the quay is close to being the sleepy waterway it was when Raffles first arrived; cargo vessels are banned from entering. You can board one of the bumboats (small launches) that offer daily 30-minute cruises along the river and into Marina Bay; it's a pleasant ride and a respite for tired feet. There are a slew of eateries along the water and there's a Sunday flea market. Thrill seekers will love the G-MAX Bungy, a reverse bungy ride at the river's edge. Ⓜ *Clarke Quay.*

❶ Collyer Quay. Land reclamation projects throughout the 19th century pushed the seafront several blocks away from Collyer Quay. At that time the view from here would have been a virtual wall of anchored ships. Today you look out on the graceful Benjamin Sheares Bridge (1981), which carries the East Coast Parkway from one landfill headland to another, enclosing what's now the Marina Bay. European traders once arrived by steamship and Chinese immigrants arrived by wind-dependent junks at **Clifford Pier,** a covered jetty with high, vaulted ceilings. Now Indonesian sailors sit around smoking clove-scented cigarettes, and seamen from every seafaring nation come ashore for liquor and duty-free electronics. Bumboats wallow in the bay, waiting to take sailors back to their ships or carry other visitors wherever they want to go for about S$30 an hour. The atmosphere can be seedy; this is one of the few places in Singapore where women might feel uncomfortable wandering by themselves.

Next to Clifford Pier is **No.1 Fullerton,** an elegant complex of offices, restaurants, nightclubs, and cafés. The **Merlion** statue has been shifted here from its former home in Merlion Park at the edge of the Anderson Bridge. In the evening the statue is floodlighted, its eyes are lighted, and its mouth spews water. You can see an even bigger one on Sentosa Island. Symbolizing courage, strength, and excellence, the Merlion is half fish, half lion and is based on the national symbol, the lion (from which the name Singapore was derived). Ⓜ *Raffles Place.*

❺ Empress Place Building. Constructed in the 1860s as a courthouse, this huge, white, neoclassical building has since had four major additions and has housed nearly every government body, including the Registry of Births and Deaths and the Immigration Department. It's now Phase II (or the second wing) of the **Asian Civilisations Museum,** the nation's first to look comprehensively at the east, south, southeast, and west Asian regions. With 10 galleries spread over three levels, each of the regions has its own thematic timeline and permanent displays. The galleries have state-of-the-art interactive features, and there's an educational center for kids. ✉ *1 Empress Pl., CBD* ☎ *6332–7798* ⊕ *www.nhb.gov.sg* 💲 *S$3* ◷ *Mon. 1–7, Tues.–Thurs. and weekends 9–7, and Fri. 9–9* Ⓜ *Raffles Place.*

FodorśChoice ★

❷ Former General Post Office. The post office has moved to the suburbs from this imposing edifice—all gray stone and monumental pillars—constructed in 1928, the heyday of the British Empire. Now it's the Fullerton Hotel, the S$400 million result of three years of painstaking restoration. The hallmarks of the old Fullerton Building, which have both historical and architectural value, have been preserved alongside current designs. There are 20-foot Doric columns, and wall motifs from the 1920s. The result is a unique contemporary hotel installed in an Edwardian exterior. ✉ *1 Fullerton Sq., CBD* ☎ *6733–8388* ⊕ *www.fullertonhotel.com* Ⓜ *Raffles Place.*

Ⓒ ㉒ **Ft. Canning Park.** Offering green sanctuary from the bustling city below, Ft. Canning is where modern Singapore's founder, Sir Stamford Raffles, built his first bungalow and experimented with a botanical garden. Massive fig trees, luxuriant ferns, and abundant birdlife—including piping black-naped orioles and chattering collared kingfishers—flourish here. The hill's trails are well marked by signs, and there are designated picnic areas. At the park's edge a private country club occupies the British military's former Singapore Command and Staff College. A lively reconstruction of the British army's former underground Far East Command Centre called the **Battle Box** highlights the hill's World War II history. Audiovisual displays shed light on the British surrender of Singapore to the Japanese on February 15, 1942. You can also see the remnants of a 19th-century **European cemetery.** Weathered tombstones, once divided into areas for Protestants and for Catholics, are now set into a wall around an open field. The volume of tombstones for young people tells of the grim conditions faced by pioneering colonials.

In the 13th and 14th centuries, the Malay rulers of the kingdom of Temasek (part of the Srivijayan empire based in Palembang, Sumatra) built their royal palaces on **Ft. Canning Rise,** as the hill has been called. No doubt they chose the spot for its freshwater spring, cool breezes, and commanding river views. Archaeological excavations on the hill have unearthed ancient gold ornaments as well as Chinese trading ceramics. The last five kings of Singa Pura, as the island came to be called, including the legendary Iskandar Shah, are said to be buried here; a sacred shrine, or *kramat* in Malay, marks the spot. Some dispute this, claiming that Iskandar Shah escaped from Singa Pura before its destruction in 1391, when Temasek succumbed to attacks from the Majapahit empire in Java and from the Ayuthia empire of Siam (Thailand).

For several hundred years the site was abandoned to the jungle. It was referred to by the Malays as Bukit Larangan, the Forbidden Hill, a place where the spirits of bygone kings roamed on sacred ground. Then Raffles came: defying Malay superstition, he established his Government House on the rise and neatly assumed the mantle of the ancient kings for colonial British rule. Later, in 1859, a fort was constructed; its guns were fired to mark dawn, noon, and night. ✉ *51 Canning Rise, Colonial Singapore* ☎ *6333–0510* 🎟 *S$8* ⊙ *Daily 10–6* Ⓜ *Dhoby Ghaut.*

| off the beaten path | **MARINA SQUARE –** This minicity has three malls and five tony hotels—the Pan Pacific, the Marina Mandarin, the Oriental, the Ritz-Carlton, and the Conrad International Centennial. Suntec City, a mammoth convention center and shopping mall, is rivaled by an even bigger mall, the Millenia [sic] Walk, with its trilevel duty-free shop. The Marina Square Shopping Mall has a mix of high-end boutiques and bargain shops. Across the street from the mall, along Queen Elizabeth Walk, is the **Esplanade–Theatres on the Bay,** a massive performing arts center. It's part of an ambitious project by the |

government to create a cultural calendar that satisfies the varied interests of Singapore's multiracial community, to cultivate the local arts scene by supporting young artists, and to play a proactive role in arts education. ⊠ *6 Raffles Blvd.* ⊘ *Daily 10–10.*

❼ Old Parliament House. George Coleman designed the Parliament House FodorsChoice in 1827 as a mansion for wealthy merchant John Maxwell. Maxwell ★ never occupied it, and instead leased it to the government, which eventually bought it in 1841 for S$15,600. It was the Supreme Court until 1939 and is considered Singapore's oldest government building. In 1953 it became the home of the then governing Legislative Assembly and then the meeting place for Parliament in 1965. The bronze elephant statue on a plinth in front was a gift from King Chulalongkorn of Siam during his state visit in 1871. The building is now **The Arts House** performance space. Film retrospectives, photo exhibitions, musicals, plays, and talks by experts are regular events. ⊠ *1 Old Parliament La. (Corner of High St. and St. Andrew's Rd.), Colonial Singapore* ☎ *6332–6900* ⊕ *www.theartshouse.com.sg* ⊠ *Free* ⊘ *Weekdays 10–9, weekends 11–8* Ⓜ *City Hall.*

❿ Padang. Used primarily as a playing field, the Padang (Malay for "field" or "plain") is behind the Singapore Cricket Club. It has traditionally been a social and political hub. Once called the Esplanade, it was half its current size until an 1890s land reclamation expanded it. During World War II the Japanese gathered 2,000 British civilians here before marching them off to Changi Prison and, in many cases, to their deaths.

Beyond the Padang's northeastern edge, across Stamford Road and the Stamford Canal, are the four 220-foot (67-meter) tapering white columns of the **Civilian War Memorial,** known locally as the Four Chopsticks. The monument honors the thousands of civilians from Singapore's four main ethnic groups (Chinese, Malay, Indian, and "others," including Eurasians and Europeans) who lost their lives during the Japanese occupation or were dispatched to build the Burma–Siam Railway.

Along the Padang's eastern edge, just across Connaught Drive, are several other monuments. **Major General Lim Bo Seng Memorial** honors a World War II freedom fighter who was tortured to death by the Japanese in 1944. The imposing **Cenotaph War Memorial** honors the dead of the two world wars. Ⓜ *City Hall.*

⓮ Raffles City. Designed by famous Chinese-American architect I. M. Pei, the difficult-to-navigate Raffles City complex of offices and shops contains two hotels, Swissôtel The Stamford and Raffles The Plaza. There's a stunning view of downtown and the harbor from the Stamford's 69th-floor Equinox restaurant. A great alternative to a Singapore Sling at the Raffles Hotel is a martini at sunset in the City Space bar on the Stamford's 70th floor. Ⓜ *City Hall.*

⓯ Raffles Hotel. This hotel began life as the home of a British sea captain. In 1887 the Armenian Sarkies brothers took over the building and transformed it into one of Asia's grandest hotels. Raffles has experienced many ups and downs, especially during World War II, when it was first a center for British refugees, then quarters for Japanese officers, and then a center for released Allied POWs. There's a delicious irony to the hotel: although it's regarded as a bastion of colonialism, it's actually an Armenian creation, and in its 130 years of hosting expatriates, it has only once had a British manager. Even so, service has been unfailingly loyal to the colonial heritage. Right before the Japanese invasion, the Chinese waiters took the silverware from the dining rooms and buried it in the Palm Court garden, where it remained safely hidden until the occupiers departed.

The hotel deteriorated after the war, surviving by trading on its heritage rather than its facilities. However, in late 1991, after two years of renovation and expansion, Raffles reopened as the republic's most expensive hotel (S$650 a night and upward). You can no longer just roam around inside. Instead you're channeled through recreated colonial-style buildings to a free museum (☉ Daily 10–7) of Raffles memorabilia and then, perhaps, to take refreshment in a reproduction of the **Long Bar,** where the famous Singapore Sling was created in 1915 by bartender Ngiam Tong Boon. The Sling here is still regarded as Singapore's best; note that the S$18.65 tab includes service and tax—if you want to keep the glass you can shell out another S$18. Some consider the new Long Bar a travesty, with manually operated *punkahs* (fans) replaced by electric-powered ones. Casual visitors are discouraged from entering the original part of the hotel, via the front reception and lobby area, and nowadays the once lovely Palm Court is not only out of bounds but, to all appearances, devoid of life. Still, the historical hotel's Tiffin Room, Empire Café, and Bar & Billiard Room are definitely worth a visit. You can also browse the arcade's 65 shops, stop by Doc Cheng's for its "transethnic" cuisine, or head to the tiny Writers' Bar for a drink. ⊠ *1 Beach Rd., Colonial Singapore* ☎ *6337–1886* ⊕ *www.raffleshotel.com* Ⓜ *City Hall.*

⓲ **St. Andrew's Cathedral.** The first church at this site was constructed in 1834, but was demolished in 1852 following two lightning strikes. Some suggested that before another place of worship was built, the spirits should be appeased with the blood from 30 heads. Thankfully, the suggestion was ignored. Indian convicts were brought in to construct this cathedral in the English Gothic style. The structure, completed in 1861, has bells cast by the firm that made Big Ben's, and it resembles Netley Abbey, in Hampshire, England. The British overlords were so impressed by the cathedral that the Indian convict who supplied the working drawings was granted his freedom. The church was expanded in 1952 and again in 1983. Its lofty interior is white and simple, with stained-glass windows coloring the sunlight as it enters. On the walls are marble-and-brass memorial plaques, including one commemorating the British who died in a 1915 mutiny of native light infantry and another in memory of 41 Australian army nurses killed in the Japanese invasion. Services are held every Sunday. A showcase of historical artifacts and a history video are in the south transept. Guided tours are available. ⊠ *11 St. Andrew's Rd., Colonial Singapore* ☎ *6337–6104* ⊕ *www. livingstreams.org.sg* ⊜ *Free* ☉ *Daily 9–5* Ⓜ *City Hall.*

⑯ Singapore Art Museum. Previously this museum was an all-boys Catholic St. Joseph's institution until 1987. It reopened as a museum in 1996 and has a 6,000-piece permanent collection that includes modern and contemporary art from all over Southeast Asia. One of the highlights is the E-Mage Gallery, which displays 20th-century art on large, high-definition monitors. A regularly rotating permanent collection shares space with visiting exhibits. ✉ *71 Bras Basah Rd., Colonial Singapore* ☎ *6332–3222/3220* ⊕ *www.nhb.gov.sg/SAM/sam.shtml* ⚏ *S$3* ☉ *Sat.–Thurs. 10–7, Fri. 10–9* Ⓜ *City Hall.*

> **need a break?** At the back of the Singapore Art Museum is the **Olio Dome** (☎ 6339–0792), a casual breakfast and lunch spot. The Dome, one of several in Singapore, serves a Western menu of soups, salads, and sandwiches—but it really specializes in coffee. You can eat outside on the curving neoclassical porch or inside in a 1920s-style bistro.

❾ Singapore Cricket Club. Founded in 1852 and housed in a charming 1884 building with 1907 and 1921 modifications, this club was for a long time the center of social and sporting life for the British community (they played cricket on the Padang at least from the 1830s). It now has a multiracial active membership of 5,500 and offers facilities for various sports, in addition to bars and restaurants. If you're going to be in Singapore for more than a couple of weeks, you can apply, with the support of a member, for a visiting membership. The club isn't open to the general public, but from the Padang you can sneak a quick look at the deep, shaded verandas, from which members still watch cricket, rugby, and tennis matches. ✉ *Connaught Dr., Colonial Singapore* ☎ *6338–9271* ⊕ *www.scc.org.sg* Ⓜ *City Hall.*

★ ㉑ Singapore History Museum. Housed in a silver-dome colonial building, this was originally opened as the Raffles Museum in 1887. Included in its collection are 20 dioramas depicting the republic's past, together with the Revere Bell, donated to the original St. Andrew's Church in 1834 by the daughter of American patriot Paul Revere; the 380-piece Haw Par Jade Collection, one of the largest of its kind; the exquisite Farquhar Collection of regional flora and fauna paintings executed in the 19th century; occult paraphernalia from Chinese secret societies; and sundry historical documents. Don't miss *The Singapore Story,* a 3-D audiovisual show, or *Rivertales,* a historical exhibition revolving around the Singapore River. (At this writing, the museum is at #03–09/17 Riverside Point, 30 Merchant Road in Colonial Singapore until early 2006 when it will return to its renovated home.) ✉ *Stamford Rd., Colonial Singapore* ☎ *6332–3659/5642* ⊕ *www.nhb.gov.sg/SHM* ⚏ *S$2* ☉ *Mon. 1–7, Tues.–Thurs. and Sun. 9–7, Fri. 9–9* Ⓜ *Clarke Quay.*

⑲ Singapore Philatelic Museum. Southeast Asia's first stamp museum is inside what was once the Anglo Chinese School. It has a top-notch collection of local and international stamps as well as an audiovisual theater, a resource center, interactive games, and a souvenir shop. ✉ *23B Coleman St., Colonial Singapore* ☎ *6337–3888* ⊕ *www.nhb.gov.sg* ⚏ *S$3* ☉ *Mon. 1–7, Tues.–Sun. 9–7* Ⓜ *City Hall.*

6 **Statue of Sir Thomas Stamford Raffles.** Raffles' likeness keeps permanent watch over the spot where he purportedly first landed in Singapore on the morning of January 29, 1819. This white statue is a replica of the bronze one, erected in 1887, inside Empress Place Building. Pause here a moment to observe the contrast between the old and the new. Previously, this river was the artery feeding Singapore's commercial life, packed with barges and lighters that ferried goods from cargo ship to dock. There were no cranes—the unloading was done by teams of laborers who tottered back and forth between lighters and riverside godowns. ⊠ *North Boat Quay, near Empress Place Bldg., Boat Quay* Ⓜ *Raffles Place.*

⓫ **Supreme Court.** In the ponderous neoclassical style so beloved by British colonials, the Supreme Court has Corinthian pillars and the look of arrogant certainty. Completed in 1939, it was the last such building to be erected in Singapore, replacing the famous Hôtel de l'Europe, a romantic venue of the Conrad era of sailors' derring-do. The pedimental sculptures of the Greek temple-style facade, by Italian artist Cavalieri Rudolfo Nolli, portray an allegory of Justice. Inside, there's an echoing hall and a magnificent staircase, and high above, the vast paneled ceiling is an exercise in showmanship. All of this was completed just in time for the Japanese to use the building as their headquarters. Thankfully, World War II preempted architect Frank Dorrington Ward's plan to demolish most of the historical buildings around the Padang in favor of a modern complex. ⊠ *1 St. Andrew's Rd., Colonial Singapore* ☎ *6337–8191* ⊕ *www.supcourt.gov.sg* ☉ *Weekdays 8:30–5:30, Sat. 8:30–1, closed Sun.* Ⓜ *City Hall.*

8 **Victoria Memorial Hall.** The hall was built in 1905 as a tribute to Queen Victoria. Along with the adjacent **Victoria Theatre,** built in 1862 as the town hall, it's the main venue for Singapore Symphony Orchestra performances. ⊠ *9 Empress Pl., Colonial Singapore* ☎ *6338–8283* ⊕ *www. nac.gov.sg* Ⓜ *Raffles Place.*

CHINATOWN

In a country where 77% of the people are Chinese, it may seem strange to name a small urban area Chinatown. But Chinatown was born nearly two centuries ago, when the Chinese were a minority (if only for half a century) in the newly formed British settlement. In an attempt to minimize racial tension, Raffles allotted sections of the settlement to different immigrant groups. The Chinese were given the area south of the Singapore River. Today the river is still the northern boundary of old Chinatown; Maxwell Road marks its southern perimeter and New Bridge Road its western one. Before 20th-century land reclamation, the western perimeter was the sea. The reclaimed area between Telok Ayer Street and Collyer Quay–Shenton Way has become the business district, whose expansion has caused Chinese shophouses to be knocked down all the way to Cross Street.

Immigrants from mainland China—many of them penniless and half-starved—were crammed inside a relatively small rectangle. Within three years of the formation of the Straits Settlement, 3,000 Chinese had arrived; this number increased tenfold over the next decade. The Hokkien people, traders from Fukien Province, made up about a quarter of the community. Other leading groups were the Teochews, from the Swatow region of Guangdong Province, and their mainland neighbors, the Cantonese. In smaller groups, the Hainanese, the nomadic Hakkas, and peoples from Guangxi arrived in tightly packed junks, riding on the northeast monsoon winds.

Most immigrants came with the sole intention of exchanging their rags for riches, then returning to China. They had no allegiance to Singapore or to Chinatown, which was no melting pot but, rather, separate pockets of ethnically diverse groups, each with a different dialect; a different cuisine; and different cultural, social, and religious attitudes. In the shophouses (bilevel buildings with shops or small factories on the ground floor and living quarters upstairs) as many as 30 lodgers would share a single room, using beds in shifts. Life was a fight for space and survival. Crime was rampant. What order existed was maintained by Chinese guilds, clan associations, and secret societies, all of which fought—sometimes savagely—for control of lucrative aspects of community life.

Not too long ago, all of Chinatown was slated for the bulldozer in the name of "progress." Selective conservation, however, is now enshrined in government policy, both as a way of generating new commercial space (skyrocketing prices reflect the popularity of old shophouses converted into offices) and as a necessary part of an enlightened tourism agenda. Besides this, in the latter part of the 20th century, both the government and citizens of Singapore have developed more pride in their heritage. They've recognized that an important way of maintaining Chinese customs and family ties is to conserve the building frameworks in which they once were nurtured. To some extent Chinatown has been recast as a place of the 21st century, but much of the old vigor survives at street level. The aim of a S$97.5 million conservation project by the Singapore Tourism Board is to evoke a sense of the past by carving Chinatown into three sectors—Historic District, Greater Town, and Hilltown—each with its own cultural focal points and identifying markers.

Districts

Chinatown has four districts: Telok Ayer, Kreta Ayer, Bukit Pasoh, and Tanjong Pagar.

Telok Ayer centers around Telok Ayer Road, which, believe it or not, once faced the open sea. The neighborhood stretches all the way to Ann Siang Hill; Thian Hock Keng Temple is its most recognizable landmark.

Kreta Ayer was named after the bullock water carts that used to ply the area supplying water to the locals. Although it developed after the Telok Ayer district, in many ways this was once the heart of Chinatown. It had a major concentration of restaurants, theaters, and brothels and these days mainly two- to three-story shophouses, of late art deco style. It centers around Pagoda, Temple, Trengganu and Sago streets.

Bukit Pasoh is predominantly residential, but several boutique hotels and restaurants have opened up here recently. It's bounded by Keong Saik, New Bridge, Kreta Ayer, Neil, and Cantonment roads. The neighborhood is linked to Tanjong Pagar, a business and residential area with some restaurants and bridal shops, which is bounded by Neil, Craig, and Tanjong Pagar roads.

Numbers in the text correspond to numbers in the margin and on the Chinatown map.

a good walk

Begin at the Elgin Bridge, built to link Chinatown with colonial Singapore. At the bridge's south end, logically enough, South Bridge Road begins. Off to the right is Upper Circular Road, on the left-hand side of which is **Yeo Swee Huat** ❶, purveyor of paper replica houses, cars, and other worldly goods intended to be burned at Chinese funerals (for the deceased to take into the other world). You'll encounter other similar shops during your walk. Backtrack along South Bridge Road and cross onto Circular Road, once lined with cloth wholesalers and now home to bars and restaurants. This is a good place to have some simple local fare, especially of the Indian and Malay variety. Walk down **Lorong Telok** ❷, with its architecturally interesting shops and clan houses, and take a right onto North Canal Road for stores that sell Chinese delicacies—dried foods, turtles for soup, sea cucumbers, shark fins, and bird nests. Also on this street is the **Speakers' Corner** ❸ modeled on the forum in London's Hyde Park, and neighboring the Kreta Ayer Neighborhood Police Post. Trace your steps back along North Canal to Chulia Street. Follow it to Phillip Street and turn right to reach the **Wak Hai Cheng Bio Temple** ❹ (1826).

Return to North Canal Road. Continue to New Bridge Road, turn left, and walk past the Furama Singapore Hotel and the People's Park Centre, now home to the Singapore Handicrafts Centre. Next to it is the **Yue Hwa Building** ❺, which sells unique but pricey Chinese arts and crafts. Cross Upper Cross Street and take a left onto **Mosque Street**—you have arrived at the core of Chinatown, also known as Kreta Ayer. The shophouses here, originally built as stables, have been redeveloped into a string of spas, traditional massage parlors, reflexology centers, and a smattering of restaurants. Turn right onto South Bridge Road; **Jamae Mosque** ❻, Singapore's oldest surviving mosque, will be on your right. On the next block is the **Sri Mariamman Temple** ❼, Singapore's oldest Hindu temple.

If you take the next right, onto **Temple Street,** you may be fortunate enough to see one of Singapore's few remaining streetside scribes. In the next lane, on Pagoda Street is the **Chinatown Heritage Centre** ❽. Trengganu Street leads to the **Chinatown Complex** ❾. Leaving the market, walk along narrow Sago Street lined with mobile stalls and small shops peddling pastries, ceramics, medicine, and knickknacks. **Smith Street,** between Sago and Temple streets, has stores that sell everything from chilies to ground rhinoceros horn. It's turned into a pedestrian zone nightly where it crosses Trengganu Street; the food and snack stalls here are open daily from 11 to 11. Gnosh on local eats before visiting the old shops, some of which are allocated to arts groups specializing in opera, theater, calligraphy, and literature.

If you turn right onto South Bridge Road, you'll come to the intersection of Tanjong Pagar, Neil, and Maxwell roads. **Jinriksha Station** ⑩, on Maxwell and Neil, was once a rickshaw depot, but now has a stretch of fine restaurants. After strolling down **Tanjong Pagar Road** to see the restored shophouses and trendy restaurants, backtrack to the intersection of Maxwell and South Bridge. Turn right onto Maxwell Road and head for the **URA Gallery** ⑪, which showcases the Urban Redevelopment Authority's conservation efforts in Singapore. From here, proceed down Maxwell, turn left onto Cecil Street, and then turn left up Telok Ayer to reach the **Al Abrar Mosque** ⑫. Farther up the street is the intriguing **Thian Hock Keng Temple** ⑬, a magnificent Taoist temple that, prior to land reclamation projects, once stood on the waterfront. **Nagore Durgha Shrine** ⑭, at Telok Ayer and Boon Tat streets, is an odd mix of minarets and Greek columns decorated with fairy lights that was built by South Indian Muslims. At Boon Tat's eastern end you'll see the **Lau Pa Sat** ⑮, meaning "Old Market" in the local Hokkien-Chinese dialect (derived from the Malay word *pasar,* for "market"), Southeast Asia's largest Victorian cast-iron structure. Here you can refresh yourself at the food court, then take the subway back to Raffles Place.

TIMING   Allow three to four hours for this walk, and even longer if you want to nose around the shops. Factor in at least an hour each for the Chinatown Heritage Centre and the Wak Hai Cheng Bio and Sri Mariamman temples. The best time to go is during the week, anytime from early morning through early evening. Most sights close around 8 PM, but markets and food stalls stay open until 11 PM. Weekends can be rather busy and you may encounter crowds of locals going about their business.

What to See

⑫ **Al Abrar Mosque.** In 1827 when the original thatch hut stood here, it was one of Singapore's first mosques for its Indian Muslims. Also known as Kuchu Palli (Tamil for "mosque hut"), the existing structure dates from 1850. Though much of the mosque's original ornamentation has been replaced, its original timber panels and fanlight windows have remained. ⊠ *192 Telok Ayer St., Telok Ayer* ☉ *Sat.–Thurs. 5 AM–9 PM, closed Fri.* Ⓜ *Tanjong Pajar.*

off the beaten path

SETTLER'S CAFÉ – For a breather, pop into Settler's Café at No. 39 North Canal Road (☎ 6535–0435), near the Clarke Quay MRT. It's one of Singapore's popular themed cafés. You can rub elbows with locals (and other travelers) while playing board games over dinner and drinks. Western food, such as burgers and pastas, come at moderate prices.

❾ **Chinatown Complex.** Typically, this market is mobbed. At the open-air vegetable and fruit stands, women—toothless and wrinkled—sell their wares. Inside, on the first floor, hawker stalls sell cooked foods, but it's the basement floor that fascinates: here you'll find a wet market—so called because water is continually sloshed over the floors to clean them—where meat, fowl, and fish are bought and sold. Some sights may spoil your appetite; at the far left corner, for example, live pigeons, furry

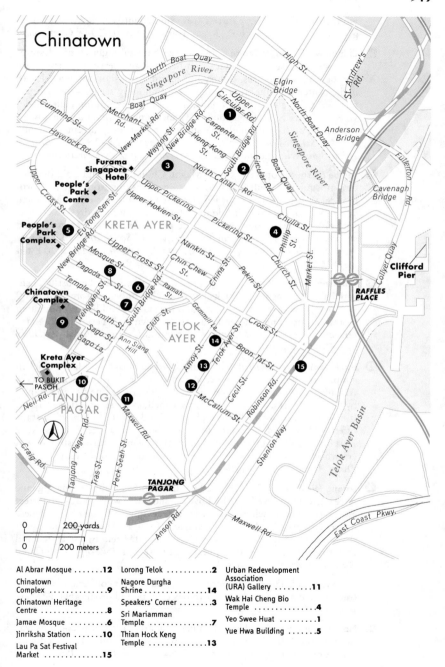

Chinatown

white rabbits, and sleepy turtles are crammed into cages, awaiting hungry buyers. ⊠ *335 Smith St., Kreta Ayer* ⊙ *Daily 10–10* Ⓜ *Chinatown.*

⑧ Chinatown Heritage Centre. These three painstakingly restored shophouses showcase Chinatown's rich heritage and serve as a repository for the area's memories, sights, and sounds. The shophouse at No. 48 is the center's highlight, with replicas of an early settler's living quarters and tailor shop. Additionally, there are 15 exhibition galleries devoted to the trials and tribulations of Chinese immigrants and Chinatown's evolution, as told through the stories of past and current residents. ⊠ *48–50 Pagoda St., Kreta Ayer* ☎ *6325–2878* ⊕ *www.chinatownheritage.com.sg* ▧ *S$8* ⊙ *Daily 10–7* Ⓜ *Chinatown.*

⑥ Jamae Mosque. Popularly called Masjid Chulia, the simple, almost austere mosque was built in 1835 by Chulia Muslims from India's Coromandel Coast. So long as it isn't prayer time and the doors are open, you're welcome to step inside for a look (you must be dressed conservatively and take your shoes off before entering; women may need shawls or scarves to cover their heads). ⊠ *218 South Bridge Rd., Kreta Ayer* ⊙ *Sat.–Thurs. 9 AM–11:30 AM and 2:30 PM–4 PM; Fri. 2:30 PM–4 PM* Ⓜ *Chinatown.*

⑩ Jinriksha Station. Built in 1903, this station was once the bustling central depot for Singapore's rickshaws, which numbered more than 9,000 in 1919. Now there's nary a one, and the station building is dominated by restaurants. This is a good place to sit down with a cool drink. ⊠ *Intersection of Neil and Tanjong Pagar roads, Bukit Pasoh* ⊙ *Daily 9–4:30* Ⓜ *Tanjong Pajar.*

⑮ Lau Pa Sat Festival Market. This market, which looks a lot like a chicken coop, is the largest Victorian cast-iron structure left in Southeast Asia. Already a thriving fish market in 1822, it was redesigned as an octagon by George Coleman in 1834 and redesigned, as we see it today, in 1894. It has been transformed into a planned food court, with hawker stalls offering all types of Asian fare. By day it's busy with office workers. After 7 PM Boon Tat Street is closed to traffic, and the mood turns festive: hawkers wheel out their carts, and street musicians perform. ⊠ *18 Raffles Quay, Telok Ayer* Ⓜ *Raffles Place.*

② Lorong Telok. Nos. 27, 28, and 29 on this architecturally fascinating lane have intricately carved panels above the shop doorways. Across the street are old clan houses whose stonework facades appear to have a Portuguese influence—possibly by way of Malacca (now Melaka), a trading post that was established by the Portuguese and later held by the Dutch and then the British in the 16th century. ⊠ *Lorong Telok, off North Canal Rd., Telok Ayer* Ⓜ *Raffles Place.*

Mosque Street. The old shophouses here have been converted into spas, traditional massage parlors, reflexology centers, and restaurants. ⊠ *Kreta Ayer* Ⓜ *Chinatown.*

⑭ Nagore Durgha Shrine. This odd mix of minarets and Greek columns was built by South Indian Muslims in 1830. Inside it's now decorated with tiny lights. ⊠ *140 Telok Ayer St., Telok Ayer* Ⓜ *Tanjong Pagar.*

Sago Street. At No. 16, Fong Moon Kee, traditional healing oils are sold to cure asthma, colds, and other ailments. A cake shop at No. 34 is extremely popular for fresh baked goods, especially during the Mooncake Festival (a.k.a. the Mid-Autumn Festival). ⊠ *Kreta Ayer* Ⓜ *Chinatown.*

❸ **Speakers' Corner.** Also known as Hong Lim Park, this spot was declared a "free speech zone" by the government in 2001. Resembling London's Hyde Park, it looks like nothing more than a small patch of grass, but from 7 AM to 7 PM on some days, you may be able to catch carefully crafted words and speeches. Those who wish to speak need to register with the police at the park station. This was intended as a place for people to express their opinions freely, but it hasn't been fully successful. You can't address religious or racial issues and having to register means that your presence has been noted. ⊠ *North Canal Rd., Kreta Ayer* Ⓜ *Raffles Place.*

★ **Smith Street.** This street transforms into a pedestrian zone nightly that brings to mind the hustle and bustle of the street hawkers from the 1970s. Sit outdoors as you sample delicious local fare at affordable prices. Pop into the Chinese Theatre Circle at No. 5 Smith Street on Friday and Saturday nights for Catonese opera performances while you dine. ⊠ *Kreta Ayer* Ⓜ *Chinatown.*

★ ❼ **Sri Mariamman Temple.** Singapore's oldest Hindu temple has a pagoda-like entrance topped by one of the most ornate *gopurams* (pyramidal gateway towers) you're likely to ever see. Hundreds of brightly colored statues of deities and mythical animals line the tiers of this towering porch; glazed cement cows sit, seemingly in great contentment, atop the surrounding walls. The story of this temple begins with Naraina Pillay, who came to Singapore on the same ship as Raffles in 1819 and started work as a clerk, Singapore's first recorded Indian immigrant. Within a short time he'd set up his own construction business, often using convicts sent to Singapore from India, and quickly made a fortune. He obtained this site for the temple, so that devotees could pray on the way to and from work at the harbor. The first temple, built in 1827 of wood and *attap* (wattle and daub), was replaced in 1843 by the current brick structure. The gopuram was added in 1936. Inside are some spectacular paintings that have been restored by Tamil craftsmen brought over from South India. This is where Hindu weddings, as well as the firewalking festival *Thimithi* takes place. You'll need to purchase tickets ($3 for cameras, $6 for camcorders) if you want to take photographs. ⊠ *244 South Bridge Rd., Kreta Ayer* ☎ *6223–4064* ⊕ *www.heb.gov.sg/temples.html* ⊙ *Daily 7 AM–9 PM* Ⓜ *Chinatown.*

Tanjong Pagar Road. The 220 shophouses here have been restored to their 19th-century appearance—or rather a sanitized, dollhouse version of it. They contain teahouses, calligraphers, mah-jongg makers, shops, bars, and restaurants. Lively when it first opened, the area has since been somewhat overshadowed by nightlife establishments at Boat Quay and Clarke Quay on the Singapore River. ⊠ *Tanjong Pagar* Ⓜ *Tanjong Pagar.*

Temple Street. Here you may be fortunate enough to see one of the few remaining practitioners of a dying profession. Sometimes found sitting on a stool along the street is a scribe, an old man to whom other elderly Chinese come to have their letters written. ✉ *Kreta Ayer* Ⓜ *Chinatown.*

⑬ Thian Hock Keng Temple. This structure—the Temple of Heavenly Happiness—was completed in 1842 to replace a simple shrine built 20 years earlier. It's one of Singapore's oldest and largest Chinese temples, built on the spot where, prior to land reclamation, immigrants stepped ashore after a hazardous journey across the China Sea. In gratitude for their safe passage, the Hokkien people dedicated the temple to Ma Chu P'oh, the goddess of the sea. It's richly decorated with gilded carvings, sculptures, tile roofs topped with dragons, and fine carved-stone pillars. The pillars and sculptures were brought over from China, the exterior cast-iron railings were made in Glasgow, and the blue porcelain tiles on an outer building came from Holland. On either side of the entrance are two stone lions. The one on the left is female and holds a cup symbolizing fertility; the other, a male, holds a ball, a symbol of wealth. If the temple is open, note that as you enter, you must step over a high threshold board. This serves a dual function. First, it forces devotees to look downward, as they should when entering the temple. Second, it keeps out wandering ghosts—ghosts tend to shuffle their feet, so if they try to enter, the threshold board will trip them.

FodorśChoice ★

Inside, a statue of a maternal Ma Chu P'oh surrounded by masses of burning incense and candles dominates the room. On either side of her are the deities of health (on the left if your back is to the entrance) and wealth. The two tall figures you'll notice are her sentinels: one can see for 1,000 miles; the other can hear for 1,000 miles. The gluey black substance on their lips—placed there by devotees in days past—is opium, meant to heighten their senses. Although the main temple is Taoist, the temple at the back is Buddhist and dedicated to Kuan Yin, the goddess of mercy. Her many arms represent how she reaches out to all those who suffer on earth. This is a good place to learn your fortune. Choose a number out of the box, then pick up two small stenciled pieces of wood at the back of the altar and let them fall to the ground. If they land showing opposite faces, then the number you have picked is valid. If they land same-side up, try again. From a valid number, the person in the nearby booth will tell you your fate, and whether you like it or not, you pay for the information. Leave the grounds by the alley that runs alongside the main temple. The two statues to the left are the gambling brothers. They will help you choose a lucky number for your next betting session; if you win, you must return and place lighted cigarettes in their hands. ✉ *158 Telok Ayer St., Telok Ayer* ☎ *6423–4616* ⊕ *www.nhb. gov.sg* ⊙ *Daily 7:30–5:30* Ⓜ *Tanjong Pagar.*

⑪ Urban Redevelopment Association (URA) Gallery. Get a bird's-eye view of Chinatown and other districts in this gallery, where you can see a 3-D model of the city. There's also an interactive display with touch-screens and hands-on exhibits. You can experience 180 years of Singaporean history through various models and get a sense of what the city will be like in the future. ✉ *45 Maxwell Rd., Tanjong Pajar* ☎ *6321–8321* ⊕ *www.ura.gov.sg* ⊙ *Weekdays 9–4:30, Sat. 9 AM–12:30 PM, closed Sun.*

❹ **Wak Hai Cheng Bio Temple.** Built in 1826 by Teochew Chinese from Guangdong Province and dedicated to the goddess of the sea, this is one of Singapore's oldest Taoist temples. The temple is also known as Yueng Hai Ching Temple, which means Temple of the Calm Sea. Traders and travelers returning from China visited the temple on disembarking—believe it or not, Philip Street was then very close to the water—to offer their thanks for a safe journey. It has been maintained by the Ngee Ann Clan Association since 1845 and was rebuilt in 1895. Inside, there's an imperial signboard presented by Qing Dynasty Emperor Guang Xu in 1907. Each of the structure's twin wings can be accessed by its own entrance, which have different ornamental features. Besides dragons and pagodas, human figurines and scenes from Chinese operas are depicted on the temple's roof. This is the only temple in Singapore with 3-D sculptural reliefs of Chinese opera scenes on its interior walls. ⊠ *30B Phillip St., Telok Ayer* ☉ *Daily 6* AM*–5:30* PM Ⓜ *Raffles Place.*

❶ **Yeo Swee Huat.** Here you'll see a cottage industry designed to help the Chinese take care of one obligation to their ancestors: making sure they have everything they need in the afterlife. Here, paper models of the paraphernalia of life—horses, cars, boats, planes, even fake money—are made for relatives of the deceased and ritually burned so that their essence passes through to the spirit world in flames and smoke. Note that although the items may tempt you to chuckle, this is a very serious Chinese custom; try not to offend the proprietors. ⊠ *15 Upper Circular Rd., Chinatown* Ⓜ *Raffles Place.*

❺ **Yue Hwa Building.** Inside this Chinese department store, you'll find plenty of unique but pricey Chinese products—silk, arts and crafts, porcelain, foodstuffs—on sale here. ⊠ *70 Eu Tong Sen St., Chinatown* Ⓜ *Chinatown* ⊕ *www.yuehwa.com.sg.*

LITTLE INDIA

Indians have been part of Singapore's development from the beginning. Although Singapore was administered by the East India Company, headquartered in Calcutta, Indian convicts were sent here to serve their time. These convicts left an indelible mark on the city, reclaiming land from swampy marshes and constructing a great deal of the infrastructure and buildings, including St. Andrew's Cathedral and many Hindu temples. The enlightened penal program permitted convicts to study a trade of their choice in the evenings. Many, on gaining their freedom, chose to stay in Singapore.

Other Indians came freely to seek their fortunes as clerks, traders, teachers, and moneylenders. Most came from southern India—both Hindu Tamils and Muslims from the Coromandel and Malabar coasts—but there were also Gujaratis, Sindhis, Sikhs, Parsis, and Bengalis. Each group brought its own language, cuisine, religion, and customs, and these divisions remain evident today. The Indians also brought their love of colorful festivals, which they now celebrate more frequently and more spectacularly than in India itself. The gory Thaipusam, in January or February, is among the most fascinating.

The area Raffles allotted to the Indian immigrants was north of the British colonial district. Little India encompasses most of Serangoon Road, the heart of this district, its side roads extending out to Jalan Besar, plus Race Course Road, which runs parallel to both. The district is bounded by Sungei Road/Rochor Canal Road to the south and Lavender Street and Perumal Road to the north. Although new buildings have replaced many of the old, the sights, sounds, and smells will convince you that you're in an Indian town.

As you walk along Serangoon, your senses will be overwhelmed by the fragrances of curry powders and perfumes, by tapes of high-pitched Indian music, by jewelry shops selling gold, and stands selling garlands of flowers. (Indian women love wearing flowers and glittering arm bangles, though once their husbands die, they never do so again.) Shops here supply the colorful dyes used for the *pottu* (dot) seen on the foreheads of Indian women. Traditionally, a Tamil woman wears a red dot to signify she's married; a North Indian woman conveys the same message with a red streak down the part of her hair. The modern trend, however, is for an Indian girl or woman to choose a dye color to match her sari or Western dress. Occasionally you'll see an unmarried woman with a black dot on her forehead: this is intended to counter the effects of the evil eye.

Numbers in the text correspond to numbers in the margin and on the Little India map.

a good walk

A good starting point is at the junction of Serangoon and Sungei roads. On the first block on the left is **Tekka Market ❶**, one of the city's largest wet markets. Adjacent to the market is the Tekka Mall, a multi-ware emporium. Down Serangoon is the Little India Arcade, a cluster of art deco–style shophouses built in 1913 that have stores selling candies, saris, and incense. The streets to the right off Serangoon Road—Campbell Lane and Dunlop Street (home of the highly regarded **Haniffa Textiles ❷**, at No. 104)—as well as **Clive Street,** which runs parallel to Serangoon, are filled with shops that sell such utilitarian items as pots and pans, rice, spices, brown cakes of palm sugar, red henna powder (a great hair dye), and sundry Indian groceries. You'll also see open-air barbershops and tailors working old-fashioned treadle sewing machines, and everywhere you go you'll hear sugar-sweet love songs from Indian movies. Along **Buffalo Road,** to the left off Serangoon, are shops specializing in saris, flower garlands, and electronic equipment. Above the doorways are strings of dried mango leaves, a customary Indian sign of blessing and good fortune. (If you detour down Dunlop Street, to the right off Serangoon Road, you'll come to the **Abdul Gaffoor Mosque ❸**, with its detailed facade of green and gold.)

A little farther down Serangoon Road on the left (opposite Veerasamy Road), you'll notice the elaborate gopuram of the **Sri Veeramakaliamman Temple ❹**, built in 1881 by indentured Bengali laborers working the lime pits nearby. Turn right on Race Course Road, well known for Singapore's most famous Indian curry restaurants, to **Farrer Park ❺**, site of Singapore's original racecourse. Farther along Race Course Road is the charming **Leong San Temple** ❻, dedicated to the goddess of mercy, Kuan Yin. On your way there, you'll pass a row of shops selling Chinese porcelain, a rather unusual feature in Little India. Across the road is Sakya Muni Buddha Gaya Temple, more commonly referred to as the **Temple of 1,000 Lights** ❼. Backtrack on Race Course Road to Perumal Road; to the left is the **Sri Srinivasa Perumal Temple** ❽. Behind you to your right is the Serangoon Plaza complex, on Serangoon Road itself, together with the famed **Mustafa's Centre** ❾, up Syed Alwi Road, a multistory emporium of goods at extremely attractive prices. If you continue along Race Course Road, you'll come to the Banana Leaf Apolo, an excellent place for a drink and a curry.

TIMING   Try to plan your walk for a weekday morning or mid to early evening when crowds are at their thinnest and temperatures at their lowest. Avoid the area on Sunday afternoon, when the neighborhood teems with people. You should be able to do this tour in three to four hours. Factor in half an hour extra for each of the temples. Start off in the morning as the temples usually close by 4 or 5 PM.

What to See

❸ **Abdul Gaffoor Mosque.** In 1979 this small, personable mosque, at No. 41 Dunlop Street became a national monument. Though it has none of the exotic, multicolor statuary of the Hindu temples, it still woos you with an intricately detailed facade in the Muslim colors of green and gold. When entering, make sure your legs are covered to the ankles, and remember to take off your shoes. Only worshipers are allowed into the prayer hall. Out of respect you shouldn't enter during evening prayer sessions or at any time on Friday. ✉ *41 Dunlop St., Little India* ☎ *6295–4204* Ⓜ *Little India.*

Buffalo Road. Shops here specialize in saris, flower garlands, and electronic equipment. Also along this short street are a number of moneylenders from the Chettiar caste—the only caste that continues to pursue in Singapore the role prescribed to them in India. You'll find them seated on the floor before decrepit desks, but don't let the simplicity of their style fool you: some of them are very, very rich.

Clive Street. On this byway off Sungei Road, you'll find shops that purvey sugar, prawn crackers, rice, and dried beans. The older Indian women you'll see with red lips and stained teeth are betel-nut chewers. Betel nuts are mild stimulants and are thought to be a panacea for a variety of ills. If you want to try the stuff, you can buy a mouthful from street vendors.

❺ **Farrer Park.** This is the site of Singapore's original racetrack. It's also where the first aircraft to land in Singapore came to rest en route from England to Australia in 1919.

❷ **Haniffa Textiles.** Try this silk shop for a cornucopia of richly colored and ornamented fabrics, scarves, bedspreads, and the like, often at surprisingly affordable prices. ✉ *104–120 Dunlop St., Little India* ☎ *6339–0926* ⊗ *Daily 9:30–9* Ⓜ *Little India.*

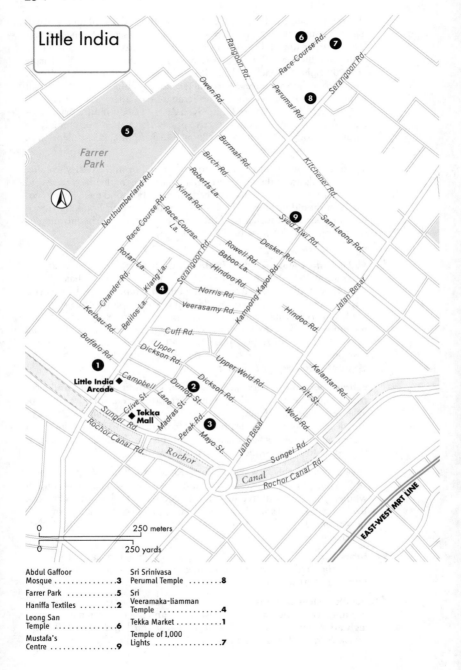

Little India

Farrer Park

Rangoon Rd.

Owen Rd.

Race Course Rd.

Serangoon Rd.

Perumal Rd.

Kitchener Rd.

Burmah Rd.

Birch Rd.

Roberts La.

Kinta Rd.

Northumberland Rd.

Race Course Rd.

Race Course La.

Sam Leong Rd.

Syed Alwi Rd.

Desker Rd.

Rowell Rd.

Baboo La.

Hindoo Rd.

Jalan Besar

Pratan La.

Chander Rd.

Klang La.

Serangoon Rd.

Norris Rd.

Kampong Kapor Rd.

Kerbau Rd.

Belilos La.

Veerasamy Rd.

Hindoo Rd.

Cuff Rd.

Buffalo Rd.

Upper Dickson Rd.

Upper Weld Rd.

Kelantan Rd.

Little India Arcade

Campbell Lane

Dunlop St.

Dickson Rd.

Pitt St.

Clive St.

Madras St.

Weld Rd.

Tekka Mall

Perak Rd.

Mayo St.

Jalan Besar

Sungei Rd.

Rochor Canal Rd.

Sungei Rd.

Rochor Canal Rd.

Rochor Canal

EAST-WEST MRT LINE

```
0          250 meters
0          250 yards
```

6 **Leong San Temple.** Its main altar is dedicated to Kuan Yin—also known as Bodhisattva Avalokitesvara—and is framed by beautiful, ornate carvings of flowers, a phoenix, and other birds. The temple, a.k.a. Dragon Mountain Temple, was built in the late 19th century. Right of the main altar is an image of Confucius to which many parents bring their children to pray for intelligence and filial piety. If you enter from the prayer hall's side doors, you'll reach the ancestral hall in the rear, where you can see tablets with the names of deceased worshippers. ⊠ *371 Race Course Rd., Little India* Ⓜ *Farrer Park.*

9 **Mustafa's Centre.** This used to be a humble store frequented only by Indian shoppers—until word spread about its low prices and mind-boggling variety of goods. These days, it's expanded to a 24-hour multilevel store, but it remains unassuming and still offers good prices. You can even buy yourself a car! ⊠ *145 Syed Alwi Rd., Little India* ☎ *6295–5855* ⊕ *www.mustafa.com.sg* ☉ *Open 24 hours* Ⓜ *Farrer Park.*

8 **Sri Srinivasa Perumal Temple.** Dedicated to Vishnu the Preserver, the temple is easy to recognize by its 60-foot-high monumental gopuram, with tiers of intricate sculptures depicting Vishnu in the nine forms in which he has appeared on earth. Especially vivid are the depictions of Vishnu's manifestations as Rama, on his seventh visit, and as Krishna, on his eighth. Rama is thought to be the personification of the ideal man; Krishna was brought up with peasants and, therefore, was a manifestation popular with laborers in Singapore's early days. Sri Srinivasa Perumal is very much a people's temple. Inside you'll find devotees making offerings of fruit to one of the manifestations of Vishnu. This is done either by handing coconuts or bananas, along with a slip of paper with your name on it, to a temple official, who'll chant the appropriate prayers to the deity and place holy ash on your head; or by walking clockwise while praying, coconut in hand, around one of the shrines a certain number of times, then breaking the coconut (a successful break symbolizes that Vishnu has been receptive to the incantation). Dress conservatively, and don't wear shoes inside. ⊠ *397 Serangoon Rd., Little India* ☎ *6298–5771* ☉ *Daily 6:30 AM–noon and 6 PM–9 PM* Ⓜ *Farrer Park.*

Fodor's Choice
★

4 **Sri Veeramakaliamman Temple.** Dedicated to Kali the Courageous, a ferocious incarnation of Shiva's wife, Parvati the Beautiful, this temple was built in 1881 by indentured Bengali laborers working at nearby lime pits. Inside is a jet-black statue of Kali, the fiercest of the Hindu deities, who demands sacrifices and is often depicted with a garland of skulls. More cheerful is the shrine to Ganesh, the elephant-headed god of wisdom and prosperity. Perhaps the most popular Hindu deity, Ganesh is the child of Shiva and Parvati. (He wasn't born with an elephant head. Shiva came back from a long absence to find his wife in a room with a young man. In a blind rage, he lopped off the man's head, not realizing he'd killed his now-grown son. The only way to bring Ganesh back to life was with the head of the first living thing Shiva saw: an elephant.) During the temple's opening hours you will see Hindus going in to receive blessings: the priests streak devotees' foreheads with *vibhuti*, the white ash from burned cow dung. ⊠ *141 Serangoon Rd., Little India* ☎ *6295–4538* ☉ *Daily 8 AM–noon and 5:30 PM–8:30 PM* Ⓜ *Farrer Park.*

❶ Tekka Market. As one of the city's largest wet markets, Tekka has a staggering array of fruits, vegetables, fish, herbs, and spices. On the Sungei Road side of the ground floor are food stalls offering Chinese, Indian, Malay, and Western foods. Upstairs are shops selling hardware, shoes, luggage, textiles, and exotic Indian clothing. ✉ *665 Buffalo Rd., Little India* ◷ *Daily 7 AM–9 PM* Ⓜ *Little India.*

❼ Temple of 1,000 Lights. The Sakya Muni Buddha Gaya is better known by its popular name because, for a small donation, you can pull a switch that lights countless bulbs around a 50-foot Buddha. The entire temple, as well as the Buddha statue, was built by the Thai monk Vutthisasala, who, until he died at the age of 94, was always in the temple, ready to explain Buddhist philosophy to anyone who wanted to listen. The monk also managed to procure relics for the temple: a mother-of-pearl-inlaid cast of the Buddha's footprint and a piece of bark from the bodhi tree under which the Buddha received Enlightenment. Around the pedestal supporting the great Buddha statue is a series of scenes depicting the story of his search for Enlightenment; inside a hollow chamber at the back is a re-creation of the scene of the Buddha's last sermon. ✉ *336 Race Course Rd., Little India* ☎ *6294–0714* ◷ *Daily 8 AM–4:45 PM* Ⓜ *Farrer Park.*

off the
beaten
path

LEMBU ROAD – Near Mustafa Centre is this open grassy space, flanked by Deskar and Syed Alwi roads, where you'll find many Indians gathering on a Sunday evening, passing the time chatting or relaxing among the food stalls. It may not be much of a tourist attraction, but the area does give you insight into life in Little India.

THE ARAB DISTRICT

Long before the Europeans arrived, Arab traders plied the coastlines of the Malay Peninsula and Indonesia, bringing with them the teachings of Islam. By the time Raffles came to Singapore in 1819, to be a Malay was also to be a Muslim. Traditionally, Malays' lives have centered on their religion and their villages, known as *kampongs*. These consisted of several wooden houses with steep roofs of corrugated iron or thatch gathered around a communal center, where chickens fed and children played under the watchful eye of mothers and the village elders while the younger men tended the fields or took to the sea in fishing boats. The houses were usually built on stilts above marshes and reached by narrow planks serving as bridges. If the kampong was on dry land, flowers and fruit trees would surround the houses.

All traditional kampongs have fallen to the might of the bulldozer in the name of urban renewal. Though all ethnic groups have had their social fabric undermined by the demolition of their old communities, the Malays have suffered the most, since social life centered on the kampong.

The area known as the Arab District, while not a true kampong, remains a Malay enclave, held firmly together by strict observance of the tenets of Islam. At the heart of the community is the Sultan Mosque, or Masjid

Sultan, originally built with a grant from the East India Company to the Sultan of Johor. Around it are streets whose very names—Bussorah, Baghdad, Kandahar—evoke the fragrances of the Muslim world. The pace of life is slower here: there are few cars, people gossip in doorways, and closet-size shops are crammed with such wares as *songkok,* the velvety diamond-shape hats worn by Muslim men; the lacy white skullcaps presented to *hajji,* those who have made the *hajj,* as the pilgrimage to Mecca is called; the tasseled, beaded, and embroidered *tudung* (head scarves) worn by devout Muslim women; Indonesian batiks; leather bags; and herbs whose packages promise youth, fertility, and beauty.

Districts

The Arab District is a small area, bounded by Beach and North Bridge roads to the south and north and spreading a couple of blocks to either side of Arab Street. The area can further be divided up into the subneighborhoods of Kampong Glam (the region around Jalan Sultan) and Bugis (the area around infamous Bugis Street). It's a place to meander, taking time to browse through shops or enjoy Muslim food at a simple café.

Numbers in the text correspond to numbers in the margin and on the Arab District map.

a good walk

This walk begins at the foot of **Arab Street,** just off North Bridge Road. Wander past the specialty shops and take a right onto Baghdad Street; watch for a dramatic view of the **Sultan Mosque ❶** where **Bussorah Street** opens to your left. Leaving the mosque, return to Arab Street and take the first left onto Muscat Street, turn right onto Kandahar Street, and then left onto Baghdad Street. At Sultan Gate you'll find **Istana Kampong Glam ❷,** the sultan's Malay-style palace, built in the 1840s. Baghdad Street becomes Pahang Street at Sultan Gate, where Chinese stonemasons create statues curbside. At the junction of Pahang Street and Jalan Sultan, turn right and, at Beach Road, left to visit the endearing **Hajjah Fatimah Mosque ❸,** built in 1845. It leans at a six-degree angle. Return to Jalan Sultan and take a right; keep walking, crossing over **North Bridge Road,** to the junction of Victoria Street and the **Malabar Muslim Jama-Ath Mosque ❹.**

Follow Victoria Street down to **Bugis Street ❺.** Three blocks beyond where Bugis Street becomes Albert Street—between the Fu Lu Shou shopping complex and the food-oriented Albert Complex—is Waterloo Street. Near the corner is the **Kwan Im Thong Hood Cho Temple ❻,** or just Kwan Im for short, one of Singapore's most popular Chinese temples.

TIMING   This walking tour shouldn't take more than two hours, including stops to look around the temples and mosques. But take your time. This is one of the friendliest areas in Singapore. It's best to go around 10 in the morning so you can catch a glimpse of the locals at the mosques. If you've got time, stop in at one of Arab Street's few hookah cafés.

What to See

★   **Arab Street.** On this street of specialty shops, you'll find baskets of every description—stacked on the floor or suspended from the ceiling. Far-

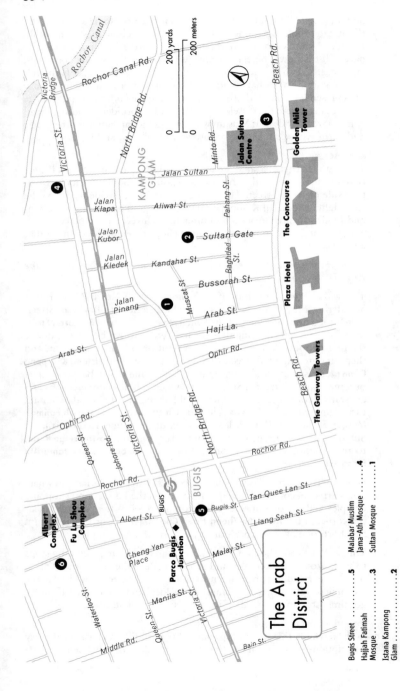

The Arab District

ther along, the road is dominated by shops that sell fabrics: batiks, embroidered table linens, rich silks, and velvets.

❺ Bugis Street. Until recently, Bugis Street was the epitome of Singapore's seedy, but colorful nightlife, famous for the transvestite beauties who paraded its sidewalks; the government wasn't delighted, though, and the area was razed to make way for the Bugis MRT station. So strong was the outcry that Bugis Street has been recreated (but not really) just steps from its original site, between Victoria and Queen streets, Rochor Road, and Cheng Yan Place. The shophouses have been resurrected; hawker food stands compete with open-front restaurants (Kentucky Fried Chicken has a prominent spot on a corner). Closed to traffic, the streets in the center of the block are *the* places to find bargain watches and CDs; across the road is the Parco Bugis Junction, an upscale shopping center that's quite a contrast to all the area's dollar stores and souvenir shops. On Saturday, there are two markets to explore: one at the junction of Queen Street and Rochor Road, and the other just behind Parco Bugis Junction.

❸ Hajjah Fatimah Mosque. In 1845 Hajjah Fatimah, a wealthy Muslim woman married to a Bugis trader, commissioned a British architect to build this mosque (*hajjah* is the title given to a woman who has made the pilgrimage to Mecca). The minaret is reputedly modeled on the spire of the original St. Andrew's Church in Colonial Singapore, but it leans at a six-degree angle. No one knows whether this was intentional or accidental, and engineers brought in to see if the minaret could be straightened have walked away shaking their heads. Islam forbids carved images of Allah. Usually, the only decorative element employed is the beautiful flowing Arabic script in which quotations from the Qur'an (Koran) are written across the walls. This relatively small mosque is an intimate oasis amid all the bustle. It's extremely relaxing to enter the prayer hall (remember to take your shoes off) and sit in the shade of its dome. French contractors and Malay artisans rebuilt the mosque in the 1930s. Hajjah Fatimah and her daughter and son-in-law are buried in an enclosure behind the mosque. ✉ *4001 Beach Rd., Kampong Glam* Ⓜ *Bugis* ⏱ *Daily 5:30 AM–10 PM.*

❷ Istana Kampong Glam. The sultan's Malay-style palace is more like a big house than a palace. It was built in the 1840s on the site of an even simpler thatched building; purportedly, the structure was designed by George Coleman. It now houses a Malay Cultural Heritage Centre. Next door is another grand royal bungalow: the home of the sultan's first minister. Notice its gateposts surmounted by green eagles. ✉ *Sultan Gate, Kampong Glam* Ⓜ *Bugis.*

❻ Kwan Im Thong Hood Cho Temple. The dusty, incense-filled interior of this popular temple (commonly known as just Kwan Im), its altars heaped with hundreds of small statues of gods from the Chinese pantheon, transports you into the world of Asian mythology. Of the hundreds of Chinese deities, Kwan Im, more often known as Kuan Yin, is perhaps most dear to the hearts of Singaporeans. Legend has it that just as she was about to enter Nirvana, she heard a plaintive cry from Earth. Filled with compassion, she gave up her place in paradise to devote herself to alleviating the pain of those on Earth; thereupon, she took the name Kuan Yin, meaning "to see and hear all." People in search of advice on anything from an auspicious date for a marriage to possible solutions for domestic or work crises come to her temple, shake *cham si* (bamboo fortune sticks), and wait for an answer. The gods are most receptive on days of a new or full moon.

For more immediate advice, you can speak to any of the fortune-tellers who sit under umbrellas outside the temple. They'll pore over ancient scrolls of the Chinese almanac and, for a few dollars, tell you your future. If the news isn't good, you may want to buy some of the flowers sold nearby and add them to your bathwater. They're said to help wash away bad luck. A small vegetarian restaurant next to the temple, of the same name, serves good food and delicious Chinese pastries. ☒ *178 Waterloo St., Bugis* Ⓜ *Bugis.*

❹ **Malabar Muslim Jama-Ath Mosque.** The land on which this mosque sits was originally granted to the *Jawi Peranakan* (the offspring of Indian Muslims and Malaysians) community in 1848, by Sultan Ally Iskander Shah, as a burial ground. The mosque they erected here was abandoned and later taken over by the Malabar Muslims (those with ancestors from India or Ceylon, now Sri Lanka), who rebuilt it in 1962. Do note that photographs shouldn't be taken here after 1 PM. ☒ *471 Victoria St., Kampong Glam* ☽ *Daily 5 AM–10 PM* Ⓜ *Bugis.*

North Bridge Road. Fascinating stores selling costumes and headdresses for Muslim weddings, clothes for traditional Malay dances, prayer beads, scarves, perfumes, and much more line this road. Interspersed among the shops are small, simple restaurants serving Muslim food. Toward the Sultan Mosque, the shops have mostly religious items, including *barang haji,* the clothing and other requisites for a pilgrimage to Mecca.

❶ **Sultan Mosque.** The first mosque on this site was built in the early 1820s Fodor$Choice with a S$3,000 grant from the East India Company. The current struc- ★ ture, built in 1928 by Denis Santry of Swan & Maclaren—the architect who designed the Victoria Memorial Hall—is a dramatic building with golden domes and minarets that glisten in the sun. The walls of the vast prayer hall are adorned with green and gold mosaic tiles on which passages from the Qur'an are written in decorative Arab script. The main dome has an odd architectural feature: hundreds of brown bottles, stacked five or more rows deep, are jammed in neck first between the dome and base. No one knows why. Five times a day—at dawn, 12:30, 4, sunset, and 8:15—the sound of the muezzin, or crier, calls the faithful to prayer. At midday on Friday, the Islamic Sabbath, seemingly every Malay in Singapore enters through one of the Sultan Mosque's 14 portals to recite the Qur'an. During Ramadan, the month of fasting, the nearby streets, especially Bussorah, and the square in front of mosque are lined with hundreds of stalls selling curries, cakes, and candy; at dusk Muslims break their day's fast in this square. Non-Muslims, too, come to enjoy the rich array of Muslim foods and the party atmosphere. The best view of the Sultan Mosque is at the junction of Bussorah Street and Beach Road. ⊠ *3 Muscat St., Kampong Glam* ⊙ *Daily 9–4* Ⓜ *Bugis.*

need a break? **Café Samat,** at No. 19 Bagdad St., is the place to sit back and take in this friendly district. Sit on the café's carpeted floor and feast on such Middle Eastern fare as grilled lamb and apple milk. Don't leave without trying the hookahs; the fruit tobaccos leave a strong taste in your mouth so start off with something pleasant such as apple or mixed berry.

ORCHARD ROAD

If "downtown" is defined as where the action is, then Singapore's downtown is Orchard Road. Here are some of the city's most fashionable shops, hotels (which often, like the Hilton, have expensive, upscale malls all their own), restaurants, and nightclubs. The street has been dubbed the 5th Avenue or Bond Street of Singapore, but, air of luxury aside, it has little in common with either of those older, relatively understated marketplaces for the wealthy. Orchard Road is an ultra-high-rent district that's very modern and very, very flashy—especially at night, when millions of light bulbs, flashing from just about every building, assault your eyes. Additionally, this is Singapore's best place for people-watching; a perfect distraction from or alternative to a shopping adventure. Relative to the other neighborhoods, there are few sites of historical interest along Orchard Road.

Numbers in the text correspond to numbers in the margin and on the Orchard Road map.

a good walk Start at the bottom of Orchard Road and head toward the junction with Scotts Road, the hub of downtown. You'll see the enormous **Istana** ❶, once the official residence of the colonial governor and now that of the president of the republic. On the other side of Orchard Road and a few steps down Clemenceau Avenue is the lovely old **Tan Yeok Nee House** ❷. Built in 1885 for a wealthy Chinese merchant, the house has served various purposes, including headquarters for the Salvation Army. It's now the Asian campus for the University of Chicago's graduate business school. Turn on Tank Road and continue to the **Chettiar Temple** ❸, which houses the image of Lord Subramaniam. Return to Orchard Road and turn left. On the right is Cuppage Road, with a market (open every morning) known for imported and unusual fruit and a row of antiques shops.

Returning once more to Orchard Road, you'll pass the block-long Centrepoint; immediately after it is **Peranakan Place** ❹. A detour up Scotts Road leads to the landmark **Goodwood Park Hotel** ❺ which offers one of the most civilized high teas in town. Farther up Scotts Road is the **Newton Circus** ❻ food hawker center.

Retrace your steps to the intersection of Scotts and Orchard roads. Walk up the left side of Orchard Road, past the Wheelock Place Building, which houses the large Borders, as much a social center as a bookstore. Taxi drivers call this section of Wheelock Place "the rocket," and you'll see why. As you continue up Orchard Road, the Palais Renaissance will be on your right. Just before Orchard turns into Tanglin, you'll find the Tanglin Shopping Centre on your left; the second floor has some of the best antiques shops in town. Tanglin Mall, at the junction of Tanglin and Napier roads, has chic boutiques and an excellent food court. Flip to the Shopping chapter for more information about Orchard Road.

TIMING   Orchard Road has so many shopping diversions that you should allow three to four hours for the walk. Set aside half an hour for the Chettiar Temple and, if you are an antiques fan, at least an hour for the Tanglin Shopping Centre. Avoid the area on Saturday if you're not big on crowds.

What to See

❸ Chettiar Temple. This southern Indian temple, home to numerous shrines, is a replacement for the original, which was built in the 19th century. The 75-foot-high gopuram, with its many colorful sculptures of godly manifestations, is astounding. The chandelier-lighted interior is lavishly decorated; 48 painted-glass panels are inset in the ceiling and angled to reflect the sunrise and sunset. ⊠ *15 Tank Rd., River Valley* ⊕ *www. nhb.gov.sg* ☉ *Daily 8 AM–noon and 5:30 PM–8:30 PM* Ⓜ *Clarke Quay.*

★ **❺ Goodwood Park Hotel.** Though it's 30 years younger than the more widely known Raffles, this hotel is just as much a landmark. Built in 1900, this hotel previously was used as a German club and as a Japanese army headquarters during World War II. The interior is modeled on European designs. The Tower Wing was named a national monument in 1989. Partaking of an elegant afternoon tea here—accompanied by live piano music—is the perfect way to take a break from all that shopping. High tea is served from 2 to 5 and costs about S$23. ⊠ *22 Scotts Rd., Scotts Road* ☎ *6737–7411* ⊕ *www.goodwoodparkhotel.com.sg* Ⓜ *Orchard.*

❶ Istana. Built in 1869, this elegant Palladian building set in extensive tropical gardens off Orchard Road once served as the British colonial governor's residence and is now the official residence of the president of the republic. *Istana* means palace in Malay. The building and grounds are open to the public only on fixed holidays: New Year's Day, Hari Raya Puasa (the end of the Muslim fasting month), Chinese New Year, Labor Day, National Day, and the Hindu festival of Deepavali. On the first Sunday of each month, a changing-of-the-guard ceremony at the main gates on Orchard Road lasts from 5:45 to 6:45. ⊠ *Orchard Rd., Dhoby Ghaut* Ⓜ *Dhoby Ghaut.*

★ **❻ Newton Circus.** This is one of the best-known hawker centers in town. (The "circus" refers to a rotary, as in Piccadilly Circus.) Some of the stalls are open all day, but the best times to go are either around 9 AM, when a few stalls serve Chinese breakfasts, or after 7 PM, when all the stores are open and the Circus is humming with the hungry. Ⓜ *Newton.*

❹ Peranakan Place. The building on the corner of Orchard and Emerald Hill roads is a somewhat diluted celebration of Peranakan culture. A conserved masterpiece of heritage architecture in the Peranakan (also

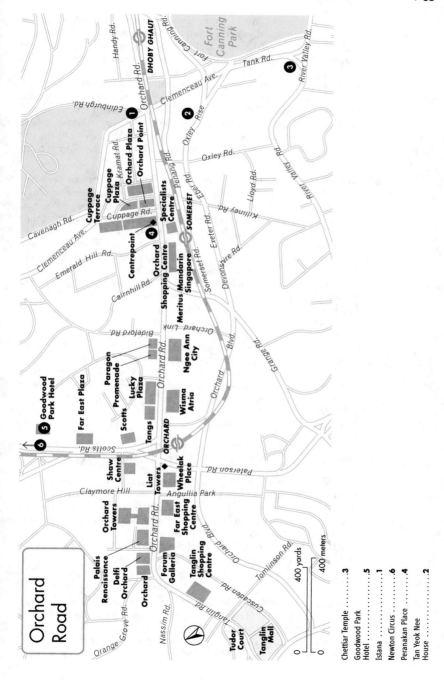

Orchard Road

called Straits-born Chinese, Baba, or Nonya) style, a blend of Chinese and Malay cultures that emerged in the 19th century as Chinese born in the then Straits Settlements (including Singapore) adopted, and often adapted, Malay fashions, cuisine, and architecture. The area is now a mix of upscale residences, with renovated shophouses doubling as bars and restaurants, as at Nos. 5 and 7 Emerald Hill. Parts of Emerald Hill, from Orchard Road through Ice Cold Beer pub, are for pedestrians only; there are several outdoor cafés and restaurants along the stretch. Stroll the arcaded street and check out fretted woodwork, pastel wash, ornate wall tiles, and other typical Peranakan touches. Note especially the unusual carved swing "fence" doors (*pintu pagar*), some with gold-leaf treatments. Ⓜ *Somerset.*

❷ **Tan Yeok Nee House.** The house was built around 1885 for Tan Yeok Nee (1827–1902), a merchant from China who began his career here as a cloth peddler and became a very wealthy man through trade in opium, gambier, and pepper. Whereas most homes built in Singapore at that time followed European styles, this townhouse was designed in a style popular in South China—notice the keyhole gables, terra-cotta tiles, and massive granite pillars. After the railway was laid along Tank Road in 1901, the house became the stationmaster's. In 1912 St. Mary's Home and School for Girls took it over. In 1940 the Salvation Army made the place its local headquarters. It's now home to the University of Chicago Graduate School of Business's Asia Campus. ✉ *101 Penang Rd., Orchard* ☎ *6835–6482* Ⓜ *Somerset.*

---

need a break?	**Crossroads Café** (✉ 320 Orchard Rd. ☎ 6735–5800), on the street level of the Singapore Marriott, serves cool cocktails as well as perky cups of coffee. Head here for a break from Orchard Road, and a bite from its extensive menu, which includes local favorites like chicken rice. Prices are on the moderate to high side. The patio is a prime perch for Singaporeans who want to see and be seen. The café is open 24 hours.

SIDE TRIPS AROUND & BEYOND SINGAPORE

On a trip outside of the city, you'll see the island's slower side, and get a more realistic view of everyday life. Hop aboard a ferry to one of the islets just off the coast. A jaunt to the nearby Indonesian islands of Bintan and Batam—with their pristine shores, mangrove swamps, and hideaway resorts—will no doubt add still more dimension to your Southeast Asia journey, illustrating the diversity of its people, culture, and traditions.

The East Coast

Two decades ago Singapore's eastern coastal area contained only coconut plantations, Malay villages, and a few undeveloped beaches. Nowadays, things are totally different. At the island's extreme northeastern tip is Changi International Airport, one of the world's finest. Legions of satellite residential developments have sprung up between

HOLLAND VILLAGE

HOLLAND VILLAGE IS AN UP-AND-COMING NEIGHBORHOOD that's just a 10-minute drive west of Orchard Road. It's bounded by Lorong Liput, Lorong Mambong, and parts of Holland Road and Holland Avenue. Regarded as the bohemian part of Singapore, the multifaceted area is both fashionably chic and casually understated at the same time. It's popular with expatriates and local yuppies, thanks to its countless bars, eateries, and cafés; the people-watching is particularly good on Sunday.

Asian furniture and antiques shops line Holland Village Shopping Centre. Lim's Arts and Crafts on the third floor is one of the best places for knickknacks and decorative pieces.

If you'd like to relax, pop into Spa Esprit just behind the center on Lorong Mambong. The Health Step Foot Reflexology Centre at 4A Lorong Mambong offers traditional Chinese therapies. Wala Wala at 31 Lorong Mambong is a popular bar–cum–café with live entertainment nightly starting at 9:30. For more upscale food, try Tango Restaurant and Wine Bar, next door to Wala Wala.

the airport and the city, and vast land-reclamation projects along the shore have created a park that's 8 km (5 mi) long, with plenty of recreational facilities. Several luxury high-rise apartments with stunning ocean views have appeared north of East Coast Park. Siglap is an up-and-coming suburb known for its relaxed atmosphere and cafés, restaurants, and shops.

Numbers in the text correspond to numbers in the margin and on the East and West Coasts & the Green Interior, and the Sentosa Island maps.

a good tour

This tour is best done by taxi, which will cost you roughly S$8–S$15 each way. Catch a cab at the junction of Nicoll Highway and Bras Basah Road, near the Raffles Hotel and Marina Square. Nicoll Highway leads onto East Coast Road, and heading east along it, you come to the Kallang area. Cross the Rochor and Kallang rivers by the Merdeka (Independence) Bridge, and you'll see to the left and right an estuary that was once the haunt of pirates and smugglers. A few shipyards are visible to the left, where the old Bugis trading schooners once anchored. (The Bugis, a seafaring people from the Celebes—now Sulawesi—Indonesia, have a long history as great traders; their schooners, called *prahus*, still ply Indonesian waters.) To the right is the huge National Stadium, where international sporting events are held. Just past it, Mountbatten Road crosses Old Airport Road, previously the runway of Singapore's first airfield. This area was previously a British colonial residential district, and is still home to the wealthy, as attested by the splendid houses in both traditional and modern architectural styles.

If you're game for a walk, ask the taxi driver to drop you at the beginning of the **East Coast Park** ❶, which is at the junction of Fort Road and East Coast Parkway. Otherwise, a practical point to begin your excursion is at McDonald's, the only one along the whole stretch (the area is also identified as the Marine Cove area). Numerous kiosks here rent in-line skates, bicycles, kayaks, and boats. For refreshments there are many cafés, pubs, and eateries offering everything from Indian *pratas* (fried bread served with meat, chicken, or vegetable curry) to Danish hot dogs. You can play an amusing game of golf at the nearby **LilliPutt** ❷, an indoor mini-golf course. Alternatively, stop at the East Coast Lagoon Food Village, an outdoor hawker center, or the **UDMC Seafood Centre.** Catch another taxi farther east to the **Changi Chapel & Museum** ❸, where you can learn about the infamous Changi Prison.

TIMING   A trip to the east coast is a relaxing way to spend a morning or afternoon. By cab, the tour should take from two to three hours. Weekends can be very crowded (surprise, surprise).

What to See

❸ **Changi Chapel & Museum.** Sprawling, squat, sinister-looking Changi Prison was built in the 1930s by the British and was used by the Japanese in World War II to intern some 70,000 POWs, who endured terrible hardships here. The prison, which now houses thousands of convicts, many of whom are here owing to Singapore's strict drug laws, is being renovated. It's where serious offenders are hanged at dawn on Friday.

The museum's walls hold poignant memorial plaques to those interned here during the war. It's a replica of one of 14 chapels where 85,000 Allied POWs and civilians gained the faith and courage to overcome the degradation and deprivation inflicted upon them by the Japanese. The museum contains drawings, sketches, and photographs by POWs depicting their wartime experiences. Organized tours take you through the old British barracks areas to the former RAF camp. Here, in **Block 151**— a prisoners' hospital during the war—you'll see the simple but striking murals painted by a British POW, bombardier Stanley Warren. The scale of military spending in the 1930s by the British—who put up these well-designed barracks to accommodate tens of thousands of men—is amazing. You can clearly see why the British believed Singapore was impregnable! This is still a military area; most of the barracks are used by Singapore's servicemen during their 2½-year compulsory duty. There are regular guided tours to give you more comprehensive information of the area depending on your interest.

✉ *1000 Upper Changi Rd. North* ☎ *6214–2451* ⊕ *www.changimuseum. com* ✎ *Free; donations accepted* ⊙ *Chapel and museum: daily 9:30–5; visitors welcome at 4:30 Sun. service* Ⓜ *Tanah Merah.*

1 **East Coast Park.** Between the highway and the sea, this park has sundry water sports and recreational facilities. A cool sea breeze makes it the best place in town for running. Locals frequent the park on weekends for bike rides and rollerblading. You can also go windsurfing, sailing, or simply take a dip in the water. There are about 80 barbecue pits, 7.5 km (4.7 mi) of sandy beaches, as well as a camp site and hawker centers. There's no MRT stop nearby, so a taxi is your best bet for getting here. ⊠ *East Coast Pkwy., East Coast.*

2 **LilliPutt.** Built to look like a miniature Singapore, this 18-hole indoor mini-golf course is definitely kitschy, but worth visiting for a good laugh. All the golf holes are modeled after familiar Singaporean landmarks, such as the Esplanade, Sentosa, and the Singapore Zoological Gardens. ⊠ *902 East Coast Pkwy., East Coast* ☎ *6348–9606* ☞ *S$12–S$18; no kids under 8* ☉ *Daily 10–10* ⊕ *www.lilliputt.com.*

need a break? | **Marine Cove** (⊠ 1000 East Coast Pkwy., East Coast), formerly known as the East Coast Recreation Centre, is where many cafés, restaurants, and bars are located. A landmark to watch for is the McDonald's—the only one on the East Coast Park stretch. There are a number of upscale restaurants, such as Mango Tree, where locals like to head on weekend afternoons for long leisurely lunches. There are also a number of shops scattered about.

UDMC Seafood Centre. This gathering of nine outdoor restaurants is a popular evening destination. Red House, Long Beach, and Jumbo are some of the seafood restaurants here, which serve local treats like chili crab. ⊠ *1216 East Coast Pkwy.*

The West Coast

The satellite city of Jurong is Singapore's main industrial area. It's estimated that more than 70% of the nation's manufacturing workforce is employed here by more than 3,000 companies. Though this may seem an unlikely vacation destination, there are actually several interesting attractions in or around Jurong. A garden environment exists here, demonstrating that an industrial area doesn't have to be ugly.

a good tour | West Coast attractions are far from the center of town and far from one another. You can arrange a tour through your hotel or take taxis alone or in combination with the MRT. A cab ride from the city center to Jurong will cost about S$17. **Haw Par Villa** **4** amusement park is much closer to town than the other sights. The nearest MRT station is Buona Vista, from which you must transfer to Bus 200 (though air-conditioned express coach service is available from hotels along Orchard Road). Haw Par Villa is also near one of the main jumping-off points to Sentosa Island, a short ride away.

On another day, you might start with a visit to **Jurong Bird Park** **5**. Next to the bird park and across the street from each other are **Jurong Crocodile Paradise** **7** and **Jurong Reptile Park** **6**. An MRT ride to Clementi will cost about S$1.50, depending on where you start your journey, and a taxi

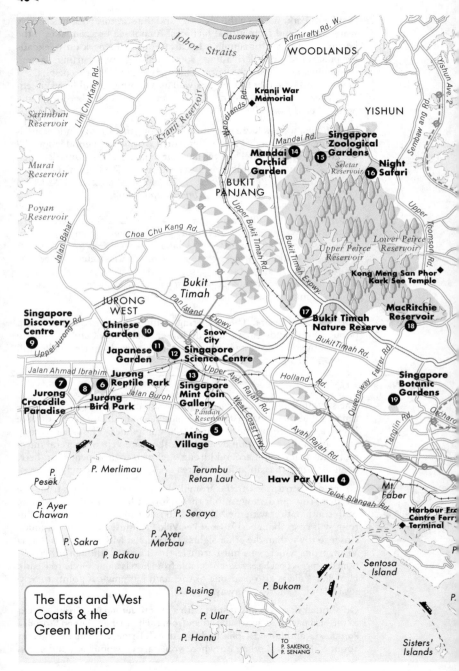

The East and West Coasts & the Green Interior

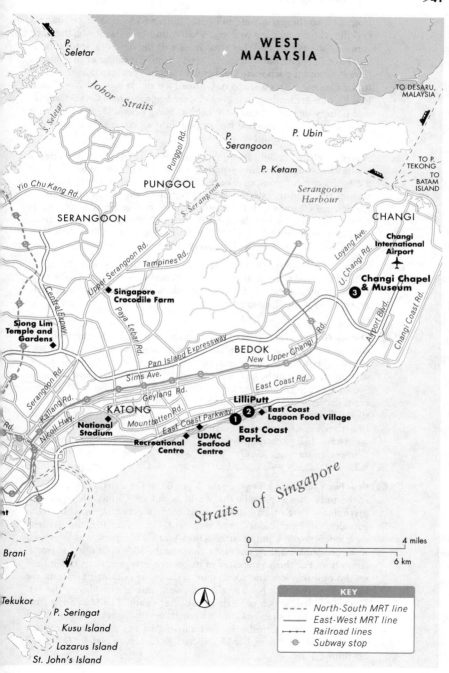

WEST
MALAYSIA

TO DESARU,
MALAYSIA

Johor Straits

S. Seletar

P.
Seletar

Yio Chu Kang Rd.

Punggol Rd.

P.
Serangoon

P. Ubin

P. Ketam

TO P.
TEKONG
TO
BATAM
ISLAND

PUNGGOL

SERANGOON

S. Serangoon

*Serangoon
Harbour*

CHANGI

Central Expwy.

Upper Serangoon Rd.

Tampines Rd.

Loyang Ave.

U. Changi Rd.

Changi International
Airport

◆ **Singapore
Crocodile Farm**

❸ **Changi Chapel
& Museum**

**Siong Lim
Temple and
Gardens** ◆

Paya Lebar Rd.

Pan Island Expressway

BEDOK
New Upper Changi Rd.

Airport Blvd.

Changi Coast Rd.

Serangoon Rd.

Sims Ave.

East Coast Rd.

Kallang Rd.

Geylang Rd.

KATONG

Mountbatten Rd.

LilliPutt

Nicoll Hwy.

**National
Stadium** ◆

East Coast Parkway

❶ ❷ ◆ **East Coast
Lagoon Food Village**

**Recreational
Centre** ◆ ◆ **UDMC
Seafood
Centre**

**East Coast
Park**

Rd.

Straits of Singapore

Brani

0   4 miles

0   6 km

Tekukor

P. Seringat

Kusu Island

Lazarus Island

St. John's Island

KEY	
-----	*North-South MRT line*
——	*East-West MRT line*
⊢—⊢	*Railroad lines*
⊝	*Subway stop*

from here to the park itself will cost another S$5 or so. If you take a taxi the whole way, plan to spend S$30 round-trip. Exploring the park is tiring, so take a break (or two) in one of the on-site restaurants. If you haven't tired of all the fauna, spend your afternoon at the **Chinese Garden** ⑩ and the **Japanese Garden** ⑪ (note that you can take the MRT to the Chinese Garden station). Or head for sights toward West Coast Road. Coins are made and displayed at the **Singapore Mint Coin Gallery** ⑬, and pottery demonstrations are held at **Ming Village** ⑤. Both of these sights can be easily reached by hopping into a taxi, it should take you no more than 10 minutes.

Alternatively, you could spend your afternoon at the **Singapore Science Centre** ⑫. If you don't want to spring for a taxi from Orchard Road (about a 20-minute ride), you can take the westbound MRT to the Jurong East station and then transfer to Bus 335, or make the 10-minute walk to the Science Centre's Omni-Theatre. A little farther away is the entertaining and educational **Singapore Discovery Centre** ⑨. To get here from the Science Centre, take the MRT from Jurong East to Boon Lay, then take Bus 182 or 193 to the Discovery Centre.

TIMING   Allow a half day for each sight (except Jurong Crocodile Paradise, which deserves an hour at most). Avoid coming here during peak traffic hours, which start at 5 PM. The gardens are best explored in early morning to avoid the heat.

What to See

♻ ⑩ **Chinese Garden.** This 32-acre reconstruction of a Chinese imperial garden (one inspiration for it was the garden of the Beijing Summer Palace) has pagodas, temples, courtyards, and bridges. Lotus-filled lakes and placid streams are overhung by groves of willows. Rental rowboats allow a swan's-eye view of the grounds, and there are refreshment facilities. Within the main garden you'll find the Ixora Garden, with several varieties of the showy flowering ixora shrub; the Herb Garden, showcasing plants used in herbal medicines; and the Garden of Fragrance, where many newlyweds have their photographs taken against stone plaques with auspicious Chinese engravings. ✉ *Off Yuan Ching Rd., Jurong* ☎ *6261–3632* 🎫 *Free* ☉ *Daily 9–7; last admission at 6* Ⓜ *Chinese Garden.*

♻ ④ **Haw Par Villa.** Also known as the Tiger Balm Gardens, Haw Par Villa is the only theme park in the world based on Chinese legends and mythology. Part of an estate owned by two eccentric brothers—the founders of Tiger Balm brand ointment—in the 1930s, the gardens were opened to the public after World War II. The park was later sold to a soft-drink bottling company that spent S$85 million on its transformation. For those interested in its bizarre interpretations of Chinese mythology, religion, and social mores, the many odd little tableaux are intriguing. The park has an infamous walk-through display of the Ten Courts of Hell, which is a tale of life after death. The **Hua Song Museum** relates the stories of Chinese immigrants throughout the world and in various time periods. ✉ *262 Pasir Panjang Rd., Buona Vista* ☎ *6872–2003* 🎫 *Free, but S$1.50 for Ten Courts of Hell* ☉ *Daily 9–7* Ⓜ *Buona Vista.*

🐣 ⑪ **Japanese Garden.** This enchanting formal garden is adjacent to the Chinese Garden and is one of the largest of its kind outside Japan. Its classic simplicity, and harmonious arrangement of plants, stones, bridges, and trees induce tranquillity (indeed, the garden's Japanese name, Seiwaen, means Garden of Tranquillity). A miniature waterfall spills into a pond full of water lilies and lotus. ☒ *Off Yuan Ching Rd., Jurong* ☎ *6261–3632* 🎫 *Free, but S$2 for the Bonsai Garden* ☉ *Daily 9–7; last admission at 6* Ⓜ *Chinese Garden.*

★ 🐣 ⑧ **Jurong Bird Park.** The region's leading bird park hosts the largest walk-in aviary in the world, with a 100-foot man-made waterfall (the world's tallest), in addition to another exquisite walk-in, Southeast Asian Birds Aviary, where a tropical thunderstorm is simulated daily at noon. More than 8,000 birds from 600 species are here, including hornbills, hummingbirds, parrots, and penguins. In stark contrast, the view from Jurong Hill is of the factories that crank out Singapore's economic success. For sweeping park vistas, consider taking a 10-minute ride on the Panorail, an air-conditioned monorail train.

If you arrive early, try breakfast at the Lodge on Flamingo Lake or catch the Lory Feeding (the first is at 9) at the huge Waterfall Aviary. The penguins, bee-eaters, and starlings are fed on a regularly scheduled basis at the Waterfall Aviary. There are also feedings in the Southeast Asian Birds Aviary and the Hornbills and Toucans Exhibit. Try to catch the JBP All-Star Bird Show at Pools Amphitheatre. One of the last shows of the day King of the Skies at 4. At the World of Darkness, you can sidle up to such nocturnal birds as owls, night herons, frogmouth, and kiwis. ☒ *2 Jurong Hill, Jurong* ☎ *6262–0022* ⊕ *www.birdpark.com.sg* 🎫 *S$14* ☉ *Daily 9–6* Ⓜ *Boon Lay.*

🐣 ⑦ **Jurong Crocodile Paradise.** Jurong Crocodile Paradise, across the street from the Jurong Bird Park, has over 2,500 crocodiles, underwater viewing areas, a breeding enclosure, and daily crocodile-wrestling shows. ☒ *241 Jalan Ahmad Ibrahim, Jurong* ☎ *6261–8866* 🎫 *$2* ☉ *Daily 9–6* Ⓜ *Boon Lay.*

🐣 ⑥ **Jurong Reptile Park.** Singaporeans seem to be fascinated with crocs, and at this 5-acre park you'll find 18-foot specimens. You can feed the crocodiles, watch muscle-bound showmen (and one showlady) wrestle with them, or buy crocodile-skin products at the shop. You can also watch the beasts through glass, in an underwater viewing gallery. But there's more: king cobra snakes, iguana lizards, colorful chameleons, and giant tortoises, for example, more than 50 species in all. A seafood restaurant and fast-food outlets provide refreshments, and there are rides for children. ☒ *241 Jalan Ahmad Ibrahim, Jurong* ☎ *6261–8866* ⊕ *www. reptilepark.com.sg* 🎫 *S$7* ☉ *Daily 9–6* Ⓜ *Boon Lay.*

⑤ **Ming Village.** At this small complex of buildings not far from the Jurong Bird Park, demonstrations of the art of Chinese pottery making are given, and copies of Ming dynasty blue-and-white porcelain are produced and sold. This is the region's largest remaining pottery center. ☒ *32 Pandan Rd., Jurong* ☎ *6265–7711* 🎫 *Free* ☉ *Daily 9–5:30* Ⓜ *Clementi.*

9 Singapore Discovery Centre. This world-class "edutainment" center makes education entertaining through countless multimedia and emotive attractions. The attractions aim to engage the senses through demonstrations and digital animation. At the Future Wonders Theatre, visitors input their dream data into devices that compile the information for a 3–5 minute multimedia presentation on their dreams. Definitely don't miss the 3-D films screened in the iWerks Theatre, or the motion simulator rides and virtual reality games. Here you can learn more about Singapore's history. ⊠ *510 Upper Jurong Rd., Jurong* ☎ *6792–6188* ⊕ *www.sdc. com.sg* 🖾 ⊘ *Tues.–Sun. & public holidays 9–7; closed Mon. unless it's a public holiday* Ⓜ *Boon Lay.*

13 Singapore Mint Coin Gallery. Close to the Singapore Science Centre and just east of the Boon Lay MRT station, you can watch minting operations. There are also displays of coins, medals, and medallions from Singapore and around the world. ⊠ *20 Teban Gardens Crescent, Jurong* ☎ *6566–2626* ⊕ *www.singaporemint.com.sg* 🖾 *Free* ⊘ *Weekdays 9:30–4:30* Ⓜ *Jurong East.*

🌙 **12** **Singapore Science Centre.** Aviation, nuclear science, robotics, astronomy, space technology, and Internet technology are entertainingly explored through 750 audiovisual and interactive exhibits. You can walk into a "human body" for a closer look at vital organs or test yourself on computer quiz games. You'll also find a flight simulator of a Boeing 747 and the Omni Theatre where movies and planetarium shows are screened. ⊠ *15 Science Centre Rd., Jurong* ☎ *6560–3316* ⊕ *www. science.edu.sg* 🖾 *S$6; Omni Theatre S$10; Virtual Voyages Ride S$6* ⊘ *Tues.–Sun. 10–6, Omni Theatre 10–8* Ⓜ *Jurong East.*

FodorsChoice ★

Snow City. Snow is a novelty when you live in a country where it's tropics all year-round. Locals endure sub-zero temperatures for a rare chance to touch and play in real snow at this indoor snow center. This place is definitely kitschy and not for all tourists. Still, it may provide an insight to the locals. ⊠ *21 Jurong Town Hall Rd., Jurong* ☎ *6337–1511* ⊕ *www.snowcity.com.sg* 🖾 *Single: S$12, Double: S$18* ⊘ *Tues.–Sun. 10:30–6:30, public holidays 9–8* Ⓜ *Jurong.*

Into the Garden Isle

Singapore is called the Garden Isle for good reason. While giving economic progress more than its fair share of attention, the government has also established nature reserves, gardens, and a zoo. If you have only a little time visit the zoo—it's truly exceptional.

To learn more about Singapore's natural habitats and plant life, contact the **National Parks Board** (☎ 6471–7361 ⊕ www.nparks.gov.sg). It manages about 4,199 acres of parks, park connectors, and open spaces as well as the 7,012 acres of the Nature Reserves, which includes the Singapore Botanic Gardens and Ft. Canning Park.

The **Nature Society (Singapore)** (☎ 6741–2036 ⊕ www.post1.com/home/naturesinsingapore) is one of the oldest nongovernment organizations in Singapore. It's dedicated to the study, conservation, and enjoyment of the natural heritage of Singapore, Malaysia, and the surrounding regions. Sponsored activities include excursions, talks, and workshops aimed at enhancing nature appreciation.

a good tour

Start at the **Mandai Orchid Garden** ⑭, a must for flower lovers; a taxi here from downtown will cost about S$16, or you can take SBS Bus 138 from the Ang Mo Kio MRT station. Spend about an hour here, then visit the **Singapore Zoological Gardens** ⑮. The taxi ride from the orchid garden will cost about S$6 (though you can also take Bus 138). If you arrive by 3 sharp, you'll be in time for tea with an orangutan. You can then get a good look at the zoo before it closes at 6 and head over to **Night Safari** ⑯ for dinner in the restaurant at its entrance (the grounds don't open until 7:30).

To reach the **Bukit Timah Nature Reserve** ⑰, take Bus 171, which departs from the Newton MRT station. From the Orchard MRT station to **MacRitchie Reservoir** ⑱ it's about a S$7 taxi ride. Plan to spend about S$4 on a cab to reach the **Singapore Botanic Gardens** ⑲ from the city center, or you can catch Bus 7, 105, 106, 123, or 174 from the Orchard MRT station.

On a trip to this area, visitors interested in Buddhism can work in visits to the **Kong Meng San Phor Kark See Temple** and the **Siong Lim Temple and Gardens**; nature lovers can check out the **Seletar Reservoir**; and history buffs can stop by the **Kranji War Memorial**.

TIMING Much of Singapore's natural world is miles from the center of the city. Because of the heat and humidity, a little walking here can be very tiring, so you probably won't be able to see all the sights in one day. Taxis or hotel tours are the favored ways of getting to the orchid garden, the zoo, and the Night Safari—all of which you can tour in the space of an afternoon and an evening. Allow yourself two hours for the Singapore Botanic Gardens, two for the MacRitchie Reservoir, and three for the Bukit Timah Nature Reserve.

What to See

★ ⑰ **Bukit Timah Nature Reserve.** If you like your nature a little wilder than what's found in manicured urban parks, then this is the place for you. In these 405 acres around Singapore's highest hill (535 feet), the rain forest runs riot, giving you a feel for how things might have been when tigers roamed the island. Wandering along structured, well-marked paths among towering trees, tangled vines, and prickly rattan palms, you may be startled by long-tailed macaques, squirrels, or tree shrews or, if you're really lucky, by a flying lemur. Hiking trails run through the rain forest; some lead to a hilltop with superb views. Wear good walking shoes—the trails are rocky, sometimes muddy. You can buy maps from the visitor center. ✉ *177 Hindhede Dr.* ☎ *1800/468–5736* ⊕ *www. nparks.gov.sg* 🎟 *Free* ☉ *Daily 8:30–6:30.*

Kong Meng San Phor Kark See Temple. The Bright Hill Temple, as it's commonly known, is Singapore's largest Mahayana temple. It's in a relatively modern complex of Buddhist temples, with much gilded carving. ✉ *88 Bright Hill Dr.* ☎ *1800/468–5736* ⊕ *www.kmspks.org* 🎟 *Free* ☉ *Daily 6:30–9* Ⓜ *Bishan.*

Kranji War Memorial. Soldiers who defended Singapore in World War II are buried in this cemetery near the causeway off Woodlands Road. Rows of Allied dead are grouped with their countrymen in plots on a peaceful, well-manicured hill. A visit here is a poignant experience, a reminder of the greatness of the loss in this and all wars. ⊠ *9 Woodlands Rd.* ☎ *6269–6158* 🕮 *Free* ◷ *Daily 7–6* Ⓜ *Kranji to Bus 170.*

🕲 ⑱ **MacRitchie Reservoir.** This 30-acre park has a jogging track with exercise areas, a playground, and a tea kiosk. The path around the reservoir is peaceful, with only the warbling of birds and chatter of monkeys to break your reverie. Crocodile spotting became a favorite pastime after baby crocs were found in the reservoir. Don't go in the water. ⊠ *Lornie Rd., near Thomson Rd.* ☎ *No phone* 🕮 *Free* ◷ *Daily dawn–dusk.*

⑭ **Mandai Orchid Garden.** Less than a kilometer down the road from the zoo (TIBS Bus 171 links the two) is a commercial orchid farm. The hillside is covered with the exotic blooms, cultivated for domestic sale and export. There are many varieties to admire, some quite spectacular, you can also buy their orchid gift-boxes as a little memento to take home. Guided tours are also available, however, since it is a good 30-minute taxi ride from downtown, unless you're an orchid enthusiast, a visit here is worth it only when combined with a visit to the zoo. The Singapore Botanic Gardens is closer to downtown and it also has orchids. ⊠ *Mandai Lake Rd.* ☎ *6739–54806* ⊕ *www.mandai.com.sg* 🕮 *S$3* ◷ *Weekdays 8:30–6:30* Ⓜ *Ang Mo Kio to Bus 138.*

🕲 ⑯ **Night Safari.** Right next to the Singapore Zoological Gardens, the safari is the world's first wildlife park designed exclusively and especially for night viewing. Here 80 acres of secondary jungle provide a home to 1,200 animals (100 species) that are more active at night than during the day. Some 90% of tropical animals are, in fact, nocturnal, and to see them do something other than snooze gives their behavior a new dimension. Night Safari, like the zoo, uses a moat concept to create open, natural habitats; areas are floodlighted with enough light to see the animals' colors but not enough to limit their normal activity. You're taken on a 45-minute tram ride along 3 km (2 mi) of road, stopping frequently to admire the beasts (some of which, like deer and tapirs, can get quite close to the tram) and their antics. On another kilometer or so of walking trails you can observe some of the small cat families, such as the fishing cat; primates, such as the slow loris and the tarsier; and the *pangolin* (scaly anteater). Larger animals include the Nepalese rhino (the largest of rhinos, with a single, mammoth horn), the beautifully marked royal Bengal tigers, which are somewhat intimidating to the nearby mouse deer, *babirusa* (pig deer with curled tusks that protrude through the upper lip), *gorals* (wild mountain goats), and *bharals* (mountain sheep). ⊠ *80 Mandai Lake Rd.* ☎ *6269–3411* ⊕ *www.nightsafari.com.sg* 🕮 *S$15.75* ◷ *Daily 7:30 PM–midnight* Ⓜ *Ang Mo Kio to Bus 138.*

FodorśChoice ★

Seletar Reservoir. The Seletar is the largest and least-developed of the island's natural areas. There's a viewing tower from which you can see the entire reservoir and a 9-hole public golf course. This parkland is largely flat and a good place for leisurely strolls or a jog. ⊠ *Mandai Rd., near zoo* ☏ *No phone* ⊡ *Free* ⊙ *Daily dawn–dusk.*

⓳ **Singapore Botanic Gardens.** The gardens were begun in 1859 and carry
Fodor'sChoice the hallmarks of Victorian garden design—gazebos, pavilions, and or-
★ nate bandstands included. This is still one of the world's great centers
of botanical scholarship, attracting international scientists to its herbar-
ium and library; the gardens' work on orchid hybridization and com-
mercialization for export has been groundbreaking. Botanist Henry
Ridley experimented here with rubber-tree seeds from South America;
his work led to the development of the region's huge rubber industry
and to the decline of the Amazon basin's importance as a source of the
commodity.

Spread over some 128 acres, the grounds contain a large lake (with black
swans from Australia), masses of shrubs and flowers, and magnificent
examples of many tree species, including fan palms more than 90 feet
high. Don't miss the 10-acre natural remnant rain forest. Locals come
here to stroll along nature walks, jog, practice tai chi, feed geese, or just
enjoy the serenity. There's an excellent visitor center and garden shop,
as well as a few restaurants. Recently, about 319 acres of the gardens
were trisected into three different zones, each with its own identity and
attractions. The ecolake extension at the Bukit Timah side of Cluny Road
is a lovely open site with interesting displays of commercial, culinary,
and medicinal crops and herbs. ⊠ *Corner of Napier and Cluny Rds.*
☏ *6471–7361* ⊕ *www.sbg.org.sg* ⊡ *Free* ⊙ *Daily 5 AM–midnight.*

Inside the Botanic Gardens is the 7.4-acre **National Orchid Garden,** where
you can see more than 700 orchids and some 2,100 hybrids, bred over
the past 70 years. ⊡ *S$5* ⊙ *Daily 8:30–7* ⊕ *www.nparks.gov.sg.*

★ ☙ **⓯** **Singapore Zoological Gardens.** You get the impressionthat animals come
here for a vacation and not, as is often the case elsewhere, to serve a
prison sentence. The zoo, which is set in the middle of natural rain forest with stunning views of nearby reservoir lakes, has an open-moat
concept, wherein a wet or dry moat separates the animals from the people. A mere 3-foot-deep moat will keep humans and giraffes apart, since
a giraffe's gait makes even a shallow trench impossible to negotiate. A
narrow water-filled moat prevents spider monkeys from leaving their
home turf for a closer inspection of visitors. Few zoos have been able
to afford the huge cost of employing this system, which was developed
by Carl Hagenbeck, who created the Hamburg, Germany, zoo at the
turn of the century. The Singapore zoo has managed by starting small
and expanding gradually. It now sprawls over 69 acres of a 220-acre
forested area.

The zoo has used its massive glass viewing windows to great effect: not
only can you watch polar bears perform "ballet" underwater and pygmy
hippos do less graceful things, but you can also observe such big cats
as lions and jaguars close up. At the reptile house, be sure to seek out
the Komodo dragons, which can grow to 10 feet in length. The primate
displays are striking, too, and the orangutan enclosure shows off the
world's largest captive orangutan group. The educational Fragile For-

est exhibit has displays of the rain forest and mangrove ecosystems. Some animals are free ranging, conditioned to stay in the zoo by territorial needs, as well as by readily available food and shelter. In all there are about 3,000 animals from around 160 species here.

Try to arrive at the zoo in time for the buffet breakfast. The food itself isn't special, but the company is: orangutans, a python, and an otter. The Jungle Breakfast (daily at 9 AM) is one of the zoo's most unique attractions.

At the primate-and-reptile show, monkeys, gibbons, and chimpanzees have humans perform tricks, and snakes embrace volunteers from the audience. There are performances by fur seals, elephants, free-flying storks, and other zoo inhabitants at various times throughout the day. The zoo's special shows and viewing galleries allow visitors to get close to its animals; a recent addition is the *Elephants of Asia,* which showcases elephants in a Burmese forest habitat. ✉ *80 Mandai Lake Rd.* ☎ *6269–3411* ⊕ *www.zoo.com.sg* ✉ *S$14; Jungle Breakfast S$18* ☉ *Daily 8:30–6* Ⓜ *Ang Mo Kio.*

Siong Lim Temple and Gardens. The largest Buddhist temple complex in Singapore was built by two wealthy Hokkien merchants between 1868 and 1908. Set among groves of bamboo, the temple is guarded by the giant Four Kings of Heaven, in full armor. There are several shrines and halls, with many ornate features and statues of the Lord Buddha. The goddess of mercy, Kuan Yin, has her shrine behind the main hall; another hall houses fine Thai Buddha images. The complex's oldest building is a small wooden shrine containing antique murals of the favorite Chinese legend "Pilgrimage to the West." ✉ *184 E. Jalan Toa Payoh* ☎ *6259–6924* ☉ *Daily, 6:30 - 9* Ⓜ *about 1 km (½ mi) east of Toa Payoh MRT station.*

Sentosa Island

This island was once a fishing village known as Pulau Blakang Mati. It was a British military fortress until 1967 when it was handed back to the newly independent Singapore government. In 1968 the government decided that Sentosa, the Isle of Peace and Tranquillity, would be transformed from the military fortress it was into a resort playground, with museums, parks, golf courses, restaurants, and hotels. A lot of money was spent on development, but the attractions were tired and dated, and the island held little interest for travelers who had come 10,000 miles to visit Asia, a fact lost on the Singapore government. Until very recently, Sentosa's only draws were the visual drama of reaching it—via cable car—and its wax museum. Billions have been spent of late to reinvigorate the area, and the island has become a popular leisure destination, providing tourists and locals alike with sights, attractions, and entertainment.

Much of Sentosa's attraction lies in its natural splendor. The island has a canopy of secondary rainforest covering 70% of its 1,200 acres, and is home to monitor lizards, monkeys, peacocks, parrots as well as other native fauna and flora. There are nature walks through jungles; campsites by the lagoon and tent rentals; and sundry recreational activities.

Play a game of volleyball, try your hand at being a trapeze artist, or swim in the lagoon and at a small ocean beach, tough owing to all the cargo ships—you'll see hundreds of them anchored off the coast—the waters leave a lot to be desired. If golf is your game, try a few rounds at the Sentosa Golf Club, or putt away on one of Sijori WonderGolf's uniquely landscaped greens.

The best way to make the 2-km (1-mi) trip to Sentosa is by cable car (small gondolas that hold four passengers each) from the HarbourFront Centre. Cable car tickets usually run from S$8–S$9. Other options include a shuttle bus (S$3) or taxi via the causeway. The island's S$2 admission price will get you into many attractions, though some have separate entrance fees. Sentosa has Southeast Asia's first monorail, which operates daily from 9 AM to 10 PM. It has stations close to the major attractions (a recording discusses each sight as you pass it), and unlimited rides are included in the price of the island admission. A free bus can also take you to most of the sights; it runs at 10-minute intervals daily from 7 AM to 11 PM. A small train runs along the south coast for about 3 km (2 mi); bicycles are available for rent at kiosks throughout the island; and, of course, you always have your own two feet. For more information about Sentosa and its facilities, call the **Sentosa Development Corporation** (☎ 6275–0388 ⊕ www.sentosa.com.sg).

Numbers in the text correspond to numbers in the margin and on the Sentosa Island map.

a good tour

Start at the HarbourFront Centre, where you can take a ferry or cable car (from the nearby station) to Sentosa. Between the ferry terminal and the cable car station on the Sentosa side are **Fountain Gardens ❶**, the **Sentosa Orchid Garden ❷**, and **Sijori WonderGolf ❸**. From the orchid garden you can follow the signs to **Images of Singapore ❹**, a combined wax, animatronics, and multimedia museum that gives you an idea of Singapore's history and cultures. Those who can handle heights should take a trip up the nearby **Carlsberg Sky Tower ❺** for breathtaking views. At 361 feet, it's Singapore's highest public viewing point. The **Butterfly Park and Insect Kingdom ❻** is also near. After seeing all the bugs, board the monorail for a trip to **Underwater World ❼**, a popular aquarium. Next to that is **Fort Siloso ❽**, an old British fort whose cannons were pointed the wrong way during World War II. From here take the monorail to the nearby swimming lagoon.

After a drink at the **Sunset Bar,** where you can sit on the wooden deck, gaze out at the view, and watch the nonstop volleyball, head up the hill behind the bar to **The Merlion & Merlion Walk ❾**, Singapore's 10-story mascot. The view from the top is good—the city and the container port on one side; the harbor, the refineries, and the Indonesian islands of Bintan and Batam on the other. Round out your trip with a stop at **VolcanoLand ❿**, which is close to the Merlion.

TIMING This tour will take three to four hours, longer if you linger at the beach or visit Sijori WonderGolf. If you don't like crowds, stay clear of Sentosa on the weekend. Come on a weekday afternoon so you can catch the sunset.

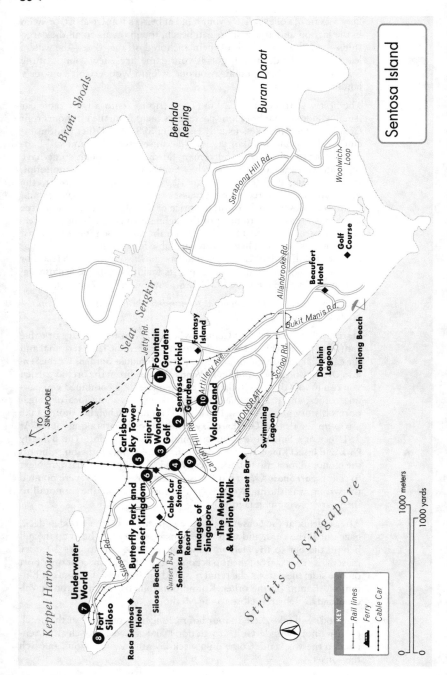

Sentosa Island

Brani Shoals

Berhala Reping

Buran Darat

Selat Sengkir

Serapong Hill Rd.

Woolwich Loop

Golf Course

Allanbrooke Rd.

Beaufort Hotel

Bukit Manis Rd.

Jetty Rd.

1 Fountain Gardens

Sentosa Orchid Garden

Fantasy Island

10 VolcanoLand

Artillery Ave.

School Rd.

Dolphin Lagoon

Tanjong Beach

TO SINGAPORE

Carlsberg Sky Tower

Sijori Wonder-Golf

5

2

3

Cable Car Station

4

9

Carlton Hill Rd.

Swimming Lagoon

MONORAIL

6

Butterfly Park and Insect Kingdom

Images of Singapore

The Merlion & Merlion Walk

Sunset Bar

Sentosa Beach Resort

Siloso Beach

Sunset Bay

Siloso Rd.

Rasa Sentosa Hotel

7 Underwater World

8 Fort Siloso

Keppel Harbour

Straits of Singapore

KEY	
+++	Rail lines
▲▲	Ferry
•••	Cable Car

0   1000 meters
0   1000 yards

What to See

⑥ **Butterfly Park and Insect Kingdom.** This park has a collection of 1,500 live butterflies from 50 species and 3,000 insects that creep, crawl, or fly. Look for tree-horn rhino beetles, scorpions, and tarantulas. The park has an Asian landscape with a moon gate, streams, and bridges. ⊠ *51A Cable Car Rd.* ☎ *6736–0013* ⊕ *www.sentosa.com.sg* ☞ *S$10* ⊙ *Daily 9–6:30.*

⑤ **Carlsberg Sky Tower.** Take a comfortable ride up this 361-foot tower for stunning views of Singapore. This is one of only 13 such towers worldwide. Each ride takes approximately seven minutes. ⊠ *Adjacent to the Sentosa cable car station* ☞ *S$10* ⊙ *Daily 9–9.*

Fodor'sChoice
★

⑧ **Fort Siloso.** The fort covers 10 acres of gun emplacements and tunnels created by the British to fend off the Japanese. Unfortunately, the Japanese arrived by land (through Malaysia) instead of by sea, so the huge guns were pointed in the wrong direction. The displays have been successfully revamped with lots of interactive high-tech audiovisual and animatronic effects. Photographs document the war in the Pacific, and dioramas depict the life of POWs during the Japanese occupation. To make your experience a more complete one, the wax figurines of Britain's General Percival and Japan's Lt. General Yamashita have been moved to Fort Siloso from the **Images of Singapore**—which has been closed for renovation until 2006—in a scene depicting the Japanese surrender to the British in World War II. ☎ *6736–0131* ☞ *S$8* ⊙ *Daily 10–6.*

① **Fountain Gardens.** Several times each evening visitors to the gardens, conveniently close to the ferry terminal, are invited to dance along with the illuminated sprays from the fountains to classical or pop music. Performances by traditional-dance groups are sometimes held. ⊠ *5 Garden Ave., near the Ferry Terminal.*

★ ④ **Images of Singapore.** This museum stands out from all the rest of Sentosa's attractions. It's best known for its excellent war-history displays, but it offers much more. Galleries trace the development of Singapore and depict the characters who profoundly influenced its history. Though the wax figures aren't the most lifelike, the scenes and the running narrative offer a vivid picture of 19th-century life in Singapore and a rare opportunity, in modern Singapore, to ponder the diversity of cultures that were thrust together in the pursuit of trade and fortune. In the Surrender Chambers wax tableaux show the surrender of the Allies to the Japanese in 1942 and the surrender of the Japanese to the Allies in 1945. Photographs, documents, and audiovisuals highlight events during the Japanese occupation and the various battles that led to their defeat. Other sections offer faithful depictions of traditional lifestyles and festivals. ☎ *6275–0388* ⊕ *www.sentosa.com.sg/a_images.htm* ☞ *S$8* ⊙ *Daily 9–7.*

⑨ **The Merlion & Merlion Walk.** This monument is the mascot of Singapore tourism; it's a 10-story off-white "lion fish" creature that emits laser beams from its eyes and smoke from its nostrils. It even glows in the dark. To get to the observation tower, you walk through a pirate cave exhibition, which uses animation and theater effects to introduce visitors to the mysteries of the sea through *The Legend of the Merlion.* ⊠ *Merlion Walk* ☎ 6736–5407 ⊕ *www.sentosa.com.sg/a_merlion.htm* ⊠ *S$8* ⊙ *Daily 10–8.*

Sentosa Orchid Garden. This exotic garden is filled with orchids from around the world. You'll also find a flower clock, a carp pond, and a Japanese teahouse. ☎ 6736–8672 ⊕ *www.sentosa.com.sg/a_orchid. htm* ⊠ *S$3.50* ⊙ *Daily 9:30–6:30.*

Sijori WonderGolf. There are 54 holes at this course where you can putt in picturesque surroundings, including caves, ravines, streams, and ponds. Three different 18-hole greens deliver different experiences and challenges. ⊠ *11 Siloso Rd.* ☎ 6736–8672 ⊕ *www.sentosa.com.sg* ⊠ *S$8* ⊙ *Daily 9–7.*

Sunset Bay. A popular hangout for expatriates and locals, you can always catch a good game of beach volleyball here as you groove to hip-hop and reggae. ⊠ *Siloso Beach* ☎ 6275–0668 ⊠ *Under 18 not admitted* ⊙ *Daily 10–10.*

need a break? You may want to take a break at **Trapizza** (⊠ Siloso Beach, near Shangri-La Hotel ☎ 6275–0100), open daily 11–11. Here you can sip a cool beverage and have a slice of pizza before (or after) you give your acrobatic skills a whirl at their on-site trapeze school. It's on Siloso Beach.

Underwater World. The traditional aquarium experience is reversed at Underwater World, where aquariums surround you. Two gigantic tanks house thousands of Asian-Pacific fish and other marine life; you walk through a 100-yard acrylic tunnel that curves along the bottom. There are sharks, giant octopuses, stingrays, moray eels, and the gorgeous little weedy sea dragons of Australia. Among the latest crowd pleasers are piranhas, electric eels, a *dugong* (sea cow), and pink dolphins. In total, there are 2,500 marine creatures from 250 species. Try to visit the **Dolphin Lagoon,** which is outside the park at Tanjong Beach. You can get really close to dolphins at this attraction, one of the island's newest. The admission price is included with your Underwater World ticket, otherwise tickets are S$17.50. You can observe and even interact with the animals in feeding and training sessions from 10:30–5 daily. ⊠ *99 Siloso Rd.* ☎ 6275–0030 ⊕ *www.underwaterworld.com.sg* ⊠ *S$17.30* ⊙ *Daily 9–9.*

VolcanoLand. This multisensory theme attraction creates a simulated journey to the center of the earth, complete with a man-made volcano that spews smoke on the half hour. There are also exhibits on Mayan civilization and a journey to prehistory to view real dinosaur eggs. ☎ 6736–8672 ⊕ *www.sentosa.com.sg* ⊠ *S$10* ⊙ *Daily 1–6.*

The Outer Islands

Singapore consists of one large island and some 60 smaller ones. Though many of the outer islands are still off the beaten track—with few facilities—some are being developed as beach destinations. Island hopping by ferry, bumboat, or water taxi is relatively easy to arrange.

Kusu

Kusu, also known as Turtle Island and sacred to both Muslims and Taoists, is an ideal weekday retreat (it gets crowded on weekends) from the traffic and concrete. The island is easily reached by a 30-minute ferry ride from HarbourFront Centre. During Kusu Season—a festival where Taoists travel to Kusu to pray for prosperity, luck, and fertility—from September 26 through October 24 the ferry leaves from Clifford Pier, which is off the Raffles Place MRT, rather than from HarbourFront Centre. There's a small coffee shop on the island, but you may want to bring a picnic lunch to enjoy in peace on the beach. A number of stories attempt to explain the association with turtles; all the tales in some way relate to a turtle that saved two shipwrecked sailors—one Chinese and one Malay—who washed up on the shore. Turtles now are given sanctuary here, and an artificial pond honors them with stone sculptures.

The hilltop **Kramat Kusu** (shrine) is dedicated to a Malay saint named Haji Syed Abdul Rahman, who, with his mother and sister, is said to have disappeared supernaturally from the island in the 19th century. To reach the shrine, you climb 122 steps that snake up through a forest. Plastic bags containing stones have been hung on the trees by devotees who have come to the shrine to pray for forgiveness of sins and the correction of wayward children. If their wishes are granted, believers must return the following year to remove their bags and give thanks.

Tua Pekong, a small, open-front Chinese temple, was built by Hoe Beng Watt in gratitude for the birth of his child. The temple is dedicated to Da Bo Gong, the god of prosperity, and the ever-popular Kuan Yin, goddess of mercy. Here she's also known by her Chinese surname, Sung Tzu Niang (Giver of Sons), and is associated with longevity, love of virtue, and fulfillment of destiny. Sung Tzu had a difficult childhood. She was determined to become a nun, but her father forbade it. When she ran away to join an order, he tried to have her killed. In the nick of time she was saved by a tiger and fulfilled her destiny. In gratitude, she cut off her arm as a sacrifice. This so impressed the gods that she was then blessed with many arms. Hence, when you see her statue in many of the Chinese temples in Singapore, she is depicted with six or eight arms. From late October to early November (or in the ninth lunar month), some 100,000 Taoist pilgrims bring exotic foods, flowers, joss sticks, and candles, and pray for prosperity and healthy children.

Pulau Ubin

Here amid the *kelongs* (fishing huts) and duck and prawn farms the lifestyle for the island's 200 residents hasn't changed much in 30 years. The name derives from the Malay word for granite, *zubin.* Indeed, there are five granite quarries on this tiny island. The mangrove and forest areas are havens for plants, birds (145 recorded species), and insects. Prior arrangements need to be made with the National Parks Board (☎ 6542–4108) before visiting Chek Jawa beach on the island's eastern tip. Granted its conservation status in 2001, the beach overflows with marine wildlife as well as colorful Thai *Ma Chor* temples—Ma Chor Poh is the patron saint of seafarers. The best way to see this island is on bicycle; you can rent one around the Changi Jetty on Changi Village Road, near Le Meridien Hotel, Changi. Accommodations can be found at **Ubin Lagoon Resort** (✉ 1000 Pulau Ubin ☎ 6542–9590), which is a cluster of kampung-style chalets. Otherwise, you can pitch tents on **Noordin beach** or **Mamam beach,** both of which offer unparalleled views of the Singapore skyline. Take a 10-minute jetty ride from Changi Point Jetty to reach Pulau Ubin.

St. John's Island

St. John's was first a leper colony, then a prison camp, and then a place to intern political enemies of the republic. Today it's a great place for picnics and camping. You can rent colonial bungalows from counters at the HarbourFront Centre. There are camping facilities as well. At the moment, the island is home to a Marine Aquaculture Centre and also operates a detention center for illegal immigrants. You can get to St. John's via the ferries at HarbourFront Centre.

Sisters' Islands

Some of the most beautiful of the southern islands are the best for snorkeling and diving. To get there, you'll have to hire a water taxi (rates are negotiable) at the Jardine Steps or Clifford Pier or take an organized day cruise (check with your hotel). Some of the boatmen know where to find the best coral reefs. If you plan to dive, be advised that the currents can be very strong.

Batam Island, Indonesia

Batam Island is just 25 minutes by ferry from Tanah Merah Ferry Terminal in Changi and is one of the most popular weekend retreats for Singaporeans. The island is one of Indonesia's industrial centers, but it's still surrounded by nature. Batam's population is a melting pot of many Indonesian ethnic groups that are heavily influenced by Malay culture. The island is separated by four ferry terminals—Sekupang, Waterfront City, Batam Centre, and Nongsa—and each locale has a distinct character to it. The two main draws are its unspoiled beaches and seafood restaurants, many of which are kelong style. Your taxi driver will probably be able to recommend a place to eat, but take care to check prices first as they may have an prior "arrangement" with certain establishments. It's worth staying overnight if you just want to escape the city without burning a hole in your pocket. Batam is popular with golfers, thanks to its respectable and affordable courses. There's also a panoply of water sports including surfing, canoeing, windsurfing, snorkeling, sailing, jet skiing, and speed boats. Equipment rental and instruction are available mostly through the resorts; they can also arrange fishing trips. In recent years, the island has come under scrutiny for its nightlife offerings, which can border on seedy. The best time for a trip to Batam is the weekend, when there's more going on. Citizens of Canada, the U.K., and the U.S. need only passports for stays in Indonesia of less than one month.

What to See

Nagoya, Batam's largest township, has a concentration of hotels, restaurants, clubs, bars, theaters, and shopping plazas, not to mention a night

WHERE TO EAT IN BINTAN

BINTAN'S LOCAL FOOD is influenced by Malay and Indonesian cuisines. There are plenty of restaurants, but the best food is found at hotel restaurants, which serve international as well as Indonesian dishes such as nasi goreng (fried rice) and gado gado (traditional salad). Seafood dishes are uncommonly good and fresh in Bintan; try the chili crab. Inform your waiter if spice is an issue. To be on the safe side, order bottled water to avoid any stomach discomfort. Credit cards are accepted at hotels; local places tend to accept cash (Indonesian rupiah or Singapore dollars).

Baan Aarya Thai Restaurant & Bar (✉ 1 Indra Maya Villas ☎ 770/692877), in the Bintan Beach International Resort, has its own botanical garden and beach. Come early to see the sunset on the verandah overlooking the South China Sea.

Alfresco **Café Helo-Helo** (✉ Pasar Oleh Oleh) serves reasonably priced local foods and offers live music and cultural performances.

Kelong Seafood Restaurant (✉ Tanjung Uban-Lagoi), a seafood restaurant in the Nirwana Gardens hotel, is built on stilts and also overlooks the South China Sea. The highlights here are the chili crab, garlic prawns, and mee goreng (Malay-style chili noodles).

Saffron Restaurant (✉ Site A4, Lagoi ☎ 770/693100) offers ocean views and is among Bintan's most exclusive restaurants. Saffron serves Thai and Indonesian dishes; try the bebek betutu (roast duck in banana leaves) or the satay.

market or two. Most bank and money changers are also here. The Buddhist temple **Vihara Budhi Bhakti,** at the eastern edge of the city, is worth a visit. Nagoya is also the center of nightlife on Batam and has many pubs and dance clubs. The scene heats up around 11 PM and continues on until 5 AM. Karaoke bars are prevalent, but note that many are fronts for prostitution. **The Sphinx** at Hotel Seruni is one of the island's most popular dance clubs. **Ozone** is among Sumatra's largest discos, with a capacity of 3,000. **Steps,** in the Melia Panorama Hotel, has a house band. On the first floor of the same hotel is **The Tavern,** a popular club favored by trendy locals and Singaporeans.

Nongsa, where most tourists go (the ferry drops you off here), is where the island's major resorts are; it has Batam's best beach, with a view of Singapore's skyline. Be sure to ask your hotel about boat trips up the Nongsa River to view the rainforest and its wildlife. For water sports enthusiasts, there are opportunities to jet ski, wakeboard, and windsurf; the operators are usually connected to the hotels. In **Batam Centre,** a planned city and Batam's commercial center, you'll find **Matahari,** a large shopping center. For a taste of old Batam, grab a bite in **Telaga Punggur,** an old-fashioned fishing village.

Bintan Island, Indonesia

Overnight trips to Bintan, more than twice the size of Singapore, can include a stay at a five-star hotel with your own private pool or a more adventurous jaunt in a sampan to the 16th-century palace of a Malaysian sultan. The *orang laut* (sea people, island inhabitants who are descendants of pirates and traders) still live in houses on stilts over the sea—an interesting contrast to the six modern beach resorts here.

The island's laidback, resort feel makes it a refreshing escape from Singapore's bustle. Most of the resorts have easy access to the beachfront. Make hotel reservations as far in advance as possible. You may also want to consider a guided tour of the island. Note that citizens of Canada, the U.K., and the U.S. need only passports for stays in Indonesia of less than one month.

What to See

Bintan's main town is **Tanjung Pinang** (a.k.a. Riau), where the primary activity is shopping on Pasar Pelantar Dua. There are several night markets, including one on Jalan Hang Tuah and another at Kedai Harapan Jaya at the end of Jalan Pelantar II. You can sample a wide array of the local fare at these markets, usually from 5 PM–2 AM nightly. Tanjung Pinang is a jumping-off point for some interesting sites nearby.

Take a tour from Tanjung Pinang's Pelentar Pier up the **Snake River** through the mangrove swamps to the oldest Chinese temple in Riau. As the boatman poles his way up the small tributary choked with mangroves, the sudden view of the isolated 300-year-old temple with its murals of hell will send chills down your spine. Have the boatman take you back down the river to Tanjung Berakit, where tiny huts perch on stilts. Friendly villagers here live in spartan homes without electricity or water—only an hour and a half from Singapore.

Another good stop by motorboat is **Pulau Penyengat** (Wasp Island), once the heart of the Riau sultanate and the cultural hub of the Malay empire. In the 16th century the Malay sultanate fled here after being defeated by the Portuguese in Malacca. The island is just 15 minutes by motorboat from Tanjung Pinang's Pelentar Pier. Sites include royal graves, the banyan-shrouded ruins of the palace, and the Mesjid Raya (Sultan's Mosque)—a bright yellow building that was plastered together with egg yolks and is considered the most important place of worship in the Riau Islands.

WHERE TO EAT

2

Updated by
Josie Taylor

OTHER CULTURES MIGHT PRIZE ATMOSPHERE, decor, and service over food, but in Singapore, the food's the thing. Bistros, eating houses, fine restaurants, and hawker centers serving home-grown Nonya, and all other conceivable cuisines, attest to this simple fact: Singaporeans live to eat.

Sundays in Singapore can be an epicurean adventure with many upscale hotels—standouts are the Conrad International, Grand Hyatt, Four Seasons, and Hilton—offering lavish value brunches (usually noon–3 for around S$80 per person). Buffets with international dishes and free-flowing champagne, wine, or soda are standard. Always make reservations and clarify times and prices, since you may get a discount if you opt for soda over champagne. High tea is also served on weekends, and occasionally during the week, usually 3–6 for about S$25–S$35 without tax or service charge at several hotels; best bets include the Ritz-Carlton and the Tiffin Room at Raffles. Singapore's spin on this British tradition comes with finger sandwiches, cakes, and scones, as well as Asian or Indian tidbits such as dim sum (a.k.a. *dian xin*), fried noodles, satays, and curry puffs.

Widespread building restoration in Singapore has given birth to several chic establishments, such as Au Jardin (French), a converted colonial residence in the botanical gardens; Flutes at the Fort (eclectic) atop Ft. Canning Park; and Saint Julien (French) in a converted boathouse overlooking the confluence of the Singapore River and the Straits of Malacca. Senso (Italian) on Club Street was formerly an ecclesiastical building, and Tanjong Pagar's Blue Ginger (Nonya) and Chinatown's Da Paolo e Judie (Italian) were once shophouses. Unique to Singapore, Penang, and Malaysia, shophouses were usually built by Southern Chinese migrants. The owners operated businesses on the ground floor and lived upstairs. Nineteenth-century shophouses are simple, bilevel buildings, but 20th-century structures are taller and more ornate. The most recognizable shophouse style, known as Chinese–Baroque, combines Georgian windows and cornices, plaster reliefs of Chinese elements, and detailed Malay wood carvings. Shophouses now very popular as homes and restaurant/bars.

Opportunities for waterside dining include the IndoChine Waterfront Restaurant at the Asian Civilisations Museum, the East Coast Seafood Centre's no-frills seafood restaurants, and One Fullerton's cafés, restaurants, and bars—highlights are the House of Sundanese Food and Pierside Kitchen and Bar. You can sample satay sticks with peanut sauce at the popular Satay Club under Esplanade Bridge (between Merlion Park and Waterboat House). Other noteworthy dining areas are Jalan Merah Saga in Holland Village—here you'll find Michelangelo's (Italian), Original Sin (vegetarian Mediterranean), Da Paolo Gastronomia (Italian), and Au Petit Salut (French)—and Chinatown's Club Street, home to trendy Da Paolo e Judie (Italian) and L'Aigle d'Or (French).

For authentic, time-honored cooking minus the linen tablecloths, head to the ethnic enclaves. Several of mainland China's provinces are represented among Chinatown's eateries. Geylang has popular Malay and Indonesian hawker stalls. In Little India you can eat at no-frills, shop-

2

Mealtimes
The restaurants listed, with exceptions noted, are open daily for lunch and dinner. Most open from noon to 2:30 or 3 for lunch, and from 6:30 to 10:30 (last order) for dinner. Singaporeans tend to eat out at lunch; food courts and restaurants are at their busiest from 1 to 2 PM.

Paying
Credit cards are widely accepted in restaurants, but are often useless at the simpler coffee shops and food stalls.

Reservations & Dress
Reservations are always a good idea, though they're noted only when they're essential or not accepted. Singaporeans don't tend to dress up for eating out—except at some of the fancier hotel dining rooms—because of the tropical weather. Bring a light jacket if you're sensitive to cold; many restaurants crank up the air-conditioning. Dress codes are mentioned when a jacket, or a jacket and tie, are required for men.

Wine, Beer & Spirits
The minimum age for purchasing alcohol is 18. There are no regulations regarding the places where or times when alcohol can be sold. Be aware that religious restrictions prevent owners of Muslim and some of the more orthodox Hindu restaurants from serving any alcohol. Singaporeans tend to favor sweet wines, such as the warm rice wine found in Chinese restaurants. If you like beer consider trying Tiger, Anchor, or another local brew. Purists may be put off by the local habit of mixing beer or wine with ice, but it chills your drink and lessens your chances of dehydration.

Prices
Competition has kept overall restaurant prices low, but liquor remains expensive. A cocktail or a glass of wine can cost S$10–S$14, and a reasonably good bottle of wine costs at least S$80. The import tax on each bottle is levied by alcohol content rather than by quality. Vintage wines may be priced similar to lesser-quality bottles. Western-style restaurants tend to have higher quality wines due to better storage conditions and closer relationships with foreign (usually Australian) vineyards. BYOB (bring your own bottle) is popular, but corkage charges (typically S$30 a bottle) negate this custom's economical side. Local and imported beers are sold at similar prices: around S$10 per glass of S$35 per jug.

Seafood is usually inexpensive, with the exception of such delicacies as shark fin, abalone, and lobster, which are sourced daily from markets where prices fluctuate. Such dishes are often charged at "market prices" rather than set prices; ask for exact rates before you order to avoid any surprises. If the prices are quoted per 100 grams, ask how much it will cost for the whole table. Don't be surprised if you're charged for napkins and pre-meal eats. Some Indian restaurants automatically bring a plate of *pappadoms* (lentil crackers) with spicy dips. Other eateries serve a *couvert* (an appetizer of such items as bread, cheese or paté, olives, quail eggs, and the like). You'll be charged extra for these, and you're perfectly within your rights to send it back if you don't want it.

	$$$$	$$$	$$	$	¢
	WHAT IT COSTS In Singapore dollars				
AT DINNER	over S$50	S$35–S$50	S$20–S$35	S$10–S$20	under S$10

Prices are for one main course at dinner.

house restaurants like Korma Vila and Banana Leaf Apolo, where you'll be rubbing elbows with locals.

Visit ⊕ http://food.asia1.com.sg for the latest information on dining in Singapore.

American/Casual

☺ **$–$$** ✕ **Brewerkz.** Across from Clarke Quay is this microbrewery, which serves homemade burgers, fried calamari, pizza, beer-battered fish-and-chips, and buffalo wings. The service is speedy and the portions are huge. You can shoot pool indoors, or kick back with your food on the expansive patio. In 2004 Brewerkz's English-style pale ale was awarded a gold medal in the Association of Brewers World Beer Cup. You can order from a late-night menu, which has finger foods, chicken Cobb salad, and spicy sausage sandwiches, on Friday and Saturday nights from 11 to midnight. There's also a snack menu from midnight to 1:30 AM these nights. ⊠ #01–05/06 Riverside Point, 30 Merchant Rd., Clarke Quay ☎ 6438–7438 ⊟ AE, DC, MC, V Ⓜ Raffles Place.

Brazilian

$$$ ✕ **Brazil Churrascaria.** Carnivores (and carb watchers) should take a 20-minute cab ride from downtown to this lively all-you-can-eat *churrascaria* (barbecue) restaurant. Waiters slice marinated beef, pork, lamb, and other types of meat off jumbo skewers onto your plate. Vegetarians can find solace in the salad bar. ⊠ 14–16 Sixth Ave., Thomson/Bukit Timah ☎ 6463–1923 ⊟ AE, DC, MC, V ☺ No lunch.

Chinese

$$$–$$$$ ✕ **Jade.** Like the precious stone it's named for, this restaurant has both
Fodor'sChoice exquisite and intriguing attributes. Inside, the theme follows an eclec-
★ tic Asian thread with Vietnamese hanging lamps and Chinese calligraphy. Similarly, the food is fundamentally Chinese but with modern and regional accents. Dip into the skewered pan-seared scallops and greens with lemongrass in mango dressing, or rich cocoa-flavored pork ribs with spinach in raspberry vinaigrette. For something light and nourishing, the homemade spinach tofu with Japanese nameko mushrooms and crispy *conpoy* (dried scallops) is popular for lunch. ⊠ The Fullerton Hotel, 1 Fullerton Square, CBD ☎ 6877–8188 ⚑ Reservations essential ⊟ AE, DC, MC, V Ⓜ Orchard.

$$–$$$$ ✕ **Golden Peony.** Join the power-lunchers at this swanky Cantonese dining room for what has been described as "maverick Hong Kong cui-

TABLE MANNERS

ALTHOUGH SINGAPOREANS ARE accepting of variations in etiquette, thanks to their nation's multiculturalism, there are a few things to keep in mind. Traditionally, your food is served family style—placed all at once on the table so everyone can dig in— or, for more formal meals, served a course at a time, again with diners sharing from a single dish. Nevertheless, some restaurants are dispensing with tradition and are instead serving individual portions. When eating with chopsticks, dip them in tea before wiping them with a tissue to clean them; never leave them upright in a rice bowl—this resembles a grave marker which is considered a bad omen. It's a sign of respect for a Singaporean to serve you during a family-style meal. It's polite to reciprocate the gesture when their bowl is nearing empty. It's not a big deal to start eating before your companions have been served; waiting until everyone is served is a western concept. Many locals may have religion-based dietary restrictions, such as only eating vegetarian or halal (Muslim) food. If you're arranging a meal with Singaporeans be sure to clarify their eating habits before deciding on a restaurant. Smoking is banned in air-conditioned restaurants and banquet/meeting rooms, but many establishments have outdoor patios and seating areas for smokers.

sine." Alongside more conventional dim sum delicacies are chef Kit Lam's crispy prawns with walnuts or golden crispy chicken stuffed with glutinous rice. There's also a full lunch and dinner menu. Popular dishes include deboned chicken with bean curd skin and Yunnan ham, and steamed crab claw in Hua Tiao wine and ginger sauce. ⊠ *Conrad International Centennial Hotel, 2 Temasek Blvd., Marina Square* ☏ *6334–8888 Ext. 7482* ▭ *AE, DC, MC, V* Ⓜ *City Hall.*

$$–$$$$ ✕ **My Humble House.** Eat at this colorful restaurant, which is the result of a collaboration between Beijing artist/musician Zhang Jin Jie and local restaurateurs, to get your creative (and digestive) juices flowing. Dispersed about the shimmering split-level interiors are whimsical curled and high-back furniture, vividly hued throws and curtains, modern artwork, and quirky flatware. Equally entertaining is the menu with its florid descriptions; "snow drops in the forest" is the colorful name for honey beans with preserved vegetables and dried scallops, of course. Alternatively, there's "smooth as velvet" (braised superior shark's fin), which is a pricier signature dish, and "the balmy breeze beckons" (baked five-spiced pork loin). ⊠ *#02–27/29 Esplanade Mall, 8 Raffles Ave., Colonial Singapore* ☏ *6423-1881* ▭ *AE, DC, MC, V* Ⓜ *City Hall.*

$$$ ✕ **Szechuan Court.** Your tastebuds may tingle even after you've left this restaurant. The culprit? Chili peppers that appear frequently in Szechuan dishes. The cuisine strives to engage all five tastes: *xian* (salty), *tian* (sweet), *suan* (sour), *la* (hot) and *xin* (pungent), and *ku* (bitter). Specialities include thinly sliced beef rolls with garlic sauce, spareribs in honey sauce, and spicy rice noodles with diced chicken. The set menus, with six dishes each, are wise options. ✉ *Raffles The Plaza, Level 3, 2 Stamford Rd., Colonial Singapore* ☎ *6431–5323* Ⓜ *City Hall.*

$$–$$$ ✕ **Hai Tien Lo.** Most of the tables at this 37th-floor restaurant grant you sweeping views of Singapore, particularly the ocean, the Padang, and City Hall. The details, Cantonese cuisine, and service combine for an elegant experience: plates change with every course, and waitresses wear cheongsams (Chinese dresses with Mandarin collars and side slits). Cantonese master chef Simon Ho prepares tempting specialties like wok-fried lobster in chili sauce with sautéed prawns and canteloupe; baked codfish with champagne sauce; and steamed bean curd with scallops, mashed prawns, and crab roe. ✉ *Pan Pacific Singapore, Level 37, 7 Raffles Blvd., Marina Square* ☎ *6826–8338* ▭ *AE, DC, MC, V* Ⓜ *City Hall.*

$$–$$$ ✕ **Lei Garden.** The menu changes daily at this bilevel restaurant, but its famed double-boiled tonic soup (highly prized for its medicinal qualities), barbecued meats, and seafood (including a variety of shark-fin dishes) are almost always available. Office workers crowd here for lunch, when dim sum is served. Must-tries at dinner are Peking duck, grilled rib-eye beef, and fresh scallops with bean curd in black bean sauce. ✉ *#01–24 Chijmes, 30 Victoria St., Colonial Singapore* ☎ *6339–3822* ▭ *AE, DC, MC, V* Ⓜ *City Hall.*

$$ ✕ **House of Mao Hunan Hot Pot.** If you've ever wondered about Chairman Mao's propaganda machine, you should take a look at this kitschy eatery's wall-to-wall propaganda posters, party flags, and giant airbrushed canvases of children waving red books. The staff's Red Army uniforms and a looped video of the late dictator complete the schema, but it's the do-it-yourself approach to food that would most impress the Chairman. Select soup stock, condiments, sauces, vegetables, seafood, and meat, and then boil it in the large pot recessed in your table. You can also order noodle side dishes. ✉ *#01–09/10 Orchard Hotel Shopping Arcade, 442 Orchard Rd., Orchard* ☎ *6733–7667* ▭ *AE, DC, MC, V* Ⓜ *Orchard.*

$$ ✕ **Imperial Herbal Restaurant.** Feeling rundown? Jet-lagged? Having problems with digestion? A Chinese herbalist at this dining hall will give you a quick checkup before making recommendations that may improve your health. More than 100 dishes have been developed with specific therapeutic purposes in mind. The braised Canadian codfish flambé with garlic and ginger is said to relieve fatigue. The candied sweet potato reportedly calms stomachs upset from too much traveling. There are also restorative tonics and teas, as well as beer and wine. If you're really impressed with the results or need some extra help, take-home herbal remedies are also available. ✉ *Metropole Hotel, Level 3, 41 Seah St., Colonial Singapore* ☎ *6337–0491* ⌕ *Reservations essential* ▭ *AE, MC, V* Ⓜ *City Hall.*

2

Nonya is Singapore's best showcase for cross-cultural foods. When Chinese settlers moved to Malaysia, their methods of food preparation underwent a slow evolution as they incorporated local ingredients and cooking styles. Simple Nonya snacks include *poh piah,* soft spring rolls stuffed with such components as bean sprouts, pork, and minced prawns. Other cross-cultural meals include the spicy Indian-style *mee goreng* (fried noodles), noted for its tomato-derived reddish color, and the **fish-head curry,** a celebrated local classic, neither of which originated from India. Spicy and simple *sop kambing* (mutton soup) is an Indonesian spin on an Indian dish. The Chinese food-derived Peking/Beijing duck isn't native to China. *Hokkien mee* (fried noodles) in the style of the Fujian people from China, packed with prawns, and the Malay *curry laksa,* a.k.a. *laksa lemak* (coconut-milk curry), are also unconventional options. Don't wear white to munch on the fiery, crunchy, messy **chili crab,** a meal of which inevitably ends with cracked shells scattered around your table.

Singaporeans love chili, but their concept of "mild" may not match yours. Pungent *sambals* (chili-based pastes), such as *sambal belacan* (chili with pungent, fermented prawn paste) may not be to everyone's taste.

Keeping healthy can be difficult when many local foods are fried, sugar is used liberally in drinks and desserts, and most Asian dishes comes with rice, noodles, or bread. A light and nutritious lunch that you can control is *yong tau foo,* a Chinese dish where you select such ingredients as quail eggs, Asian vegetables, and soybean curd to mix in a clear soup (noodles are optional).

Note: Wine isn't always the best accompaniment to local cuisines—whiskey or beer is often preferred. If you're dining on European fare, consider Australian wines—they seem to survive the tropics better than do the French labels. If you want wine with Cantonese fare, check the wine list for Chinese wine (be sure that it's made from grapes and not rice).

Chinese

Cantonese. This cooking style is known for its fresh, delicate flavors, and is the best-known regional Chinese cuisine. Characteristic dishes are stir-fried beef in oyster sauce, steamed fish with slivers of ginger, and deep-fried duckling with mashed taro.

Teochew. Though the cooking of the Teochew (or Chao Zhou), mainly fisherfolk from Swatow in the eastern part of Guangdong Province, has been greatly influenced by the Cantonese, it's quite distinctive. Chefs cook with clarity and freshness, often steaming or braising, with an emphasis on fish and vegetables. Such Cantonese cooking staples as oyster sauce and sesame oil don't appear much in Teochew meals.

Characteristic dishes are *lo arp* and *lo goh* (braised duck and goose), served with vinegary chili-and-garlic sauce; crispy liver or prawn rolls; stewed, preserved vegetables; black mushrooms with fish roe; and a unique porridge called *congee,* which is eaten with small dishes of salted vegetables, fried whitebait, black olives, and preserved-radish omelets.

Szechuan. The Szechuan style of cooking is distinguished by the use of bean paste, chilies, and garlic, as well as a wide, complex use of nuts and poultry. The pungent dishes are harmoniously blended and spicy hot. Simmering and smoking are common forms of preparation, and noodles and steamed bread are preferred accompaniments. Characteristic dishes are hot-and-sour soup, sautéed chicken or prawns with dried chilies, tea-smoked duck, and spicy string beans.

Pekingese. This cuisine, also known as Beijing style, originated in the Imperial courts and makes liberal use of strong-flavored roots and vegetables, such as peppers, garlic, ginger, leeks, and coriander. Meals usually come with noodles or dumplings and baked, steamed, or fried bread. The most famous meal is Peking duck: the skin is lacquered with aromatic honey and baked until it looks like dark mahogany and is crackly crisp.

Hainan. One of the most celebrated contributions made by arrivals from China's Hainan island, off the north coast of Vietnam, is "chicken rice": whole chickens are poached with ginger and spring onions; then rice is boiled in the liquid to fluffy perfection and eaten with chopped-up pieces of chicken, which are dipped into sour-and-hot chili sauce and dark soy sauce.

Fukien. Soups and stews with rich, meaty stocks are emphasized in this cuisine. Wine-sediment paste and dark soy sauce are used, and seafood is prominent. Try the braised pork belly served with buns, fried oysters, and turtle soup.

Hunanese. Sugars and spices dominate this semi-rustic cooking style. One of the most famous dishes is beggar's chicken: a whole bird is wrapped in lotus leaves and baked in a sealed covering of clay; when it's done, a mallet is used to break away the hardened clay.

Hakka. This provincial food uses ingredients not normally found in other Chinese cuisines. Red-wine dregs are used to great effect in dishes of fried prawns or steamed chicken, producing delicious gravies.

Indian

Southern Indian. This chili-hot cuisine generally relies on strong spices like mustard seed, and uses coconut milk liberally. Meals are very cheap, and eating is informal: just survey the displayed food, point to your choice, then take a seat at a table. A piece of banana leaf will be placed before you, plain rice will be spooned out, and the rest of your food will be arranged around the rice and covered with curry sauce. Generally, these meals are vegetarian because of the predominantly Hindu population in Southern India.

Northern Indian. These meals are more likely to include meats because of the region's Muslim population. This food is less hot and more subtly spiced than southern, and cow's milk is used as a base instead of coconut milk. Yogurt is used to tame the pungency of the spices; pureed tomatoes and nuts are used to thicken gravies. The signature dish is tandoori chicken (marinated in yogurt and spices and cooked in a clay urn) and fresh mint chutney, eaten with naan, *chapati*, and *paratha* (Indian breads). Northern Indian dishes may cost more because of the meat ingredients.

Malay and Indonesian

Malay. Turmeric root, lemongrass, coriander, *blachan* (prawn paste), chilies, and shallots are among this hot and rich cuisine's key ingredients; coconut milk is used to create fragrant, spicy gravies. A basic cooking method is to gently fry the *rempah* (spices, herbs, roots, chilies, and shallots ground to a paste) in oil and then add meat and either a tamarind liquid, to make a tart spicy-hot sauce, or coconut milk, to make a rich spicy-hot curry sauce. Dishes to look for are *gulai ikan* (a smooth, sweetish fish curry), *telor sambal* (eggs in hot sauce), *empalan* (beef boiled in coconut milk and then deep-fried), *tahu goreng* (fried bean curd in peanut sauce), and *ikan bilis* (fried anchovies). The best-known Malay dish is *satay*—slivers of marinated meats threaded onto thin coconut sticks, barbecued, and served with spicy peanut sauce.

Indonesian. This cuisine is very similar to Malay; both are based on rice and don't use pork (except for dishes prepared by the non-Muslim Indonesians). *Nasi padang* consists of various dishes, such as curried meat and vegetables with rice, and offers a range of tastes from sweet to salty to sour to spicy. *Nasi goreng* (fried rice), and *ayam bakar* (grilled chicken) or *ikan bakar* (grilled fish) are ubiquitous.

Nonya (Nyonya or Peranakan)

When Hokkien immigrants settled on the Malay Peninsula, they acquired the taste for Malay spices and soon adapted Malay foods. Nonya (the cuisine was given this title, which is the Malay for word "woman" or "wife," because cooking was considered a feminine art) food is one manifestation of the marriage of the two cultures. Nonya cooking combines the finesse of Chinese cuisine with the spiciness of Malay cooking. Many Chinese ingredients are used—especially dried ingredients like Chinese mushrooms, anchovies, lily flowers, soybean sticks, and salted fish.

Nonya cooks use preserved soybeans, garlic, and shallots to form the rempah needed to make *chap chay* (a mixed-vegetable stew with soy sauce). Other typical dishes are *husit goreng* (an omelet fried with shark fin and crabmeat) and *otak otak* (a sort of fish quenelle with fried spices and coconut milk). Nonya cooking features such sour and hot dishes like *garam asam*, a fish or prawn soup made with pounded turmeric, shallots, *galangal* (a hard ginger), lemongrass, shrimp paste, and preserved tamarind.

Thai

Although influenced by Chinese, Indian, Indonesian, and Malaysian cooking styles, Thai cuisine has a distinctly different taste. Its characteristic flavors come from fresh mint, Thai basil, coriander, and citrus leaves; extensive use of lemongrass, lime, vinegar, and tamarind keeps a sour-hot taste prevalent. On first tasting a dish, you may find it stingingly hot (tiny chilies provide the fire), but the taste of fresh herbs will soon surface. Not all Thai food is hot; a meal is designed to have contrasting dishes—some spicy, others mild. Traditionally, salt isn't used in Thai cooking. Instead, *nam pla* (fish sauce) is served on the side, which you add to suit your taste.

Popular Thai dishes include *mee krob*, crispy fried noodles with shrimp; *tom yam kung*, hot and spicy shrimp soup, and *tom kha gai*, small pieces of chicken in a coconut-based soup; *gai hor bai toey*, fried chicken wrapped in pandanus leaves; and *pu cha*, steamed crab with fresh coriander root and coconut milk. Thai curries may contain coconut milk and are often served with garnishes and side dishes. Most meals come with rice and soup. Accompany your meal with *o-liang*, a very strong, black, iced coffee sweetened with palm-sugar syrup.

$$ ╳ **Soup Restaurant.** Soup isn't the only thing on the menu at this home-style eatery. Slowly cooked meals, which are Singapore's version of comfort food, also have a place. The *Samsui* chicken is a piece of Singapore food history. Female construction workers in early Singapore who hailed from China's Samsui province sent most of their earnings back home and were, thus, known for their frugality. At Chinese New Year, however, they'd hold a feast where they ate boiled chicken that had been marinated in ginger. The shredded ginger would then be prepared as a dip. Like the Samsui women, you can feast on boneless pieces of chicken dipped in ginger sauce and wrapped in lettuce. Equally tempting are the tofu prawns with mild chili gravy and Penang fried noodles. There are several branches within busy shopping areas, such as complexes on Orchard Road, which makes them ideal for a quick bite. ⊠ *25 Smith St., Chinatown* ☎ *6222–9923* ▤ *AE, DC, MC, V* Ⓜ *Tanjong Pagar* ⊠ *#02–01 DFS Scottswalk, 25 Scotts Rd., Orchard* ☎ *6333–8033* Ⓜ *Orchard* ⊠ *#B1–44 Paragon, 290 Orchard Rd., Orchard/Somerset* ☎ *6333–6228* Ⓜ *Orchard* ⊠ *#B1–59 Suntec City Mall, 3 Temasak Blvd., Colonial Singapore* ☎ *6333–9886* Ⓜ *City Hall.*

$–$$ ╳ **Grand Shanghai.** This restaurant, formerly known as Ye Shanghai, tries to recreate the glamour of 1930s Shanghai. Sumptuous decorations and a jazz crooner lend to its mellow mood. The extensive menu includes soups, noodles, seafood (charged by the gram), meats, and dim sum. Some selections, such as smoked eel or crispy Shanghai roast duck, must be ordered at least a day in advance. Request a table away from the speakers if you want to talk. ⊠ *#01–01 Kings Centre, 390 Havelock Rd., Havelock* ☎ *6836–6866* ▤ *AE, DC, V* ◷ *Closed Mon.* Ⓜ *Orchard.*

¢–$ ╳ **Crystal Jade Kitchen.** Order by number from the 150-dish menu/placemat at this authentic Cantonese restaurant. It's short on glamour, but the food's fresh and cooked to order. Munch on the deep-fried bean curd in spice salt, the glutinous rice dumpling, or the braised crispy noodles with seafood. Adventurous types should order the pig's giblet *congee* (rice porridge) or marinated chicken feet. Ask for a table along the footpath for people-watching opportunities down in Holland Village. Tim Sum (dim sum) on Sunday is very popular—be prepared for a line if you arrive after 10 AM. ⊠ *2 & 2a Lorong Mambong, Holland Village* ☎ *6469–0300* ▤ *AE, DC, MC, V* Ⓜ *Orchard.*

¢–$ ╳ **Da Dong.** When its doors opened in 1928, Da Dong was one of Chinatown's first eateries, popular with visiting merchants and officials. Now its location makes it a pleasant place to take a break from the chaos of sightseeing and shopping. Request a table near this converted shophouse's upper-level windows for a lively view of Chinatown's intersections, markets, and pedestrian walkways. The wooden floors, floor-to-ceiling window shutters, and congenial service effectively accompany the flavorful Cantonese food. Try the pork ribs, Peking duck, or steamed fish head. Dim sum service begins at 7 AM on weekends and holidays. Many older Chinatown locals still refer to this restaurant by its original name, Tai Tong. ⊠ *39 Smith St., Chinatown* ☎ *6221–3822* ▤ *AE, DC, V* Ⓜ *Tanjong Pagar.*

AROUND THE CLOCK EATS

ARLY BIRDS CAN BREAKFAST IN LITTLE INDIA, Geylang, and Malay areas, especially around Arab Street. Starbucks, Coffee Bean & Tea Leaf, Delifrance, and McDonald's are scattered throughout major tourist centers and open for breakfast around 8.

Breakfasts vary with respect to Singapore's multicultural population: noodles, dumplings, or chok/congee (rice porridge with shredded meats and veggies) for the Chinese, nasi lemak (coconut rice) with fish and egg, meat curries, or roti (breads) for the Indians. For something closer to a western-style breakfast, try kaya (egg-and-coconut jam) toast with coffee. More-elaborate lunch options include Chinese dim sum, where small dishes are wheeled around on trolleys, and the Indonesian nasi padang, where rice is accompanied by meats and vegetables.

Late-night makan (eating) is a big thing, especially in suburban estate areas, the ethnic quarters of Chinatown, Geylang, and Little India/Serangoon, and the island's quiet backstreets. Geylang's *Boon Tat Street*, next to the 24-hour Lau Pa Sat market off Robinson Road, is packed with outdoor food stalls open nightly. Night owls can also be found at 24-hour **Kopitiam** (coffee shop) outlets on Waterloo Street and Orchard Road (in the Le Meridien Singapore's basement). The Muslim and Indian outdoor restaurant at the corner where "Food Alley" (Murray Street) crosses Maxwell Road (close to the junction with Tanjong Pagar/Neil Road) is good for late-night roti prata (bread with curry), known as roti canai in Malay. The restaurants in the **Clarke Quay and Boat Quay** areas open fairly late. Malay restaurants tend to close early, while more formal Chinese restaurants close almost on the dot at 10 PM; western-style restaurants usually take their last order around 10:30 PM.

Continental

$$$$ ✕ **Morton's of Chicago.** When this Morton's opened in 1998, it was the first of its kind outside the U.S. It has since become an adopted favorite among Singaporean carnivores. The characteristic dark-wood paneling, linen napkins and tablecloths, and subdued lighting are all here. Morton's menu is known for its USDA prime aged beef, flown in from Chicago. Dishes to try include the spicy Cajun rib eye and the signature porterhouse steak. Portions are huge and pricey. If you have room for dessert, dig into a key lime pie or a Godiva hot chocolate cake. ⊠ *Mandarin Oriental, Level 4, 5 Raffles Ave., Marina Square* ☎ *6339–3740* ▭ *AE, DC, MC, V* ☉ *No lunch* Ⓜ *City Hall.*

Eclectic

$$–$$$ ✕ **Club Chinois.** The minimalist interior at this sleek restaurant is accented with splashes of fuschia, lime green, yellow, and turquoise; soft furnishings; and fine European tableware. Like the lighting, the superior service is subtle, but turned on in just the right places. East meets West in such dishes as crispy Beijing duck skin with five-spiced foie gras, and rack of lamb accompanied by chili-mint chutney. For dessert try the warm

Valhrona chocolate mousse. In a word: delicious. ⊠ *#02–18 Orchard Parade Hotel, 1 Tanglin Rd., Orchard* ☎ *6834–0668* ⌂ *Reservations essential* ⊟ *AE, DC, MC, V* Ⓜ *Orchard.*

$$–$$$ ✕ **Doc Cheng's.** Unlike its namesake, a charismatic 1920s physician with
Fodor'sChoice a penchant for alcohol, this first-rate fusion restaurant has few flaws.
★ The eatery is styled in colonial meets European details, and is known for its attentive service and subtle, yet mouthwatering, food. Best bets include the crab cakes with Malay turmeric sauce, the spit-roasted beef tenderloin drizzled with vindaloo jus, and, for dessert, the caramelized macadamia and chocolate crunch bars with Hawaiian berries. Opt for the booths with white curtains for extra privacy. ⊠ *Raffles Hotel Arcade, Level 2, 1 Beach Rd., Colonial Singapore* ☎ *6337–1886* ⊟ *AE, DC, MC, V* ⊘ *No lunch weekends* Ⓜ *City Hall.*

$–$$$ ✕ **mezza9.** Indecisive diners will appreciate this restaurant's many options.
Fodor'sChoice Dishes come from each of mezza9's "kitchens"—deli, sushi and sashimi,
★ Thai, grill, yakitori, Chinese steamboat, patisserie, martini bar, and shop (with upscale provisions)—distributed throughout the dining area. Deep-fried soft-shell crabs, duck with anise seed and fennel spices, chargrilled tuna with niçoise salad, and the m9 signature dish (nine dessert samples on a silver platter) are among the most popular choices. Another option is the nine-course ultimate menu for $99. You can also check out the wine cellar or sit at the martini bar. ⊠ *Grand Hyatt Hotel, Mezzanine, 10 Scotts Rd., Orchard* ☎ *6416–7189* ⊟ *AE, DC, MC, V* Ⓜ *Orchard.*

$–$$ ✕ **Crossroads Café.** Take a break from shopping along crowded Orchard Road at this stylish eatery on the Singapore Marriott's ground floor. If you have shopping bags, the staff can arrange for them to be left with the concierge. Then you can people-watch unencumbered from tables near the windows as you're cooled by large overhead fans. Western breakfasts are served until 1 PM, and both the lunch and dinner menus have such international options as salads, sandwiches, burgers, and Mexican wraps. If you feel like a glass of wine, there are meal and drink pairings; for example, a glass of chardonnay coupled with the grilled ahi tuna with a California roll and mustard aioli. ⊠ *Singapore Marriott, 320 Orchard Rd., Orchard* ☎ *6735–5800* ⊟ *AE, DC, MC, V* Ⓜ *Orchard.*

$ ✕ **Blood Café.** Singaporean foodies are grateful that the owners of trendy
Fodor'sChoice Project Shop Blood Brothers didn't go through with Plan A to trans-
★ form the back of their clothing store into a hair salon. Taste the food, and you'll understand their sentiments. The Blood Caesar salad has been voted the island's best by readers of an expat magazine; equally scrumptious is the homemade bread. Other highlights include the *laksa pesto* (pasta with laksa leaf and sunflower seed pesto, sambal, and fish cakes) and the chicken burger with sesame and Szechuan peppercorn dressing. Finding the place is tricky as there's no café sign; look for the store sign and make a beeline past the register. ⊠ *#02–33/44 Paragon, 290 Orchard Rd., Orchard* ☎ *6735–6765* ⊟ *MC, V* Ⓜ *Orchard/Somerset.*

French

$$$$ ✕ **Au Jardin.** Absorb panoramic views at this former colonial home in the Singapore Botanical Gardens. An outdoor patio terrace and a small eating area make Au Jardin ideal for intimate occasions. The extensive à la carte menu takes a backseat to the prix-fixe options. There's the three-course *table d'hôte* and the awe-inspiring seven-course *dégustation* menu, which includes scallops with pistachio and coriander, Wagyu beef (a Japanese delicacy), and chocolate soufflé with earl grey ice cream. The black-tie waiters provide impeccable service, and there's brunch service on Sunday. ⊠ *EJH Corner House, Singapore Botanical Gardens, 1 Cluny Rd., Tanglin* ☎ *6466–8812* ⌁ *Reservations essential* ▤ *AE, DC, MC, V* ☉ *No lunch* Ⓜ *Orchard.*

$$$$
Fodor'sChoice
★

✕ **Les Amis.** Mingle with Singaporean tycoons and celebrities at the island's finest French restaurant. Chef Gunther Hubrechsen has created sublime à la carte options—standouts are langoustines with Iranian caviar cream, and roasted suckling pig with truffles—as well as three-course business lunch, six-course *table d'hôte,* and vegetarian dinner menus. Admire the adjoining bar's chandelier and curtain-draped wine cabinets before adjourning to the dining area, which has tables surrounded by subtle screens. There's an impressive wine list, as this is Singapore's only restaurant to have won *Wine Spectator's* Grand Award. Enter from the street on Claymore Hill. ⊠ *#02–16 Shaw Centre, 1 Scotts Rd., Orchard* ☎ *6733–2252* ⌁ *Reservations recommended* ▤ *AE, DC, MC, V* Ⓜ *Orchard.*

$$–$$$$

✕ **Amuse Bouche.** The menu at this smart and showy-colored restaurant does indeed "tease the palate." An attentive staff delivers great picks, like the creamy, yet light, mushroom soup served like a cappuccino, veal cheek in Madeira sauce, and Maine lobster tagliarini in aromatic oil. Theatergoers can nosh on post- or preshow tapas at the bar up front. To get here, walk through the underground City Link and up to the ground level Raffles Link; look for a small sign on the left. ⊠ *#01–03 Raffles Link, 1 Raffles Link, Colonial Singapore* ☎ *6338–6881* ▤ *AE, DC, MC, V* Ⓜ *City Hall.*

$$–$$$

✕ **Saint Julien.** The days when boats arrived here to collect fresh water are long gone, as this boathouse has been transformed into a first-class French restaurant captained by chef Julien Bombard. Preparations are, as he describes them, "reminiscent of a bourgeois Paris that no longer exists," and include extravagant entrées. For example, there's the duck with zesty orange sauce and polenta pancake with pine nuts—that's one course. The six-course dinner *menu gourmet* mixes traditional and original dishes. You can arrange to dine in private group or two-person rooms. ⊠ *The Water Boathouse, 3 Fullerton Rd., CBD* ☎ *6225–6897* ⌁ *Reservations essential* ▤ *AE, DC, MC, V* ☉ *Closed Sun.* Ⓜ *Raffles Place.*

$$

✕ **L'Angelus.** Pass the potted plants that line this casual-and-chic eatery's entrance to get to the traditional French food inside. The dining area is simple, the daily specials are scrawled on chalkboards, and French movie posters line the walls from floor to ceiling. Alongside cream sauces and assorted meats are such Gallic specialties as escargot and prawns with garlic and pastis. For dessert try the sticky nougat or lemon sherbet with vodka. ⊠ *85 Club St., Chinatown* ☎ *6225–6897* ▤ *AE, DC, MC, V* ☉ *Closed Sun. No lunch Sat.* Ⓜ *Chinatown.*

Indian

$$–$$$

✕ **Vansh.** If Austin Powers designed an Indian restaurant, he would probably come up with the groovy lounge atmosphere of this waterfront restau-

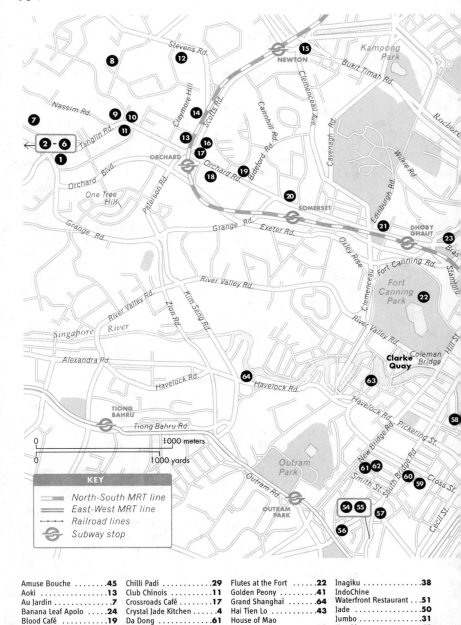

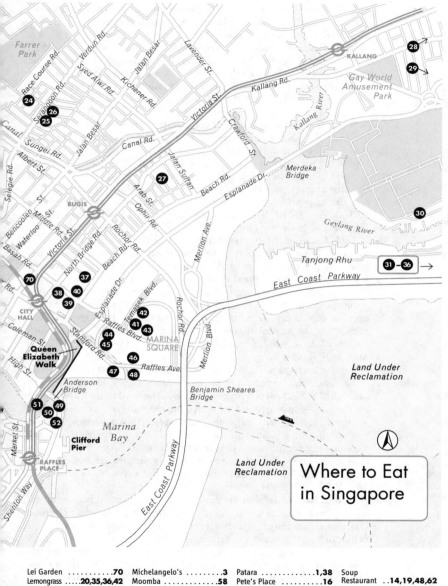

Where to Eat in Singapore

rant. The waiters—who virtually recline on side couches to take orders—and the chefs working in the open stainless-steel kitchen have a serenity that comes from unhyped professionalism. Some of the food is presented in styles borrowed from other cultures; sample the Indian tapas menu, or slightly larger entrées served in Japanese crockery. All the main dishes come with dhal, basmati rice, a daily side dish, and baby naan. Meals start with stylishly rolled *papadam* (deep-fried lentil crackers) and three chutneys. ⊠ #01–04 Singapore Indoor Stadium, 2 Stadium Walk, East Coast/Kallang ☎ 6345–4466 ▭ AE, DC, MC, V Ⓜ Kallang.

$–$$ ✕ **Mango Tree.** For food from Goa and Kerala, on India's southwest coast, head to this beachside restaurant on Singapore's east coast. The most popular tables are in the outdoor area towards the water. Get here before 7 PM to watch the sunset over a pre-dinner drink. The Indian seafood meals—including mint-flavored Lahore fish, *moily jhingdi* (prawns and coconut curry), and the generous Malabar seafood platter—are staggeringly good when paired with mango naan flat bread. ⊠ 1000 East Coast Pkwy., Block 23, East Coast ☎ 6442–8655 ▭ AE, DC, MC, V ⊘ Closed Sun.

$–$$ ✕ **Shahi Maharani.** Maharajas and maharinis are as welcome in this lavish north Indian restaurant as any Joe. Ponderous doors, teak tables, gold-plated chairs, Indian artifacts, and live Nepalese music combine for a regal experience. Food is categorized as mild, spicy, or very spicy, but the cook will honor requests to turn up or tone down the intensity. As it is with Mogul royalty, your wish is the staff's command. Stellar options include any of the biryani or tandoori meals. Fill your wineglass with any of the Australian, French, or Italian labels served here. ⊠ Raffles the Plaza, Level 3, Colonial Singapore ☎ 6235–8840 ▭ AE, DC, MC, V Ⓜ Raffles City.

¢–$ ✕ **Banana Leaf Apolo.** Rub elbows with the locals at this cafeteria-style
Fodor'sChoice   restaurant, which specializes in fish-head curry (the most expensive
★   dish is S$18–S$25, depending on the size). The food is good and downright spicy—you may wind up with tears in your eyes. You'll be given a large piece of banana leaf with steaming rice, two papadam, and two vegetables, with delicious spiced sauces. If it gets too spicy for you, ask for some *curd* (traditional yogurt) or *raita* (yogurt with cucumber) to cool things down. Eating with your hands is encouraged, but cutlery is available. ⊠ 54–58 Race Course Rd., Little India ☎ 6293–8682 ▭ AE, MC, V Ⓜ Little India.

¢–$ ✕ **Madras New Woodlands Restaurant.** With its quiet and no-fuss atmosphere, this restaurant has attracted a dedicated loyal following. The food is vegetarian, mainly Punjabi style. For a full meal, order a *thali*: a large platter of *dosai* (pancakes) with three spiced vegetables, curd, dhal, *rasam* (hot and sour soup), *sambar* (spicy sauce), sweet raita, and papadam. Also tempting is the *paper dosai*, which is a thin, crispy rice flour crepe in an enormous roll; it's served with two spicy coconut sauces and rasam. ⊠ 12–14 Upper Dickson Rd., Little India ☎ 6297–1594 ⚑ Reservations not accepted ▭ No credit cards Ⓜ Little India.

¢–$ ✕ **Samy's Curry.** Among Singapore's best-kept secrets—there's no way
Fodor'sChoice   to stumble on it by chance—is this south Indian restaurant in a private
★   civil-service clubhouse. The airy colonial edifice has wooden-louver

windows and overhead fans, but no air-conditioning. The simple banana-leaf eats, delivered by a parade of shuffling waiters, come with spoonfuls of zesty curries, fragrant rices, breads, and other assorted condiments. Dinner is Samy's strongest meal; arrive before 7 PM, when it starts getting crowded, for the best selection. You'll need to get a S$2 temporary membership to the Singapore Civil Service Club to eat here. ⊠ *Singapore Civil Service Club House, Block 25, Dempsey Rd., Holland Village* ☎ *6472–2080* ⌲ *Reservations not accepted* ⊟ *AE, DC, V* ⊗ *No dinner Thurs.* Ⓜ *Orchard.*

¢ ✕ **Komala Vilas.** Among Little India's oldest and best-known stops is this noisy south Indian eatery. Most meals come with curries, rice, dhal, condiments, Indian breads, or special sauces. Upstairs, which is quieter with slightly larger tables and a more expansive menu, you can order biryiani and daily specials. Be prepared to share tables downstairs when it's busy. There's also a well-stocked Indian sweets counter here. ⊠ *76–78 Serangoon Rd., Little India* ☎ *6293–6980* ⌲ *Reservations not accepted* ⊟ *AE, MC, V* Ⓜ *Little India.*

Italian

\$\$–\$\$\$ ✕ **Da Paolo e Judie.** Escape from chaotic Chinatown to this tranquil and elegantly converted shophouse, serviced by an attentive staff. The palatable *tagliolini alla aragosta* (pasta in light tomato sauce with lobster) is like a mouthful of sunlight. Other highlights include trim-cut lamb with lavender sauce and, for dessert, warm soft-centered chocolate cake with homemade ice cream. You can almost stand your spoon vertically in the espressos. Smokers can take to the terrace. ⊠ *81 Neil Rd., Chinatown* ☎ *6225–8306* ⊟ *AE, DC, MC, V* Ⓜ *Chinatown.*

\$\$–\$\$\$ ✕ **Michelangelo's.** Chef Angelo Sanelli puts his innovative spin on Italian eats—from the bruschetta to the veal—at this enticing restaurant, which has won almost every food and wine award in Singapore, including *Wine Spectator's* "Award of Excellence" for several years in a row and inclusion in several best restaurant lists. A warm and professional staff will serve you generous portions and selections from the expansive wine list. Fresco paintings and fabric-draped ceilings create a cozy atmosphere inside, or you can sit outside and dine by candlelight, with fans to keep you cool. At lunch, the three-course prix-fixe menu is an excellent value. ⊠ *#01–60 Chip Bee Gardens, 44 Jalan Merah Saga, Holland Village* ☎ *6475–9069* ⊟ *AE, DC, MC, V.*

\$\$–\$\$\$ ✕ **Zambuca.** This alluring restaurant's dining room has filtered lighting that trickles over the thousands of bottles laid in wine racks to create walls between seating areas. Oversize vintage posters and a sparkling floor-to-ceiling black quartzite wall reinforce the elegance. The outstanding menu has some very enticing selections, including, for starters, the foie gras with apple compote, peppered fig, and port wine jus, or, as an entrée, the *merluzzo croccante ai gamberetti* (baked black cod and prawns atop green pea mash with prawn sauce and summer salad). ⊠ *Pan Pacific Singapore, Level 3, 7 Raffles Blvd., Marina Square* ☎ *6337–8086* ⌲ *Reservations essential* ⊟ *AE, DC, MC, V* Ⓜ *City Hall.*

♻ \$\$ ✕ **Sistina.** More than 20 pizzas are on the menu at this kid- and parent-friendly restaurant. The home-style Italian menu also has ample pasta, salad, meat, seafood, and dessert options. You can choose from an astounding 2,000-plus wine selection. The kitchen opens early (3 on weekdays and 11:30 on weekends) to accommodate families. ⊠ *#01–58 Chip Bee Gardens, 44 Jalan Merah Saga, Holland Village* ☎ *6476–7782* 🖃 *AE, DC, MC, V* ⊗ *No lunch weekdays* Ⓜ *15-minute walk from the Buona Vista MRT.*

🖑 **$–$$** ✕ **Pete's Place.** Neither the main menu, nor the photos of the international celebrities who've eaten here have changed much in three decades. Famed for its antipasto, pizza, and pasta, Pete's also has an enormous soup-and-salad buffet complete with warm breads and homemade butter. The restaurant's dark, cozy aura plays second fiddle to its food. Families are very welcome here. ⊠ *Grand Hyatt Singapore, Basement, 10 Scotts Rd., Orchard* ☎ *6730–7113* 🖃 *AE, DC, MC, V* Ⓜ *Orchard.*

$–$$ ✕ **Senso.** Should you eat alfresco—flanked by pillars, balconies, and statues—in the stone quadrangle of this converted colonial convent and orphanage, you may feel as if you're in an Italian opera. Nevertheless, the contemporary Italian creations are unquestionably the main acts here. Best bites include the panfried buffalo mozzarella wrapped in Parma ham, olive pesto, and chili mayonnaise, and the *manzo* (beef fillet in rocket and Gorgonzola sauce). Some popular dishes appear consistently, though the menu changes monthly. If you start your evening at the neighboring W Wine Bar, you can arrange for your drinks to be bought to your table. ⊠ *#01–04, 21 Club St., Chinatown* ☎ *6224–0147* 🖃 *AE, DC, MC, V* Ⓜ *Tanjong Pagar.*

Japanese

$$$$ ✕ **Keyaki.** On the roof of the Pan Pacific Hotel is this Japanese restaurant, set within a tranquil Japanese garden—complete with koi pond, stone lanterns, bamboo surrounded by pebbles, and a pavilion. Here you'll be served by kimono-clad waitresses and waiters in *happi* coats. The menu's traditional Japanese fare includes what is perhaps Singapore's best *teppanyaki* (meat and vegetables stir fried at your table). ⊠ *Pan Pacific Singapore, Level 4, 7 Raffles Blvd., Marina Square* ☎ *6442–8265* 🖃 *AE, DC, V* Ⓜ *City Hall.*

$$$–$$$$ ✕ **Inagiku.** Most regulars at this upscale restaurant don't know that it's a branch of the original Inagiku that opened in Japan in 1866 and developed a style of food preparation where food is prepared in front of guests in private Tatami rooms. Rather, they come to feast on some of the island's most authentic Japanese food. Many Japanese expatriates assert that this modern establishment serves Singapore's freshest sashimi platters. Also enticing is the light, crisp tempura; the teppanyaki comes with a heavenly prawn dipping sauce and savory garlic fried rice. À la carte prices can add up very quickly here, so opt for a prix-fixe menu if you're on a tight budget. ⊠ *Swissôtel The Stamford, Level 3, 2 Stamford Rd., Colonial Singapore* ☎ *6431–5305* 🖃 *AE, DC, MC, V* Ⓜ *City Hall.*

$$–$$$$ ✕ **Aoki.** You'll join Japanese Emperor Akihito as one of chef Aoki's customers once you eat at this sleek restaurant. Aoki serves such beautifully presented cuisine as *kaiseki* (a formal banquet), *sukiyaki* (skillet-grilled beef and veggies), *shabu shabu* (hot pot), and sake sherbets. Fish is flown in from Tokyo's prestigious fish market four times a week. There are hinoki wood counters and elegant kimono-clad servers. A pink glass sliding door leads to an adjoining bar. There's no English-language sign outside; look for the fabric-covered doorway opposite the HSBC building on Claymore Hill. ⊠ *#02–17 Shaw Centre, 1 Scotts Rd., Orchard* ☎ *6333–8015* ⊟ *AE, MC, V* ⊗ *Closed last Sun of the month. No lunch Sun.* Ⓜ *Orchard.*

$$–$$$$ ✕ **Nadaman.** Unlike other Japanese restaurants in Singapore, this refined restaurant has a somewhat casual atmosphere due in part to its split-level open dining area. You can order sushi and sashimi, tempura, or kaiseki, and watch the teppanyaki chef perform his culinary calisthenics while you eat. Try one of the prix-fixe *bento* (box) lunches. The service is discretely attentive; note that the staff may try to steer you toward such tourist-friendly eats as tempura or grilled foods rather than more-traditional meals. If you're eating in a group, ask for a private room at the far end of the dining area for the most attentive service. ⊠ *Shangri-La Hotel, 22 Orange Grove Rd., Orchard* ☎ *6737–3644* ⊟ *AE, DC, MC, V* Ⓜ *Orchard.*

Malay & Indonesian

$–$$ ✕ **House of Sundanese Food.** The waiters here will happily give you a lesson in how Sundanese food differs from other Indonesian foods, before trying to persuade you to sample at least one of the regional specialities. At the top of their list is a charcoal dish, preferably the delicious barbecue fish, with several smaller dishes to share. You might start with *keredok* (vegetables in spicy peanut dressing), continue with *taupok goreng isi* (bean-curd-skin rolls stuffed with scallops, prawns, water chestnuts, and mushrooms); and *sedap ikan snapper bakar* (broiled red snapper in sweet sauce). ⊠ *55 Boat Quay, Boat Quay* ☎ *6534–3775* Ⓜ *Raffles Place* ⊠ *#B1–063 Suntec City Mall, Fountain Terrace, 3 Temasek Blvd., Marina Square* ☎ *6334–1012* Ⓜ *City Hall* ⊟ *AE, DC, MC, V.*

$ ✕ **Bumbu.** Coffee chicken, soft-shell crab, curried seafood in a hollow coconut, and olive rice are among the unusual dishes at this homey Arab District shophouse, which serves Indonesian and Peranakan food with a touch of Thai. The salads—particularly the spicy and sour Thai-style pomelo, and the green mango—are great sides. The portions are small, so it's easy to try multiple dishes. Pair your order with a refreshing lemongrass iced drink—you won't regret it. ⊠ *44 Kandahar St., Arab District* ☎ *6392–8628.* ⊟ *AE, DC, MC, V* Ⓜ *Bugis.*

¢–$ ✕ **Rendezvous Restaurant.** Previously, this was a small coffee shop, which doubled as a meeting point for Australian, New Zealand, Irish, and British troops stationed in Singapore. After the troops left the island in the 1950s, the eatery's menu switched from western-style foods to *nasi padang* (rice cooked in banana leaves) from western Sumatra. Order multiple plates of *beef rendang* (beef curry), *sayur lodeh* (vegetable in spicy coconut milk), *sambal sotong* (chili squid), and *sambal brinjal* (spicy eggplant). Servings are small and meant to be shared like tapas. Meat and seafood are charged by the piece. ⊠ *Rendezvous Hotel, Level 2, 9 Bras Basah Rd., Colonial Singapore* ☎ *6339–7508* ⊟ *AE, DC, MC, V* Ⓜ *Doby Ghaut.*

Mediterranean

$–$$$ ✕ **Esmiralda.** Break off a hunk of steaming garlic baguette and tap along with the locals to the Gypsy Kings. This festive Mediterranean eatery is favored for its moussaka, couscous, paella, big salads, and skewered lamb, beef, and seafood. A warning: night patrons may wind up dancing on the floor or on empty tables. A small bar serves bar snacks. ⊠ *Orchard Hotel, 422 Orchard Rd., Orchard* ☎ *6735–3476* ⊟ *AE, DC, MC, V* Ⓜ *Orchard.*

Modern Australian

$$ ✕ **Flutes at the Fort.** Frangipani perfumes the air as you ascend the steps to this former colonial residence in Ft. Canning's gardens. Built in 1908, it was home to Singapore's fire chiefs for most of the 20th century before being transformed into a modern Australian restaurant. Opt for a seat on the balcony where you can admire the garden, which twinkles with subtle fairy lights at night, or admire the exceptional photographs of Singapore. The menu changes regularly, but staples include homemade breads, lobster bisque, lamb with Parmesan crust, and Roma tomato tart. The cheese platter is one of the few in Singapore that includes quince paste. Enter from the Singapore Philatelic Museum's parking lot for the shortest walk. ⊠ *Ft. Canning Park, 21 Lewin Terrace, Ft. Canning* ☎ *6338–8770* ⊟ *AE, DC, MC, V* Ⓜ *Clarke Quay/ Somerset.*

$$ ✕ **Moomba.** Arrive ready to chow on food prepared Down Under style at this eatery, named from an aboriginal word meaning "to come together to have fun." Whet your appetite on squid cakes with spicy Thai mango salad or Middle Eastern–inspired starters. Select from some of Australia's best wines to accompany the barbecued kangaroo, then follow with the devilishly good sticky date pudding. Don't overlook the large traditional Aboriginal dot murals at the front of the restaurant. ⊠ *52A Circular Rd., Boat Quay* ☎ *6438–0141* ⊟ *AE, DC, MC, V* ⊘ *No lunch weekends* Ⓜ *Raffles Place.*

Nonya

¢–$$ ✕ **Blue Ginger.** Come to this nostalgically restored shophouse for reliable Malaysian/Chinese fare, such as *udang goreng tauyu lada* (sautéed prawns with pepper in sweet soy sauce), *ayam panggang Blue Ginger* (grilled boneless chicken grilled in spiced coconut milk), or *ngo heong* (rolls of minced pork and prawns seasoned with five spices). Perhaps only the brave should order the dessert made from the infamous durian, a thorny fruit that smells like old gym socks, but actually tastes like caramel. ⊠ *97 Tanjong Pagar Rd., Tanjong Pagar* ☎ *6222–3928* ⊟ *AE, DC, MC, V* Ⓜ *Tanjong Pagar.*

FodorśChoice ★

¢–$ **Chilli Padi.** Let's cut to the chase: the dishes here are fiery, spicy, and, most importantly, mouthwatering delicious. Most meals are prepared with generous amounts of homemade chili paste and fresh herbs, so be sure to specify exactly how tongue tingling you want your food to be. The Straits Chinese menu is extensive and unabashedly authentic. Try

HAWKER CENTERS

What?
"Hawkers" originally referred to wandering food vendors who advertised their arrival by sounding horns, knocking bamboo sticks, or shouting. Once alerted, people dashed over to place their orders. Several years ago Singapore's strict government hygiene regulations collected hawkers into large centers, where everything is very clean. At these centers you can sample colorful local eats on the cheap.

How?
Feel free to sit anywhere: tables don't belong to particular stalls. Sharing tables is common when it's busy. Vendors will bring your order to you in some centers, while in others you'll have to wait for the food to be prepared. Sometimes drink vendors wander between tables taking orders. Paying when you order is the norm, though in some places you'll pay post-meal. Most dishes cost S$4 or slightly more; for around S$12 you can get a meal, drink, and fresh fruit dessert. Specify your desired portion when you order; most dishes have several sizes priced accordingly. Generally, credit cards aren't accepted at hawker centers.

Where?
Experience the raucous 24-hour **Newton Circus** (⊠ intersection of Newton, Scotts, and Bukit Timah Road Rds. Ⓜ Newton), near Orchard Road, but avoid the seafood stalls, which are notorious for fleecing tourists. Instead, opt for stalls that have prominently displayed prices and offer traditional one-dish meals. The financial district's historic **Lau Pa Sat Festival Market** (⊠ 18 Raffles Quay Ⓜ Raffles Place) is an outdoor center. There's also the **Maxwell Road Hawker Centre** (⊠ intersection of Maxwell and South Bridge Rds.), near Tanjong Pagar. In an effort to revive the old tradition, roads like Chinatown's Smith Street close at 7 nightly so that modern-day nomadic hawkers can roam the area.

Major shopping centers have "food courts," which are indoor, air-conditioned, and slightly pricier hawker centers. In the Orchard Road area you can visit Picnic, in Scotts Centre's basement, or the Food Chain, in the basement of the Orchard Emerald, which faces the Meritus Mandarin Singapore hotel. The food court in Tanglin Mall's basement has a baby grand piano.

Typical Hawker Foods
char kway teow: flat rice noodles fried with chili paste, fish cakes, and bean sprouts.
chicken rice: chicken served with rice cooked in chicken stock. Often voted Singapore's favorite local dish, it's also called Hainanese chicken rice.
Hokkien prawn mee: wheat noodles in prawn-and-pork broth.
laksa: rice noodles in coconut gravy served with a garnish of steamed prawns, rice cakes, and bean sprouts.
rojak: a Malay word for "salad." Chinese rojak consists of cucumber, lettuce, pineapple, bangkwang (jicama), and deep-fried bean curd—tossed with dressing made from salty shrimp paste, ground toasted peanuts, sugar, and rice vinegar. Indian rojak consists of deep-fried lentil and prawn patties, boiled potatoes, and bean curd, all served with a spicy dip.
roti prata: an Indian breakfast pancake served with curry sauce or sugar.
satay: small strips of meat marinated in fresh spices and threaded onto short skewers.
thosai: an Indian rice-flour pancake that's popular for breakfast and eaten with curry powder or brown sugar.

the *kepetin bak wan* (minced crab and pork soup), assam fish head (fish head in spicy gravy), chicken curry, and the *ayam sio* (chicken with coriander). Seafood lovers can try the *udang mesak nanas* (prawns cooked with tamarind and pineapple), and squid with sambal. Save room for dessert for the cooling taste of sago pudding with palm sugar. ✉ #01-03, 11 Joo Chiat Place, East Coast ☎ 6275 1002 🖃 AE, MC, V Ⓜ Bedok.

Pan-Asian

\$\$–\$\$\$\$ ✕ **Equinox.** You can see Malaysia *and* Indonesia from this 70th-floor restaurant. The service is reserved and the elegant freestanding carved screens create intimacy without sacrificing light. Diners seeking a calm evening can select from either the western or the Asian menu. Start off with the Iranian caviar or the sesame-crusted tuna before moving on to such signature dishes as cod marinated in *yuzu* (a sour Japanese fruit) or grilled beef with foie gras. For dessert, the chocolate fantasy sampler and the Asian crème brûlée are certainly indulgent. ✉ *Swissôtel The Stamford, Level 70, 2 Stamford Rd., Colonial Singapore* ☎ *6431–5669* ⌕ *Reservations essential* 🖃 *AE, DC, MC, V* Ⓜ *City Hall.*

★ **\$\$–\$\$\$** ✕ **IndoChine Waterfront Restaurant.** Rare Shan and Thai Buddha statues and a stunning view of the Singapore River, accompany the amazing Cambodian, Vietnamese, and Laotian food. Owner Michael Ma is so intent on creating authentic cuisine that he regularly flies his aunt from Laos to work with the kitchen staff. The lemongrass, chili, mint, and curry flavors are subtle, though the beef ragout is far spicier than its French ancestor. Arrive by 7 to enjoy the sunset over the river. ✉ *Asian Civilisations Museum, 1 Empress Pl., CBD* ☎ *6339–1720* ⌕ *Reservations essential* 🖃 *AE, DC, MC, V* ☉ *No lunch weekends* Ⓜ *City Hall.*

\$\$ ✕ **Nude.** Sashay over a transparent catwalk, above illuminated running
Fodor's Choice water, toward a 20-meter-long aquarium. Welcome to Nude, a chic
★ eatery favored by visiting rock stars and local celebrities. All of the ingredients are prepared free of any preserved, stored, or artificial additives. Try the *tuna tataki* (marinated tuna with Japanese seasoning, wasabi dressing, and salmon roe), duck breast with shiitake mushroom and duck liver sauce, or light lemongrass seafood pasta. If you bring friends and want to be noticed, request the elevated—and internally lit—central table. In lieu of standard washbasins the bathrooms have spectacular aquariums. It looks as though tap water will fall into the tanks, but a sloped, thin glass plate forces it to drizzle down the back wall outside the tanks. ✉ *#01–18 Wisma Atria, 435 Orchard Rd., Orchard* ☎ *6333–5003* ⌕ *Reservations recommended* 🖃 *AE, DC, MC, V* Ⓜ *Orchard.*

Seafood

\$\$–\$\$\$\$ ✕ **Pierside Kitchen and Bar.** Overlooking the point where the Singapore River meets the Straits of Malacca is this crisp waterfront restaurant with whitewashed interiors and floor-to-ceiling glass doors. The à la carte menu has pasta and other non-seafood options, but the seafood dishes are far superior. Try the zesty cumin-spiced crab cakes or oysters with

DINING WITH CHILDREN

ALL HAWKER CENTERS, *food courts, and snack bars are used to serving young children and will usually accommodate their special requests. Chicken rice, fluffy steamed pork buns (a dim sum dish), and fresh fruit juices are ever popular with Singaporean kids. Many food courts have western-style stalls that serve eats like deep-fried breaded chicken and chunky fries.*

On virtually every block in the shopping areas you'll spot familiar fast-food chains: **McDonald's, Burger King, KFC, Pizza Hut.** *Some items have slightly spicier sauces, but the menus are fundamentally unchanged. You'll also see* **Subway, Starbucks, Coffee Bean & Tea Leaf,** *and the local* **Delifrance** *chain, which serves light meals. Snacks such as banana fritters are available from roadside stalls.*

There are also several family restaurants on the island. **Jumbo** *or any of the eateries at the* **UDMC Seafood Centre** *are good bets. The grassy areas, beach, and adjoining East Coast Parkway are perfect for energetic children either before or during the meal.* **Brewerkz,** *opposite Clarke Quay, has kid-size menu options. A step up is* **Sistina** *in Holland Village, which has a kid-friendly staff and tasty pizzas. Additionally, parents may find some relief in the reasonably priced wine list.*

chili-lime granita. Fish-and-chips are popular at lunch. A variety of Australian wines and beers is also available. ⊠ *#01–01 One Fullerton, 1 Fullerton Rd., CBD* ☎ *6238–0400* ⊟ *AE, DC, MC, V* Ⓜ *Raffles Place.*

$$–$$$$ ✕ **Tung Lok Seafood Gallery.** A step above the island's more roughhewn seafood centers is this smart East Coast restaurant. The daily catch is imported: you'll find Maine Atlantic lobster, Alaskan king crab, and Australian barramundi among the pickings. The iridescent green dipping sauce that accompanies the wasabi and mango prawns can be a shock initially, but the combination eventually melts in your mouth. The pepper crabs come with whole fresh peppercorns. Walk your meal off along the boardwalk afterwards. ⊠ *East Coast Recreation Centre, Block B, 1000 East Coast Pkwy., East Coast* ☎ *6246–0555* ⊟ *AE, MC, V* Ⓜ *Eunos.*

★ ♻ $ ✕ **Jumbo.** What Jumbo lacks in polish, it makes up for in food quality, and competitive prices. This restaurant has some of the East Coast's best seafood, which includes crab—over 2,000 kilograms of Sri Lankan crab is served weekly—either in rich chili gravy or black-pepper seasoning, deep-fried whole fish in Nonya sauce, or inventive scallops in yam rings. Arrive before 7 to watch the sunset. The outdoor seating area is family friendly, and children can play on the adjoining grassy areas or walk down to the beach. ✉ *#01–07/08 East Coast Seafood Centre, Block 1206, East Coast* ☎ *6342–3435* ⊟ *AE, MC, V* Ⓜ *Kallang.*

🐾 ¢–$$ ✗ **UDMC Seafood Centre.** You *must* visit this East Coast Parkway venue to comprehend the Singaporean dining experience, and to savor the island's cheapest seafood prices. Peruse the open-front restaurants before you decide on a place. Bring insect repellant if you plan to sit outside. Dishes are prepared using various Asian styles. Each eatery has its own speciality, but all serve local beers, and have a seafood base. Restaurants include **Chin Wah Heng** (☎ 6444–7967), **Gold Coast Seafood** (☎ 6448–2020), **Golden Lagoon Seafood** (☎ 6448–1894), **Jumbo Seafood** (☎ 6442–3435), **Lucky View Seafood Restaurant** (☎ 6242–1011), and **Red House Seafood Restaurant** (☎ 6442–3112). ✉ *East Coast Pkwy., East Coast* ⌲ *Reservations not accepted* ⊟ *AE, DC, MC, V* ☉ *No lunch* Ⓜ *Tanah Merah.*

Thai

$$ ✗ **Thanying.** Some of the most royally good Thai food in Singapore is
Fodor'sChoice served here. Feast on *gai kor bai toey* (marinated chicken in pandanus
★ leaves), an exquisite Thai salad like *yam sam oh* (shredded pomelo tossed with chicken and prawns in lime sauce), or *pla khao sam rod* (grouper deep-fried until it's so crispy you can eat the bones). Make sure you leave room for the dessert buffet with its 15 varieties of sweets. ✉ *Amara Hotel, Level 2, 165 Tanjong Pagar Rd., Tanjong Pagar* ☎ *6222–4688* ⊟ *AE, DC, MC, V* Ⓜ *Tanjong Pagar.*

$ ✗ **Naam.** Tempted by Thai, but can't decide what to order? The Naam sampler set includes seafood *tom yam* (hot and sour soup), mango salad, fried prawn cakes, green curry chicken, garlic-pepper king prawns, fried rice, and a dessert platter. Alternatively, try the curry dishes, the *tah hu pad phrik* (fried tofu in spicy sauce), or the *plamak yang* (barbecue cuttlefish). Most dishes are prepared with homemade spice pastes and a minimum of oil and coconut milk. Let the kitchen know if you're sensitive to spicey foods. ✉ *#02–22 Plaza Singapura, 68 Orchard Rd., Orchard* ☎ *6339–9803* ⊟ *AE, MC, V* Ⓜ *Dhoby Ghaut.*

$ ✗ **Patara.** Sample specialties like green curry, pineapple rice, or deep-fried pomfret (a small, white fish) with tamarind sauce at friendly and serene Patara. This popular Thai restaurant is famed for its garlic-and-pepper spareribs and fish cakes with cucumber dip. There are also lots of vegetarian dishes on the menu. Ask the staff about seasonal specials. ✉ *#03–14 Tanglin Mall, 163 Tanglin Rd., Orchard* ☎ *6737–0818* ⊟ *AE, DC, MC, V* Ⓜ *10-minute walk from the Orchard MRT* ✉ *Swissôtel The Stamford, Level 3, Colonial* ☎ *6339–1488* Ⓜ *Orchard.*

¢–$ ✗ **Lemongrass.** Ask to sit in the elevated wooden pavilion at the front of this modest restaurant. Here you'll be surrounded by wooden pillars and Thai silk furnishings, the perfect environment to choose from an extensive menu of over 60 dishes. Chicken with basil, soft-shell crab with garlic, prawn patties, and dry green curries are among the eatery's perennial Thai favorites. Vegetarian dishes are also available; no pork or lard is used in any of the meals. The chef can prepare meals according to your tolerance for spice, be it mild or fiery. ✉ *#05–02 The Heeren, 260 Orchard Rd., Orchard* ☎ *6736–1998* ⊟ *AE, MC, V* Ⓜ *Somer-*

set ✉ #03–03 *The Village Centre, 3 South Buona Vista Rd., East Coast* ☎ 6873–2112 Ⓜ *Harbourfront* ✉ *899 Upper East Coast Rd., East Coast* ☎ 6443–1995 Ⓜ *Bedok* ✉ #01–41 *NTUC Lifestyle World-Downtown East, 1 Pasir Ris Close* ☎ 6583–2112 Ⓜ *Pasir Ris.*

Vegetarian

$$ ✕ **Original Sin.** Singapore's first western-style vegetarian restaurant attracts plenty of non-vegetarians for its hearty Greek, Italian, Spanish, and Mediterranean eats. Start by sharing the mezza plate (a platter of Middle-Eastern eats), before moving on to the piquant Lentil Tower (layers of char-grilled eggplant, roasted capsicum, cherry tomatoes, mesclun, and Haloumi cheese drizzled with mint vinaigrette), ricotta spinach cakes, or sundry pastas and pizzas. Some dishes are prepared free of any animal products, making them ideal for vegans. An expansive wine list complements the colorful menu. ✉ #01–62 *Chip Bee Gardens, Block 43, 43 Jalan Merah Saga, Orchard* ☎ 6475–5605 ▭ *AE, DC, MC, V.*

WHERE TO STAY

3

Updated by
Tracey Furniss

OVER THE YEARS SINGAPORE HAS BEEN TRANSFORMED from a popular vacation destination to a conventioneers' mecca teeming with tour groups and delegates. Singapore's lodging has visibly changed to accommodate this clientele: extensive refurbishment and growth with more varied services has been the trend. Luxury still abounds, and there are still places where exceptional personal service hasn't fallen by the wayside. Indeed, in 2004 Singapore was one of only three cities (along with Chicago and Bangkok) to have three of its hotels ranked in *Travel & Leisure's* annual "100 World's Best Hotels" poll. The hotels making the cut were the Four Seasons, Raffles, and the Ritz-Carlton Millenia.

Prices rival those in New York or London—a superior double room in a deluxe hotel can run more than S$400 a night; one with a private bath in a modest hotel, about S$150 a night. During conventions and the peak months of June through September and December, rooms are scarce, and prices rise. Still, there are enough discounts and deals that no thrifty visitor should ever have to pay the published price (if you use a travel agent, make sure that he or she asks for a discount). There are also budget hotels with rates less than S$95 a night. The Geylang area east of City Hall has many low-cost hotels with rooms between S$49 and S$100 a night. And if all you're looking for is a bunk, walk along Bencoolen Street, where there are dormitory-style guest houses that charge no more than S$25 a night, although they seem to be on the way out. (For more information on affordable lodgings, contact the Singapore Tourism Board, or STB [*see* Visitor Information *in* Smart Travel Tips A to Z]for its annually updated brochure "Budget Hotels.")

Booking ahead—particularly for stays in June through September and December—will probably save you money and will definitely save you headaches. If, however, you gamble and arrive without reservations, the Singapore Hotel Association has two counters at Changi Airport that are staffed by people who can set you up with a room—often at a discount—with no booking fee.

Establishments in the $$$–$$$$ range offer such amenities as international direct dial (IDD) phones with bathroom extensions, TVs with international cable, room service, minibars, data ports for modems, no-smoking rooms or floors, in-room safes, and business and fitness centers loaded with the latest equipment. Several hotels have wireless Internet in common areas or in some executive rooms and suites. These hotels have facilities for travelers with mobility problems; however, some smaller budget hotels do not, so ask before you book. Some properties, particularly those in converted shophouses, have a few rooms that lack windows, so be sure to ask for one that has windows. All rooms have air-conditioning and private baths unless otherwise stated.

Singapore City

Singapore's hotels have developed in clusters. The best-known grouping is at the intersection of Orchard and Scotts roads. In Raffles City the megalithic Westins—the Plaza and the Stamford—stare down at the

Raffles, the grande dame of the city's hotels, and the InterContinental's black-and-white marble gleams alongside turn-of-the-century shophouses. At the south end of the Shenton Way commercial district are a group of business-oriented hotels; to the south of the Singapore River is another cluster, one with boutique hotels as well as the Raffles-owned Merchant Court. Marina Square—a minicity created by a reclamation project that pushed back the seafront to make way for the Suntec City convention complex, more than 200 shops, and many restaurants—is near a half dozen hotels.

If you like shopping and nightlife, then the Orchard and Scotts roads area is for you. If you're attending a convention or simply want an urban landscape with open spaces and river views, Marina Square is the logical choice. If you're doing business in the financial district, a hotel close to Shenton Way is ideal; if your business plans include a trip to the industrial city of Jurong, then a hotel on the Singapore River is best. Regardless of where you stay, it's easy to get around this compact city. Taxis and public transportation, especially the subway, make it possible to travel between areas swiftly, and no hotel is more than a 30-minute cab ride from Changi Airport.

★ **$$$$** ▦ **Four Seasons Hotel Singapore.** The luxuries at this quiet, refined hotel are intended to outshine the city's older, more renowned digs. Rooms are spacious, with sumptuous fabrics, Asian art, and large bathrooms. The Cantonese restaurant, Jiang-Nam Chun, prepares exotic fare and has a stunning interior, which blends art deco and art nouveau styles. Some of the tennis courts are air-conditioned, and there's a golf simulator and in-room exercise equipment. Parents can request a childproof guest room, along with a complimentary stroller or baby carrier; board and video games are available for older kids. The hotel is linked to Orchard Road via an elevated passageway to the Hilton. ✉ *190 Orchard Blvd., Orchard, 248646* ☎ *6734–1110* 🖷 *6733–0682* ⊕ *www. fourseasons.com* ⇌ *254 rooms, 41 suites* ♨ *3 restaurants, room service, in-room data ports, in-room fax, in-room safes, minibars, cable TV with movies and video games, in-room VCRs, golf privileges, 4 tennis courts, 2 pools, health club, spa, billiards, bar, library, shops, babysitting, dry cleaning, laundry service, concierge, Internet, business services, convention center, travel services, free parking, no-smoking rooms* ▤ *AE, DC, MC, V* ⦶ *EP* Ⓜ *Orchard.*

$$$$ ▦ **Goodwood Park.** What began in 1900 as a club for German expatriates is now a national monument, which has hosted the likes of the Duke of Windsor, Edward Heath, Nöel Coward, and the great Anna Pavlova, who performed here. The Parklane Suites, each with a bedroom and a living-dining room, can be rented for less than a double room in the main hotel; it's a short walk to the main hotel lobby. The elegant poolside suites have French windows opening directly to the Balinese-style pool. Service is extremely efficient down to the smallest detail, from the nightly bed turn down to the flashlight in the vanity drawer. Restaurants—which are popular with local diners—include the Gordon Grill and Min Jiang. ✉ *22 Scotts Rd., Orchard, 228221* ☎ *6737–7411, 800/772–3890 for reservations in the U.S.* 🖷 *6738–4579*

Facilities

All hotels listed have room TVs, private baths, and air-conditioning unless otherwise noted. Singapore's hotels are generally opulent, with a wide range of high-quality facilities both inside and outside the rooms.

Assume that hotels operate on the European Plan (EP, with no meals) unless we specify that they use the Continental Plan (CP, with a Continental breakfast), Breakfast Plan (BP, with a full breakfast), Modified American Plan (MAP, with breakfast and dinner), or the Full American Plan (FAP, with all meals).

3

Many hotels are social centers for ordinary Singaporeans and aren't mere tourist islands removed from local reality. The emphasis is on service from the staff, so you won't always find as many "do it yourself" features (e.g., tea-making equipment, irons and ironing boards, etc.) in your room as you might in a country like Australia for example.

Reservations

Notwithstanding its seemingly incalculable number of hotel rooms, Singapore can be short on rooms due to its frequent conventions. During the peak convention times between February and April, September and October, as well as the peak tourism season between June and September (when the weather is less humid) hotel rooms are difficult to come by. Book well in advance if you plan to visit the island at these times.

Prices

There are always great deals on-line if you book ahead; you shouldn't ever have to pay the published rate. Hotel Web sites often have special packages, which can include breakfast, spa specials, restaurant discounts, and more. Weekends are typically more expensive than weekdays during off-peak seasons. Most hotels offer free parking.

We always list the facilities that are available, but we don't specify whether they cost extra. When pricing accommodations, always ask what's included and what costs extra.

	WHAT IT COSTS in Singapore dollars				
	$$$$	**$$$**	**$$**	**$**	**¢**
FOR 2 PEOPLE	over 475	325–475	200–325	100–200	under 100

Prices are for a standard double room.

⊕ *www.goodwoodparkhotel.com.sg* 📲 *171 rooms, 64 suites* 🍴 *5 restaurants, coffee shop, room service, in-room data ports, in-room safes, minibars, cable TV with movies, tennis court, 3 pools, health club, hair salon, spa, baby-sitting, dry cleaning, laundry service, concierge, Internet, business services, convention center, travel services, free parking, no-smoking rooms* ▤ *AE, DC, MC, V* 🍽 *BP* Ⓜ *Orchard.*

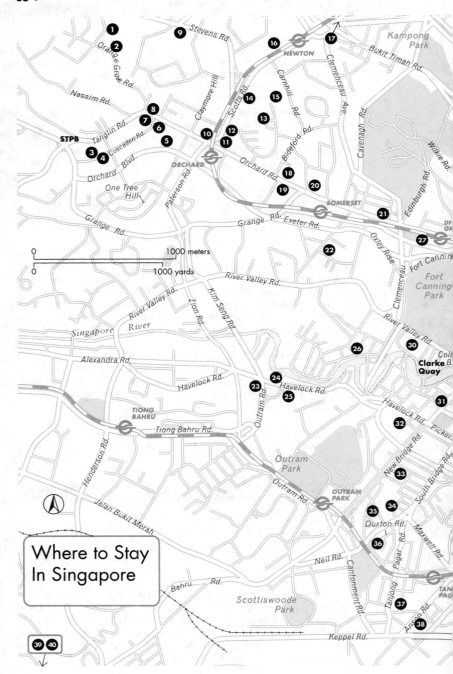

Where to Stay
In Singapore

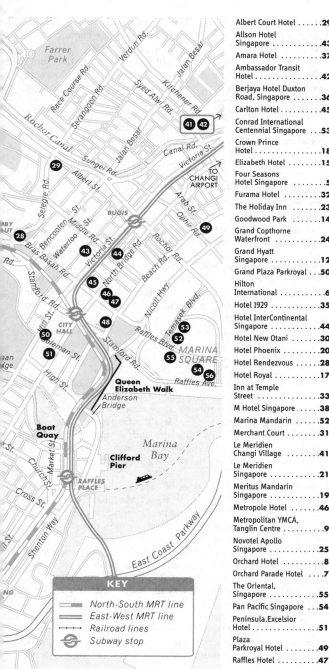

$$$$ 🏨 **Grand Hyatt Singapore.** The recently renovated Grand Wing consists of one-, two-, and three-room apartments with two-line phones, extra bathrooms, work areas, and private mailboxes; the Grand Club executive floor has relocated to the tranquility of the 21st floor with breathtaking skyline views. The smallish standard rooms are painted in soft hues against dark carpeting. The deluxe rooms in the Terrace Wing have glass enclosed alcoves with views. The hotel has convenient amenities for travelers with disabilities. The gardens on the fourth- and fifth-floor terraces have cascading water falls and Asian landscaping. Dine at Pete's Place for excellent pasta dishes, mezza9 for authentic Asian, or stop at Scotts Lounge for afternoon tea. ⊠ *10–12 Scotts Rd., Orchard, 228211* ☎ *6738–1234* 🖷 *6732–1696* ⊕ *http://singapore.grand.hyatt.com* 📤 *266 rooms, 427 apartments* ♨ *4 restaurants, coffee shop, room service, in-room data ports, in-room fax, in-room safes, minibars, cable TV with movies, 2 tennis courts, pool, health club, hair salon, spa, badminton, squash, bar, nightclub, baby-sitting, dry cleaning, laundry service, concierge, Internet, business services, convention center, travel services, free parking, no-smoking rooms* ▤ *AE, DC, MC, V* ℺ *EP* Ⓜ *Orchard.*

$$$$ 🏨 **Hotel InterContinental Singapore.** With its Chinese paintings, wooden paneling, British colonial furnishings, elegant chandeliers, and little foyers, this Bugis Junction hotel exudes old Singapore. Nevertheless, all the latest amenities are here, including on-call "cyber-relations" officers to assist with your computer needs. The Shophouse rooms are in a Peranakan style (a distinctive Malay-Chinese-European mix) and each is different from the next; they cost more than other rooms, but have the same amenities. Standard guest rooms have classical, clean European lines. There's a "kids eat free" policy for children under six in the Olive Tree restaurant. ⊠ *80 Middle Rd., Bugis, 188966* ☎ *6338–7600* 🖷 *6338–7366* ⊕ *www.intercontinental.com* 📤 *350 rooms, 56 suites* ♨ *3 restaurants, coffee shop, room service, in-room data ports, in-room fax, in-room safes, minibars, cable TV with movies, golf privileges, pool, health club, hair salon, bar, shops, baby-sitting, dry cleaning, laundry service, concierge, Internet, business services, convention center, travel services, free parking, no-smoking rooms* ▤ *AE, DC, MC, V* ℺ *EP* Ⓜ *Bugis.*

$$$$ 🏨 **Raffles Hotel.** Opened by the Sarkies brothers in 1887 and visited by **Fodor'sChoice** such writers as Rudyard Kipling and Somerset Maugham, Raffles was ★ the belle of the East during its heyday in the '20s and '30s and was declared a national monument in 1987. True to form in this planned republic, millions of dollars were spent replacing Singapore's old noble appeal with a sanitized version of colonial ambience. The new Raffles is a glistening showpiece, especially from the outside; inside, antique furniture blends with modern conveniences. The lobby is divided into two areas: one exclusively for in-house guests and the other for the constant flow of curious tourists. Suites have high ceilings, overhead fans, and '20s-style furnishings. ⊠ *1 Beach Rd., Colonial Singapore, 189673* ☎ *6337–1886* 🖷 *6339–7650* ⊕ *www.raffleshotel.com* 📤 *103 suites* ♨ *6 restaurants, 2 cafés, patisserie, room service, in-room data ports, in-room fax, in-room safes, minibars, cable TV with movies, pool,*

LODGING ALTERNATIVES

Apartment Rentals

If you want a home base that's roomy enough for a family and comes with cooking facilities, consider a furnished rental. These can save you money, especially if you're traveling with a group. Short-lease (usually a month minimum) serviced apartments are an attractive option. The centrally located ones, however, can be luxurious and more expensive.

International Agents Hideaways International ⊠ 767 Islington St., Portsmouth, NH 03801 ☎ 603/430–4433 or 800/843–4433 ⊟ 603/430–4444 ⊕ www.hideaways.com, annual membership $145.

Local Agents The Ascott ⊠ 6 Scotts Rd. ☎ 6735–6868. **City Developments** (for Le Grove Apartments in Orange Grove Rd., and others) ☎ 6221–2266. **Far East Organization** ☎ 6235–2411. **Midpoint Properties** (for the Great World Serviced Apartments in Kim Seng Rd., off River Valley Rd., and others) ☎ 6736–0100. **Pidemco Land** (for The Orchard apartments on Orchard Rd., and others) ☎ 6820–2188, 6735–0500. Somewhat more affordable, closer to S$3,000 a month, are the **Metropolitan YMCA Apartments** ⊠ 58 Stevens Rd. ☎ 6737–7755, 6731–0730, and **Newton Service Apartments** ⊠ #04–02, 9 Surrey Rd. ☎ 6254–2818.

Hostels

You can save on lodging costs by staying at hostels. There are YMCAs (International House and the Metropolitan) as well as some new hostels. The **Summer Tavern** (⊠ 31 Carpenter St., Clarke Quay ☎ 6535–6601 ⊕ www.summertaven. com), a converted shophouse in the heart of the city, serves breakfast. It costs S$22 for the dorms and S$60 for a double room. **Betel Box Hostel** (⊠ 200 Joo Chiat Rd., Geylang Serai ☎ 6247–7340

⊕ www.betelbox.com) is in the Katong and Geylang Seria district near the Paya Lebar subway. Beds are S$18 a night and the facilities are clean with Internet access and lockers. It's easy to find out about the Singapore hostel and backpacker scene online.

Hostelling International (HI), the umbrella group for a number of national youth-hostel associations around the world, offers single-sex, dorm-style beds and, at many hostels, rooms for couples and family accommodations. Membership, open to travelers of all ages, allows you to stay in HI-affiliated hostels at member rates; one-year membership is about $28 for adults (C$35 for a two-year minimum membership in Canada, @15 in the U.K., A$52 in Australia, and NZ$40 in New Zealand); hostels charge about $10–$30 per night. Members have priority if the hostel is full; they're also eligible for discounts around the world, even on rail and bus travel in some countries.

Hostelling International HI–USA ⊠ 8401 Colesville Rd., Suite 600, Silver Spring, MD 20910 ☎ 301/495–1240 ⊟ 301/495–6697 ⊕ www.hiusa.org. **HI–Canada** ⊠ 205 Catherine St., Suite 400, Ottawa, Ontario K2P 1C3 ☎ 613/237–7884 or 800/663–5777 ⊟ 613/237–7868 ⊕ www.hihostels.ca. **YHA England and Wales** ⊠ Trevelyan House, Dimple Rd., Matlock, Derbyshire DE4 3YH, U.K. ☎ 0870/870–8808, 0870/770–8868, 0162/959–2600 ⊟ 0870/770–6127 ⊕ www.yha.org.uk. **YHA Australia** ⊠ 422 Kent St., Sydney, NSW 2001 ☎ 02/9261–1111 ⊟ 02/9261–1969 ⊕ www.yha.com.au. **YHA New Zealand** ⊠ Level 1, Moorhouse City, 166 Moorhouse Ave., Box 436, Christchurch ☎ 03/379–9970 or 0800/278–299 ⊟ 03/365–4476 ⊕ www.yha.org.nz.

health club, hair salon, spa, billiards, 3 bars, shops, baby-sitting, dry cleaning, laundry service, concierge, Internet, business services, convention center, travel services, free parking, no-smoking rooms ☰ *AE, DC, MC, V* ⍜ *EP* Ⓜ *City Hall.*

$$$$ ⊞ **The Ritz-Carlton, Millenia Singapore.** The most dramatic of the luxury

FodorsChoice hotels in Marina Bay has 32 floors of unobstructed harbor and city views,

★ as well as sculptures by Frank Stella and limited-edition prints by David Hockney and Henry Moore. All rooms are unusually large with sofas, bathrooms whose tubs have pillows, and have large octagonal windows. Ritz-Carlton Club is on the 32nd floor with personalized concierge service. The three restaurants are Snappers for seafood, the Summer Pavilion for Cantonese cuisine, and the Asian- and European-accented Greenhouse. There's live jazz in the lobby lounge every evening. ✉ *7 Raffles Ave., Marina Square, 039799* ☎ *6337–8888* 🖷 *6338–0001* ⊕ *www.ritzcarlton.com* ⤶ *609 rooms, 80 suites* ⅋ *3 restaurants, coffee shop, room service, in-room data ports, in-room fax, in-room safes, minibars, cable TV with movies, tennis court, pool, health club, hair salon, spa, bar, lounge, shop, baby-sitting, dry cleaning, laundry service, concierge, Internet, business services, convention center, travel services, free parking, no-smoking rooms* ☰ *AE, DC, MC, V* ⍜ *EP* Ⓜ *City Hall.*

$$$$ ⊞ **Sheraton Towers.** Just a quick walk from Orchard Road is this relaxed hotel. The pastel guest rooms are homey, include deluxe conveniences such as daily newspapers and data ports, and have small sitting areas with a sofa and easy chairs. The six Cabana Rooms on the fifth floor have balconies. The best vantage point for the Sheraton's dramatic cascading waterfall (the rocks are fiberglass) is from the Dining Room restaurant or the lobby lounge where a pianist plays in the afternoon and a live band performs in the evening. Other restaurants are Domvs, for Italian, and Li Bai for refined Cantonese. The hawker stalls at Newton Circus are within walking distance. ✉ *39 Scotts Rd., Orchard, 228230* ☎ *6737–6888* 🖷 *6733–4366* ⊕ *www.starwoodhotels.com* ⤶ *606 rooms* ⅋ *3 restaurants, coffee shop, room service, in-room data ports, in-room safes, minibar, cable TV with movies, pool, health club, hair salon, spa, lounge, dance club, shop, baby-sitting, dry cleaning, laundry service, concierge, Internet, business services, convention center, travel services, free parking, no-smoking rooms* ☰ *AE, DC, MC, V* ⍜ *EP* Ⓜ *Newton.*

$$$–$$$$ ⊞ **The Oriental, Singapore.** Inside this pyramid-shape Marina Square hotel,

FodorsChoice the level of service is second to none. Subdued, modern elegance and

★ personal attention are the hallmarks here. Rooms are understated, with soft hues of peach and green, handwoven carpets, and paintings of old Singapore. Of special note are the Italian-marble-tile bathrooms with phones, radio, and TV speakers. One-bedroom suites have lovely sitting rooms and separate washrooms. Café des Artistes has international fare with a daily buffet, and the Gallery Lounge has a panoramic city view and vivid works by local artists adorning the walls. ✉ *5 Raffles Blvd., Marina Square, 039797* ☎ *6338–0066* 🖷 *6339–9537* ⊕ *www. mandarinoriental.com* ⤶ *463 rooms, 60 suites* ⅋ *3 restaurants, coffee shop, room service, in-room data ports, in-room fax, in-room safes, minibars, cable TV, golf privileges, 2 tennis courts, pool, health club,*

LODGING WITH CHILDREN

MOST HOTELS IN SINGAPORE allow children under a certain age to stay in their parents' room at no extra charge, but others count them as extra adults; be sure to **find out the cutoff age for children's discounts.** Some hotels allow children under a certain age to eat for free or at a discounted price. For example, there's a "kids eat free" policy at the restaurants in the **Hotel InterContinental Singapore** (✉ 80 Middle Rd., Bugis ☎ 6338–7600 ⊕ www.intercontinental.com).

The **Four Seasons** (✉ 190 Orchard Blvd, Orchard ☎ 6734–1110 ⊕ www.fourseasons.com) offers video and board games and complimentary strollers and baby carriers. The **Conrad International Centennial** (✉ 2 Temasek Blvd, Marina Square ☎ 6334–8888 ⊕ www.conradhotels.com) has a fun playhouse for young children during Sunday brunch. The **Orchard Parade Hotel** (✉ 1 Tanglin Rd., Orchard ☎ 6737–1133 ⊕ www.orchardparade.com.sg) has Singapore's best rooms for traveling families, especially those with young children.

massage, sauna, bar, shop, baby-sitting, dry cleaning, laundry service, concierge, Internet, business services, meeting rooms, travel services, free parking, no-smoking rooms ⊟ AE, DC, MC, V ¶Ol BP Ⓜ City Hall.

★ **$$$–$$$$** 🖼 **Shangri-La Hotel, Singapore.** For 30 years the Shangri-La has been one of Singapore's top hotels. Presidents have stayed here, but all travelers are treated to the same excellent service. Often referred to as "Singapore's other botanical garden," the hotel has 15 acres of flowers and plants, visible through the glass wall that encloses the lobby and dining areas. The Coffee Garden, styled after an English conservatory, has light meals and a lunch buffet; you'll find haute Cantonese cuisine in Shang Palace, fine California eats with late-night jazz at Blu, and Japanese at Nadaman. ✉ 22 Orange Grove Rd., Orchard, 258350 ☎ 6737–3644, 020/8747–8485 for reservations in the U.K., 800/942–5050 for reservations in Canada and the U.S. 🖷 6737–3257 ⊕ www.shangri-la.com ↪ 823 rooms ⚹ 4 restaurants, coffee shop, room service, in-room data ports, in-room safes, minibars, cable TV with movies, putting green, 4 tennis courts, pool, health club, hair salon, spa, squash, bar, shops, baby-sitting, dry cleaning, laundry service, concierge, Internet, business services, convention center, travel services, free parking, no-smoking rooms ⊟ AE, DC, MC, V ¶Ol BP Ⓜ Orchard.

$$$ ▦ **Carlton Hotel.** Raffles City, Chijmes, the arts and cultural district, the convention and business areas, and major public transportation are all near this understated and classy modern hotel. The black-and-white marble lobby is interspersed with palm trees; lounges to the side are quiet enclaves for sipping afternoon tea. The red-and-black guest rooms have bay windows and such amenities as flat-screen TVs. This is a good value for your money. ⊠ *76 Bras Basah Rd., Colonial Singapore, 189558* ☎ *6338–8333* 🖷 *6339–6866* ⊕ *www.carlton.com.sg* ➹ *463 rooms, 14 suites ♣ 2 restaurants, café, room service, in-room safes, minibars, cable TV with movies, pool, health club, hair salon, spa, bar, lobby lounge, baby-sitting, dry cleaning, laundry service, concierge, Internet, business services, convention center, travel services, free parking, no-smoking rooms* ▤ *AE, DC, MC, V* ⑩ *EP* Ⓜ *City Hall.*

$$$ ▦ **Conrad International Centennial Singapore.** Convenience is key here—nearby are the Singapore International Convention and Exhibition Centre, Suntec City, three national museums, and the CBD. Public spaces and accommodations alike are brightened by original Asian-influenced artwork. Guest rooms have lots of little extras, such as a pillow menu (you can choose a pillow to suit your needs), a Conrad teddy bear, and bath salts. The 24-hour business center has well-equipped meeting rooms. Oscar's Café is also open around the clock and is known for its popular wine buffet. Golden Peony Where to Eat serves yummy Cantonese dim sum. ⊠ *2 Temasek Blvd., Marina Square, 038982* ☎ *6334–8888* 🖷 *6333–9166* ⊕ *www.conradhotels.com* ➹ *484 rooms, 25 suites ♣ 2 restaurants, coffee shop, room service, in-room data ports, in-room safes, minibars, cable TV with movies, golf privileges, pool, health club, spa, bar, lobby lounge, shops, baby-sitting, children's programs (ages 12 and under), dry cleaning, laundry service, concierge, Internet, business services, convention center, travel services, free parking, no-smoking rooms* ▤ *AE, DC, MC, V* ⑩ *BP* Ⓜ *City Hall.*

$$$ ▦ **Crown Prince Hotel.** The location rather than the facilities are what makes this hotel popular with repeat travelers. The lobby is large and sparse with Italian marble and glass chandeliers. Dramatic glass elevators run along the outside of the building so you can check out Orchard Road on the way to your room. Though the pastel rooms are neat and trim, efficiency outweighs warmth here. Long Jiang Szechuan restaurant serves Szechuan food from a set menu, and Sushi Nogawa is Japanese-owned. ⊠ *270 Orchard Rd., Orchard, 238857* ☎ *6732–1111* 🖷 *6734–9137* ⊕ *www.crownhotels.com* ➹ *302 rooms, 9 suites ♣ 3 restaurants, coffee shop, room service, in-room data ports, in-room safes, minibars, cable TV with movies, pool, gym, sauna, spa, bar, shop, baby-sitting, dry cleaning, laundry service, concierge, Internet, business services, convention center, travel services, free parking, no-smoking rooms* ▤ *AE, DC, MC, V* ⑩ *BP* Ⓜ *Tanjong Pagar.*

$$$ ▦ **Grand Copthorne Waterfront.** Large windows throughout this hotel give full focus to the Singapore River. Standard rooms have a resort feel with their parquet floors and rattan furniture. The bathrooms have showers, but no tubs. All rooms are wheelchair accessible. Guests in the Executive Club rooms have access to an exclusive bilevel lounge with personalized services, breakfast, and cocktails. A 24-hour business center has state-of-the-art offices and a boardroom. Chopsticks serves pan-Asian food, and an Italian restaurant, Pontini, offers authentic northern Italian cuisine. ⊠ *392 Havelock Rd., Havelock, 169663* ☎ *6733–0880* 🖶 *6737–0880* ⊕ *www.millenniumhotels.com* ⤴ *537 rooms ♿ 2 restaurants, cafe, room service, in-room data ports, in-room fax, in-room safes, minibars, cable TV with movies, golf privileges, tennis court, pool, health club, hair salon, 2 bars, shop, baby-sitting, dry cleaning, laundry service, concierge, Internet, business services, convention center, free parking, no-smoking floors* ▤ *AE, DC, MC, V* ❜O❛ *EP* Ⓜ *Outram.*

$$$ 🏨 **Grand Plaza Parkroyal.** Just a 10-minute walk from notorious Bugis Street, where sailors once strolled with ladies of the night, you'll find the Grand Plaza. The rooms are a good value and have plush furnishings and floor-to-ceiling windows overlooking the city or pool. The excellent facilities include a first-class pool and the 7,000-square-foot St. Gregory Javana Spa, which offers Balinese-style massages and facials. The Orchid Club floors have such special services as fax machines and butler service for pampered travelers. ⊠ *10 Coleman St., Colonial Singapore, 179809* ☎ *6336–3456* 🖶 *6339–9311* ⊕ *http://grandplaza. singapore.parkroyalhotels.com* ⤴ *348 rooms ♿ 3 restaurants, coffee shop, room service, in-room data ports, in-room fax, in-room safes, minibars, cable TV with movies, pool, health club, hair salon, spa, bar, lounge, shops, baby-sitting, dry cleaning, laundry service, concierge, Internet, business services, convention center, travel services, free parking, no-smoking rooms* ▤ *AE, DC, MC, V* ❜O❛ *EP* Ⓜ *City Hall.*

$$$ 🏨 **Hilton International.** At the Hilton you can expect all the modern in-room amenities characteristic of more luxurious properties in Singapore. Some of Singapore's most exclusive boutiques are in its shopping arcade. Guests have access to nearby sports and water sports facilities for squash, bowling, jet skiing, and golf. The lodgings are spacious and those on the street side have city views, but rooms at the back are blocked by the adjacent Four Seasons. The Executive Club floors have 72 rooms and suites with Jacuzzis, and a clubroom, which serves food and cocktails. The hotel's eateries include Checkers Brasserie; rooftop and poolside dining; and the Harbour Grill, which has seafood and French cuisine. ⊠ *581 Orchard Rd., Orchard, 238883* ☎ *6737–2233* 🖶 *6732–2917* ⊕ *www.singapore.hilton.com* ⤴ *312 rooms, 16 suites, 95 executive rooms ♿ 3 restaurants, room service, in-room data ports, in-room safes, minibars, cable TV, golf privileges, pool, health club, hair salon, 2 bars, shops, baby-sitting, dry cleaning, laundry service, concierge, Internet, business services, convention center, travel services, free parking, no-smoking rooms* ▤ *AE, DC, MC, V* ❜O❛ *EP* Ⓜ *Orchard.*

$$$ 🏨 **Hotel New Otani.** Off by itself on the north bank of the Singapore River (the front desk can arrange for a river cruise), this orange-brick-fronted hotel is striking against the greenery of Ft. Canning Park. It attracts many Japanese travelers as it's part of the Liang Court complex, which houses more than 40 specialty shops. Rooms come with a PC and MS Office software as well as coffee-, tea-, and soup-makers. The hotel's location is ideal for business travelers who need to be close to Shenton Way. ⊠ *177A River Valley Rd., Clarke Quay, 179031* ☎ *6338–3333*

⊞ 6339–2854 ⊕ *www.newotanisingapore.com* ⇌ *423 rooms, 22 suites* ⌂ *2 restaurants, room service, in-room data ports, in-room safes, minibars, cable TV, pool, health club, bar, shops, dry cleaning, laundry service, Internet, business services, convention center, travel services, free parking, no-smoking rooms* ⊟ *AE, DC, MC, V* ⍤ *EP* Ⓜ *City Hall.*

$$$ ⬚ **Hotel Phoenix.** Type A personalities—including frenzied businesspeople—will appreciate the Phoenix: all rooms have PCs with Internet access and exercise equipment; executive rooms and suites also have computerized massage chairs. Business Executive rooms can be converted into offices during the day. Standard rooms only have showers, but the Super Deluxe rooms have a combined shower and bathtub. There's no on-site health club, but guests can use the nearby California Fitness Center for free. The Phoenix Garden Café serves international fare, but gets noisy at dinner due to its basement location. The hotel is in the heart of the Orchard Road area, not far from the convention center. ⊠ *277 Orchard Rd., Orchard, 238858* ☎ *6737–8666* ⊞ *6732–2024* ⊕ *www. hotelphoenixsingapore.com* ⇌ *290 rooms, 22 suites* ⌂ *Restaurant, patisserie, room service, in-room data ports, in-room safes, minibars, cable TV with movies and video games, in-room VCR, hair salon, lounge, wine bar, nightclub, shops, baby-sitting, laundry facilities, Internet, business services, meeting rooms, travel services, free parking, no-smoking rooms* ⊟ *AE, DC, MC, V* ⍤ *EP* Ⓜ *Somerset.*

$$$ ⬚ **Hotel Rendezvous.** With its mix of colonial and modern architecture, this hotel retains its '30s charm. The rooms are Peranakan in style, with warm, bright colors; the retro bathroom tiles reflect shades of days gone by. The lobby and courtyard are peaceful places with plenty of sunlight. You can wine and dine at the Straits Café by the Park, which has an Asian buffet. High tea is served on Saturday, and the Sunday brunch is very popular. The Gourmet Gallery in the courtyard operates several shops, a spa, an Internet cafe, and The Rendezvous Restaurant. ⊠ *9 Bras Basah Rd., Colonial Singapore, 189559* ☎ *6336–0220* ⊞ *6337–3773* ⊕ *www.rendezvoushotels.com* ⇌ *300 rooms* ⌂ *Restaurant, 2 cafés, coffee shop, room service, in-room data ports, in-room safes, minibars, cable TV with movies, pool, health club, spa, bar, shop, baby-sitting, dry cleaning, laundry service, Internet, business services, convention center, travel services, parking (fee), no-smoking rooms* ⊟ *AE, DC, MC, V* ⍤ *EP* Ⓜ *Dhoby Ghaut.*

$$$ ⬚ **Le Meridien Singapore.** The atrium-like lobby of this hotel, which is on one of the quieter stretches of Orchard Road, captivates guests with a cascade of flowers descending from the upper floors. Pastel and floral rooms have such Asian touches as silk-screen murals; some rooms have balconies loaded with potted plants. Quarters on Le Club Président concierge level have extra amenities, like CD players and fax machines. The hotel's dining includes rotisserie buffets, local specialties, and Western fare in the relaxed Café Georges. Keep in mind that the entrance isn't obvious from the road. ⊠ *100 Orchard Rd., Orchard, 238840* ☎ *6733–8855* ⊞ *6732–7886* ⊕ *www.lemeridien-singapore.com* ⇌ *382 rooms, 25 suites* ⌂ *2 restaurants, café, room service, in-room data ports, in-room fax, in-room safes, minibars, cable TVs with movies, pool, gym, hair salon, bar, lounge, baby-sitting, dry cleaning, laundry* *service, concierge, Internet, business services, convention center, travel services, parking (fee), no-smoking rooms* ⊟ *AE, DC, MC, V* ⦿| *EP* Ⓜ *Somerset.*

$$$ ⊡ **Marina Mandarin.** The relatively peaceful lobby here has a John Portman–designed atrium that narrows as it ascends 21 floors to a tinted skylight. Pastel guest rooms are modern and smart; for the best view, request a room overlooking the harbor. Rooms on the concierge floor— the Marina Club—cost about 25% more and have such extras as terry cloth robes, butler service, and free breakfast and cocktails. The on-site Peach Blossoms restaurant serves Chinese cuisine and the Ristorante Bologna has northern Italian fare; the Cricketer pub is a pleasant place for an evening drink. ⊠ *6 Raffles Blvd., Marina Square, 039594* ☎ *6338–3388* 🖷 *6339–4977* ⊕ *www.marina-mandarin.com.sg* ⇗ *575 rooms* ⚴ *3 restaurants, room service, in-room data ports, in-room safes, minibars, cable TV with movies, golf privileges, 2 tennis courts, pool, health club, hair salon, spa, squash, lounge, pub, shops, baby-sitting, dry cleaning, laundry service, concierge, Internet, business services, convention center, free parking, no-smoking rooms* ⊟ *AE, DC, MC, V* ⦿| *EP* Ⓜ *City Hall.*

$$$ ⊡ **Merchant Court.** The trend toward developing no-frills hotels for business travelers led the Raffles Group to open Merchant Court, in the Boat Quay district. Standard rooms, albeit small, are comfortable; larger executive rooms have a few more amenities, and the Premier Rooms have balconies. A stay in a Merchant Club room gets you free use of laptop computers and fax machines as well as complimentary breakfast and cocktails. Ellenborough Market Café offers international, local, and Straits Chinese cuisine. There are excellent fitness facilities, and you can take a free shuttle bus from here to Raffles City. ⊠ *20 Merchant Rd., Boat Quay, 058281* ☎ *6337–2288* 🖷 *6334–0606* ⊕ *www.swissotel-merchantcourt. com* ⇗ *470 rooms, 6 suites* ⚴ *Café, in-room data ports, in-room fax, in-room safes, minibar, cable TV with movies, pool, gym, hair salon, spa, 2 bars, shops, dry cleaning, laundry facilities, laundry service, concierge, Internet, business services, meeting rooms, travel services, free parking, no-smoking rooms* ⊟ *AE, DC, MC, V* ⦿| *EP* Ⓜ *City Hall.*

$$$ ⊡ **Meritus Mandarin Singapore.** The grand main lobby has black-and-white Italian marble and a huge mural, *87 Taoist Immortals*, which is based on an 8th-century Chinese scroll. Guest rooms have Asian themes with modern amenities and the upper floors command fabulous views of the harbor, the city, and Malaysia. Deluxe rooms have separate shower cubicles. Tour groups are the mainstay here though. The eateries are frequented by locals and include the Pine Court; the Top of the M, a revolving restaurant; Triple 3, a buffet restaurant; as well as the 24-hour Chatterbox coffeehouse. ⊠ *333 Orchard Rd., Orchard, 238867* ☎ *6737–4411* 🖷 *6732–2361* ⊕ *www.mandarin-singapore.com* ⇗ *1,200 rooms and suites* ⚴ *3 restaurants, café, coffee shop, room service, in-room data ports, in-room fax, in-room safes, minibars, cable TV with movies, tennis court, pool, health club, hair salon, squash, bar, lounge, shops, baby-sitting, dry cleaning, laundry service, concierge, Internet, business services, convention center, travel services, free parking, no-smoking rooms* ⊟ *AE, DC, MC, V* ⦿| *EP* Ⓜ *Somerset.*

$$$ 🏨 **Orchard Hotel.** Its proximity to the activity on Orchard Road, several embassies, and the Botanic Gardens has no doubt contributed to this hotel's popularity. Guest rooms are comfortable and functional, and there are facilities for people with disabilities. Rooms in the Orchard Wing are larger and more expensive than standard rooms. Premier and Harvesters' Club rooms on the top floors have separate check-in, in-room fax services, and complimentary breakfast and evening cocktails. The formal Hua Ting restaurant offers Cantonese and Shanghainese dishes, and the Orchard and Sidewalk cafés serve light fare until 1 AM. ⊠ *442 Orchard Rd., Orchard, 238879* 🕾 *6734–7766* 🖷 *6733–5482* ⊕ *www. orchardhotel.com.sg* ⇆ *680 rooms* ৬ *2 restaurant, 2 cafés, snack bar, room service, in-room data ports, in-room safes, minibars, cable TV with movies, pool, health club, hair salon, spa, bar, nightclub, shops, baby-sitting, dry cleaning, laundry service, concierge, Internet, business services, convention center, travel services, free parking, no-smoking rooms* 🚭 *AE, DC, MC, V* ❉ *EP* Ⓜ *Orchard.*

$$$ 🏨 **Pan Pacific Singapore.** The vast 35-story atrium of this luxury hotel is filled with greenery and has an exterior elevator that offers staggering city views. Guest rooms on the upper levels have not only great vistas, but also great amenities; for example, butler service and complimentary breakfast and cocktails. The Duplex Suite has a private sauna and spa bath. Guest rooms have high-speed Internet access, and "cyberbutlers" will be happy to assist you with any technical difficulties. Dining options include a rooftop Chinese restaurant and the Japanese and Italian dining rooms. The hotel is connected to the Suntec Centre via a covered walkway. ⊠ *7 Raffles Blvd., Marina Square, 039595* 🕾 *6336–8111* 🖷 *6339–1861* ⊕ *www.singapore.panpacific.com* ⇆ *784 rooms, 37 suites* ৬ *4 restaurants, café, snack bar, room service, in-room data ports, in-room safes, minibars, cable TV with movies, 2 tennis courts, pool, health club, spa, lounge, baby-sitting, dry cleaning, laundry service, concierge, Internet, business services, convention center, travel services, free parking, no-smoking rooms* 🚭 *AE, DC, MC, V* ❉ *EP* Ⓜ *City Hall.*

☾ **$$$** 🏨 **Orchard Parade Hotel.** Previously known as the Ming Court Hotel, this 30-year-old property at the corner of Tanglin and Orchard roads has a warm and colorful Mediterranean resort feel to it. The rooms are spacious, especially the Junior suites, and the family rooms have extra single beds and a dining area, which makes the hotel one of Singapore's best options for travelers with young children. The location makes it a favorite with leisure travelers, and all the on-site restaurants are leased to well-known eateries. Club Chinois adds a touch of elegance, while the Devil's Bar @ Red Cafe Nightlife & the Arts is more raucous, with live music. ⊠ *1 Tanglin Rd., Orchard, 247905* 🕾 *6737–1133* 🖷 *6733-0242* ⊕ *www.orchardparade.com.sg* ⇆ *368 rooms, 19 suites* ৬ *4 restaurants, coffee shop, room service, in-room data ports, in-room fax, in-room safes, minibars, cable TV with movies, pool, gym, hair salon, spa, bar, nightclub, shops, baby-sitting, dry cleaning, laundry service, concierge, Internet, business services, convention center, travel services, free parking, no-smoking rooms* 🚭 *AE, DC, MC, V* ❉ *EP* Ⓜ *Orchard.*

$$$ ⊞ **The Regent.** A good 10-minute walk from Orchard and Scotts roads, the Regent appeals to those who want quiet. Relaxed, comfortable public rooms are decked out with Asian carpets and wood paneling. The second-floor cocktail lounge, the Bar, is a refuge within a refuge. Rooms have big beds, writing desks, and marble bathrooms; some have balconies. The Tea Lounge serves high tea daily. Capers has an alfresco setting for its international cuisine, the Summer Palace serves Cantonese cuisine prepared by Hong Kong chefs, and Maxim's de Paris has belle epoque decor and French cuisine. ⊠ *1 Cuscaden Rd., Orchard, 249715* ☎ *6733–8888* 🖷 *6732–8838* ⊕ *www.regenthotels.com* ↪ *393 rooms, 48 suites* ♨ *3 restaurants, patisserie, room service, in-room data ports, in-room fax, in-room safes, minibars, cable TV with movies, in-room VCRs, pool, health club, hair salon, spa, bar, lobby lounge, shops, baby-sitting, dry cleaning, laundry service, concierge, Internet, business services, convention center, travel services, free parking, no-smoking rooms* ⊟ *AE, DC, MC, V* ⦿ *EP* Ⓜ *Orchard.*

$$$ ⊞ **Royal Plaza on Scotts.** The lobby here makes a statement with Italian marble floors, two grand staircases, Burmese teak paneling, stained-glass skylights, and tapestries. Rooms, done in soft hues and pastels, can look somewhat old and worn; still, they do come with a free minibar, which is restocked with one beer, mineral water, and 4 soft drinks daily. The Executive Club floor has a private lounge for complimentary breakfast and evening cocktails. The Palm Café on the roof terrace serves Italian pizzas and salads. ⊠ *25 Scotts Rd., Orchard, 228220* ☎ *6737–7966* 🖷 *6737–6646* ⊕ *www.royalplaza.com.sg* ↪ *495 rooms* ♨ *Restaurant, 2 cafés, patisserie, room service, in-room data ports, in-room safes, minibars, cable TV with movies, pool, gym, sauna, spa, bar, lounge, shops, baby-sitting, dry cleaning, laundry service, concierge, Internet, business services, meeting rooms, travel services, free parking, no-smoking rooms* ⊟ *AE, DC, MC, V* ⦿ *EP* Ⓜ *Orchard.*

$$$ ⊞ **Singapore Marriott.** This striking 33-story, pagoda-inspired property anchors Singapore's "million-dollar corner"—the intersection of Orchard and Scotts roads. There's a 24-hour business center, in addition to a 24-hour fitness center, and nearby sports facilities with opportunities for golf, tennis, squash, sailing, and kayaking. Rooms are Western style, with light-gray carpets, pink-vinyl wallpaper, pink-gray upholstery, and ample wood; there are amenities for people with disabilities. The hotel's location—rather than its character—is its selling point. The Crossroads Café is a popular people-watching spot. ⊠ *320 Orchard Rd., Orchard, 238865* ☎ *6735–5800* 🖷 *6735–9800* ⊕ *www.marriott.com.sg* ↪ *364 rooms, 19 suites* ♨ *2 restaurants, 2 cafés, patisserie, room service, in-room data ports, in-room safes, minibars, cable TV with movies, golf privileges, pool, health club, hair salon, spa, shop, baby-sitting, dry cleaning, laundry service, concierge, Internet, business services, convention center, free parking, no-smoking rooms* ⊟ *AE, DC, MC, V* ⦿ *EP* Ⓜ *Orchard.*

$$$ ⊞ **Swissôtel The Stamford and Raffles The Plaza.** Catering to business executives, the 70-story twin towers of the Stamford and the Plaza are among the tallest hotels in the world. Attracting tours and conventions, these hotels are a hub of their own, with a dozen restaurants—the Compass Rose Restaurant is the highlight—more than 100 shops, and convention facilities (including the largest column-free meeting rooms in the world). All rooms have balconies and cater to travelers with disabilities. The 29 Stamford Crest suites are extremely well appointed, sharing a private dining room and exercise room. ☒ *2 Stamford Rd., Colonial Singapore, 178882* ☎ *6339–6633* 🖷 *6336–5117* ⊕ *www. rafflescityhotels.com* ⇨ *Stamford, 1,234 rooms, 29 suites; Plaza, 764 rooms, 29 suites* ⚭ *12 restaurants, room service, in-room data ports, in-room safes, minibars, cable TV with movies, 6 tennis courts, 2 pools, health club, hair salon, spa, squash, bar, lounge, dance club, shops, babysitting, dry cleaning, laundry service, concierge, Internet, business services, convention center, travel services, parking (fee), no-smoking floors* ▭ *AE, DC, MC, V* ⧪ *EP* Ⓜ *City Hall.*

★ **$$**   ▥ **Albert Court Hotel.** Rare in Singapore are small hotels that have gone to the expense and effort of restoring existing structures and of installing facilities for people with disabilities. The Albert Court, which is only a few minutes' walk from Little India, is one. Furnishings are simple, and wood paneling lends warmth. The staff is enthusiastic, and this attitude infects the mostly European guests. You can dine on Nepalese food in the Shimmahal Restaurant or venture out into the adjoining mall, where there are sundry food outlets. ☒ *180 Albert St., Little India, 189971* ☎ *6339–3939* 🖷 *6339–3253* ⊕ *www.albertcourt.com. sg* ⇨ *182 rooms, 1 suite* ⚭ *Restaurant, café, room service, in-room safes, minibars, cable TV with movies, bar, shops, baby-sitting, laundry service, business services, meeting rooms, travel services, free parking, no-smoking rooms* ▭ *AE, MC, V* ⧪ *EP* Ⓜ *Kandang Kerban.*

$$
Fodor'sChoice
★   ▥ **Berjaya Hotel Duxton Road, Singapore.** Formerly known as the Duxton, the nation's first boutique hotel offers an intimate whiff of Singapore's character before it sold out to steel girders and glass. Rooms are in eight converted shophouses in Chinatown's Tanjong Pagar district. Standard rooms, at the back of the building, are small with colonial reproduction furniture; the duplex suites are a better option. The karaoke bar across the street may keep you awake at night. Breakfast is included, and afternoon tea is served in the lounge. The excellent French restaurant L'Aigle d'Or is off the lobby. ☒ *83 Duxton Rd., Tanjong Pagar, 089540* ☎ *6227–7678, 800/272–8188 for reservations in the U.S.* 🖷 *6227–1232* ⊕ *www.berjayaresorts.com.my* ⇨ *38 rooms, 11 suites* ⚭ *Restaurant, room service, in-room data ports, in-room safes, minibars, cable TV with movies, bar, baby-sitting, dry cleaning, laundry service, business services, no-smoking rooms* ▭ *AE, DC, MC, V* ⧪ *BP* Ⓜ *Tanjong Pagar.*

$$ ▥ **Furama Hotel.** This modern curvilinear building stands out on Chinatown's threshold, amid the surrounding shophouses. The dated beige lobby belies the comfortable, contemporary guest rooms. Tour groups and Japanese businessmen call this place home. There are data ports by the pool, in the Tiffany Coffee House, and elsewhere. The helpful staff will direct you to interesting sights, and there are daily guided walking tours through Chinatown. After hoofing it around, you can rest at the popular poolside café. ☒ *60 Eu Tong Sen St., Kreta Ayer, 059804* ☎ *6533–3888* 🖷 *6534–1489* ⊕ *www.furama.com* ⇨ *356 rooms* ⚭ *Restaurant, café, room service, in-room data ports, minibars, room*

TVs *with movies, pool, gym, hair salon, outdoor hot tub, bar, baby-sitting, dry cleaning, laundry service, concierge, Internet, business services, convention center, travel services, free parking, no-smoking rooms* ▤ *AE, DC, MC, V* ❑❘ *EP* Ⓜ *Outram Park.*

$$ ⊞ **Holiday Inn Atrium.** Once appropriately called the Glass Hotel, the Holiday Inn Atrium has a glass canopy that curves down from the ninth story over the entrance, facing southeast for good fortune. Decorated in autumn hues, rooms are modern and have standard amenities. A stay on one of the three executive floors gets you complimentary breakfast and cocktails. For dining and entertainment there's a Chinese restaurant, which frequently has floor shows; the Melting Pot Café, serving international fare; and a lobby lounge with live music. The hotel lies just south of the Singapore River and west of the business district. ✉ *317 Outram Rd., Havelock, 169075* ☎ *6733–0188* 🖷 *6733–0989* ⊕ *www.ichotelsgroup.com* ⟿ *511 rooms, 4 suites* ⟑ *Restaurant, café, room service, in-room safes, minibars, cable TV with movies, tennis court, pool, gym, massage, sauna, steam room, 2 lounges, shops, baby-sitting, dry cleaning, laundry facilities, Internet, business services, convention center, travel services, free parking, no-smoking rooms* ▤ *AE, DC, MC, V* ❑❘ *EP* Ⓜ *Tiong Bahru Plaza.*

$$ ⊞ **Le Meridien Changi Village.** It's only 10 minutes from the airport, and near many attractions, including a beach, boat rides to other islands, cafés, pubs, shops, golf facilities, and a museum; free shuttle buses are available to the airport and downtown. Rooms are small with minimalist furnishings and high ceilings to generate an illusion of more space. Some rooms have bay windows. The small rooftop pool has a great view. Saltwater restaurant offers fusion alfresco dining next to the golf course. ✉ *1 Netheravon Rd., Changi, 508502* ☎ *6379–7111* 🖷 *6545–0112* ⊕ *www.changivillage.lemeridien.com* ⟿ *374 rooms, 6 suites* ⟑ *Restaurant, coffee shop, room service, in-room data ports, in-room safes, minibars, cable TVs with movies, golf privileges, pool, gym, spa, bicycles, bar, lounge, baby-sitting, dry cleaning, laundry service, concierge, Internet, business services, convention center, free parking, no-smoking rooms* ▤ *AE, DC, MC, V* ❑❘ *EP* Ⓜ *Tampines.*

$$ ⊞ **M Hotel Singapore.** The dull exterior contradicts the modern and stylish interior of this business hotel. Though it's near the business district, the M hotel is removed from all the hurly-burly. Rooms are small, neat, and contemporary with separate showers and bathtubs. All rooms have CD players, and the suites rival those of 5-star hotels—the living areas have large flat-screen TVs, and the bedrooms have a TV, DVD player, and Bose stereo. The Tea Bar serves a wide selection of premium teas. There's live jazz in the new J Bar, the Buffet has a nightly hot pot buffet, and Café 2000 has Asian and Western eats. ✉ *81 Anson Rd., CBD, 079908* ☎ *6224–1133* 🖷 *6222–0749* ⊕ *www.mhotel.com.sg* ⟿ *404 rooms, 9 suites* ⟑ *2 restaurants, café, room service, in-room data ports, in-room fax, in-room safes, minibars, cable TV with movies, golf privileges, pool, gym, sauna, spa, library, nightclub, baby-sitting, dry cleaning, laundry service, concierge, Internet, business services, convention center, travel services, free parking, no-smoking rooms* ▤ *AE, DC, MC, V* ❑❘ *BP* Ⓜ *Tanjong Pagar.*

$$ ▦ **Novotel Apollo Singapore.** Upon entering the hotel, you're greeted by the Waterfall Lounge, a relaxing little spot with a view of small man-made waterfalls. The marble foyer, with its huge pillars, is art deco–inspired. The rooms are bright but simple, and those on the Executive Floor have data ports. A terrace with a sundeck, a hot tub, a wading pool, and a tennis court are amid a garden. The Kintamani Restaurant serves Indonesian food, and the Square has 60 global cuisine choices that change daily. Close by are Clarke Quay and the infamous "pub row" on Mohamed Sultan Road. ⊠ *405 Havelock Rd., Havelock, 169633* ☎ *6733–2081* 🖷 *6732–7025* ⊕ *www.accorhotels-asia.com* ⇋ *480 rooms, 23 suites, 135 deluxe rooms* ☖ *2 restaurants, room service, in-room safes, minibar, cable TV with movies, tennis court, pool, gym, outdoor hot tub, bar, lounge, baby-sitting, laundry facilities, Internet, business services, convention center, travel services, free parking, no-smoking rooms* ▭ *AE, DC, MC, V* ⦿| *EP* Ⓜ *Outram Park.*

$$ ▦ **Plaza Parkroyal Hotel.** Rooms here are spacious and have wood floors, simple decor, and high ceilings. Service is friendly though a bit too laid-back at times. There's a Balinese-style pool and a well-equipped gym. Check out the automated rock climbing wall, which simulates a real climb. Si Chuan Dou Hua Seafood Restaurant serves Cantonese and authentic Sichuan cuisine and Café Plaza has Western and regional fare. With a full house the hotel can be quite lively. Club 5 plays nostalgic '50s and '60s music starting up at 3 PM. ⊠ *7500A Beach Rd., Kampong Glam, 199591* ☎ *6298–0011* 🖷 *6296–3600* ⊕ *www. parkroyalhotels.com* ⇋ *342 rooms, 3 suites* ☖ *Restaurant, café, room service, in-room data ports, in-room safes, minibars, cable TV with movies, pool, health club, hair salon, spa, bar, dance club, shops, baby-sitting, dry cleaning, laundry service, concierge, Internet, business services, convention center, travel services, free parking, no-smoking rooms* ▭ *AE, DC, MC, V* ⦿| *EP* Ⓜ *Bugis.*

★ **$$** ▦ **Traders Hotel.** Connected to the Tanglin Mall, this hotel has all the necessary comforts—including those for travelers with disabilities. Rooms are comfortable, with plenty of light from their bay windows. Room service is available 24 hours, and scores of restaurants and a supermarket are just steps away. An hourly shuttle to Orchard Road and the MRT station is available for tired sightseers. For seafood and local dishes by the pool, check out Ah Hoi's Kitchen famous for its chili crab; Rumpoles serves lunch, snacks, and drinks. ⊠ *1A Cuscaden Rd., Orchard, 249716* ☎ *6738–2222, 020/8747–8485 for reservations in the U.K., 800/942–5050 for reservations in Canada and U.S.* 🖷 *6831–4314* ⊕ *www.shangri-la.com* ⇋ *531 rooms, 12 suites* ☖ *Restaurant, coffee shop, room service, in-room data ports, in-room safes, minibars, cable TV with movies, pool, health club, hair salon, spa, shops, baby-sitting, dry cleaning, laundry service, Internet, business services, meeting rooms, travel services, free parking, no-smoking rooms* ▭ *AE, DC, MC, V* ⦿| *BP* Ⓜ *Orchard.*

$$ ▦ **York Hotel.** Despite its closeness to busy Orchard Road, this classic European hotel is characteristically quiet and placid. The tower only has suites, and the poolside wing has split-level cabanas and rooms surrounding a garden. All guest quarters have two queen-size beds. The

White Rose Café serves Asian and Western fare. ⊠ *21 Mt. Elizabeth, Mt. Elizabeth, 228516* ☎ *6737–0511* 🖶 *6732–1217* ⊕ *www.yorkhotel. com.sg* ↪ *335 rooms, 69 suites* ♿ *Café, coffee shop, room service, in-room safes, minibars, cable TV with movies, pool, health club, hair salon, spa, bar, shops, baby-sitting, dry cleaning, laundry service, Internet, business services, convention center, travel services, free parking, no-smoking rooms* 🚭 *AE, DC, MC, V* ⏀ *EP* Ⓜ *Orchard.*

$ 🖭 **Allson Hotel Singapore.** This hotel is a good value compared to similar hotels, such as the nearby Carlton. All rooms have a Chinese touch (rosewood furniture, for one) and such extras as coffee- and tea makers and IDD phones. Rooms on the Excellence Floor are more expensive but more spacious. This hotel has a central location: it's near Raffles City Tower, Marina Square, the historic colonial district, Little India, Bugis Street, the Arab District, and it's only a 10-minute subway or bus ride to Orchard Road. ⊠ *101 Victoria St., Bugis, 188018* ☎ *6336–0811* 🖶 *6339–7019* ⊕ *www.allsonhotels.com* ↪ *450 rooms* ♿ *Restaurant, café, room service, in-room safes, minibars, cable TV with movies, pool, health club, hair salon, bar, shops, baby-sitting, laundry facilities, Internet, business services, meeting rooms, travel services, free parking, no-smoking rooms* 🚭 *AE, DC, MC, V* ⏀ *EP* Ⓜ *Bugis.*

$ 🖭 **Amara Hotel.** At the business district's south end is this value-price 18-story hotel, convenient to the train station and the commercial and port facilities. It's a soothing place thanks to a minimalistic lobby, Balinese-style pool and spa, and spacious guest rooms decorated in earth-tones and timber. The hotel is part of a vibrant shopping and entertainment complex, and is close to Chinatown's Tanjong Pagar. The Royal Club concierge floor has butler service. ⊠ *165 Tanjong Pagar Rd., Tanjong Pagar, 088539* ☎ *6224–4488* 🖶 *6224–3910* ⊕ *www.amarahotels.com* ↪ *380 rooms* ♿ *5 restaurants, 2 cafés, room service, in-room data ports, in-room safes, minibar, cable TV with movies, tennis court, pool, health club, spa, shop, baby-sitting, dry cleaning, laundry service, Internet, business services, convention center, travel services, parking (fee), no-smoking rooms* 🚭 *AE, DC, MC, V* ⏀ *EP* Ⓜ *Tanjong Pagar.*

$ 🖭 **Elizabeth Hotel.** This hotel is in a residential area surrounded by greenery behind Orchard Road's main shopping district. Superior and deluxe rooms are done in an English country style with Tudor furnishings. The lobby lounge has floor-to-ceiling glass panels that overlook a landscaped waterfall garden. The poolside Greenhouse Café serves international food. Travelers with disabilities will be comfortable here. ⊠ *24 Mt. Elizabeth, Mt. Elizabeth, 228518* ☎ *6738–1188* 🖶 *6732–3866* ⊕ *www.theelizabeth.com* ↪ *247 rooms* ♿ *Restaurant, coffee shop, room service, in-room data ports, in-room safes, minibars, cable TV with movies, pool, gym, sauna, spa, bar, baby-sitting, dry cleaning, laundry service, Internet, business services, meeting rooms, travel services, free parking, no-smoking rooms* 🚭 *AE, DC, MC, V* ⏀ *BP* Ⓜ *Orchard.*

$ 🖭 **Hotel 1929.** Comprising five converted shophouses, built in 1929, this hotel successfully blends old-style architecture with a modern interior. Rooms are small and really only big enough for one person, furnishings are of classic and retro design. Flat-screen TVs and CD players are standard, and the bathrooms are of the latest trend in clear glass washbasins. Each of the two suites has an outdoor rooftop bathtub overlooking Chinatown. Ember juggles its duties as a coffee shop, bar, lounge, and dining room. ☒ *50 Keong Saik St., Chinatown 089154* ☏ *6347–1929* 🖷 *6327–1929* ⊕ *http://hotel1929.com* ↝ *32 rooms, 2 suites* ♻ *Restaurant, in-room data ports, in-room safes, minibars, cable TV, hot tub, laundry services, Internet, business services, travel services, no-smoking rooms* ▭ *AE, DC, MC, V* ⑂ *EP* Ⓜ *Outram Park.*

$ 🖼 **Hotel Royal.** The rooms at this modest hotel are spacious but in need of a face-lift. On the premises is an international forwarding service that can be useful for sending excess baggage or new purchases back home. The hotel is near Newton Circus and is a 20-minute walk from Orchard Road. ☒ *36 Newton Rd., Bukit Timah, 307964* ☏ *6253–4411* 🖷 *6253–8668* ⊕ *www.hotelroyal.com.sg* ↝ *316 rooms, 15 suites* ♻ *3 restaurants, coffee shop, room service, in-room data ports, in-room safes, minibars, room TVs with movies, pool, gym, bar, nightclub, dry cleaning, laundry service, Internet, business services, meeting rooms, travel services, free parking, no-smoking rooms* ▭ *AE, DC, MC, V* ⑂ *EP* Ⓜ *Novena.*

$ 🖼 **Peninsula Excelsior Hotel.** The hotel is easily accessible from the financial, shopping, and entertainment districts. The interior design of the fairly spacious guest rooms seems to be stuck in the '80s. The rooms on and above the 17th floor have good views. The lobby lounge has glass walls looking into the depths of the pool, and you can literally watch guests swim right by you. There's no proper restaurant, but Coleman's Café serves around-the-clock international eats, and there are several reasonably priced restaurants nearby. ☒ *3 Coleman St., Colonial Singapore, 179804* ☏ *6339–0708* 🖷 *6339–3847* ⊕ *www.ytchotels.com.sg* ↝ *508 rooms, 8 suites* ♻ *Café, room service, in-room data ports, in-room safes, minibars, cable TV with movies, pool, gym, spa, bar, lounge, nightclub, shops, baby-sitting, dry cleaning, laundry facilities, Internet, business services, convention center, travel services, free parking, no-smoking rooms* ▭ *AE, DC, MC, V* ⑂ *EP* Ⓜ *City Hall.*

$ 🖼 **RELC International Hotel.** This is less a hotel than an international conference center often used by Singapore's university for seminars. The upper floors, however, contain bargain guest rooms that are large and basically comfortable with balconies and plenty of light. There are two floors of serviced apartments for long-term guests. The building is in a residential neighborhood, up a hill beyond the Shangri-La hotel, a 10-minute walk from the Orchard and Scotts roads intersection. Breakfast is included, and the rooms have coffeemakers. Because the hotel is such a good value, reservations well in advance are strongly advised. ☒ *30 Orange Grove Rd., Nassim Hill, 258352* ☏ *6737–9044* 🖷 *6733–9976* ⊕ *www.relc.org.sg* ↝ *142 rooms and suites* ♻ *Restaurant, café, in-room data ports, minibars, cable TV, laundry service, business services, convention center, free parking, no-smoking rooms* ▭ *AE, DC, MC, V* ⑂ *EP* Ⓜ *Orchard.*

Fodor'sChoice
★

$ 🖼 **Robertson Quay Hotel.** This 10-story circular hotel is in a serene neighborhood just a short walk from Chinatown and bustling Clarke and Boat quays. You won't find superfluous luxury here, but you'll be comfortable. The two-room suites are roomier and ideal for families. Rooms above the seventh floor have great river and city views. There's a putting green and small pool overlooking the river. The Home Beach Bar downstairs is equipped with darts, pool, and other table games. ⊠ *15 Merbau Rd., Robertson Quay, 239032* ☎ *6735–3333* 🖷 *6738–1515* ⊕ *www.robertsonquayhotel.com.sg* ⇆ *150 rooms, 10 suites* ☖ *Restaurant, café, in-room data ports, in-room safes, cable TV, putting green, pool, gym, hot tub, spa, bar, lobby lounge, baby-sitting, laundry service, meeting room, travel services, free parking, no-smoking rooms* ▤ *AE, DC, MC, V* ¶◎¶ *EP* Ⓜ *Dhoby Ghaut.*

$ 🏨 **Royal Peacock.** Living up to its name, this brightly painted shophouse hotel is on the once notorious Keong Saik Road (it was known for its red lanterns and ladies of the night, who are now in state-controlled brothels). The standard rooms don't have windows, so ask for a deal on a superior or deluxe rooms. Breakfast, coffee, tea fixings are included in all rates. ⊠ *55 Keong Saik Rd., Kreta Ayer, 089518* ☎ *6223–3522* 🖷 *6221–1770* ⊕ *www.royalpeacockhotel.com* ⇆ *76 rooms* ☖ *Restaurant, café, room service, in-room data ports, in-room fax, in-room safes, minibars, cable TV with movies, bar, dry cleaning, laundry service, business services, no-smoking rooms* ▤ *AE, DC, MC, V* ¶◎¶ *BP* Ⓜ *Outram.*

$ 🏨 **Sha Villa.** This white building from the 1950s once housed the Singapore Ballet Company. The boutique hotel's rooms have hardwood floors and teak furniture. The bathrooms have white and pink tiles. Orchard Road is only a five-minute walk away. The Rosette restaurant is known for its international cuisine. ⊠ *64 Lloyd Rd., Orchard, 239113* ☎ *6734–7117* 🖷 *6736–1651* ⊕ *www.sha.org.sg* ⇆ *40 rooms* ☖ *Restaurant, room service, in-room safe, minibar, cable TV, laundry service, Internet, travel services, free parking* ▤ *AE, DC, MC, V* ¶◎¶ *EP* Ⓜ *Somerset.*

Fodor's Choice
★

¢–$ 🏨 **YMCA International House.** This well-run YMCA at the bottom of Orchard Road offers hotel-like accommodations for men and women—choose from single (S$98) rooms or three-bed family rooms (S$130)—as well as dormitory-style quarters (S$25); S$5 will buy you a temporary YMCA membership. All rooms have private baths, color TVs, and IDD phones. In addition to an impressive gym, you'll find a rooftop pool and squash and badminton courts. There's also a McDonald's at the entrance. ⊠ *1 Orchard Rd., Orchard, 238824* ☎ *6336–6000* 🖷 *6337–3140* ⊕ *www.ymca.org.sg* ⇆ *111 rooms* ☖ *Café, in-room safes, pool, gym, badminton, billiards, squash, laundry service, business services, convention center, travel services, no-smoking floors* ▤ *AE, DC, MC, V* ¶◎¶ *BP* Ⓜ *Dhoby Ghaut.*

¢ 🏨 **Ambassador Transit Hotel.** At last: a lodging truly geared to bleary-eyed travelers en route to still another destination. This hotel is *inside* Changi Airport, on Level 3 of the departure lounge in both Terminals 1 and 2. (Note: if you stay here, you don't go through immigration control.) Rooms are clean, fresh, and basic. Rates are for six-hour periods and include use of the swimming pool, sauna, and fitness center. Nonguests may also use the pool (S$10), the sauna and showers (S$10), or just the shower (S$5). ⊠ *Changi Airport* ☎ *6541–9106 for Terminal 1, 6541–9107 for Terminal 2, 0800/96–3562 for reservations in the U.K., 800/690–6785 for reservations in the U.S.* 🖷 *6542–4875 for Ter-*

minal 1, 6542–6122 for Terminal 2 🌐 *www.airport-hotel.com.sg* 👍 *Restaurant, cable TV, pool, gym, hair salon, sauna, spa, bar, business services, meeting rooms* 💳 *AE, DC, MC, V* 🍽 *EP.*

★ ¢ **Inn at Temple Street.** The Inn at Temple Street occupies five beautifully restored shophouses. The attractive Peranakan decor recalls the neighborhood's rich cultural traditions. Ask for a room with a view of the street below, which is slated to become a pedestrian mall. ✉ *36 Temple St., Kreta Ayer, 058581* ☎ *6221–5333* 📠 *6225–5391* 🌐 *www.theinn.com.sg* 🛏 *42 rooms* 👍 *Coffee shop, room service, in-room safes, minibars, room TV, bar, lounge, shops, dry cleaning, laundry service, concierge, business services, meeting rooms, travel services* 💳 *AE, DC, MC, V* 🍽 *EP* Ⓜ *Outram Park.*

¢ **Metropole Hotel.** This very modest, very basic hotel near Raffles City has simply furnished rooms. Rare in budget lodgings, you'll find both a helpful staff and room service. The Imperial Herbal Restaurant serves northern Chinese cuisine, and herbal physicians are on hand to advise you on health matters. The Barn Steak House and Restaurant prepares inexpensive lunches. ✉ *41 Seah St., Colonial Singapore, 188396* ☎ *6336–3611* 📠 *6339–3610* 🌐 *www.metrohotel.com* 🛏 *48 rooms, 2 suites* 👍 *2 restaurants, coffee shop, room service, room TVs, laundry service, meeting rooms, free parking* 💳 *AE, DC, MC, V* 🍽 *BP* Ⓜ *City Hall.*

¢ **Metropolitan YMCA, Tanglin Centre.** A 10-minute walk from Orchard Road, this YMCA (which admits women) has rooms with air-conditioning and private baths. There are even a few suites. The budget restaurant offers wholesome English breakfasts as well as Chinese, Malay, Nonya, and Western meals. ✉ *60 Stevens Rd., Stevens Road, 257854* ☎ *6737–7755* 📠 *6235–5528* 🌐 *www.mymca.org.sg* 🛏 *93 rooms* 👍 *Restaurant, coffee shop, minibars, cable TV, pool, gym, shop, laundry service, laundry facilities, business services, meeting rooms, travel services, free parking, no-smoking floors* 💳 *AE, DC, MC, V* 🍽 *EP* Ⓜ *Orchard.*

Batam Island, Indonesia

$–$$$ **Batam View.** Batam's first and largest resort is on the island's northeast tip and has over 240 acres of gardens as well as a private beach and watersports. Rooms have cream-color fabrics, shiny wood floors, and cane furniture. A live band performs nightly at 7 in the lounge. ✉ *Jalan Hang Lekir, Nongsa* ☎ *627/7876–1740* 📠 *627/7876–1747* 🌐 *www.batamviewresort.com* 🛏 *161 rooms, 16 suites, 18 villas* 👍 *3 restaurants, 18-hole golf course, tennis court, pool, massage, spa, snorkeling, windsurfing, jet skiing, fishing, basketball, squash, lounge, nightclub, meeting rooms* 💳 *AE, D, MC, V* 🍽 *CP.*

$–$$ **Turi Beach Resort.** This five-level resort is in Nongsa, on the island's northeastern side, spread over 45 oceanfront acres. The Balinese bungalows are surrounded by natural jungle, with striking views of the deep blue ocean. There's an on-site karaoke lounge. ✉ *Nongsa* ☎ *627/7876–1084* 📠 *627/7876–1043* 🌐 *www.nongsaresorts.com* 🛏 *130 rooms* 👍 *3 restaurants, golf course, tennis courts, pool, massage, volleyball, pub, meeting rooms* 💳 *AE, DC, MC, V* 🍽 *BP.*

¢–$ ⊞ **Novotel Batam.** In this value-priced hotel by the sea the rooms are basic, clean, and modern. You have easy access to golf courses, shopping, and the entertainment district in Nagoya. Common areas have Western-style decorations. ⊠ *Jalan Duyung, Sei Jodoh* ☎ *627/7842–5555* 🖷 *627/ 7842–6555* ⊕ *www.novotel.com* ☙ *254 rooms* 🖒 *Restaurant, cable TV, putting green, pool, health club, hot tub, massage, 2 bars, pub, shops, baby-sitting, children's programs (ages 3 and up), meeting rooms* ☱ *AE, DC, MC, V* ⓞⓘ *CP.*

Bintan Island, Indonesia

Bintan's resorts dot wide sandy beaches on the northern coast; book as far in advance as possible. On weekends Singaporeans and expats take full advantage of the island's clean waters, just 45 minutes from one of the world's busiest ports.

The resorts accept Singapore dollars for rooms and for meals (price categories assigned below are based on Singapore dollars), though credit card purchases for other items may be charged in Indonesian rupiahs at, no doubt, a better rate of exchange. All resorts have their marketing offices in Singapore; for more information contact **Bintan Resort Management** (☎ 6543–0039 ⊕ www.bintan-resorts.com). If for some reason you need to dial an establishment directly, the country code for Indonesia is 62, and the area code for Bintan is 771.

Free shuttles run every half hour between Nirwana Hotel and Bintan Lagoon Resort. Shuttles linking other resorts are independently owned by hotels and aren't free. If you have to rely on a taxi to get around, you need to book it in advance from a car-rental agency at the ferry terminal. Ask the front-desk staff of your hotel to help with the arrangements.

★ $$$$ ⊞ **Banyan Tree Bintan.** Overlooking a horseshoe-shape bay, this resort is composed of Balinese-style villas perched on stilts. Fifty-five of the villas have a decktop whirlpool tub that faces the South China Sea. The more luxurious Pool Villas have either a private swimming pool or a plunge pool with king-size beds, and a kitchen. Additionally, the Banyan Tree's three restaurants are among the best in Bintan. There's access to a beautiful beach and you can easily arrange excursions to Bintan's sights. ⊠ *Site A4, Lagoi, Tanjong Said* ☎ *6462–4800 in Singapore, 770/ 693100 in Bintan* 🖷 *6462–2800 in Singapore, 770/693200 in Bintan* ⊕ *www.banyantree.com* ☙ *72 villas* 🖒 *3 restaurants, cable TV, 18-hole golf course, 2 tennis courts, 2 pools, outdoor hot tub, spa, beach, dive shop, dock, snorkeling, windsurfing, waterskiing, fishing, meeting rooms* ☱ *AE, MC, V.*

$$–$$$$ ⊞ **Bintan Lagoon Resort Hotel and Golf Club.** Japanese visitors and golfers alike are drawn to this enormous villa complex. Although it's on the beach, this hotel isn't as aesthetically appealing or relaxed as some other resorts. Still, it *is* a golfer's paradise, with two 18-hole courses— one designed by Jack Nicklaus, the other by Ian Baker-Finch. There are two pools—one of them *very* large—water-sports facilities, a mah-jongg hall, and a children's center. ⊠ *Pasir Panjang Beach, north coast*

☎ 6226–3122 *in Singapore, 770/691388 in Bintan* 🖷 *6223–0693 in Singapore, 770/691399 in Bintan* ⊕ *www.bintanlagoon.com* 🛏 *416 rooms, 57 villas* ♨ *7 restaurants, 2 driving ranges, 2 18-hole golf course, 2 putting greens, 4 tennis courts, 2 pools, health club, massage, spa, beach, jet skiing, waterskiing, water sports, fishing, bicycles, billiards, Ping-Pong, volleyball, dance club, baby-sitting, children's programs (ages 4–12), playground, laundry service, business services, meeting rooms, travel services* ⊟ *AE, DC, MC, V.*

$$$ 🖃 **Club Med Ria Bintan.** Typical of Club Med, the range of activities is the big draw—there's even a circus school for children. As the resort is frequented by Europeans, Japanese, and Club Med junkies from around the world, its staff members are multilingual. The general feeling here is that you never need to leave the resort for anything; everything is very well organized (great if you want to be involved, not so great if you're seeking solitude). The rooms are comfortable and have balconies and stunning sunset views. ⊠ *North coast* ☎ *6738–4222 in Singapore, 770/692801 in Bintan* 🖷 *6738–0770 in Singapore, 770/692829 in Bintan* ⊕ *www.clubmed.com* 🛏 *302 rooms* ♨ *4 restaurants, 2 tennis courts, 2 pools, aerobics, health club, spa, beach, archery, bar, cabaret, dance club, baby-sitting, children's programs (2 years and up), playground, laundry facilities, meeting rooms* ⊟ *AE, MC, V* ⏏ *FAP.*

$$ 🖃 **Mayang Sari Beach Resort.** On a bay with an exquisite palm-lined beach, the relaxed, friendly Mayang Sari is a quiet retreat—the perfect place to read a novel or go beachcombing. There's a rustic feel to its chalet-style cabins, which have high ceilings, Indonesian teak furnishings, large beds, and private verandas. This, Bintan's first resort property, is reminiscent of Bali in the 1960s: tall palm trees lining the beach, friendly service, decent prices, gentle breezes. The on-site Mayang Terrace restaurant serves delicious Indonesian dishes at affordable prices. ⊠ *Northwest coast at Tanjong Tondang* ☎ *6372–1308 in Singapore, 778/323088 in Bintan* 🖷 *6372–1318 in Singapore, 778/323080 in Bintan* 🛏 *50 cabins* ♨ *Restaurant, beach, 2 bars, recreation room, baby-sitting, laundry service, meeting room* ⊟ *AE, MC, V.*

¢–$ 🖃 **Mana Mana.** Young Europeans and Australians, many of them college students, flock to this resort for its affordable rates; water-sports enthusiasts of all ages are drawn by the facilities at its beach club, which holds a beach party every Saturday night. Accommodations are in small huts in a garden setting; only the lobby and alfresco restaurant-bar front the beach. ⊠ *North coast* ☎ *6339–8878 in Singapore* 🖷 *6339–7812 in Singapore* ⊕ *www.manamana.com* 🛏 *50 rooms in 25 huts with television and air-conditioning* ♨ *Restaurant, beach, snorkeling, windsurfing, boating, bar* ⊟ *AE, MC, V.*

Sentosa Island

☾ **$$$** 🖃 **Rasa Sentosa Resort.** It's a vast, arc-shape building facing the sea that's popular with both conventions and Singaporean families escaping to the beach for the weekend. The motel-like rooms are small, but all have balconies; ask for a room facing the water, or else your view will be of a grassy knoll. The main restaurant serves Cantonese fare, and the café dishes up western and Asian food. Children love this place for its pool with water slides, and adults can rock climb (on a wall), golf, or windsurf. A free shuttle bus from the Shangri-La Hotel will bring you here. ✉ *101 Siloso Rd., Sentosa Island, 098970* ☎ *6275–0100, 020/8747–8485 for reservations in the U.K., 800/ 942–5050 for reservations in Canada and the U.S.* 🖷 *6275–0355* ⊕ *www.shangri-la.com* ➷ *441 rooms, 18 suites* ♨ *3 restaurants, café, room service, in-room data ports, in-room safes, minibars, cable TV with movies, pool, health club, massage, windsurfing, boating, Ping-Pong, bar, lobby lounge, recreation room, video game room, shops, playground, dry cleaning, laundry service, business services, convention center, free parking, no-smoking rooms* ⊟ *AE, DC, MC, V* ❏ *MAP* Ⓜ *World Trade Centre.*

$$$ 🏨 **The Sentosa Resort and Spa.** The remote location of this resort is ideal for business seminars and leisure visitors who wish to escape. The best feature is its pool, which overlooks the Malacca Straits and is flanked by a romantic, open-air seafood restaurant. Deluxe rooms aren't very large (though bathrooms are of a good size) and have nondescript pastel furniture, but they look on to tropical parklands. The Garden rooms have larger bedrooms and work areas with better-quality furniture such as handmade tortoiseshell desks, mosaic tables, and French banquette sofas. There are four luxurious two-bedroom villas, each with its own pool. ✉ *2 Bukit Manis Rd., Sentosa Island, 099891* ☎ *6275–0331, 800/ 637–7200 for reservations in the U.S.* 🖷 *6275–0228* ⊕ *www.beaufort. com.sg* ➷ *175 rooms, 34 suites, 4 villas* ♨ *3 restaurants, room service, in-room data ports, in-room safes, minibars, cable TV, golf privileges, 2 tennis courts, pool, gym, spa, squash, volleyball, bar, lounge, dry cleaning, laundry service, concierge, Internet, business services, convention center, parking (fee), no-smoking rooms* ⊟ *AE, DC, MC, V* ❏ *BP* Ⓜ *World Trade Centre.*

NIGHTLIFE & THE ARTS

4

Updated by
Ilsa Sharp

A WARM, TROPICAL CLIME ENABLES SINGAPOREANS TO STAY OUT AT ALL HOURS. Considering their long working hours (the government just ended Saturday half-days for civil servants), it seems only natural that locals would want to unwind in their free time. Nevertheless, business networking at bars, clubs, and restaurants is second nature to most locals; not all of the fun is as simple and straightforward as it may look. Taxis tend to go into hiding before the 50% midnight surcharge kicks in, so people who don't go home by 10 PM usually stay out until well after midnight. The nightlife and arts scene in Singapore is lively, although local recession and international terrorism scares (with consequent security warnings about spots frequented by Westerners) have somewhat affected it. The government's decision to relax nightlife restrictions, specifically by sometimes permitting 24-hour entertainment, has encouraged the scene's survival.

NIGHTLIFE

Nightclubs and discos are glitzy and pricey, targeted chiefly at the young or those on the prowl, and are very, very loud, making conversation near impossible. The action stays focused on geographically separated clusters. The more established districts are still going strong: the lively Singapore River quayside scene (Boat, Clarke, and Robertson quays, together with Chinatown's Tanjong Pagar district); the touristy hotel strip of Orchard Road; and the nineteenth-century former convent, the Chijmes complex, near the Singapore History Museum off Stamford and Bras Basah roads.

The sleazier, more colorful action on the east coast—from Kallang to Katong (e.g., the Joo Chiat Road strip around the old Joo Chiat Police Station and Dunman Market food center), and around Serangoon, out to Changi Village—gratifies with its rough-and-ready charms and authentic local food. In recent years, as authorities have eased up on the nightlife scene, so the sleaze quotient has escalated, although once-bawdy Bugis Street is now sanitized as New Bugis Street. Be aware that this underworld still exists in parts of Geylang, around the numbered *lorongs* (streets or lanes) off Geylang Road, and along Desker Road, off Jalan Besar, Serangoon.

Typically, red-light districts are illuminated by red lanterns and have large, backlit red-on-white house numbers. Soliciting for prostitution is illegal, but the deed itself isn't; it's actually tolerated, monitored, and contained, with most prostitutes registered and subject to regular medical checks. Perhaps uniquely in Southeast Asia, however, this scene doesn't menace visitors who don't want to get involved and it's still closely monitored by the police.

If karaoke is what you seek, beware that it may come with many "extras" in the Singapore context. To some extent, there have always been intensely local (and usually Chinese) bars with "sexual action on the side." In the past, these were merely darkly lit shops where patrons were relieved of large sums of money by obliging hostesses (and there are still some of these venues around). This genre has now been recast in the karaoke bar mold. One bizarre new feature of some bars, including several along the Mohamed Sultan stretch, is the specially widened bar counter, now custom-made for bar-top dancing, a government-sanctioned activity since August 2003.

The gay scene is also increasingly active and out of the closet, though technically illegal (cruisers beware entrapment). The relatively new trend of dedicated gay bars has continued apace and centers particularly on the Chinatown district of Tanjong Pagar.

Ethnic enclave bars are a new trend in Singapore. Indian pubs purvey Bollywood-style music, Hindi pop, hip-hop, and Punjabi-style bhangra dancing and Malay-oriented establishments serve the raw hard rock favored by young Malay Singaporeans. Catch the local band Unwanted playing at O'Reilly's Irish Bar (not very Irish) at 86 East Coast Road, or stop in on a weeknight at the fabled Anywhere bar in Orchard's Tanglin Shopping Centre to hear Malay-style rock music.

Jazz and the blues have always been minority interests in Singapore. With the lamented demise of Somerset's, only a few venues have kept the flag flying: Harry's Quayside Cafe (a.k.a. Harry's Bar) and Jazz@Southbridge on Boat Quay for jazz, Crazy Elephant on Clarke Quay and Roomful of Blues on Prinsep Street for blues.

Bars & Pubs

★ **Balaclava.** Smartly dressed executives and twentysomething professionals hang loose after hours in this sophisticated chill-out bar. It's close to the Esplanade complex, and about as downtown CBD as you can get. Lounge in leather armchairs to live music some nights (call to check when). No casual threads here, there's a dress code: no shorts, jeans, T-shirts, or rubber sandals. ⊠ #01–01B Suntec City Convention Centre, 1 Raffles Blvd., CBD ☎ 6339–1600 ☉ Mon.–Thurs. 3 PM–1 AM; Fri., Sat., and holiday eves 3 PM–2 AM; closed Sun.

Bar Opiume. Movers and shakers take pause here relaxing to spectacular views of the Singapore River and business district skyline. The opulent—if a little confused—decor includes massive Czechoslovakian crystal chandeliers and towering gold-leaf Buddhas. The bar declares itself Asia's first prosecco (sparkling white wine) and vodka bar. It's part of Indo-Chine, so there's Indo-Chinese finger food, such as spring rolls and prawns on sugarcane. ⊠ Asian Civilisations Museum, 1 Empress Pl., Colonial Singapore ☎ 6339–2876, 6339–1720 ⊕ www.indochine.com.sg/baropium.html ☉ Sun.–Thurs. 5 PM–2 AM, Fri. and Sat. 5 PM–3 AM.

Barcelona. Get a taste of Spain's most exciting city at this bar with a Catalan flavor. Dip into the salsa music, fine wines, and tapas-style finger foods; fall into the plush, comfy couches. Starting at 8:30 PM Wednesday through Saturday there's live world music. ⊠ #01–30/31, 11 Unity St., Robertson Quay ☎ 6327–8327, 6235–3456 ⊕ www.uno-restaurant.com.sg ☉ Sun.–Thurs. 5 PM–1 AM, Fri. and Sat. 5 PM–2 AM.

Bisous. This is a sophisticated, but relaxed bar for the mature who like to converse, not shout. If you come for an early drink, you can also enjoy a set three-course Mediterranean or Mexican lunch. Tuesday is Trivia Night; Friday is Disco Night. ⊠ #01–01 Capital Square Three, 25

Age Restrictions

Age restrictions are imposed by individual bars for their own reasons; some dance bars won't admit anyone below 16. The only legal restrictions are that you must be at least 18 to drink alcohol.

Dress

Almost everywhere—except at posher hotels—dress codes are relaxed, even casual, thanks to the heat and humidity.

Hours

Most clubs open in the early evening around 5 PM and close their doors by 1 or 2 AM on weekdays. On the weekend, they tend to stay open until 3 or 4 AM.

4

Prices

Cover charges, which sometimes include a first drink, can run from S$20 to S$30. Unless noted otherwise, the bars listed don't have cover charges. It's more common for nightclubs and discos to have such fees.

Happy hours offering discount drinks exist here, so calling ahead to find out when they are could save you some money. Many places welcome women for free or at a reduced rate.

Liquor prices are inflated by the government's high excise and import taxes (no import duty on wine, but the excise is about S$10 per liter). Most beers cost about S$8, spirits are a bit more, and a glass of wine can set you back S$10 to $S15. Wine bottles usually cost at least S$40. Buying wine from a supermarket may save you some, but these prices still run high and BYOB isn't universally accepted.

Safety

Groups of ladies out for a night on the town are a common sight, but drinking alone isn't that easy for a woman—it's seen as an invitation for someone to approach. Public confrontation isn't very common so a firm and fairly loud "Get lost!" should remedy the situation. Never use foul language or prolong the scene more than needed. When in doubt, ask for help from the management or the bouncers.

Church St., off Raffles Pl., CBD ☎ *6226–5505* ⊕ *www.bisous.com.sg* ⊙ *Mon.–Thurs. 11:30 PM–1 AM, Fri. 11:30 PM–2 AM, Sat. 5 PM–2 AM, closed Sun.*

★ **Brewerkz.** Beer lovers home in on this large open-plan brewery, which brews its own beers, bitters, and ales. The most popular brew is the India Pale Ale. The pub's English-style real ale (a.k.a. cask ale) is a rarity in Southeast Asia. This bar claimed a gold medal in the Association of Brewers World Beer Cup 2004. The kitchen serves American fare. ✉ *#01–05/06 Riverside Point, 30 Merchant Rd., Robertson Quay* ☎ *6438–7438* ⊕ *www.brewerkz.com* ⊙ *Sun.–Thurs. noon–3 AM, Fri. and Sat. noon–1 AM.*

Brix. Globetrotters, local lovelies, and sundry fun seekers come here for the whiskey, wine, music, and singles scene. The music includes the familiar Top 40, disco, soul, R&B, and jazz standards, with a live band starting at 9 PM nightly, at which time the dance floor gets packed. ✉ *Grand Hyatt Singapore, 10–12 Scotts Rd., Orchard* ☎ *6416–7107* ⊕ *http://restaurants.singapore.hyatt.com/brix/brix_intro.html* 🎫 *Cover: S$25 Thurs.–Sat. after 9 PM* ☽ *Sun.–Thurs. 5 PM–2 AM, Fri. and Sat. 5 PM–3 AM.*

★ **Carnegie's.** The after-work crew jams this bar. No wonder, since there are specials galore: at the weekday 6–7 PM Crazy Hour all drinks are S$6, Tuesday through Saturday 9–10 PM there are Power Hour drinks for S$3, on Wednesday ladies get free champagne after 9 PM. Quiz nights are on Monday and Latino dance nights are on Tuesday. There's good food to be had and a weekend brunch. ✉ *#01–01 Far East Square, 44/45 Pekin St., Chinatown* ☎ *6534–0850* ⊕ *http://carnegies.net* ☽ *Sun. and Mon. 11 AM–midnight, Tues.–Thurs. 11 AM–2 AM, Fri. and Sat. 11 AM–3 AM.*

Devil's Bar @ Red Cafe. Soccer-crazy Singaporeans gather here to celebrate England's premier soccer team, Manchester United (a.k.a. the Red Devils). Big TV screens guarantee that patrons won't miss a single goal. Tiger Beer in hand, you can relax in the Chill Out Zone, listen to live music in the Live Room, dance in the Dance Bar, or play pool in the Sports Bar. This bar pioneered the "daring" bar-top dancing. You can pick up soccer souvenirs in the attached megastore. ✉ *#02–01 Orchard Parade Hotel, 1 Tanglin Rd., Orchard* ☎ *6732–0819, 6733–7676* 🎫 *Cover: (includes 1 drink) weekdays S$12 and weekends S$20 for men; Fri. and Sat. S$12 for women* ☽ *Chill Out Zone: daily 11 AM–3 AM; Dance Bar: daily 9 PM–3 AM; Live Room: daily 5 PM–5 AM; Sports Bar: daily 5 PM–3 AM; Megastore: daily 11–9.*

Embargo. Wash down your tapas with sangria while taking in a stunning harbor view in this airy seafront bar, near the Esplanade complex. The cool and young crowd lounges on velvet sofas, grooving to drum'n'bass and smooth-sounding tracks from one of the resident DJs. ✉ *One Fullerton, Level 1, 1 Fullerton Rd., Colonial Singapore* ☎ *6220–6556* ☽ *Sun.–Thurs. 5 PM–2 AM, Fri. and Sat. 5 PM–3 AM.*

Father Flanagan's. Aptly (or inaptly?) located in the historic 19th-century Chijmes convent complex, this Irish pub serves fish-and-chips or beef and Guinness pie at lunch; seafood at dinner; and a variety of brews all day (try the pub's own label, Monk's Brew, an Irish red ale). ✉ *#B1-06 Fountain Court, Chijmes complex, 30 Victoria St., Colonial Singapore* ☎ *6333–1418* ⊕ *www.fatherflanagan.com* ☽ *Daily 11 AM–2 AM.*

Hard Rock Café. Hamburgers and large portions of Tex-Mex fare are served at this split-level music pub–café. A live band plays from 10:30 PM nightly, with jam sessions on Sunday night—and Kumar, a gifted local comedian/female impersonator, struts his stuff during a campy show on Monday at 10:30 PM. It's much like other establishments in the chain: casual, festive, and filled with rock memorabilia. ✉ *#05–01 HPL House, 50 Cuscaden Rd., Orchard* ☎ *6235–5232* ⊕ *www.hardrock.com.sg* 🎫 *Cover: S$23 Sat.* ☽ *Sun.–Thurs. 11 AM–2 AM, Fri. and Sat. 11 AM–3 AM.*

4

Cultural Centers

Several foreign government-supported cultural centers have buoyed local talent by, among other things, networking Singapore's artists abroad. These centers have exceptional libraries and lively programs showcasing the performing and visual arts of their countries and of Singapore, as well as excellent movie festivals. Membership isn't always required, and many events are open to the public and free. These include: **The Alliance Française** (⊠ 1 Sarkies Rd., Bukit Timah ☎ 6737–8422 ⊕ www. alliancefrancaise.org.sg); **The British Council** (⊠ 30 Napier Rd., Orchard ☎ 6473–1111 ⊕ www.britishcouncil.org/sg.htm); and **The Goethe Institut.** (⊠ #05–01 Winsland House, 163 Penang Rd., Orchard ☎ 6735–4555 ⊕ www.goethe.de/so/sin/enindex.htm).

Multimedia

Arts Explosion, an arts and current events magazine, is published by the TV corporation MediaCorp, with support from the NAC and the Singapore Tourism Board (STB). You can find it online at ⊕ http://pdf.todayonline.com/index_pdf.htm. Alternatively, you can tune into Passion 99.5 FM, Singapore's only arts radio station.

Tickets

Tickets typically run around S$25 to S$35, sometimes cheaper. Tickets to a concert by the Singapore Symphony Orchestra usually range from S$12 to S$60. Big-name acts from abroad can set you back S$80 to S$100. Cinema tickets cost about S$7 or S$8.

Two agencies dominate the ticketing scene: **SISTIC** (☎ 6348–5555 ⊕ www. sistic.com.sg) and **TicketCharge** (☎ 6296–2929 ⊕ www.ticketchargeasia. com). Both have counters at shopping centers, such as Centrepoint on Orchard Road and Raffles City in Colonial Singapore.

Venues

Singapore's arts venues are widely scattered. Not all are easily accessed via public transport—the Kallang/National Stadium area is an example.

A 95-foot (29-meter) high glass roof and restored colonial architecture make **AR-Trium@MICA** (⊠ MICA Bldg., 140 Hill St., Colonial Singapore ☎ 6837–9561 ⊕ www.nac.gov.sg/tbo) an interesting space for both visual and performing arts.

The **Centre for the Arts** (⊠ The National University of Singapore, 10 Kent Ridge Crescent, West Coast ☎ 6874–6114, 6874–1224, or 6874–4041 ⊕ www. nus.edu.sg/cfa) has an auditorium; music, dance, electronics, and pottery studios; and an extensive library of scores, scripts, and recordings. At the library you can see a collection of Western and Asian musical instruments on request. The 579-seat **DBS Auditorium** (⊠ DBS Bldg., Tower One, 3rd floor, 6 Shenton Way, CBD ☎ 6224–9633) is always hosting some kind of music or theater event.

The **Esplanade–Theatres on the Bay** (⊠ Esplanade Co. Ltd., 1 Esplanade Dr. ☎ 6828–8389/8377 ⊕ www.esplanade.com) is as iconic a Singapore landmark as Sydney's Opera House. The controversial S$600 million structure has been dubbed "The Durian" (after the prickly, smelly local fruit) in reference to its faceted, prickled, and domed architecture. The complex sits on a nearly 15-acre site and it has a 2,000-seat, horseshoe-shape theater, a 1,600-seat concert hall, outdoor performance spaces, studios, and many stores and restaurants.

Jubilee Hall (⊠ Raffles Hotel Arcade, 3rd floor, 328 North Bridge Rd., Colonial Singapore ☏ 6412–1319) is a cozy 388-seat theater modeled on an early-20th-century English music hall. The **Kallang Theatre** (⊠ Stadium Walk, East Coast/Kallang ☏ 6345–8488 ⊕ www.nac.gov.sg), near the National Stadium, has over 1,700 seats and often hosts big, imported shows and musicals. The landmark **National Stadium** (⊠ 15 Stadium Rd., East Coast/Kallang ☏ 6345–7111) is a massive facility chiefly for sports, which also accommodates cultural events.

The modern **Kreta Ayer People's Theatre** (⊠ 30-A Kreta Ayer Rd., Chinatown ☏ 6391–2183) seats 1,102 people for traditional Chinese opera, martial arts presentations, and acrobatic shows. With its 12,000 seats and striking architecture by Japanese architect Kenzo Tange, the **Singapore Indoor Stadium** (⊠ 2 Stadium Walk, East Coast/Kallang ☏ 6344–2660 ⊕ www.sis.gov.sg) can accommodate anything from a Bollywood extravaganza to a Russian circus. Quality performances of all kinds, from Western and Chinese opera to Indian classical dance and Western plays, take place at the old 904-seat **Victoria Theatre** (⊠ 9 Empress Pl., Colonial Singapore ☏ 6338–8283). In the same gracious old wedding-cake building as the Victoria Theatre is the 937-seat **Victoria Concert Hall** (⊠ 11 Empress Pl., 2nd floor, Colonial Singapore ☏ 6338–1239, 6338–1230), home of the Singapore Symphony Orchestra.

Adjacent to the Victoria theatre complex, in Singapore's Old Parliament Building, is **The Arts House** (⊠ 1 Old Parliament La., Colonial Singapore ☏ 6332–6900/6919 ⊕ www.theartshouse.com.sg). It contains a 72-seat movie theater, a 160-seat music chamber, and a 120-seat black-box theater, as well as a rehearsal studio and visual arts gallery. In deference to the building's past, there's also a constitutional history display.

★ The "fringe" rules at the young, avant-garde, vibrant **Substation** (⊠ 45 Armenian St., Colonial Singapore ☏ 6337–7535 for information, 6337–7800 for tickets ⊕ www.substation.org). It has a dance studio, art shop and gallery, and theater. Actors, artists, and musicians gather in the rear courtyard for alfresco drinks. Check out the bulletin boards and leaflet racks for more information.

★ **Hooha Café.** Music industry insiders, club owners, and musicians congregate at this club in the small but lively Pasir Panjang Village entertainment hub. The Saturday night jamming and sing-along action may go into the wee hours upstairs, behind closed doors, with people leaving the bar to go directly to morning mass. There's no band, but drumsets and guitars are strategically available upstairs. Downstairs there's a bar and restaurant—the tenderloin steaks are famous and there's even ostrich, too! ⊠ *220 Pasir Panjang Rd., West Coast* ☏ *6475–2210* ⊕ *www.hoohacafe.com* ☉ *Daily noon–11:30* PM.

THE SLING IS THE THING

IKE THE LEGENDARY SHOOTING OF SINGAPORE'S *last wild tiger under the billiard table at Raffles Hotel (that's for another time), the Singapore Sling is part of Singaporean folklore. The consensus is that Ngiam Tong Boon, a Raffles Hotel bartender, created the pink-colored drink with thirsty ladies in mind. That's where the agreement ends: some claim the first Sling was concocted in 1915, others contend that it was given life in 1913, and the hotel insists that it was created prior to 1910. Many purists insist that the original recipe was lost in the 1930s. They contend that the drink, in its current incarnation, is based on the memories of retired bartenders. The hotel's museum shop has what it claims is the safe where Mr. Ngiam locked away his recipe books, and the original Sling recipe. Leave the debate to the die-hards. Order a tall glass at the peanut shell–covered* Long Bar at Raffles Hotel or make your own version with these ingredients:

1½ ounces gin
½ ounce Cherry Herring brandy
¼ ounce Cointreau
¼ ounce Benedictine
4 ounces pineapple juice
½ ounce lime juice
⅓ ounce grenadine
a dash of bitters

Shake the mix with ice, pour it into a chilled glass, and garnish the drink with cherries or pineapple. Sip with care: the juices often mask the gin, brandy, Cointreau, and Benedictine.

— Josie Taylor

Fodor's Choice ★ **Ice Cold Beer.** Noted for its Straits-Chinese architecture, this 1910 townhouse is a bustling pub that attracts European expats. The bar serves some 35 international beers (ice cold from vast ice tanks), ranging from S$10 to S$12 a pop, and nine-inch hot dogs are available for S$6. Upstairs is the pub's cozy Stellar Bar, modeled on the Interbrew headquarters in Belgium, with tall mirrors and warm earth tones. All of the classic Interbrew beers are served here, including Stella Artois and Hoegaarden. Rock music from the '70s and '80s provides the soundtrack. There are cheap beer promotions all day Sunday. ⊠ *5 Emerald Hill Rd., Orchard* ☎ *6735–9929* ⊕ *www.emerald-hill.com/main/icb_about_us.htm* ⊡ *No one under 25 admitted* ☼ *Sun.–Thurs. 5 PM–2 AM, Fri. and Sat. 5 PM–3 AM.*

InkClub. This chic cocoon hasn't yet inherited the reputation of Somerset's Bar, the jazz club it supplanted, since it doesn't have live music. From 5 PM–8 PM nightly, champagne is served for S$15 a glass, cocktails S$10, and beer S$9, but don't forget that standard bills here come with various taxes on top of the actual price. ⊠ *Raffles The Plaza, 2 Stamford Rd. Marina Square* ☎ *6431–5315* ☼ *Lounge: daily 9 AM–5 PM; Bar: daily 5 PM–3 AM; Club (DJ music): weekdays 5 PM–3 AM, Saturdays 5 PM–4 AM.*

Les Amis Wine Bar. Wine is an expensive taste in Singapore, where high import duties up the ante. So if you're going to have it, you might as well do it right. There's some premium stuff here: limited-edition eiswein and top choices from France, Italy, Spain, Germany, Australia, and California. This classy bar serves fine French cuisine as well. ✉ #02–16 Shaw Centre, 1 Scotts Rd., Orchard ☎ 6733–2225 ⊕ www.lesamis.com.sg ⊘ Mon.–Sat. 5 PM–1 AM, closed Sun.

★ **Molly Malone's Irish Pub.** It's an Emerald Isle pub that offers several beers, hearty sandwiches, and free pies during televised soccer or rugby matches. Molly's Chipper upstairs serves such eats as British sausage and french fries. ✉ 42 Circular Rd., Boat Quay ☎ 6536–2029 ⊕ www.mollymalone.com ⊘ Sun. and Mon. 11 AM–midnight, Tues.–Thurs. 11 AM–1 AM, Fri. and Sat. 11 AM–2 AM.

Muddy Murphy's. This pub was built in Dublin, Ireland, before it was reassembled in Singapore. Famed for its wine and cheese promotions, Sunday Roast lunches (S$20), and live Irish-Celtic bands, the pub also offers whiskeys, draft Kilkenny Ale and Guinness Stout, and Cuban and Dutch cigars. The upstairs is modeled to look like an early-20th-century Dublin grocery store. ✉ #B1–01/06 Orchard Hotel Shopping Arcade, 442 Orchard Rd., Orchard ☎ 6735–0400 ⊕ www.gaelicinns.com.sg ⊘ Sun.–Thurs. 5 PM–2 AM, Fri. and Sat. 5 PM–3 AM.

Fodor'sChoice **New Asia Bar.** Atop Singapore's highest building, which is also Southeast Asia's tallest hotel, is this 180-seat bilevel spot. The bar is on the 71st and 72nd floors, but you'll need advance reservations to access the 72nd level, where striking views are enhanced by the way the floors slant 20 degrees downwards. There are Asian food options in the grill section, as well as shellfish and sushi stations. The vibrant decor features strong colors and unusual designer furnishings. A DJ pushes up the beat with disco music on the weekend. ✉ Swissôtel The Stamford, 2 Stamford Rd., Colonial Singapore ☎ 6431–5681, 6837–3322 ⊞ Cover: S$20 Fri. and Sat. ⊘ Sun.–Wed. 3 PM–1 AM, Thurs.–Sat. 3 PM–3 AM.

No. 5 Emerald Hill Cocktail Bar. Inside an early-20th-century, bilevel Straits-Chinese shophouse is No. 5, a relaxed bar where you're free to lounge on the floor cushions and carpets. You can listen to live blues and jazz while shooting pool here. Adventurous types may try house specialty No. 5 Vodka infusions.Bar snacks and pizzas range from S$8 to S$15. ✉ 5 Emerald Hill, Orchard ☎ 6732–0818 ⊕ www.emeraldhill.com/no5.htm ⊘ Mon.–Thurs. noon–2 AM, Fri. and Sat. noon–3 AM, Sun. 5 PM–9 PM.

★ **Que Pasa.** Wine lovers lounge in deep Chesterfield chairs at this bar resembling a Spanish provisions store. You can have tapas to accompany a glass of wine, which goes for S$11–S$16. The upstairs lounge is for bottles only (S$45–S$53), or you can order a jug of sangria for S$30. For a nominal fee, you can attend the bar's monthly wine tasting and appreciation talks. ✉ 7 Emerald Hill Rd., Orchard ☎ 6235–6626 ⊕ www.emeraldhillgroup.com/qp.htm ⊘ Sun.–Thurs. 6 PM–2 AM, Fri. and Sat. 6 PM–3 AM.

Tivoli Beer Bar. Favored by soccer fans for its big-screen televised matches, Tivoli is a friendly and casual European-style bar. Happy hour is twice daily from 5 PM to 9 PM, and from 1 AM until 3 AM. ✉ #01–23/

24 Robertson Walk, 11 Unity St., Mohamed Sultan ☎ *6738–1318* ⊕ *www.emeraldhillgroup.com/tivoli.htm* ☉ *Mon.–Sat. 5 PM–3 AM, Sun. 6 PM–3 AM.*

★ **Wala Wala.** In the hip nook of Holland Village, somewhat off the Orchard axis, is this wildly popular bar with live music upstairs (from 9:30 PM on weekends and from 6:30 PM on weekdays) and a bustling bar and table games downstairs. There's an outdoor sitting area with a welcome boulevardier feel to it, not to mention good western eats like pizza and steak. It's always crowded, partly thanks to the two-for-one happy hour from 4 PM–9 PM daily. ✉ *31 Lorong Mambong, Holland Village* ☎ *6462–4288* ☉ *Sun.–Thurs. 4 PM–1 AM, Fri. and Sat. 4 PM–2 AM.*

Dance Clubs

China Black. Teak paneling and Chinese calligraphy adorn the interior of this 10,000-square-foot penthouse disco, where dancers let loose on the large dance floor and a DJ plays Top 40 pop, techno, and house music. Strange cocktails—try the Shaolin Fist—add perspective to the views of the city skyline. The crowd is young, and the lines to get in are usually long. ✉ *Pacific Plaza Penthouse, 12th floor, 9 Scotts Rd., Orchard* ☎ *6734–7677* ⊕ *http://chinajump.hotspots.com* ▭ *Cover: Fri. and Sat. S$18 for men, S$15 for women* ☉ *Wed.–Sat. 8 PM–3 AM, closed Sun.–Tues.*

★ **China Jump.** What's by day a Tex-Mex restaurant becomes a busy club after dark. Veteran band Jive Talking plays every night but Wednesday starting at 10:30 PM; there's also a DJ who spins disco tunes. The decor is fashionable contemporary Chinese with soft colors, wooden screens, and a marble staircase. ✉ *#B1–07/08 Fountain Court, Chijmes, 30 Victoria St., Colonial Singapore* ☎ *6338–9388* ▭ *Cover: S$20, free for women on Wed.* ☉ *Daily 6:30 PM–3 AM.*

★ **Coccolatte.** Unconventional creative types and many entertainment executives frequent this bilevel disco. On the first floor is a latte lounge, upstairs is the DJ station. The music is always cutting edge, with a hip-hop and R&B slant on the weekend. A sophisticated Japanese-style mural in the lounge is complemented by sparkling mood lighting and low modular furniture. There's original artwork all over the place and the themed decor in the upstairs dancing area changes bimonthly (recent theme, "the world's oldest profession"). Wednesday is ladies night, and Thursday is gay night. ✉ *#01–09 Gallery Evason Hotel, 76 Robertson Quay Rd., Robertson Quay* ☎ *6735–0402* ⊕ *www.coccolatte.com* ☉ *Mon.–Wed. 5 PM–1 AM; Thurs., Fri., and Sun. 5 PM–3 AM; Sat. 5 PM–4 AM; dance floor closed Tues.–Thurs.*

dbl-O. Different styles of high-energy dancing, dance music each night, and beautiful girls are among the draws at this glitzy club. Drinks cost only S$3 and a jug or pitcher of beer runs about S$12. ✉ *#01–24 Robertson Walk, 11 Unity St., Mohamed Sultan* ☎ *6735–2008* ⊕ *www.emeraldhillgroup.com/dblO/index.htm* ▭ *Cover: Weds. S$25 for men, free for women; Thurs. S$10 for men, free for women; Fri.–Sun. S$20 for men, S$15 for women* ☉ *Wed.–Fri. and Sun. 8 PM–3 AM, Sat 8 PM–4 AM, closed Mon. andTues.*

★ **Lempicka.** Taking its name from Polish artist Tamara De Lempicka (1898–1980), the club showcases some serious, and seriously valuable, art deco works. The interior is infused with a warm, cozy sensuality, and the music is New Age and tribal sprinkled with Top 40 tunes. The mature and elegantly casual crowd probably appreciates the club's dedication to maintaining a decibel level that permits conversation without yelling, a blessing indeed. Saturday is salsa night. ⊠ *14 Mohamed Sultan Rd., Mohamed Sultan* ☎ *6325–0316* ⊕ *www.clubconcepts.com. sg* ☞ *No women under 21 or men under 25 admitted.* ☉ *Tues. and Wed. 6 PM–2 AM, Thurs.–Sat. 7 PM–3 AM, closed Sun. and Mon.*

★ **Liquid Room.** Consistently packed, this club has DJ-spun house, tribal, and trance music, along with occasional live acts, including foreign hip-hop artists. Arrive early on weekends, when lines start appearing at 10 PM. Most patrons dress with attitude, so you can push the envelope a bit yourself if you like. ⊠ *#01–05 The Gallery Evason Hotel, 76 Robertson Quay, Robertson Quay* ☎ *6333–8117* ⊕ *www.liquidroom.com.sg* ☉ *Wed.–Fri. and Sat. 11 PM–3 AM, closed Sun.–Tues.*

Madam Wong's 2. Oriental decorations adorn this club, which plays mostly retro and Top 40. There's a happy hour buffet (S$20) from 5 PM–9 PM Thursday through Sunday; you can get specials on draft beer (S$45 for three jugs) or spirits during this time. ⊠ *#01–02/03 Central Mall, 5 Magazine Rd., Chinatown* ☎ *6557–0828* ☞ *No women under 19 or men under 22 admitted. Cover: Fri. and Sat. S$15.* ☉ *Mon.–Thurs. 7 PM–3 AM, Fri. and Sat. 7 PM–4 AM, closed Sun.*

Music Underground. Locals lounge on couches and sip from stemware at the adjacent wine bar in this popular spot. A youngish crowd dances the evening away to a live band every night but Monday. ⊠ *#B1–00 International Bldg., 360 Orchard Rd., Orchard* ☎ *6834–1221* ☞ *Cover: Fri. and Sun. S$10 for men, Thurs.–Sat. S$15 for men* ☉ *Mon.–Thurs. 7.30 PM–3 AM, Fri. and Sat. 8 PM–5 AM, closed Sun.*

Sparks. Here you'll find live music for a chipper young crowd and 18 karaoke rooms. Everything about Sparks is big: gigantic sound system, huge dance floor, and a spectacular laser show. ⊠ *#05–19 Orchard Plaza, 150 Orchard Rd., Orchard* ☎ *6735–6133* ☞ *Cover: Wed. and Thurs. S$8, Fri. and Sat. before 10 PM S$8, after 10 PM S$15* ☉ *Sun., Wed., and Thurs. 8 PM–3 AM; Fri. and Sat. 8 PM–6 AM; closed Mon. and Tues.*

Fodor'sChoice
★ **Zouk, Velvet Underground, and Phuture.** The doyen of local clubs continually reinvents itself. The huge dance emporium borne of renovated riverside warehouses is actually four venues in one: Zouk for the young; Velvet Underground for sophisticated disco divas; jam-packed Phuture for hip lovers and frenetic dancers; and Wine Bar for cooling out. Visiting international DJs serve as hosts, and the club consistently gets rave reviews overseas. ⊠ *17 Jiak Kim St., Robertson Quay* ☎ *6738–2988* ⊕ *www. zoukclub.com.sg* ☞ *Cover varies: Velvet Underground (includes 2 drinks) S$20–S$23, but Fri. and Sat. S$25 for women, S$35 for men; Zouk/Phuture: S$20–S$25 (S$12 before 9 PM)* ☉ *Wine bar: Sun.–Mon. 6 PM–1 AM, Tues.–Sat 6 PM–3 AM; Velvet Underground: Tues.–Thurs. 9 PM–3 AM, Fri. and Sat. 9 PM–4 AM, closed Sun. and Mon.; Zouk/Phuture Weds. 9 PM–3 AM, Fri. and Sat. 9 PM–4 AM, closed Mon., Tues., Thurs., and Sun.*

Music Clubs

JAZZ **Bar & Billiard Room.** Light, acoustic jazz plays nightly at this urbane watering hole inside Singapore's best-known and most historical hotel. A well-off and mature set frequents the bar, which has wood paneling, brass fittings, Victorian billiard tables, and something of a gentleman's-retreat feel. The weekday buffet lunch, Sunday brunch, and afternoon high tea regales are lavish and scrumptious. There's live music Thursday through Saturday beginning at 9 PM as well as during Sunday brunch. ⊠ *Raffles Hotel, 1 Beach Rd., Colonial Singapore* ☎ *6412–1194* ☉ *Lunch: Mon.–Sat. 11:30 AM–2 PM; Dinner: Mon.–Sat. 7 PM–10 PM; Brunch: Sun. 11:30 AM–2:30 PM; High Tea: Mon.–Sat. 3:30 PM–5 PM, Sun. 4 PM–5:30 PM; Cocktails: daily 11:30 AM–12:30 AM.*

Fodor'sChoice
★

Harry's Quayside Cafe. At this veteran jazz, blues, and rock haven by the water you can hear local and visiting music stars Tuesday through Sunday. English-style lunches (fish-and-chips, bangers and mash, bread pudding with rum sauce) are served upstairs on weekdays; bar eats and tapas are dished daily until 11:30 PM. Expats dominate the crowd, which spills out onto the sidewalk on the weekend. The bar has cloned itself at two other locations, the Esplanade theatre complex and Changi Airport. ⊠ *28 Boat Quay, Boat Quay* ☎ *6538–3029* ⊕ *www.harrys-bar.com.sg/harrysbar.htm* ☉ *Sun.–Thurs. 11 AM–1 AM, Fri. and Sat. 11 AM–2 AM.*

Jazz@SouthBridge. This dimly lit den showcases talented acts, often imported. Sink into the soft sofas with one of the bar's two vodka-based signature cocktails, either the Deep Purple or the Green Dolphin, both S$16, while tapping along to slick jazz tunes. Sunday is jam night. ⊠ *82B Boat Quay, Boat Quay* ☎ *6327–4671/4672* ⊕ *www.southbridgejazz.com.sg* 🎟 *Cover: varies, but usually around S$10* ☉ *Sun.–Thurs. 5:30 PM–1 AM, Fri. and Sat. 5:30 PM–2 AM, closed Mon.*

Ethnic Clubs

Asoka Music Lounge. Come to hear pulsating bhangra, Bollywood soundtracks, and also international hip-hop hits. This Indian bar is very welcoming and perfect for those wanting to try something new. There's live music after 9 PM nightly. ⊠ *#03–02A Kallang Leisure Park, 5 Stadium Walk East Coast* ☎ *6440–4200, 6346–0523* ☉ *Sun.–Thurs. 7 PM–3 AM, Fri. 3 PM–3 AM, Sat. 3 PM–4 AM.*

Happy Days. For some good, clean, retro fun, head to this spacious lounge where each night revolves around a different theme: Monday is Indian Night, Tuesday and Friday are Malay Nights, Wednesday is Talk Show Night, Thursday is Hokkien Night, and Saturday is Canto-pop Night. The music and decorations are straight out of the 1970s–80s, and the environment is family-friendly. Singapore's branch of the National Trades Union Congress (NTUC) runs this club along with several others. ⊠ *Block 510, 3rd Level, Bishan St. 13, Toa Payoh* ☎ *6356–6166* ⊕ *www.ntucclub.com.sg* 🎟 *Cover: non-NTUC members S$12* ☉ *Daily 6 PM–midnight.*

Kairali Bistro. Dedicated to Malayali (a.k.a. Kerali) culture of the southern Indian state of Kerala, this bilevel café–bar has frequent performances by Malayali comedians, singers, and musicians. Malayali tapas are served, along with alcohol, despite the traditional prohibitions on such beverages. There's a resource center and reading room upstairs with English-language materials on Malayali culture. ⊠ *#02–01, 1 Dalhousie*

La., Little India ☎ 6292–7392 ⊙ *Mon.–Thurs. 6 PM–midnight, Fri.–Sun. 6 PM–1 AM.*

Rock

Fodor's Choice **Anywhere Restaurant & Lounge.** With its powerful renditions of cover songs,
★ Tania, the resident band fronted by Alban (the one with the false eye-lashes) and Zul, has been a local legend for more than 20 years. Nowa-days the band plays only on weekends; other bands, usually playing Malay rock, take the stage on weekdays. You'll find wall-to-wall humans, pre-dominantly lone expat males, in this smoke-filled room. ⊠ *#04–08 Tanglin Shopping Centre, 19 Tanglin Rd., Orchard* ☎ 6734–8233 ⊙ *Weekdays 6 PM–2 AM, Sat. 8 PM–3 AM, closed Sun.*

★ **Bar None.** Six-foot-tall photos of musicians adorn the walls of this large split-level bar, which is home to sassy 1970s-style band Douglas O (for Oliveiro) and 9Lives. The club models itself on the ambience at New York's Blue Note and asserts that it's fighting against Singapore's myr-iad techno and karaoke clubs, opting instead for quality rock and R&B. Local bands showcase their talent on Monday nights. ⊠ *Marriott Hotel, basement level, 320 Orchard Rd., Orchard Road* ☎ 6831–4656/4657 ⊕ *www.barnoneasia.com* ⊠ *Cover charge: Fri. and Sat. S$26* ⊙ *Sun.–Thurs. 7 PM–3 AM, Fri. and Sat. 7 PM–4 AM.*

Fodor's Choice **Crazy Elephant.** Dedicated to the blues, with occasional forays into R&B
★ and rock, this popular, yet laid-back bar hosts Sunday night jam sessions that draw gifted musicians. Music breaks are possible on the quayside terrace, and there's a casual dining area—called the Elephant Bar and Grill—with such straightforward meals as steak and hamburgers. ⊠ *#01–07 (Trader's Market), Clarke Quay* ☎ 6337–1990 ⊕ *www. crazyelephant.com* ⊙ *Sun.–Thurs. 5 PM–1 AM, Fri. and Sat. 5 PM–2 AM.*

Roomful of Blues. Blues lovers, many of them local musicians, come to hear all styles of blues music; Sunday jam sessions are especially popu-lar. Try the appropriately named Muddy Waters coffee, the Mississippi Catch fish-and-chips, or the Aerosmith Flaps (chicken wings doused in whiskey). ⊠ *72 Prinsep St., Colonial Singapore* ☎ 6837–0882 ⊙ *Mon.–Thurs. 5 PM–1 AM, Fri. and Sat. 5 PM–2 AM, closed Sun.*

Tanglin Community Centre Blues Jams. Blues musicians come here every Saturday to jam; sometimes in the evening, but this is becoming more of an afternoon affair. It's a loose arrangement at the moment, perhaps better suited for participant musicians than spectators, but visiting mu-sicians are more than welcome to join in. The sessions are pretty inti-mate with room for just 30 inside, but "3,000 outside" say the organizers. ⊠ *Tanglin Community Centre Club, Underground Studio, 245 Whit-ley Rd., Bukit Timah* ☎ 6251–3922, 6252–6757 ⊙ *Sat. 2 PM–6 PM or 6 PM–10 PM* ⊠ *Free.*

Nightclubs

Neptune Theatre Restaurant. At this sumptuous bilevel club you can dine on Cantonese food or sit in the nondiner's gallery. Singaporean, Taiwanese, and Filipino singers entertain in English and Chinese, joined occasion-ally by a mischievous European dance troupe. It's the only nightclub in Singapore licensed to feature occasional topless cabaret shows. On a more traditional note, there's ballroom and social dancing every Tuesday night. ✉ *Overseas Union House, 7th floor, 50 Collyer Quay, CBD* ☎ *6224–3922/3203* ⊙ *Daily 7 PM–11 PM.*

THE ARTS

Singapore is a crossroads of international business and cultural traffic. The island balances the traditional with the contemporary, and it nurtures experimentation, ancient traditions, and fusions of the two. As the National Arts Council (NAC) puts it, Singapore's aspiration is to become "a global city of the arts." Since 2000 millions of dollars have been allocated to develop the artistic communities through training and grants, financial assistance schemes, subsidized (90%) housing for artists, and arts festivals. Private sector arts funding has been in the millions and there have been active arts education in schools since 1993.

To discover and showcase local and international talent, the NAC organizes such major events as the Singapore Writers' Festival and the Singapore River Buskers' Festival. Following its mission to create accessible "Arts for All," the NAC conducts outreach in housing estates and other public spaces; programs include the Concert in the Park series as well as Poems on the MRT.

The hubbub is paying off as Singaporean artists take their place on the world stage. Singaporean animators worked on the *Lord of the Rings* films. Among the Hollywood-based special-effects wizards in *The Matrix Reloaded* was Singaporean Nickson Fong, now back in Singapore founding his Egg Story Creative Production company. Other notables include writer Mohamed Latif bin Mohamed who won the 2001 Southeast Asia Writer Award; Ong Keng Sen, Artistic Director of Theatreworks, who was invited to Denmark in 2002 to produce his pan-Asian version of Hamlet (for which he won Singapore's 2003 Cultural Medallion award); and renowned Singaporean painter Tan Swie Hian, winner of the 2003 World Economic Forum Crystal Award.

Ever since the 2002 debut of the waterfront Esplanade–Theatres on the Bay, new arts venues have popped up across the country, most notably, The Arts House in the Old Parliament Building on the riverside, next to the similarly vintage Victoria Theatre and Concert Hall. These are all part of a plan to create a continuous arts precinct from the second building of the Asian Civilisations Museum at Empress Place out to the Esplanade.

Nearly contiguous to this precinct is another arts zone in Bras Basah–Stamford, anchored by the Singapore Management University campus, the first building of the Asian Civilisations Museum at Armenian Street, the Singapore History Museum, and the Singapore Art Museum, all under the shadow of the historic Ft. Canning. Just off the Bras Basah side, there's a new Drama Centre within the National Library building at Middle Road. Contributing to this frenzy of almost complete self-renewal, the two premier arts colleges—the Nanyang Academy of Fine Arts and the LaSalle-SIA College of the Arts—have both been in the throes of expansion and relocation to new buildings and campus.

The local arts community has a noticeable preference for such edgy contemporary forms as installation art. The annual Singapore Arts Festival emphasizes contemporary Asian artists and performers. Theater here leans to the experimental, notably in its introspective explorations of local issues. Comedy borders on slapstick, uses intensely local references, and also favors the Singlish patois, largely impenetrable to foreign visitors.

Chinese Opera

Dramatic *wayangs* (operas) reenact Chinese legends through powerful movement, lavish costumes, startling face-paint masks, and clashing gongs and pounding drums, punctuated by wailing flutes and stringed lute- or zitherlike instruments. Performances are held on temporary stages set up near temples, in market areas, or on the walkways outside apartment complexes and shops. The backstage area is open to view and you can watch the actors putting on their costumes and applying their heavy makeup. Wayangs are staged all year, but are held most frequently in August and September, during the Festival of the Hungry Ghosts. Street performances—such as those at Clarke Quay (Gas Lamp Square) held on Wednesday, Thursday, and Friday at 7:45 PM—are free.

With local Chinese TV programming mostly delivered in Mandarin nowadays, street wayangs—spoken in dialect—have become popular with the older generation, who rarely have a chance to be entertained in their own language. You can get further information about the unforgettable wayangs at the **Chinese Opera Society** (⊠ #03–03 Stamford Arts Centre, 155 Waterloo St., Colonial Singapore ☎ 6541–4792).

Fodor'sChoice ★ You'll need to buy tickets to shows by the leading groups, such as the 30-strong **Chinese Theatre Circle** (⊠ 5 Smith St., Chinatown ☎ 6323–4862, 9630–2886 ⊕ http://ctcopera.com.sg ⊠ S$35 including set Chinese dinner, tea, and dessert; or S$20 for admission and tea with snacks ☺ 7 PM–9 PM with dinner, or 8 PM–9 PM for show only), though they sometimes give free demonstrations at places like Clarke Quay. Many of the bigger groups work hard to make their performances easily accessible to non-Chinese, offering English subtitles. The Circle also does an excellent introduction workshop on Chinese opera every Friday and Saturday for English-speaking novices.

The **Chinese Cultural Arts Centre** (⊠ #01–09 Telok Ayer Performing Art Centre, 182 Cecil St., Chinatown ☎ 6222–0760, 9023–1333) was established in 2002 to promote Chinese arts and culture, particularly Cantonese opera.

Dance

Odyssey Dance Theatre (⊠ #04–08/09 Telok Ayer Performing Arts Centre, 182 Cecil St., Chinatown ☎ 6221–5229, 6257–1738 ⊕ www.odysseydancetheatre.com) is home to a mesmerizing contemporary dance troupe. With a reputation for more than just contemporary dance, **Practice Performing Arts** (⊠ #02–08 Stamford Arts Centre, 155 Waterloo St., Colonial Singapore ☎ 6337–2525 ⊕ www.ppas.edu.sg) is another innovative group. Singapore's main ballet company is the **Singapore Ballet Academy** (⊠ Ft. Canning Centre, 2nd floor, Cox Terrace, Colonial Singapore ☎ 6337–9125). Periodic performances by **Singapore**

Dance Theatre (✉ Ft. Canning Centre, 2nd floor, Cox Terrace, Colonial Singapore ☏ 6338–0611 ⊕ www.singaporedancetheatre.com), as well as other dance groups, are given in Ft. Canning Park—"Ballet Under The Stars," for example, takes place in June.

Dance Ensemble Singapore (✉ 60 Waterloo St., Colonial Singapore ☏ 6334–7192) is a traditional Chinese dance group. The **Kala Mandhir** (Temple of Fine Arts; ✉ #02–11 Excelsior Hotel & Shopping Centre, 5 Coleman St., Colonial Singapore ☏ 6339–0492 ⊕ http://temple-offinearts.org/sg), run by a Hindu religious group, emphasizes appreciation for arts, culture, and education. Bhaskar's Arts Academy runs the **Nrityalaya Aesthetics Society** (✉ #01–09 Stamford Arts Centre, 155 Waterloo St., Colonial Singapore ☏ 6336–6537 ⊕ www.bhaskarsartsacademy.com) dedicated to Indian arts. **Sriwana** (✉ #03–03 Telok Ayer Performing Arts Centre, 182 Cecil St., Chinatown ☏ 6323–1956, 6880–6361 ⊕ www.sriwana.com) is renowned for its creative spins on traditional Malay dances. Popular **Sri Warisan Som Said Performing Arts** (✉ 47 Kerbau Rd., Little India ☏ 6225–6070 ⊕ www.sriwarisan.com) is a traditional Malay dance troupe.

Film
For information on the film industry contact the **Singapore Film Commission** (✉ #04–01 MICA Bldg., 140 Hill St., Singapore River ☏ 6837–9943 ⊕ www.sfc.org.sg), which was established in 1999 to nurture local cinema. Since then it's funded more than 40 films. The respected **Singapore Film Society** (✉ #03–01 Marina Leisureplex, 5A Raffles Ave., CBD ☏ 6350–3002, Hotline 90–170–160 ⊕ www.sfs.org.sg) screens art-house and foreign films. Everything in Singapore goes through the censors who usually let these films go uncut as a gesture to the nation's small but serious film-buff community. Generally, sexual activity, especially homosexuality, and certain political topics are the first to be cut.

★ The nation's annual film festivals include **Singapore International Film Festival** as well as the **Asian Film Symposium**. There's also a **Starlight Cinema** outdoor movie series in June and July. Learn more about these in *Arts Festivals Close Up*.

Orchestras
The 90-member, nearly three-decades-old **Singapore Symphony Orchestra** (✉ Victoria Memorial Hall, 11 Empress Pl., Colonial Singapore ☏ 6338–1230, 6348–5555 for tickets ⊕ www.sso.org.sg) regularly delivers a mix of Western classical music and new Asian compositions. It also makes a point of including lighter music. Tickets range from S$12 to S$60; they're also available from the Esplanade–Theatres box office at the mezzanine level.

★ The 64-member **Singapore Chinese Orchestra** (✉ Singapore Conference Hall, 7 Shenton Way, CBD ☏ 6440–3839 ⊕ www.sco.com.sg/english/main.asp) is the island's Chinese orchestra. Maestro Tsung Yeh is committed to making Chinese music more accessible to non-Chinese Singaporeans.

The 85-member **Singapore National Youth Orchestra** (✉ CCA Branch, 21 Evans Rd., Orchard ☏ 6460–9834 ⊕ www1.moe.edu.sg/ccab/music2003/

CloseUp

SINGAPOREAN CINEMA: PUSHING THE ENVELOPE

SINGAPORE'S FILM INDUSTRY IS STILL FLEDGLING, but it's noteworthy for its energy, individuality, and rapid development since about 1991. More than 30 local movies have been made since then. Some have been quirky and revealing enough to garner recognition abroad.

For example, Song of the Stork (2003) is a Singaporean–Vietnamese production that was released in Vietnam and won the Best Feature Film award at Italy's Milano Film Festival. Dirty Laundry (2002), Stamford Hall (2000), and Hype (2001) are notable Singaporean films. Hype was shown at the Deauville Asian Film Festival in France. Miss Wonton (2001), which won an award at Italy's Locarno Film Festival, was directed by a Singaporean.

One new director, 26-year-old Royston Tan, ruffled official feathers with his gritty film debut about Singaporean youth rejecting social norms. In 15, Tan used streetwise kids, not actors, looked frankly at local drug culture, and provoked the censorship board into requests for 27 cuts. The movie was given an R(A) rating (21 and over), the strictest classification available at the time. The film won a Special Achievement Award at the 2002 Singapore International Film Festival and attracted international attention at the London and Venice Film Festivals.

Tan's response to the censorship was to create Cut lampooning the censors in musical form. This bizarre short—just 13 minutes long—is jammed with local celebrities, many of whom participated for free, and is widely interpreted as the artistic community's protest against censorship. Cut has, however, escaped the censors' cut. In 2004 the government also relaxed its classifications with new M18 (18 and over) and R21 (21 and

over) categories to increase access to films with more mature themes.

Among the local films worth tracking down are director Eric Khoo's 12 Storeys, a hard-edged social commentary on life in Singapore's high-rise blocks; Mee Pok Man, a black comedy about the relationship between a noodle seller and a prostitute; and One Leg Kicking, a feel-good soccer farce that explores the working class–rich social dynamics. Also worth checking out are director Jack Neo's Money No Enough and his hugely popular I Not Stupid (a moving account of Singapore's high-pressure school system); director Ong Keng Sen's rite-of-passage saga about national service, Army Daze; Chee Kong Cheah's very Singaporean take on Romeo and Juliet called Chicken Rice Wars, set among street-side food stalls; and Glen Goei's disco comedy Forever Fever.

Learn more about Singapore's growing film industry from some of the leading filmmakers' Web sites: **Zhao Wei Films** (⊕ www.zhaowei.com) and **Raintree Pictures** (⊕ www.mediacorpraintree.com).

SNYO.htm) is composed of players under 25 who perform publicly about three times a year, usually in April, July, and December.

The **Singapore Lyric Opera** (✉ #03–06 Stamford Arts Centre, 155 Waterloo St., Colonial Singapore ☎ 6336–1929 ⊕ www.singaporeopera. com.sg) specializes in Western operas.

Theater

★ **The Necessary Stage** (✉ The Necessary Stage Black Box, #B1–02 Marine Parade Community Bldg., 278 Marine Parade Rd., East Coast ☎ 6440–8115 ⊕ www.necessary.org), noted for the work of its directors, Alvin Tan and Haresh Sharma, puts on original performances, often with a social, sometimes socialist message. The highly respected **Practice Performing Arts School** (✉ #02–06 Stamford Arts Centre, 155 Waterloo St., Colonial Singapore ☎ 6561–4809 ⊕ www.ppas.edu.sg), founded by the late Chinese–English director Kuo Pao Kun, is an innovative cross-cultural institution. The popular **Singapore Repertory Theatre** (✉ DBS Arts Theatre, 20 Merbau Rd., Robertson Quay ☎ 6733–8166 ⊕ www.srt.com.sg) stages plays and musicals. Its subsidiary, The Little Company, produces children's plays.

★ **Theatreworks** (✉ The Black Box, Ft. Canning Centre, Cox Terrace, Ft. Canning Park, Colonial Singapore ☎ 6338–4077 ⊕ www.theatreworks. org.sg), noted for the work of director Ong Keng Sen, is an internationally known theater company. It has staged daring cross-cultural productions, such as Asian versions of *King Lear* and *Desdemona* (derived from *Oth-*
★ *ello*), and has traveled to Denmark to workshop *Hamlet*. **Wild Rice** (✉ 3A Kerbau Rd., Little India ☎ 6292–2695 ⊕ www.wildrice.com. sg) pushes the boundaries of performance art under controversial director Ivan Heng.

Visual Arts

Museums and galleries typically open Tuesday through Sunday from 9 AM to 6 PM, but close on Monday. This is particularly true for larger institutions, such as the Asian Civilisations Museum. Establishments farther away from downtown, like the National University of Singapore Museums, are likely to open Monday through Saturday from 9 AM to 5 PM, and close on Sunday. Private gallery hours are usually 10 AM to 6 PM Monday through Friday, and by appointment only on the weekend.

Painters and sculptors are a rare and rarefied community here, but there are established names who've drawn on more than half a century of art reflecting innovative styles that don't simply hark back to mother cultures in Malaysia, Indonesia, China, or India. Some great names of the recent past have been Chen Wen Hsi, Georgette Chen, and Liu Kang, while older generation artists include Thomas Yeo, Goh Beng Kwan, and Ong Kim Seng. In terms of quality, output, versatility, and international acclaim, the doyen of this community is the many laureled Tan Swie Hian, an intriguing, multidisciplinary creator who bases much of his work on his Buddhist convictions and his devotion to the inner rather than the outer life. Many selections from Tan Swie Hian's considerable

Fodor's Choice oeuvre reside within Singapore's first private art museum, the **Tan Swie**
★ **Hian Museum** (✉ 460 Sims Ave., East Coast ☎ 6744–3551).

ARTS FESTIVALS

THE ANNUAL *Singapore River Buskers' Festival* (⊕ www.singapore-buskers.com), in mid-November, brings together all manner of street performers, from musical buskers to stiltwalkers and sword-swallowers. The weeklong festival gets underway after sunset and happens in various locations: along the riverbank (especially at Clarke and Robertson Quays), on Orchard Road, and even in Changi Airport.

The biennial **Singapore Writers' Festival** (⊕ www.singaporewritersfest.com.sg) celebrates literature in Singapore's four main languages: English, Chinese, Malay, and Tamil (from India). The festival happens in August and attracts international writers. Its talks, forums, breakfasts, and similar events are spread throughout several venues, including the Asian Civilisations Museum.

The annual, weeklong **Singapore International Comedy Festival** (☎ 6250–3347) in March and April lures global talents, handpicked from such events as the Edinburgh Fringe Festival.

The 17-year-old **Singapore International Film Festival** (✉ 45A Keong Saik Rd., Chinatown ☎ 6738–7567, 6225–7417 ⊕ www.filmfest.org.sg), held in April and May, screens films from more than 40 countries, paying special attention to movies from Asia and the developing world.

Staged annually for three weeks from May through June, the **Singapore Arts Festival** has a kaleidoscope of international and local acts. Tickets for individual events range from S$15 to S$80. The festival is coordinated out of the NAC offices; you can also get information from the ArtsFest Hotline (☎ 6837–9589 ⊕ www.singaporeartsfest.com).

Starlight Cinema (☎ 6296–2929 ⊕ www.starlightcinema.com.sg ✉ S$90 for a comprehensive season pass; S$10–S$15 per ticket) is a month-long series of outdoor screenings (of mostly mainstream films) with surround sound on Ft. Canning Green in June and July. For more information contact the Singapore Tourism Board.

WOMAD (World of Music Arts and Dance; ✉ 35A Duxton Rd., Chinatown ☎ 6220–2676 ⊕ www.womadsingapore.com) organizes a spectacular, international ethnic arts showcase on historical Ft. Canning Hill, in Ft. Canning Park. The three-day event usually takes place on the first weekend of September, sometimes the last weekend of August. A one-day ticket costs S$33, but the package ticket (S$82) for all three days is your best bet; it allows you to wander from one show to another.

The National University of Singapore's Centre for the Arts stages its annual **Dance Reflections** festival of Asian and Western dance in September. The annual **Asian Film Symposium** (✉ The Substation, 45 Armenian St. ☎ 6337–7535, 6337–7800 for tickets ⊕ www.sfs.org.sg ✉ S$5 per show) showcases the best Asian cinema over five days in mid-September and is part of The Substation arts center's ongoing Moving Images program with screenings, workshops, and seminars.

Colorful Indian music, drama, and dance performances are staged during major festivals at several prominent temples. For information on such Indian cultural events, contact the **Hindu Endowments Board** (✉ 397 Serangoon Rd., Little India ☎ 6296–3469).

Singapore's **Art Galleries Association** (☎ 6235–4113 ⊕ www.agas.org.sg) is the umbrella for many of the leading art galleries, and it publishes a useful Gallery Guide. **Art Forum** (✉ 82 Cairnhill Rd., Orchard ☎ 6737–3448 ⊕ www.artforum.com.sg), in an elegant townhouse, has an eclectic collection, seen by appointment only, which is dominated by paintings and drawings, including some by such local artists as Goh Beng Kwan and Earl Lu. **Art-2 Gallery** (✉ #01–03 MICA Bldg., 140 Hill St., Colonial Singapore ☎ 6338–8713 ⊕ www.art2.com.sg) dedicates itself to showcasing work by young Asian artists. **Gajah Gallery** (✉ #01–08 MICA Bldg., 140 Hill St., Colonial Singapore ☎ 6737–4202 ⊕ www.gajahgallery.com) specializes in Southeast Asian creations. **LaSalle-SIA College of the Arts Singapore** (✉ 90 Goodman Rd., East Coast ☎ 6344–4300 ⊕ www.lasallesia.edu.sg), which offers a range of degree-level courses in the fine and performing arts to its 1,500 students, is home to the **Earl Lu Gallery** (☎ 6340–9102/9116), an important space for contemporary Singaporean and Asian art.

To visit several art galleries in one stop head for the ARTrium space at the **MICA Building** (Ministry of Information and the Arts; ✉ 140 Hill St., Singapore River ☎ 6270–7988), where events are also staged, including monthly lunchtime concerts. This is also home to **Singapore's National Arts Council** (✉ #03–01 MICA Bldg., 140 Hill St., Singapore River ☎ 6746–4622 ⊕ www.nac.gov.sg). It's a 15-minute walk from here to the Singapore History Museum. A seminal influence on Singapore's fine arts scene has been the **Nanyang Academy of Fine Arts** (✉ 111 Middle Rd., CBD ☎ 6337–6636 ⊕ www.nafa.edu.sg). After visiting the Singapore Art Museum, Singapore History Museum, and the Asian Civilisations Museum (⊕ www.museum.org.sg/MCC)—all of which have impressive art collections—you may not be in the mood for more museum hopping, but if you've got the energy, you should take a trip to the **NUS Museums** (✉ National University of Singapore, 50 Kent Ridge Crescent, West Coast ☎ 6874–4616, 6874–4617, or 6874–4618 ⊕ www.nus.edu.sg/museums) on the National University of Singapore campus at Kent Ridge. At any one time NUS displays some 1,000 objets d'art from a collection of about 10,000 pieces. Admission is free; the museum is open Monday through Saturday from 9–5.

Fodor'sChoice
★

Some quirky galleries are clustered around the Kerbau Road district of Little India, which is a pleasant area, well supplied with watering holes, restaurants, and shops. **Plastique Kinetic Worms** (✉ 61 Kerbau Rd., Little India ☎ 6292–7783 ⊕ http://pkworms.org.sg) is a small community gallery that acts as a platform for young, struggling artists. The management is casual here and the gallery could be closed when you get there: phone ahead.

Sculpture Square (✉ 155 Middle Rd., CBD ☎ 6333–1055 ⊕ www.sculpturesq.com.sg) is on the site of a 19th-century Methodist church. The **Singapore Tyler Print Institute** (✉ 41 Robertson Quay, Singapore River ☎ 6336–3663 ⊕ www.stpi.com.sg), an American-inspired venture dedicated to print-, paper-making, and paper-based artwork, has a free admission gallery.

SPORTS &
THE OUTDOORS

5

Updated by
Ilsa Sharp

DESPITE THE HEAT AND HUMIDITY, Singapore is one of Asia's best cities for outdoor activities, since it's relatively unpolluted (but watch out for "the haze," which may drift over between August and November from forest fires in neighboring Indonesia, making strenuous activity inadvisable). The government has set aside a significant portion of the island for recreation and 5% for nature conservation, so you can waterski or scuba dive, play beach volleyball or take a jungle hike. Public facilities include 22 swimming complexes, 18 stadiums, and 12 squash and tennis centers. A growing fascination with holistic health has led to the opening of dozens of spas. Virtually all hotels have swimming pools, and there are several private clubs.

Notwithstanding all these conveniences, long working hours (until recently, civil servants had five-and-a-half-day work weeks) and hectic social calendars prevent most Singaporeans from devoting much time to sports. In a bid for worldwide recognition, the government has been recruiting foreign talent for its national teams. So far, the nation has had the most luck in swimming, table tennis, and badminton. Singapore's favorite sport, however, is soccer, and many locals avidly follow British teams. Through extreme activities, which are becoming very popular with younger generations, the Singapore Tourism Board hopes to promote Singapore's image as a lively, fun place. For example, in 2004, Singapore hosted its first Skydiving Festival—highlighted by someone parachuting off The Swissôtel The Stamford—as well as an Action Asia Challenge race (⊕ www.actionasia.com). The government also sanctioned bungee jumping in 2003.

Singapore's more traditional Asian sports include the ancient Malay *Sepak Takraw,* a.k.a. *Sepak Raga.* The modern version, a sort of "kick volleyball" with players on opposite sides of a net, evolved from the original game in which players stood in a circle and passed a rattan ball using any part of their body but their hands. Visit ⊕ www.sepaktakraw.org for more information about this game. Martial arts—especially Kung Fu, South Indian Kalari Payat, and Malay Silat—along with offshoots like Chinese lion and dragon dancing are ever popular here. Chinese dragon boat racing is an ancient tradition that's showcased every June at the International Dragon Boat Festival in Marina Bay (⊕ www.sdba.org.sg), as well as every November at the Singapore River Regatta (⊕ www.sdba. org.sg). Kite flying is fondly preserved by the Chinese and the Malays; the Malay version involves aggressive kite-fighting in which glass shards may be used to sever an opponent's kite. Chinese checkers is a less physical, but much loved pastime. Tables of intent players bent over their boards at street-side restaurants line Geylang Road on the East Coast.

In addition to its stadium structures, including the iconic 60,000-seat National Stadium, Singapore has several sports *padangs* (Malay for open field). The stately Singapore Cricket Club, founded in 1852 for British colonials, faces a sweeping Padang (⊕ www.scc.org.sg). The Singapore Recreation Club (⊕ www.src.org.sg), founded in 1883 for Eurasians, also has a field, which flanks the cricket club's Padang. Ethnic organizations—such as the Singapore Indian Association, Ceylon Sports Association, Singapore Khalsa Association (Sikhs from India), and Straits Chinese Recreation Club—share a field on Balestier Road in the Serangoon area, all of which date to the 1920s. Watching white-clad cricket teams from a club veranda recalls Singapore's colonial era. There's a more open policy for visitors to the Balestier Road clubs, but you'll need a membership or a friendly member to sign you in as a guest before you can tour the older colonial clubs.

When doing anything outside, drink lots of water, be prepared for rain (especially in the November–February rainy season), and try to schedule strenuous activities for early morning or late afternoon. For general sports information contact the **Singapore Sports Council** (⊠ National Stadium, 15 Stadium Rd., East Coast/Kallang ☏ 6345–7111 ⊕ www.ssc. gov.sg). Learn about outdoor activities from the **Nature Society (Singapore)** (⊠ #02–05 The Sunflower, 510 Geylang Rd., East Coast/Geylang ☏ 6741–2036 ⊕ www.nss.org.sg), an organization with considerable expertise on birding and botanical and marine conservation. The group hosts lively programs and puts together several publications. The **Singapore Environment Council** (⊠ 52A Duxton Rd., Chinatown ☏ 6337–6062 ⊕ www.sec.org.sg) issues *The Green Map of Singapore,* a valuable guide to Singapore's natural habitats and runs the Green Volunteers' Network.

★ Although it's off the beaten track, the natural history collection at the **Raffles Museum of Biodiversity Research** (⊠ National University of Singapore, Dept. of Biological Sciences, Faculty of Science, Block S6, Level 3, Science Dr. 2, West Coast ☏ 6874–5082 ⊕ rmbr.nus.edu.sg) is worth a visit. It opens 9–5 on weekdays, 9–noon on Saturday, and is closed Sunday; admission is free. Many of the local animals and plants collected by Sir Stamford Raffles and his associates are here, along with some more recent acquisitions; it's a museum of enormous scientific significance in tropical biology circles.

BEACHES & PARKS

Singapore's beaches are characteristically rocky and lined with mangrove swamps, mudflats, and dark sand. The beaches at the East Coast Sea Sports Club in the Marina area, and off Changi Village at Changi Point to the northeast, are good finds, as are the carefully nurtured beaches of Sentosa, the Southern Islands, and Pulau Ubin off Changi Point. Other small beaches worth visiting include Labrador Park on the West Coast, but Singapore lacks the white-sand, palm-fringed beaches found in other parts of Southeast Asia. There are some very attractive coastal parklands here, such as the East Coast Parkway, which stretches out to Changi Airport and Changi Village.

Bintan Island, Indonesia. A quick side trip to Indonesia from Singapore is a snap—the north of Bintan Island is only 45 minutes from Singapore's east coast Tanah Merah Ferry Terminal (TMFT), its southern half 90 minutes from the HarbourFront Ferry Terminal on the southwest coast at Maritime Square. The island is a resort haven. You can frolic on its beaches, play golf, enjoy traditional massage and herbal healing, and experience Indonesian cuisine and culture.

↻ **East Coast Park.** This park is on reclaimed land alongside the seafront road on the southeastern coast leading to the airport. It has a 7.5-km (4.5-mi) sandy beach, restaurants, food stalls, barbecue pits, daily rental holiday chalets, changing facilities and restrooms, and almost every recreational facility known to man, including a water-sports lagoon where you can rent sailboards, canoes, kayaks, and sailboats. There are a 12-km (7-mi) cycle track, a 15-km (9-mi) jogging track, bicycle and rollerblade rentals, and fishing points.

Nearby Islands. The southern islands of St. John's, Sisters, Seringat, and Lazarus have been enlarged and partly joined by land reclamation projects, in preparation for a multimillion dollar resort, which will link these islands to Sentosa. The resort will host Singapore's first casino, a very controversial issue. Seringat's 800-m (half-mile) manmade beach is one of Singapore's longest. Kusu has small beaches, swimming facilities, and religious shrines—beware the ninth lunar month (approximately October and November) when hordes of Taoists head for the Tua Pekong Temple. Take the ferry from HarbourFront to reach the southern islands.

↻ **Sentosa Island.** Billed as Singapore's leisure resort, Sentosa (⊕ www.sentosa. com.sg) offers a range of recreational facilities in addition to its museums, musical fountain, World War II sites, and other attractions. Pleasingly natural in patches but also meticulously landscaped in others, Sentosa is one of the few places in Singapore where you can get up close and personal with three species of carnivorous pitcher plants, monkeys, edible-nest swiftlets, and such immigrant exotica as Australian cockatoos. There's also a white-sand beach, as well as a swimming lagoon. At **Underwater World** (⊠ 80 Siloso Rd. ☎ 6275–0030 ⊕ www. underwaterworld.com.sg ☑ S$17.30 ⊙ Daily 9–9), you can feed dolphins at Dolphin Lagoon, take in panoramic views from the Carlsberg Sky Tower, or experience the thrill of flying, supervised by instructors, on the Flying Trapeze. **Sijori Wondergolf** (⊠ 23 Beach View ☎ 6271–2002 ⊕ www.sijoriresort.com.sg ☑ S$8 ⊙ Daily 9–9) is a miniature golf park with 54 landscaped greens in three 18-hole courses. Sentosa also has opportunities for cycling, horseback riding, and camping. Be forewarned: the island gets very crowded on weekends.

NATURE RESERVES

Generous provision of parkland and a total of 7,017 acres of wild nature reserve land, combined with Singapore's naturally lush tropical vegetation, make Singapore much more of an environmental haven than most people realize. Marine reserves include four coral reefs off the southern islands, and there are 1,235 acres of mangrove forests along the northern coastline and offshore islands. Bird watchers can look for about 350 recorded species. The total biodiversity includes some 60 mammal, 26 amphibian, 400 crab, 130 reptile (including 90 snake), 660 spider, and 1,700 native seed plant species. The government's "clean and green garden city" motto has stimulated the planting of more than five million trees and shrubs along the roads and sidewalks since 1970. To encourage the free movement of wildlife, there are nearly 300 km (186 mi) of green park connectors or corridors linking natural areas to each other.

Singapore has four major nature reserves: Bukit Timah Natural Reserve, Central Catchment Natural Reserve, Labrador Park, and Sungei Buloh Wetland Reserve. You can contact the **National Parks Board** (⊠ Singapore Botanic Gardens, 1 Cluny Rd., Holland Village ☎6471–7808, 1800/471–7300 ⊕ www.nparks.gov.sg ✉ Free) for more information.

Fodor'sChoice **Bukit Timah Nature Reserve** (⊠ Hindhede Dr., Upper Bukit Timah Rd.,
★ Bukit Timah ☎ 1800/468–5736) is a pocket-size rain forest with superior trails that's surprisingly close to the city. The reserve is open daily from 7 AM to 7 PM; the visitor center's hours are daily 8:30 AM to 6:30 PM. Take the North–South MRT to Newton, then switch to SMRT (TIBS) bus 171, and get off at Upper Bukit Timah Road opposite the Bukit Timah Shopping Centre, cross the road and find your way through the intersecting highways over to the hill with its prominent signal relay towers, entered via Hindhede Drive.

★ **Bukit Batok Nature Park** (⊠ Bukit Batok East Ave. 2) is lit from 7 PM to 7 AM. The park is a converted quarry and is also known as Little Guilin, after a site in China similarly renowned for its scenic beauty, lakes, and towering cliffs and peaks. This 104-acre park is packed with interesting forest vegetation and bird life, as well as fitness corners and shelters. Buses 61, 66, 157, 178, 852, and 985 come here—get off at Bukit Batok Avenue 6.

It's actually possible to get lost in the **Central Catchment Nature Reserve's** (⊠ MacRitchie-Peirce) 5,000 acres of forest land. Visitor facilities are minimal, so it's best not to go in too deep without a knowledgeable local guide. From time to time there may also be army exercises in the deeper forest, so stay within sight of the MacRitchie Reservoir and follow obvious trails at all times. It's not as pristine as the Bukit Timah Reserve, but this reserve has some of Singapore's most important reservoirs. You can enter the forest from a trail in Lower Peirce Park (take SBS bus 167 to Upper Thomson Road, the trail is along this road) or from a trail in the MacRitchie Reservoir park (take SBS bus 130, 132, or 167 to the Little Sisters of the Poor stop).

★ On the southwest coast, away from the city, is the 4.5-acre **Labrador Nature Reserve** (⊠ Labrador Villa Rd., off Pasir Panjang Rd., West Coast). It's somewhat deserted and out of the way, but the reserve has interesting vegetation, a striking seafront promenade offering spectacular sunsets, and a rocky beach worth visiting at low tide. Additionally, there are fascinating fortifications, gun emplacements, and tunnels from World War II. The park is lit from 7 PM to 7 AM. From Orchard Road, take SBS bus 143, get off at Pasir Panjang Road, then walk up Labrador Villa Road for about 10 minutes.

Fodor'sChoice At **Pulau Ubin Recreation Area,** on an island off Singapore's northeast coast,
★ you might spot a pied hornbill, straw-headed bulbul, magpie robin, or jungle fowl—all of which are rarely seen on the mainland. You can also see hefty mangrove swamps, as well as picturesque coconut plantations, which recall 1960s Singapore. Tanjung Chek Jawa, a fragile tidal mudflat, reveals fascinating shore life at low tide, but can only be visited by small groups under National Parks Board supervision. You can reach

Pulua Ubin via a 10-minute boat trip (S$2) from the Changi Point jetty; take SBS bus 2 or 29 to the Changi Point bus interchange, which is near the jetty.

★ In the far north, the 215-acre **Sungei Buloh Wetlands Reserve** (⊠ 301 Neo Tiew Crescent, Kranji ☎ 6794–1401 ⊕ www.sbwr.org.sg) has large monitor lizards, great bird-watching opportunities (especially during the north–south migrations from October through April), and parts of a mangrove forest that once encircled Singapore. The educational visitor center has a gift shop and café. After touring the reserve, you can take a walk through the Kranji wetlands. Sungei Buloh opens daily 7:30–7, and there's a S$1 admission. From the Woodlands bus interchange or Kranji MRT, take SMRT (TIBS) bus 925 to the reserve's entrance on Sunday and public holidays; weekdays and Saturday, the bus goes to the Kranji Reservoir Car Park, from which it's a 20-minute walk to the entrance.

SPORTS

Archery

The **Archery Association of Singapore** (⊠ 303 Upper Serangoon Rd., North East ☎ 6773–4824 ⊕ www.archerysingapore.com ⊠ 9 Lantana Ave. ☎ 6468–1813) founded in 1967, has 20 affiliated clubs, most of which welcome enthusiasts. The range is closed on Monday, but open 4 PM–9 PM on Tuesday and Thursday, 7 AM to noon on Wednesday and Friday, and 10 AM–6 PM on weekends. There's a S$25 fee for visitors.

Bicycling

Signed **bicycle kiosks** dot designated bike paths. You can rent bikes for about S$4–S$9 an hour (mountain bikes cost more), often with a refundable deposit of S$20–S$50. There are many such kiosks at **East Coast Park** (☎ 6448–7120, 6443–3489); **West Coast Park** (☎ 6872–2406); **Sentosa Island** (☎ 6275–0388); **Pasir Ris** (☎ 6583–4723, 6583–4803); **Bishan** (☎ 6451–5905); and **Pulau Ubin** (☎ 6542–4108), an island off Singapore's northeast coast that offers mountain or dirt biking. An exciting 12-km (7.5-mi) dirt-biking trail curves around the perimeter of the rain forest at Bukit Timah Nature Reserve. Call the National Parks Board (☎ 6471–7808, 1800/471–7300) for more information.

Bowling

There are more than 20 bowling centers in Singapore, most of which have at least 20 lanes. Some in the Marina South area are open 24 hours, but most are open from 9 AM to 2 AM. The cost for a game ranges S$2–S$3 before 6 PM and S$3–S$4 after 6 PM, usually excluding shoe rental. For general information contact the **Singapore Tenpin Bowling Congress** (☎ 6440–7388).

There are several **Cathay Bowl** outlets (☎ 6238–2088), but the one at **Cineleisure Orchard** (⊠ Level 9, Cathay Cineleisure Orchard, 8 Grange

Rd., Orchard ☎ 6238–2088) is the most convenient. It has 22 lanes and links to an entertainment center with dance floors. **Kallang Bowl** (✉ #02–08 Leisure Park, 5 Stadium Walk, East Coast/Kallang ☎ 6345–0545) is a major venue close to the National Stadium. **Super Bowl Marina South** (✉ 15 Marina Grove, Marina South, East Coast/Marina ☎ 6221–1010) has 36 lanes and is open 24 hours.

Boules & Petanque

This French sport was first introduced to Singapore in 1985 as the ideal sport for senior citizens. In early 2004 it was accepted as an official school sport. Boules is the French name for the ancient (back to 9000 BC) Roman game of bocce, which involves rolling balls along the ground; petanque derives from boules and was born in France in 1910. It involves throwing balls to knock other balls out of position. **Sports Boules Singapore** (✉ #01–02 Toa Payoh Swimming Complex, 301 Toa Payoh Lorong 6, Thomson ☎ 6356–5093 ⊕ sportsboules.org.sg) is the National Sport Association for boules and petanque in Singapore. It holds regular practice sessions on Tuesday and Thursday from 6:30 PM to 9 PM and on Saturday from 4 PM to 7 PM.

Bungee Jumping

New Zealand's **G-Max** (✉ 3 E. River Valley Rd., Clarke Quay ☎ 6338–1146 ⊕ www.gmax.co.nz) imported its reverse bungee jumping method into Singapore after the government decided to permit bungee jumping. You can play astronaut for S$30 per jump and experience the G Force 5, which hurtles you 200 feet (160 meters) into the air in a three-person capsule slung between two towers. G-Max is open Monday through Thursday from 3 PM to midnight, Friday from 3 PM to 1 AM, and on weekends from noon to 1 AM.

Canoeing

You can rent canoes at Changi Point, at East Coast Park, or on Sentosa Island. You'll pay about S$10 for a single-seater and S$12 for a double-seater. Advice is available from the **Singapore Canoe Federation** (✉ #18–32, 32 River Valley Close, Orchard ☎ 6732–4358 ⊕ www.scf. org.sg).

Climbing

Climbing has been popular in Singapore ever since its first Mt. Everest Expedition in 1998 where two team members successfully reached the mountain's summit. For a natural climbing site, you can try the **Hindhede Quarry** at Bukit Timah Nature Reserve, but be prepared to jump through hoops for permission to climb. The Singapore Mountaineering Federation (✉ SAFRA Toa Payoh, 293 Lorong 6 Toa Payoh, Thomson/ Toa Payoh ☎ 6355–4502 ⊕ smf_nsa.tripod.com) oversees the site, and you'll need to provide them with proof of prior climbing instruction and membership to a recognized club. If you're approved, you can climb on weekends and public holidays for S$10 a day.

Colleges—Singapore Polytechnic, Temasek Polytechnic, Nanyang Polytechnic, and the National University of Singapore to name a few—and SAFRA (Singapore Armed Forces Reservist Association) clubhouses have artificial climbing walls, which are often accessible to visitors. **SAFRA Bukit Merah** (⊠ 5200 Bukit Merah Rd., West/Bukit Merah ☎ 6278–6011 ⊕ www.safra.org.sg) has a five-story high wall, as well as a bouldering zone in a converted squash court. The wall opens daily from 9 AM to 11 PM; rates are S$8.40 for a two-hour session before 6 PM or S$10.50 after 6 PM. Reservations are only required for the climbing wall. Another clubhouse, **SAFRA Yishun** (⊠ 60 Yishun Ave. 4, North/Yishun ☎ 6852–8220/8221), calls itself the National Rock Climbing Centre and has a six-faced, 59-foot (15-meter) wall, which is Singapore's highest outdoor artificial wall open to the public. The clubhouse is open from 9 AM to 9:30 PM on weekdays, and from 9 AM to 6 PM on weekends. You can use the facilities for S$10 for four hours. **Climb Adventure (Pacific)** (⊠ #01–04/05 Keppel Towers, 10 Hoe Chiang Rd., South/Tanjong Pagar ☎ 6220–3305 ⊕ www.climbadventure.com) has a 5,400 square-foot (501 square-meter) climbing area with an abseiling tower. This facility opens from 10 AM to 9 PM on weekdays, and from 10 AM to 6 PM on weekends. There's a S$10 climbing fee.

Cricket

Fodor'sChoice ★

From March through September matches take place every Saturday at 1:30 and every Sunday at 11 on the Padang in front of the **Singapore Cricket Club** (⊕ www.scc.org.sg). Entry to the clubhouse itself during matches is restricted to members, but you can watch from the sides of the playing field. Note that the club, not dedicated solely to cricket, runs lively rugby, soccer, hockey, squash, and other sports events. For more information contact the **Singapore Cricket Association** (⊠ 31 Stadium Crescent, Kallang ☎ 6348–6566 ⊕ www.cricket.org.sg).

Fitness Facilities

Hotels

If you absolutely *have* to work out in a gym, consider staying at one of these hotels with first-rate fitness facilities. Because many hotel clubs offer annual memberships to Singaporeans, you'll find the facilities busy in the early morning, at midday, and in the early evening.

Four Seasons. Peter Burwash International pros offer tennis lessons here on four indoor, air-conditioned courts for S$63 an hour. You'll also find two pools on the third (adults only) and 20th floors, a fully equipped fitness center with aerobics videos, a billiards room, a golf simulator, saunas, and steam rooms. The spa offers a wide range of massage techniques, skin treatments, and equipment such as flotation tanks. Hotel guests only. ⊠ 190 Orchard Blvd., Orchard ☎ 6734–1110 ⊙ 6 AM–10 PM.

Marina Mandarin. Guests can play squash for S$5 per hour and then take a dip in the outdoor pool at this luxurious downtown hotel. There's a fully equipped gym (free to guests) as well as a sauna. You can also try massage therapy for S$105 per hour. ⊠ 6 Raffles Blvd., CBD ☎ 6845–1188.

The Oriental. This hotel has a fifth-floor health club as well as a splendid outdoor pool with an underwater sound system and a view of the harbor. Some of the weight-training stations are outdoors. There are massage, facial, manicure, and pedicure services, as well as foot reflexology. Access to the center is available to non-guests for a flat fee of S$25 per visit. Runners should try the waterfront path on the Esplanade across the street from the hotel; maps are provided in your room. ⊠ *5 Raffles Ave., CBD* ☎ *6338–0066, 6885–3072.*

The Ritz-Carlton, Millenia Singapore. The health and fitness club here is for hotel guests only. You'll have access to a state-of-the-art gym, an outdoor pool and Jacuzzi, hot-cold plunge pools, a sauna, and steam facilities. ⊠ *7 Raffles Ave., CBD* ☎ *6337–8888, 6235–2498* ⊙ *Daily 6 AM–10 PM.*

Shangri-La. Amenities here include a large outdoor pool and a smaller indoor one; a health club; saunas, steam rooms, and Jacuzzis; and a three-hole golf green where you can jog in the early morning, all free to guests. The three tennis courts (one hard, the others artificial grass) cost S$10 per hour. Facilities are reserved for hotel guests and club members. The "Energize and Enrich" programs include Thai bowing, yoga, and culinary skills training. ⊠ *22 Orange Grove Rd., Orchard* ☎ *6737–3644* ⊙ *Fitness center: daily 6 AM–11 PM; pool: daily 6 AM–10 PM.*

Kallang ClubFitt Gym. For facilities outside the luxury hotels, your best bet is this gym, which is one of several Singapore Sports Council Club-Fitt gyms. These gyms have very affordable rates and various discounts, including one for people over 55. ⊠ *National Stadium, 15 Stadium Rd., East Coast/Kallang* ☎ *6340–9667, 6348–1258* ⊕ *www.ssc.gov.sg* ⊙ *Weekdays 7 AM–10 PM; weekends 7 AM–8 PM.*

YMCAs/YWCAs

What were once upon a time the simple lodging houses of the Young Men's Christian Association (YMCA) and the Young Women's Christian Association (YWCA) are now very comfortable middle-bracket hotels with fitness facilities that offer temporary memberships.

Metropolitan YMCA. The most well-appointed of the three Ys, this one at the heart of the shopping and tourist area, has a swimming pool and free gym use for hotel guests. Non-guests can use the facilities if they are YMCA members, which costs S$200 annually—each use of the pool then costs another S$1.55, while the gym is another S$60 per month or S$15 per entry. ⊠ *60 Stevens Rd., Orchard* ☎ *6839–8333.*

YWCA Ft. Canning. The greenery of Ft. Canning Hill makes this Y ideal for a more relaxed workout. Only members can access the pool and a tennis court. Temporary membership (S$3.62) is available only if you book a hotel room. Otherwise membership costs S$105 a year. ⊠ *6 Ft. Canning Rd., Colonial Singapore* ☎ *6338–4222.*

YMCA International House. In the heart of the cultural and museum district in the city center, this Y has a rooftop pool, squash courts, a gym, and billiards, free to guests and members. Note that the general environment has been compromised by massive construction nearby. Visitors must pay S$10 per month for temporary membership, as well as

S$1.05 for each pool use and S$5.25 for each gym use before 6 PM, S$10.50 after 6 PM. ⊠ *1 Orchard Rd., Colonial Singapore* ☎ *6336–6000.*

Spas

Singaporeans can't get enough of seaweed wraps and sea-salt body scrubs, reflexology, aromatherapy, massage, and holistic health treatments. As a result, the city is just bursting with self-pampering options. Shop around, since prices are on the high side, averaging around S$150–S$200 for an hour session. Spas that have joined the Singapore Gold Circle, a quality recognition program supervised by the Singapore Tourism Board, are a safe bet.

Amrita Spa Raffles City. This huge (more than 50,000 square feet, 4,645 square meters) spa and health center has meditation alcoves, whirlpools, yoga and aerobics studios, two swimming pools, six tennis courts, plus a restaurant and bar. Hydrotherapy, steam capsules, and various other treatments are also available. ⊠ *Raffles The Plaza, Level 6, 2 Stamford Rd., Colonial Singapore* ☎ *6336–4477* ☉ *Daily 5:30 AM–11 PM; spa treatments daily 10–9; gym open for hotel guests 24 hours.*

Esthetica. Fitness and self-indulgence converge at this spa in the middle of busy Orchard Road. After making use of the 820-foot (250-meter) heated indoor pool, gym, aerobics studio, Jacuzzi, and saunas, you can relax with such treatments as a detoxifying seaweed body wrap and a stress-relieving massage. A café serves light food. ⊠ *#04–17/18 Takashimaya Shopping Centre, 391A Orchard Rd., Orchard* ☎ *6733–7000* ☉ *Weekdays 10–8:30, weekends 10–6:30.*

Estheva. The perfumed air announces a dedication to sensuality at this spa inspired by Italian traditions of thermal hydrotherapy. Estheva offers facials, massages, thermal-mud body wraps, hydrotherapy, and foot reflexology as well as "jet lag relief." The spa is for women only. ⊠ *Palais Renaissance, Level 3, 390 Orchard Rd., Orchard* ☎ *6733–9300* ⊕ *www.estheva.com* ☉ *Weekdays 10–10, weekends 10–6.*

Mayuri Ayurvedic Spa. This spa offers massages and other body treatments, which borrow from age-old Indian healing traditions and ancient Ayurvedic texts. ⊠ *#02–10, 11 Unity St., Robertson Quay* ☎ *6737–5657* ⊕ *www.mayurispa.com* ☉ *Weekdays 11–9, Sat. 10–8, Sun. 10–5.*

Phytomer Spa Rasa Sentosa. For maximum relaxation remove yourself from the hubbub of the main island—Phytomer is happily installed in one of Sentosa Island's beach resorts. It's fitting that the spa pushes thalassotherapy, which uses the therapeutic properties of seawater. There are a gym, saunas, and an outdoor spa pool pavilion. Complimentary transportation to the island is available from designated pickup points. ⊠ *Shangri-La Rasa Sentosa Resort, Level 1, 101 Siloso Rd., Sentosa* ☎ *6275–0100* ☉ *Daily 9:30–9.*

Renewal Day Spa–The Next Millennium. The wisdom of East and West intermingle here—the spa has traditional Indonesian herbal treatments renowned for their slimming effects, Asian foot reflexology, and western specialties such as the German Kneipp therapy, which supposedly eases migraines and insomnia and improves concentration. ⊠ *#04–15 UE Square Shopping Mall, 81 Clemenceau Ave., Robertson Quay* ☎ *6735–5665* ☉ *Daily 10–10.*

★ **Spa Botanica.** This S$10 million megaspa in the classy Sentosa Resort and Spa draws heavily on garden and plant themes amid the green landscape and beaches of Sentosa Island. It has 14 indoor treatment rooms, six outdoor pavilions, a flotation pool, and two mud pools (the mud is from Indonesia and Europe) for exfoliation and detoxification. There's even a spiral labyrinth for meditative walks. ☒ *2 Bukit Manis Rd., Sentosa* ☎ *6371–1318* ⊕ *www.spabotanica.com* ☯ *Daily 10–10.*

St. Gregory Javana Spa. The theme at this downtown spa is strongly Indonesian—both Javanese and Balinese. Treatments use eastern spices like cinnamon, nutmeg, and ginger, as well as milk, scented oils, and traditional herbs. ☒ *Plaza Hotel, Level 4, 7500A Beach Rd., Arab District* ☎ *6290–8028* ⊕ *www.stgregoryspa.com* ☯ *Weekdays 9 AM–10 PM, weekends 9–9.*

Golf

Golf is largely the sport of a members-only elite in Singapore, so be aware that Singapore's private golf clubs can be very swanky and expensive spots. Most are fully appointed social clubs, with restaurants, bars, and fitness centers. Dress codes prevail: most commonly, a collared shirt with trousers or short pants is required, along with proper golf shoes. Some courses don't allow spiked shoes. Most clubs are open daily 7–7; some offer night golfing until 11. Clubs usually have driving ranges, which offer practice for as little as S$2 for 50 balls.

Some top hotels will make arrangements for their guests to golf at the local courses. You might check before leaving home to see whether your club has any reciprocal arrangements with a Singapore club. Several courses accept nonmembers, though some limit this to weekdays. Fees will be cheaper if you can enter as a member's guest. The greens fees cited here are applicable to unaccompanied foreign visitors. In most cases the only certification required is based on your handicap—proficiency tests are available if you're not sure where you stand. Differing handicaps are catered to by multiple tee-off positions at most clubs.

Golfing just across the water on Indonesian resort islands like Bintan and Batam and in Malaysia's southern state of Johor is a convenient option—the Singapore Tourism Board promotes golf travel packages and lists several travel agents specializing in such tours on the its Web site (www.visitsingapore.com/sections/3a/0,1138,348,00.html).

Private Courses

Changi Golf Club. This hilly 9-hole, par-34 course on 50 acres is open to non-members on weekdays only. ☒ *20 Netheravon Rd., Changi* ☎ *6545–5133* ☯ *Mon. noon–5, Tues.–Thurs. 8:30–5* ☒ *Greens fees: S$80 for 18 holes; caddy: S$10–25; club rental: S$20.*

Jurong Country Club. Here you'll find an 18-hole, par-72 course on 120 acres, as well as a driving range. Half the holes are on flat terrain; the other nine are on small hills. It's open to non-members; book by phone one week in advance. ☒ *9 Science Centre Rd., West Coast/Jurong* ☎ *6560–5655, 6568–5186/5187/5188* ⊕ *www.jcc.org.sg* ☯ *Daily 7–7:30* ☒ *Greens fees: weekday mornings S$90, afternoons S$105, weekends S$180; caddy: S$25; club rental: S$25.*

★ **Keppel Club.** This historic club was founded in 1904. Non-members are welcome at the 18-hole, par-71 course. ⊠ *10 Bukit Chermin Rd., West Coast* ☎ *6375–5570* ☉ *Closed Mon.; Tues.–Sun. 7 AM–9 AM; noon–2 PM; 4:45 PM–6 PM* ⛳ *Greens fees (includes golf cart): weekdays S$102.90, weekends S$207.90; club rental: S$40.*

Raffles Country Club. Although it's in an industrial estate, this course is pleasingly rural, with the forgiving 18-hole Lake Course and the more challenging 18-hole Palm Course. Both are par 72, designed by Robert Trent Jones, Jr. Visitors can golf here on weekdays only. Book by phone one week in advance. ⊠ *450 Jalan Ahmad Ibrahim, West Coast/Jurong* ☎ *6861–7649* ⊕ *www.rcc.org.sg* ☉ *Daily 7 AM–6:30 PM* ⛳ *Greens fees (includes buggy): mornings S$126.50, afternoons S$136.50; club rental: S$35.*

Seletar Country Club. This 18-hole, par-72 golf club has such additional facilities as a gym, Jacuzzi, and swimming pool. It also has a two-tier driving range with 52 bays. Other than guests of members, visitors aren't permitted here. ⊠ *101 Seletar Club Rd., Seletar* ☎ *6486–0801* ☉ *Daily 7 AM–10:30 PM* ⛳ *Greens fees: Mon. and Tues. mornings S$65, Wed.–Fri. mornings S$80; weekday afternoons S$100; weekends and holidays S$180; golf carts S$15–20.*

Sembawang Country Club. Because of its hilly terrain, this 18-hole, par-72 course is known as the "commando course." Note that golfers are asked to wear soft spikes. ⊠ *Sembawang Airbase, 249 Sembawang Rd., Sembawang* ☎ *6751–0320, 6751–0328* ☉ *7 AM–11 PM* ⛳ *Greens fees (includes buggy): weekday mornings S$94.50, afternoons S$115.50, weekends S$41.75; club rental: S$30.*

★ **Sentosa Golf Club.** The Tanjong course (available to visitors on Tuesdays only), on the island's southeastern tip, is a challenging course with many water obstacles and occasional panoramic views of the South China Sea. The 18-hole, par-72 Serapong course is set against the backdrop of Singapore's harbor. Bookings by fax are accepted. ⊠ *27 Bukit Manis Rd., Sentosa* ☎ *6275–0022* 🖷 *6275–0654* ☉ *7–7* ⛳ *Greens fees (includes buggy): weekdays S$231; weekends S$315; club rental: S$21.*

Public Courses

Singapore has four public golf courses. They're open to the public and allow walk-in bookings, though it may be necessary to show your passport or some identification. Public courses usually lack the luxurious clubhouses and ancillary facilities such as gyms, restaurants, and pools that are common in private courses.

Executive Golf Course. Beginners can feel at ease on this jungle-fringed 9-hole, par-29 course near the Seletar Reservoir. ⊠ *Upper Seletar Reservoir, Mandai Rd. Track 7, Mandai* ☎ *6556–0600* ☉ *Daily 7 AM–6:15 PM* ⛳ *Greens fees: weekdays S$21, weekends S$31.50; club rental S$10; trolley rental: S$3.*

Green Fairways. Set in suburban Bukit Timah not too far from Orchard Road and Holland Village, this 9-hole, par-32 course is straightforward and simple. ⊠ *60 Fairways Dr., off Eng Neo Ave., Bukit Timah* ☎ *6468–7233* ☉ *Daily 7 AM–5:30 PM* ⛳ *Greens fees: weekdays S$42, weekends S$52.50; club rental: S$20–S$30; trolley rental: S$3.*

Royal Tanglin Golf Course. This 9-hole course has a par 15 rating and is frequented by golfers up for a short game and beginners. Golf carts and equipment aren't available to rent here. ☒ *130E Minden Rd., Tanglin/ Holland Village* ☎ *6473–7236* ☺ *Daily 7–7* ☜ *Greens fees: S$10 for two rounds, S$15 on weekends.*

Seletar Base Golf Club. This is considered Singapore's best 9-hole course. To play it, you need a handicap of 24 (men) or 36 (women), as certified by golf clubs affiliated with USGA or R&A of Scotland. Bring your passport for identification. ☒ *244 Oxford St., Seletar Airbase* ☎*6481–4745* ☺*7 AM–5:30 PM* ☜*Greens fees: S$31.50 weekdays, S$42 weekends; club rental: S$20 (deposit S$50); trolley rental: S$4.*

Horseback Riding

Riding for pleasure has a long established history in Singapore. The **Bukit Timah Saddle Club** (☒ 51 Fairways Dr., off Eng Neo Ave./Dunearn Rd., Bukit Timah ☎ 6466–2782 ⊕ www.btsc.org.sg), on the old Singapore Turf Club (⇨ *below*) site, has courses in beginner horseback riding, dressage, and show jumping.

Horse Racing

FodorśChoice
★

Horse racing is a serious preoccupation in Singapore. You'll find on-site racing as well as live telecasts of Malaysian races at the **Singapore Turf Club** (☒ Singapore Racecourse, 1 Turf Club Ave., Kranji ☎ 6879–1000/1719 ⊕ www.turfclub.com.sg), 30 minutes out of town—take the MRT to Kranji station. Local races are held on selected Friday nights and weekend afternoons. There's a strict dress code: shorts, sleeveless T-shirts, and sandals aren't allowed, even in the public stands (S$3–S$7 for the air-conditioned zone); smart casual or better (no jeans or any short trousers) is the way to go in the air-conditioned members' enclosures (for which foreigners need a passport to enter). Visitors can purchase a S$20 ticket to the Hibiscus Lounge on Level 3 of the Grandstand, or a S$15 entry to the Gold Card Room on Level 2; no children are allowed. The club is open Friday 6:30 PM–10 PM, Saturday 2 PM–10 PM, and Sunday 1:30 PM–6 PM.

Kite Flying

For information on this traditional Southeast Asian sport, contact the **Singapore Kite Association** (☒ #10–08, 30 Tanah Merah Kechil Rd., East Coast/Changi ⊕ welcome.to/s_k_a). On Sunday, kite flyers gather at Pasir Ris Park on the East Coast, as well as at Marina South, near the sea and the CBD. There's usually a kite festival day in February.

Polo

FodorśChoice
★

The historic **Singapore Polo Club** (☒ 80 Mt. Pleasant Rd., off Thomson Rd., Thomson ☎ 6256–4530) has local and international matches. Spectators are welcome to the matches starting at 5:30 PM on Tuesday and Thursday, and at 5 PM on the weekend. Malaysian royalty may be spotted here playing the occasional chukka—the designated 7½-minute polo session.

Rugby

Rugby is played on the **Padang** grounds in front of the Singapore Cricket Club (⊕ www.scc.org.sg). Kickoff is usually on Saturday at 3:15 PM and 5:30 PM from July through November. There are 10 teams in the local league. In early November the rugby scene is enlivened with the Singapore International Rugby Sevens tournament, which lures international stars to play on the Padang. You can learn more about the sport from the **Singapore Rugby Union** (⊠ Toa Payoh Swimming Complex, 301 Toa Payoh Lorong 6, Toa Payoh ☎ 6467–4038 ⊕ www.sru.org.sg).

Running

Singapore is a great place for runners: there are manifold parks, and many leading hotels give out jogging maps. The National Parks Board's sundry jogging paths and Park Connector Network (PCN), which links Singapore's major parks, makes for easy urban jogging; consult the board's Web site at ⊕ www.nparks.gov.sg, for detailed maps. Serious runners can tackle the 15-km (9.3-mi) East Coast Parkway track, then cool off with a swim at the park's sandy beach. One of the most enjoyable places to run is the Singapore Botanic Gardens (off Holland Road or off Bukit Timah Road, and not far from Orchard Road), where you can jog until 11 PM. It's safe for women to run alone in most areas, but caution is advised in the more forested spots, especially at night and just before dawn. Look right when crossing the road—Singaporeans drive on the left. There are big-race events during the year, such as the annual Singapore International Marathon in December.

Sailing

Sailboats can be rented for about S$20 an hour with a S$30 deposit. Windsurfing equipment costs about S$20 for two hours with a S$10 deposit. Sailboat rentals are also available on Sentosa Island. Most sailing facilities are in the Changi/East Coast area.

Folks at the **Changi Sailing Club** (⊠ 32 Netheravon Rd., Changi ☎ 6545–2876 ⊕ www.csc.org.sg) can provide general information about sailing. An important sailing facility and information source is the East Coast–based **National Service Resort & Country Club Sea Sports Centre (NSRCC)** (⊠ 10 Changi Coast Walk, Changi ☎ 6542–8288, 6546–5880 ⊕ www.nsrcc.com.sg).

Scuba Diving

Divers usually see Singapore as a springboard to more exotic diving spots off Malaysia, Indonesia, and the Philippines. Nevertheless, some interesting diving can be found closer to home at some of the small islands right off Singapore's coast, though the currents are treacherous and visibility is low. Costs can run anywhere from S$350 to S$600 (including equipment) for weekend regional dives, but dives around Pulau Hantu, off Singapore's southern coast, cost about S$60–S$80 per person for two dives (about half a day) including a guide.

The **Singapore Underwater Federation** (✉ River Valley Swimming Complex, 1 River Valley Rd., Orchard ☎ 6334–5519), the umbrella organization for diving in Singapore, has a lot of information about scuba diving in Singapore. The **Marine Conservation Group, Nature Society (Singapore)** (✉ #02–05 The Sunflower, 510 Geylang Rd., Geylang ☎ 6741–2036) knows just about everything about Singapore waters, and publishes the book *Singapore Waters: Unveiling Our Seas*.

Big Bubble Centre (✉ 51 Neil Rd., South/Tanjong Pagar ☎ 6222–6862 ⊕ www.bigbubble.com) is PADI certified and owned by a diving veteran with 25 years of experience. The center organizes travel arrangements, training, equipment repair, and boat charters. **Marsden Bros** (✉ 113 Holland Rd., Orchard ☎ 6475–0050 ⊕ home1.pacific.net. sg/~marsbros) is an experienced dive outfit led by a marine biologist who knows how to spot interesting sites. Marsden operates under PADI standards and teaches at its pool near Orchard Road.

Snow Sports

Hard to believe, but there's a place for snow sports in tropical Singapore. **Snow City Singapore** (✉ 21 Jurong Town Hall Rd., Jurong ☎ 6560–2306 ⊕ www.snowcity.com.sg) is a S$6 million permanent indoor facility in the Jurong industrial estate area of Singapore's far west. Snowboarding, snow-tubing, and skiing are available. It's open Tuesday through Sunday 10:30 AM–6:30 PM; admission is S$12 for one hour and S$18 for two hours.

Soccer

Soccer is the major sport of Singapore, with the added thrill of legalized soccer betting (*Score!*) via the national lottery, Singapore Pools; important matches take place in the **National Stadium** at Kallang. Games are played by 10 territorially based home clubs within the local S-League. Details are published in the daily papers, and ticket reservations can be made through the Singapore Sports Council (⇨ *above*). The main season is March through September. Two major annual contests are the S-League's Singapore Cup and the Singapore Cricket Club's Soccer Sevens. For more information contact the **S-League/Football Association of Singapore** (✉ Jalan Besar Stadium, 100 Tyrwhitt Rd., Northeast/ Serangoon ☎ 6348–3477, 6293–1477 ⊕ www.sleague.com).

Tennis & Squash

Several hotels have their own tennis and squash courts, and there are quite a few public squash courts as well. Unless otherwise noted, all the complexes cited below are administered by the **Singapore Sports Council** (☎ 6345–7111 or 6342–5203) and are open daily 7 AM–10 PM. Rates for tennis are usually S$3.50 per off-peak hour (weekdays 7 AM–6 PM) and S$9.50 per peak hour (weekdays 6 PM–10 PM, weekends 7 AM–10 PM); rates of S$3 and S$6 are on the same basis for squash. Only the Kallang squash courts and the School of Physical Education's competition squash courts charge a higher rate, S$5–S$10.

The **Burghley Squash & Tennis Centre** (⊠ 43 Burghley Dr., Northeast/ Serangoon Garden ☎ 6283–1251), in the old and genteel suburb of Serangoon Garden, has four tennis and five squash courts. **Farrer Park Tennis Centre** (⊠ 1 Rutland Rd., Little India ☎ 6299–4166) has eight courts and two practice walls. The **Kallang Squash and Tennis Centre** (⊠ National Stadium, 52 Stadium Rd., Kallang ☎ 6348–1291 for tennis, 6440–6839 for squash) is convenient to the CBD and has seven squash courts, eight tennis courts, and two tennis walls.

The **School of Physical Education Squash & Tennis Centre** (⊠ 21 Evans Rd., Bukit Timah ☎ 6468–8393 ⊙ Weekdays 6 PM–10 PM, Sat. 2 PM–10 PM, Sun. 7 AM–10 PM) is a well-appointed facility at the Nanyang Technological University with five tennis and four squash courts. The **Singapore Tennis Centre** (⊠ 1020 East Coast Pkwy., East Coast ☎ 6449–9034) has 10 all-weather outdoor tennis courts, as well as arcades and restaurants. Rates range from S$10.50 to S$14.50 per hour. Near Kallang and Little India, the **St. Wilfred Squash & Tennis Centre** (⊠ 3 St. Wilfred Rd., Toa Payoh ☎ 6293–3452) has four tennis and two squash courts.

Track & Field

Major events are held in the **National Stadium** at Kallang, but there are actually 17 other stadiums in Singapore, in addition to nine athletic centers with tracks. International meets are usually detailed in the daily press. For information and details on how to book seats for major meets, call the **Singapore Sports Council** (☎ 6345–7111 ⊕ www.ssc.gov.sg).

Waterskiing

The key regions for waterskiing in Singapore are Ponggol (sometimes spelled Punggol), Sembawang, and the downtown Kallang Riverside Park area near the National Stadium, home to the national waterskiing organization, **Singapore Waterski & Wakeboard Federation** (⊠ 10 Stadium La., Kallang ☎ 6344–8813), which oversees the **Singapore Waterski & Wakeboard Centre**. Ponggol, formerly a sleepy fishing village in northeastern Singapore, is now a smart marina complex. **Ponggol Seasports** (⊠ 600 Ponggol 17th Ave., Ponggol ☎ 6386–3891 ⊙ Daily 10–6) in Ponggol Marina charges S$70 per hour on weekdays and S$80 per hour on weekends for an inboard motor boat and ski equipment. **William Water Sports Center** (⊠ Ponggol Point, 35 Ponggol 24th Ave., Ponggol ☎ 6257–5859 ⊕ www.williamwatersports.com.sg) opens daily 9–6 and offers equipment rental and lessons. Its hourly rates are S$70–S$95 on weekdays and S$75–S$100 on weekends. Sembawang, like Ponggol, is also in Singapore's far north. It's home to **ProAir Watersports** (⊠ Ponggol Marina, 600 Ponggol 17th Ave., Ponggol ☎ 6756–8012 ⊕ www.proairwatersport.com), which has an hourly rate of S$80–S$105 on weekdays and S$90–S$105 on weekends, and is open daily 9–6.

Windsurfing

Windsurfing is popular here, though Singapore isn't quite windy enough for the sport's more thrilling dimensions. As with all water sports in Singapore, you have to be mindful of how close Indonesia and Malaysia are, and ensure you don't drift out of Singapore waters and across international borders. Equipment rental usually costs about S$20–S$30 for two hours, with a $10 deposit, while lessons run around S$78–S$130. The governing body for windsurfing is the **Board Sailing Association, Singapore** (☎ 6780–5805). The **Singapore Sailing Federation** (✉ #01–01 National Sailing Centre, 1500 East Coast Pkwy., East Coast ☎ 6448–0485 ⊕ www.sailing.org.sg) offers sailing and windsurfing courses, which are usually two weekends long, for around S$154–S$206.

Fodor'sChoice
★ The **East Coast Sailing Centre** (✉ 1212 East Coast Pkwy., East Coast ☎ 6449–5118 ☉ Daily 9:30–6) also offers lessons. The **East Coast Sea Sports Centre** (✉ 1390 East Coast Pkwy., East Coast ☎ 6444–0409 ⊕ www.passc.gov.sg ☉ Mon. 9:30–1 [no rentals], Wed.–Fri. 9:30–6, weekends 9–6, closed Tues.) offers a smattering of courses, particularly in windsurfing, at non-member rates ranging from S$78–290. Windsurfing instruction is available at the **National Service Resort & Country Club Seasports Centre, Changi** (✉ 10 Changi Coast Walk, East Coast/Changi ☎ 6546–5880) for S$78–S$130. The center is open Tuesday through Sunday 9:30–7.

SHOPPING

6

BEST UPSCALE MALL
Ngee Ann City ➪*p.156*

BIGGEST SELECTION UNDER ONE ROOF
Mustafa Centre ➪*p.158*

SUPER MARKET
Chinatown Complex ➪*p.161*

QUIRKIEST OBJETS D'ART
Evolution Prehistoric Art Gallery ➪*p.161*

CHICEST BOUTIQUE
Club 21 ➪*p.164*

Updated by
Josie Taylor

IF SHOPPING WERE AN OLYMPIC SPORT, SINGAPORE WOULD BE A NATION OF GOLD MEDALISTS. Brand worship and a growing disposable income have turned retail therapy into a national pastime. Servicemen in their fatigues carry luxury label paper bags, young girls clutch what looks like their body weight in purchases. On weekends the enterprising Sanctuary Bar on Orchard Road tends to those left behind by shoppers with their "Men-Minding Service." Recently, United Overseas Bank launched a Visa mini credit card that can be worn on a necklace to facilitate the transaction process.

Singapore is brilliantly set up for shoppers within a centralized geographical area. Air-conditioned underground walkways run along most of Orchard Road as well as from Raffles City to Suntec and surrounding areas, but you may prefer to walk on the street if you dislike shuffling crowds. Khmer objets d'art, funky Indian housewares, Chinese calligraphy, Indonesian teak furniture, Thai silk, Indian spices, and Vietnamese lacquerware are as easy to find as cutting-edge laptop computers and digital cameras. If you're loathe to lug your parcels around, you can send your purchases back to the hotel in a taxi (drivers are very trustworthy). Ask the store to call a taxi for you, then call your hotel to forewarn them. You'll need to pay your fare, based on the driver's estimation, when you hand over your parcels. Make sure your name, hotel, and room number are clearly marked. It's always a good idea to give them a few extra dollars in case they get stuck in traffic.

If you're interested in thumbing through haute couture, head to the Orchard and Scotts roads area to browse the designer boutiques at the Hilton Shopping Gallery, which is connected by an underground walkway to the Four Seasons Hotel arcade. The Paragon, a few blocks east, has local and imported high-end brands. The Heeren is on the next block, and across the road from The Paragon is the Wisma Atria. Trendy outfits can be found on the cheap at the Far East Plaza on Scotts Road.

Orchard Road is composed almost exclusively of mall after mall and is Singapore's prime shopping strip, especially for clothes and shoes. It's more than a mile long, but there are three MRT stops—Dhoby Ghaut, Somerset, and Orchard—that cover about two-thirds of it. The Tanglin Shopping Centre, with its distinctive antiques shops, is a 15-minute walk west from the Orchard MRT. A five-minute taxi ride from Tanglin are the former army officers' quarters on Dempsey Road. Here you'll find a selection of warehouses selling antiques, art, and rattan and teak furniture.

To avoid crowds and high prices, head for a suburban mall that's next to an MRT station. Junction 8, for example, is beside the Bishan MRT, and Tampines Mall and Century Square are next to the Tampines MRT.

The shops around Temple and Sago streets in Chinatown, Serangoon Road in Little India, Joo Chiat Road in the East Coast's Malay areas, and Arab Street market local baubles and tokens, herbal medicine, traditional housewares, antiques, religious sculptures, Chinese movie posters, and Indian tiffin boxes (stainless-steel lunch boxes). Generally speaking, the quality rivals that of the products found in the more

6

Shops in multilevel buildings and malls are often listed as "#00–00." The first part of the address (#00) indicates what floor the shop is on. The second part (–00) indicates its location on the floor.

Shops in the Orchard area tend to open daily by 10:30. Specialty malls such as Sim Lim Square tend to open between 10 and noon; these can get crowded in the afternoon, when people are avoiding the midday heat. Stores usually close by 9 nightly.

Bargaining

Department stores, chains, and some independents don't negotiate individual discounts, but bargaining is common in Singapore. Shops that don't offer discounts usually have a FIXED-PRICE STORE sign in their windows. Places that allow bargaining may have signs or price tags that read RECOMMENDED PRICE. Local shops in upscale complexes or malls tend to give a 10–15% discount on clothes. At jewelry stores, the discount can be as high as 40%; carpet dealers also give hefty reductions. At less upscale complexes the discounts tend to be greater. Stalls and shops around visitor attractions have the highest initial asking prices, so bargaining here yields deep discounts.

To bargain with any measure of success, you need to understand the value of the thing you want; you may want to visit department stores to get an idea of established prices. Everyone has his or her own method of bargaining, but in general, when a vendor tells you a price, ask for the "best" price, then offer even less. The person will probably reject your offer but come down a few dollars. With patience and good humor this can continue and earn you a few more dollars off the price.

Complaints

Look for the CASE TRUST logo in store windows. These retailers have been distinguished by the Consumers Association of Singapore (CASE) for their excellent service and fair pricing. If you have complaints about a shopkeeper or defective merchandise call the **Singapore Tourist Promotion Board** (☎ 1800/736–3366).

Electrical Goods

Singapore's current is 220–240 volts at 50 cycles, like that in Australia and Great Britain. Canada and the U.S. use 110–120 volts at 60 cycles, so before you buy appliances, verify that you can get special converters, if required, and that these won't affect performance. These days electrical goods sold are 110–220 volts compatible. Check the sticker on the apparatus you're about to buy to ensure that it's dual voltage. Square three-pin plugs are most commonly used in Singapore.

Guarantees & Receipts

Make sure you get international guarantees and warranty cards with your purchases. Check the serial number of each item against its card, and don't forget to mail the card in. Sometimes guarantees are limited to the country of purchase. If the dealer can't give you a guarantee, he's probably selling an item intended for the market in its country of manufacture; if so, he has bypassed the authorized agent and should be able to give you a lower price. Though your purchase of such an item isn't illegal, you have no guarantee on it.

Ask for receipts, both for your own protection and for customs. Though shop-keepers might offer to state false values, it's not worth the risk of potential penalties, fines, and even prosecution if you get caught.

How to Pay

All department stores and most shops accept traveler's checks and major credit cards. Check the exchange rates before agreeing to any price because some store owners try to squeeze extra profits by giving unfair rates. If you use a card, they may try to charge you the commission charged by the credit card company. This is particularly true of American Express due to their higher merchant fees.

Imitations

Copyright laws passed in early 1987 impose stern penalties on the selling of pirated music and computer software. This has pushed counterfeit items underground rather than out. Some stores will load a just-purchased computer with all the pirated software you want. Pirated CDs and DVDs can be found at certain market stalls, as can incredibly authentic-looking designer wristwatches.

Restrictions

Any weapons (even swords bought as souvenirs) you've purchased must be accompanied by export permits issued by the **Singapore Arms and Explosives Branch** (✉ #02–701 Police Cantonment Complex, 391 New Bridge Rd. ☎ 6557–5822 ⊕ www.spf.gov.sg). Singapore has restrictions on items made from endangered species such as ivory and skins; many other countries restrict the import of such goods, if in doubt check with your national consulate whether a permit is required before you bring such an item home.

Shipping

Check whether the shop has insurance covering both loss and damage in transit. You might find you need additional coverage. If you're sending your purchases home by mail, check with **Singapore Post** (☎ 800/222–5777 ⊕ www.singpost.com.sg), the national postal service, about regulations.

Solicitors

Soliciting business by approaching people on the street with offers of free shopping tours and special discounts is illegal. It occasionally happens inside one or two shopping centers, especially Lucky Plaza. Avoid all solicitors and the shops they recommend; a reputable shop doesn't need them.

Taxes

The 5% Goods & Services Tax (GST) you pay with each purchase is refundable through the international financial services company **Global Refund** (⊕ www.globalrefund.com). Look for stores that have a TAX-FREE SHOPPING sticker displayed in their front windows. They'll issue you a Global Refund check when you spend a minimum of S$100. As long as you have receipts to prove that you spent more than S$300 and you take the goods out of the country within two months of purchase, you'll be able to claim a GST refund when you leave Singapore. You can cash your check at either Changi Airport, when you leave, or at the Downtown Refund Counter on the second level of Funan–The IT Mall (✉ 109 North Bridge Rd., Colonial Singapore). At both places you'll need to bring your checks, receipts, and passport.

touristy Orchard area, but because the overhead is much lower in the ethnic areas, the savings are passed on to you.

Bargain hunters should time a visit to Singapore with the annual mid-year Great Singapore Sale, which usually runs from late May through early June. During this eight-week extravaganza, all shopping centers and boutiques extend considerable discounts (up to 80%). This is a serious sale: zealous shoppers from around the region fly in, hotels and airlines offer bargain packages, and *The Straits Times* publishes supplements profiling the best deals. Hit the sale when it starts for the best bargains.

When you're tired of shopping, you can take a break at any of the eateries sprinkled around the shopping areas. There are reflexologists set up in malls to soothe your aching feet—and prime them for more pavement pounding.

SHOPPING DISTRICTS

Orchard Road

Orchard Road is lined with deluxe hotels and modern shopping complexes filled with exclusive boutiques. The road stretches from Plaza Singapura, in the east, to Tanglin Mall, in the west, and between these two points are such retail stalwarts as Centrepoint, The Heeren, Takashimaya, Wisma Atria, and the Paragon. At Scotts Road, which crosses Orchard Road, you can find the Scotts Shopping Centre and Far East Plaza.

Department stores anchor virtually every Orchard Road shopping center. Inside these complexes are multipurpose stores which sell anything from electronic goods, cigarette lighters, and fine jewelry to Mickey Mouse watches, Chinese paper kites, and antique Korean chests. Most also have money changers (usually with better rates than you'll find at banks) and a food court.

Shopping on Orchard Road can be more expensive than in other districts due to the area's astronomical rent prices; however, the department stores have the same fixed prices here as at all their branches. Shops away from the Orchard area have slightly cheaper prices.

Chinatown

Vibrant Chinatown is rife with bargains and unexpected finds. The area's old shophouses have been restored as part of the ongoing heritage conservation programs. Focus your attention on Smith, Temple, and Pagoda streets, which are a mix of pedestrian walkways and narrow alleys with small stores full of bargains. This is the area to shop for Peranakan antiques and furniture (blending Malay and Chinese styles). Intriguing Chinese kitchenware can be found on Temple Street; unusual plates, teapots, and lacquered chopsticks in bamboo pouches are among the reasonably priced wares. Stalls along Pagoda Street sell carpets, cheongsams (traditional Chinese dresses), and old local and Hong Kong movie posters.

Chinatown's smaller streets can also yield some interesting finds. Visit Sago Street to see where kite- and paper-lantern makers live and work.

There are some famous furniture craftspeople on Ann Siang Hill, which is on the other side of South Bridge Road. Just around the corner, on Club Street, are several wood-carvers who specialize in creating idols of Chinese gods. On Merchant Road, towards Clarke Quay, you can browse Chinese opera costumes, while on Chin Hin Street you can pick up fragrant Chinese tea. The area's **Chinatown Night Market** starts nightly at 6 PM. Pagoda, Trengganu, and Sago streets are lined with a mélange of stalls, which offer contemporary items alongside traditional China-town merchandise. Tradesmen of vanishing crafts, such as clog makers, fortune tellers, paper cutters, and opera mask painters, continue to produce their wares here.

Little India

Serangoon Road, the heart of Little India, is filled with sandalwood fra-grances and Hindi pop music, which makes any shopping expedition here a full sensory experience. Take the MRT to the Little India stop and you'll be near the **Little India Arcade** (☒ 48 Serangoon Rd., between Campbell La. and Hastings Rd.). At the arcade you can browse over 50 stores worth of such Indian products as henna powder, elephant-shape door handles, and bargain-priced fabrics. Walk north along Serangoon Road, passing a myriad of stores selling saris and local foodstuffs that are often stacked from the floor to the ceiling, until you reach Syed Alwi Road. Turn right on this road to reach the famed **Mustafa Centre,** an Indian department store that's open 24 hours and sells everything from cars to bath mats at very reasonable prices. You can also wander through such side streets as Race Course Lane, Kerabu Road, and Upper Dick-son Road, to browse in colorful, no-fuss stores. Look for fresh herbs, such as saffron, at inexpensive prices, and racks of CDs and DVDs on the streets. Most of the CDs are Hindi pop favorites, though you can sometimes find unusual lounge music.

At dozens of sari shops you can run your hands through the voile, Kashmiri silk, or embroidered Benares silk necessary to fashion a sari. Prices are very low considering the variety, quality, and beauty of the fabrics. You can also browse Indian costumes, like long or short *kur-tas* (collarless men's shirts) and Punjabi trouser sets. There are several luggage shops on Serangoon Road where you can buy an old-fashioned tin trunk to store your booty.

Arab Street

The shopping segment of Arab Street begins at Beach Road, opposite the Plaza Hotel. Though it covers a relatively small area, this old-fash-ioned street has some genuinely good deals, particularly at its basket and rattan shops. You can pick up competitively priced baskets, fans, hats, and mats. There are quite a few jewelers, and many shops with loose gems and garnet or amethyst necklaces. Batiks, lace, brassware, prayer rugs, carpets, and leather slippers are among the street's wares. You can eat and shop at **Golden Mile Food Centre** (☒ 505 Beach Rd.), a few minutes walk north up Beach Road from where it intersects Jalan Sultan, with its lower floors devoted to food products, and its upper floors to antiques and local trinkets. For excellent batiks head to **Jalan Sul-tan's Textile Centre** (☒ 200 Jalan Sultan, near North Bridge Rd.).

Grab your MRT card and enough cash for cab fare to lug all your packages home from these shopping itineraries.

Ethnic Homewares
Take a cab to the Holland Road Shopping Centre. **Lim's Arts and Living,** upstairs, is jam-packed with such reasonably priced items as elephant-shape teapots, coconut candle holders, and dim sum baskets (they double as jewelry boxes); allow yourself at least an hour to browse. On the same floor is **Island & Archipelago,** where you can find the proper materials to add a Balinese touch to your home. After you've browsed this center, cross the street and head towards the POSB Bank on the corner of Holland Avenue and Taman Warna Road. Walk down Taman Warna for 50 feet until you reach Jalan Merah Saga. Here you'll find **Galerie Cho Lon,** which sells upscale Southeast Asian collectibles. Take a cab to River Valley Road, making sure not to miss the mod, Asian **Jewel Ashley Gallery,** then walk down Mohamed Sultan to the corner of Kim Yam Road and poke around **John Erdos Gallery's** four shophouses. Either take a taxi or an MRT to the Little India station; if you're on the MRT, get off at Tekka Centre/Serangoon Road. Cross over Serangoon Road to the funky **Little India Arcade.**

A Slice of Singapore
Start at the **Raffles Hotel Arcade** and visit the hotel shop on the ground floor for a good selection of mementos featuring the iconic hotel: Singapore Sling glasses, coasters, and T-shirts. Take the stairs up to **Blue Ginger Design Centre** for high-quality ready-to-wear batik outfits. For more souvenirs, cross Bras Basah Road to Raffles City where you can take the City Hall MRT north one stop to Dhoby Ghaut, switch to the Northeast Line heading south, and get off two stops later at the Chinatown station. Wander the stalls on Smith, Temple, or Pagoda streets. Double back to the Chinatown MRT and take the train back two stations to Dhoby Ghaut. Change to the North-South Line, going north, and exit two stops later at Orchard. You can pick up a gold-dipped Orchid, which is Singapore's national flower, from **Tang's.** Hail a cab to the Tanglin Shopping Center where you can peruse old maps of Singapore at **Antiques of the Orient.**

IT Indulgence
Start your gadget collection with stops at Singapore's two behemoth technology malls. Catch a train to the City Hall station, get off at the St. Andrew's Cathedral exit, and walk south on North Bridge Road until you reach **Funan–The IT Mall,** which has more than 50 stores specializing in PCs and related components. You'll see many familiar brands; Asian-brand PCs or laptops can be purchased on the cheap here. At the **Challenger Superstore,** upstairs, you can get an indication of typical prices before you head downstairs to bargain at the smaller stores. If you know what you want, take a 10-minute taxi ride to **Sim Lim Square.** These stores are more modest than at Funan, and merchants will readily undercut prices, so business is brisker here. Bargain hard for MP3 Players, PDAs, or PCs. Head upstairs for computer and CD stores. Audio equipment and digital cameras are on the lower floors.

Katong

This East Coast suburb is a 15-minute cab ride northeast from downtown via the Pan Island Expressway (a.k.a. the PIE). Katong is a residential area previously dominated by wealthy Straits Chinese families who traditionally spared no expense to acquire fine furnishings and ornaments. It's now an ideal place to shop for Peranakan clothes, artwork, and food. East Coast Road's main stretch has old-fashioned shophouses, some selling antiques and children's clothes. Look for *Nonya kebayas* (a sheer top for women), exquisitely beaded slippers and handbags, *kerongsangs* (three chained-brooches), and large *pendings* (belt-buckles). Off the main street is the more traditional Joo Chiat Road, which gets exponentially more interesting as it approaches the red-light district of Geylang Road. Its shops sell Chinese kitchenware, antiques, baby clothes, and loads of such offbeat items as beaded cigarette lighters and kitschy wedding baskets. A short walk down Joo Chiat Road is the Parkway Parade, a suburban complex composed of hawker stalls and modern stores similar to those on Orchard Road. Through an underpass next to this mall, is the East Coast Park, where you can dig your toes in the sand after a lengthy shopping trip.

Holland Village

A 10-minute taxi ride west from downtown is this relaxed community of expats and local artists, fondly dubbed HV by locals. The compact shopping precinct borders on Holland Avenue and is great for unusual and inexpensive Asian items. Plus, there are plenty of cafés and restaurants where you can replenish your energy between stores. Many stores here specialize in housewares. Look for the Holland Road Shopping Centre, on Holland Avenue. Among its stores is **Lim's Arts and Livings**, which sells Chinese, Thai, and Balinese items, and **Shaw Sisters**, which sells freshwater pearls and trendy costume jewelry. Smaller stores in the center sell such trinkets as shell-encrusted handbags, lightweight clothing, and fragrant candles. On Jalan Merah Saga (which runs parallel to Holland Avenue and can be reached by crossing behind the POSB Bank) are art galleries, boutiques, and food stores. Among these stores is **Galerie Cho Lon**, selling one-of-a-kind furniture and jewelry from Vietnam and Rajasthan, India. Visit ⊕ www.hollandvillage.com.sg for more information.

River Valley Road

A few years ago River Valley Road and Mohamed Sultan Road, its cross street, were known for their lively bar scenes, perilous open drains, and poor lighting—one misplaced step and you might wind up eight-feet underground, ankle deep in sewage. It's still a popular haunt for young night owls, but its chic galleries are lending to its reputation as a good place for art and home furnishings. **Jewel Ashley Gallery**, on River Valley Road, sells lacquerware, vividly hued silk lanterns, and glass and porcelain sculptures. The **Red Sea Gallery** displays canvasses by up-and-coming Singaporean artists. A short stroll up Mohamed Sultan Road is the **John Erdos Gallery**, which sells contemporary Asian furnishings from a stunning shophouse.

Dempsey Road

Hidden above a lush green rise that's littered with abandoned colonial buildings, you'll find one of the best areas for Southeast Asian furniture, carpets, and exotic artifacts. At the hill's peak are the former English army barracks, most of which have been converted into warehouses. Here you'll find teak outdoor table sets and pearl-inlaid rosewood beds at a fraction of what you'd pay elsewhere. There are stores that specialize in Burmese and Thai Buddha images, modern Javanese furniture, and other artworks. Always ask for a discount in this area, even at the most upscale stores. Stores can arrange for your purchases to be shipped home.

CENTERS & COMPLEXES

Centrepoint. This impressive center is anchored by the Robinson's department store, and has a basement supermarket and more than 30 shops, including Mango, Esprit, and The Metropolitan Museum of Art Store. ⊠ *176 Orchard Rd., Orchard* ⊕ *www.centrepoint.com.sg/malls/cp/ index.asp.*

CitiLink. This air-conditioned underground mall connects the City Hall MRT station to Marina Square and the Suntec City Mall. Look for FCUK and Links of London. ⊠ *1 Raffles Link, Colonial Singapore.*

Delfi Orchard. Among Delfi's 80 shops are crystal and china boutiques, art galleries, and jewelry stores. Highlights include Royal Selangor Pewter and Waterford Wedgwood. ⊠ *402 Orchard Rd., Orchard.*

Far East Plaza. The young and financially challenged gather here to see and be seen. This is the place to pick up cheap streetwear and CDs. In the forecourt are fast-food restaurants, outdoor tables, and people-watching opportunities. ⊠ *14 Scotts Rd., Orchard* ⊕ *www.fareast-plaza.com/directory.htm.*

Forum The Shopping Mall. Young families with disposable incomes shop here; parents can browse Calvin Klein or Max Mara, while kids can explore Toys "R" Us or OshKosh B'Gosh. ⊠ *583 Orchard Rd., Orchard.*

Funan–The IT Mall. On North Bridge Road and High Street, near the Peninsula Hotel, is this shopping center geared toward computer and information-technology buffs. If your time is limited, head to the all-encompassing Challenger Superstore on the top level. ⊠ *109 North Bridge Rd., Colonial Singapore* ⊕ *www.funan.com.sg.*

The Heeren Shops. Visit this complex at Orchard and Cairnhill roads for more unusual wardrobe finds. The Annexe, on the upper levels, has 50 small and independently run vintage and streetwear shops. Independent European labels are featured at stores here, such as The Changing Room, which sells quality Spanish labels. There's also a huge HMV music store. ⊠ *260 Orchard Rd., Orchard* ⊕ *www.heeren.com.sg.*

Hilton Shopping Gallery. This a standout, trilevel hotel gallery with such designers as Giorgio Armani, Gucci, Paul Smith, and Valentino. Follow the underground passage to the Four Seasons Hotel for other high-end selections. ⊠ *581 Orchard Rd., Orchard.*

Holland Road Shopping Centre. Singapore's expats frequent this shopping complex, where they pick up lightweight clothes perfect for tropical

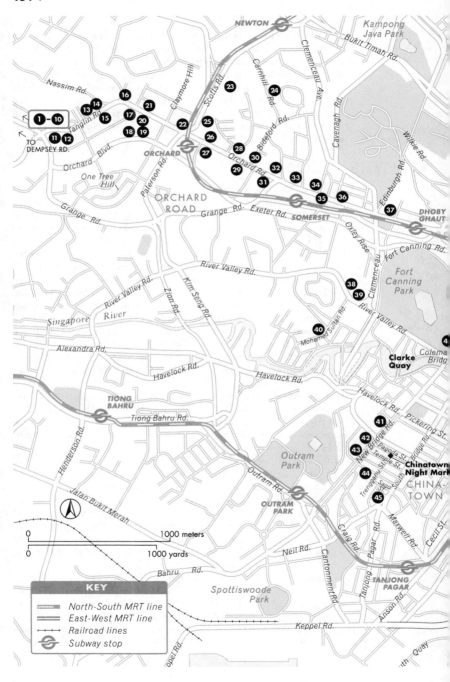

Singapore
Shopping Complexes
& Markets

weather, coral-encrusted handbags and flip flops from Bali, jewelry, and second-hand books. Lim's Arts and Crafts carries Southeast Asian houseware, furniture, and linen and rattan. ⊠ *211–213 Holland Ave., Holland Village.*

Lucky Plaza. You can "bargain for bargains" at this touristy plaza, which has stores selling trinkets, clothing, luggage, and watches of questionable origin. Plan to negotiate furiously, particularly with the jewelers who are involved in a perpetual price-cutting war. ⊠ *304 Orchard Rd., Orchard.*

Marina Square. With more than 250 shops, this is one of the largest complexes in Singapore. Major tenants include Metro department store, Golden Village Cineplex, NTUC FairPrice supermarket, and a large food court. Through underground walkways you can easily access Suntec City, Millenia Walk, Esplanade–Theatres on the Bay, and five five-star hotels: Marina Mandarin Singapore, The Oriental, Singapore, Pan Pacific Singapore, Ritz Carlton Millenia, and Conrad International Centennial Singapore. ⊠ *6 Raffles Blvd., Colonial Singapore* ⊕ *www. marinasquare.com.sg.*

★ **Millenia Walk.** If you're shopping in the Suntec City area this designer-studded mall is just a stroll away. Fendi and Burberry's are here along with other similarly upscale shops. ⊠ *9 Raffles Blvd., Colonial Singapore.*

Fodor'sChoice   **Ngee Ann City.** Japanese department store Takashimaya dominates this
★ complex, but there are also 130 other stores, including Tiffany & Co. and Chanel, several dozen food outlets, and one of Asia's largest bookstores, Books Kinokuniya. Special sales are held almost weekly in the large basement-level square. ⊠ *391 Orchard Rd., Orchard* ⊕ *www. ngeeanncity.com.sg.*

Orchard Point. Here you'll find a good range of moderately priced cosmetics, handbags, mens- and women's wear, and luggage. The lower floors are dominated by local department store **OG**. Look for special promotions of local designers on the third level. ⊠ *150 Orchard Rd., Orchard.*

Palais Renaissance. Across the street from the Hilton is this extravagantly marbled emporium where you can peruse luxury labels free from crowds. DKNY, Prada, and other high-end brands vie for space here with Singapore's first high-end Indian fashion and lifestyle store **Mumbai Se.** ⊠ *390 Orchard Rd., Orchard.*

Paragon. Glossy Paragon is worth visiting whether you're window shopping or making serious purchases at such high-end fashion boutiques as Gucci and Ermenegildo Zegna. It also has a Metro department store. Local boutiques like projectshopBLOODbros, M)phosis, and GG5 seek a slice of the pie as well. There's also a new wing of spas, including Spa Esprit, which does a five-minute instant tan that lasts for a week. ⊠ *290 Orchard Rd., Orchard.*

Parco Bugis Junction. Designed to replicate 19th-century Singaporean streets, this complex's shophouse facades and cobblestone streets are enclosed under glass domes and cooled with arctic strength air-conditioning. Even midday, you'll be cool as a cucumber. Look for affordable streetwear boutiques, a movie theater, cafés, and the Japanese department store **Seiyu.**

This center connects to the Hotel InterContinental and the Bugis MRT station. ⊠ *200 Victoria St., Bugis* ⊕ *www.parcobj.com.sg.*

Parkway Parade. Shop the trendy and affordable fashions at this six-level center in peace and quiet during the week, but it's uncomfortably crowded on the weekend. Stores tend to open around noon, and it's a 15–20 minute trip east from downtown via the East Coast Parkway (ECP) expressway to get here. ⊠ *80 Marine Parade Rd., East Coast* ⊕ *www. parkwayparade.com.sg.*

People's Park Centre. Come here to browse hundreds of lively stalls selling everything from Chinese herbs to cheap clothing. Shopkeepers are very aggressive, so if you haven't done your homework, you can get taken. ⊠ *101 Upper Cross St., Chinatown.*

People's Park Complex. Similar to the People's Park Centre on the next block, this complex also sells such traditional products as Chinese herbs, Malaysian and Indonesian textiles, religious icons, and paper effigies used at Chinese funerals. ⊠ *1 Park Rd., Chinatown.*

Plaza Singapura. This nine-story complex is a hub for families seeking entertainment, food, and shopping. ⊠ *68 Orchard Rd., Orchard* ☎ *6332–9298.*

Raffles City. Bordered by Stamford, North Bridge, and Bras Basah roads, this multilevel complex has several fashion boutiques (including Brooks Brothers and Australia's Country Road), the Times bookshop, and a basement supermarket. ⊠ *252 North Bridge Rd., City Hall* ⊕ *www. rafflescity.com.*

Raffles Hotel Arcade. More than 60 boutiques selling high fashion, art, and perfume are in the Raffles Hotel complex. **Escentials,** on the ground floor, sells limited-edition European scents. At **Evolution Prehistoric Art Gallery** you can sift through and purchase ancient fossils. ⊠ *328 North Bridge Rd., Colonial Singapore* ⊕ *www.raffleshotel.com/ arcade.html.*

Scotts Shopping Centre. One of Singapore's best places for affordable fashion just short of haute couture, Scotts has a basement food court, plus activities and demonstrations to keep shoppers entertained. ⊠ *6–8 Scotts Rd., Orchard.*

Shaw House. Isetan, a large Japanese department store, anchors this complex. The Kinokuniya bookstore has an excellent collection of volumes on Japan. There's also a **Lido** multiplex cinema here. ⊠ *350 Orchard Rd., Orchard.*

FodorśChoice ★ **Sim Lim Square.** There are over 400 stores here, all geared toward electronic and technology buffs. None of the goods here are price-tagged, so do your research beforehand and come prepared to bargain. ⊠ *1 Rochor Canal Rd., Colonial Singapore.*

Suntec City Mall. At the corner of the Nicholl Highway and Raffles Boulevard in the Marina Bay area, this large complex is divided into four zones: the Tropics (lifestyle products and services), the Entertainment Centre (with the French superstore Carrefour), the Fountain Terrace (an array of restaurants, pubs, and a food court), and the Galleria (high-end boutiques). It's large and confusing, but well worth a visit. ⊠ *3 Temasek Blvd., Colonial Singapore* ⊕ *www.sunteccity.com.sg.*

CloseUp

DEPARTMENT STORES: BIG IS BEAUTIFUL

STEP INTO ONE OF THESE STORES, with their superior shopping and people-watching opportunities, and you'll begin to see why they're so popular. When Robinson's department store announced that it intended to close its 146-year-old flagship store at Centrepoint, Singaporeans were up in arms and presented the management with a petition signed by thousands to keep it open. It worked. The clothing selection at **Robinson's** (⊠ Centrepoint, 176 Orchard Rd., Orchard ☎ 6733–0888) is among Singapore's best and there's also an ever-expanding Asian-style housewares section.

Singapore has one homegrown chain, **Metro,** that offers affordable fashions and household products. This place is a good bet for locally designed and manufactured fashion as well as brands such as Esprit. Designs are trendy and prices are good by international standards. Look for Metros in Far East Plaza, Marina Square, and the Paragon Centers & Complexes.

Multifarious **Mustafa Centre** (⊠ 145 Syed Alwi Rd., Little India ☎ 6295–5855 ⊕ www.mustafa.com.sg) can satisfy shoppers needing new sheets or kitchen utensils, and people with a hankering to peruse cars at 2 AM. Inside the modest exterior are several floors retailing an apparently infinite variety of goods at some of Singapore's lowest fixed prices.

Locally owned **Tang's** (⊠ 320 Orchard Rd., Orchard ☎ 6737–5500), a.k.a. Tang's Superstore or C. K. Tang's, is connected to the Marriott Hotel and subterranean shopping via underground passageways. Notable here are the shoes and accessories, particularly the costume jewelry. Upstairs, you'll find clothing for men and women; in the basement is a peerless collection of household products.

Overseas Emporium, a Chinese department store, is in the People's Park Complex

(⊠ #04–21 People's Park Complex, 1 Park Rd., Chinatown ☎ 6535–0555). You can find anything Chinese here: silk fabrics and blouses, brocade jackets, handcrafts, and chinaware.

Japanese department stores are popular for their packaged snacks, fashion, and housewares designed for small living spaces. **Isetan** (⊠ Parkway Parade, 80 Marine Parade Rd., East Coast ☎ 6345–5555 ⊠ Shaw House, 350 Orchard Rd., Orchard ☎ 6733–1111 ⊠ Wisma Atria, 435 Orchard Rd., Orchard ☎ 6733–7777) always has deals on its jam-packed fashion sections. **Sogo** (⊠ 252 North Bridge Rd., City Hall ☎ 6339–1100), in Raffles City, caters to a more upscale clientele with its pricy fashions and cosmetics. **Seiyu** (⊠ #03–01, 230 Victoria St., Bugis ☎ 6223–2222), in the Parco Bugis Junction Complex, carries casual wear aimed at young professionals.

Japanese icon **Takashimaya** (⊠ Ngee Ann City, 391 Orchard Rd. ☎ 6739–9323) is among Singapore's best department stores. You could easily spend a few hours wandering all of its seven floors, where you'll find a Harrods tearoom, an aromatherapy center, more than a dozen eateries, several small jewelers, a hair salon, a photo developing center, and a bookstore. The basement carries discounted sales items.

Most of the clothing at **John Little** (⊠ #05–05 Specialists' Centre, 277 Orchard Rd., Orchard ☎ 6737–2222 ⊕ www.johnlittle.com.sg ⊠ #03–11/12 Plaza Singapura, 68 Orchard Rd., Orchard ☎ 6835–9776 ⊠ #01–34 Parkway Parade, 80 Marine Parade Rd., East Coast ☎ 6447–0339) is aimed at the young and trendy. They also carry toiletries, bedding, and kitchenware.

Tanglin Mall. Crowds tend to bypass this mall, at the beginning of Orchard Road, in favor of the shops farther down the street, though there are goodies (and a yummy food court) inside. You can browse the international foods at Tanglin Market Place or housewares at Barang Barang. ⊠ *163 Tanglin Rd., Orchard.*

Tanglin Shopping Centre. This center has a selection of antiques shops, such as Moongate, one of Singapore's oldest fine antique porcelain dealers, and **Antiques of the Orient**, Singapore's only shop specializing in antique maps. ⊠ *19 Tanglin Rd., Orchard.*

Wisma Atria. Come here if only to see the aquarium that wraps around the elevator. If you want to shop as well, this center has such grand names in fashion as **Dior** and **Fendi.** You'll also find the Isetan department store. British High Street fashions can be found at **Topshop** and **Warehouse.** ⊠ *435 Orchard Rd., Orchard* ⊕ *www.wismaonline.com.*

Yue Hwa. Inside this five-level Chinese department store, you'll find plenty of unique, pricey products: silk, arts and crafts, porcelain, food stuffs. Most have been sourced from mainland China. If you spend more than S$300 in a single receipt, they'll deliver to your hotel free of charge. ⊠ *70 Eu Tong Sen St., Chinatown* ⊕ *www.yuehwa.com.sg.*

SPECIALTY SHOPS

Antiques & Curios

Begin your search for antiques on **Dempsey Road** (a 10-minute drive west from Orchard Road), which previously accommodated some British army barracks. The area is now a haven for warehouses selling Southeast Asian furniture, art, carpets, and artifacts. Burmese teak cabinets are crammed next to rosewood tables and Balinese settees. You'll need a taxi to get here; ask the driver to take you up the hill until you come to the warehouses. The stores are spread across the original barracks, which are linked by looping narrow roads. Look for the directional street signs at intersections for building numbers.

Somewhere between souvenirs and antiques are curios; these eclectic items are in shops scattered throughout the ethnic neighborhoods and in most shopping complexes. Reverse-glass paintings, porcelain vases, cloisonné, wood carvings, jewelry (agate, jade, lapis lazuli, malachite), ivory carvings, embroidery, and idols represent a fraction of the treasures you might encounter. Keep in mind that some curio dealers market their wares as antiques, as do certain vendors who sell rosewood items or reproduction furniture. Antiques in Singapore are defined as items that are more than 80 years old. Storekeepers are usually very honest about whether their goods are antique or reproductions. There's no central verification system, nor any export restrictions in place. Some stores provide a self-issued certificate of age and origin.

Teak or Asian-style furniture is sold at more reasonable prices in Singapore than what you would pay back home. You can find contemporary styles or antiques from India to Indonesia. Before you make a purchase check the furniture's hidden parts, such as the bottom and the back of the drawers, for any noticeable differences in wood grain or color. Veneers or cheaper materials are sometimes used to produce or repair furniture.

Most furniture shops will ship your goods home. Ask them to oil or wax the piece a few days before it's packed; you should repeat the process when it arrives. This keeps the wood from drying out during shipping.

Asiatique (✉ #01–14, 14–18 Dempsey Rd., Orchard/Holland Village ☎ 6471–1853) is a small, friendly store that specializes in modern Javanese furniture and home accessories made of recycled wood. **Journey East** (✉ #01–04, 13 Dempsey Rd., Orchard/Holland Village ☎ 6473–1693)sells furniture made of loom, a rattan-like fiber woven from craft paper reinforced with wire. Loom is stronger than rattan and less likely to scratch your skin or clothes. **Renaissance Antique Gallery** (✉ #01–06, 15 Dempsey Rd., Orchard/Holland Village ☎ 6474–0338) is one of the few air-conditioned shops on the hill; stop in to browse its high-quality Tibetan chests, Chinese wedding beads, and 15th-century Ming figurines.

Antiques of the Orient (✉ #02–40 Tanglin Shopping Centre, 19 Tanglin Rd., Orchard ☎ 6734–9351), in the Tanglin Shopping Centre, sells 16th-through 18th-century Buddhist artifacts and other Asian collectibles. Next door at Tudor Court, **Pagoda House Gallery** (✉ 143–145 Tanglin Rd., Orchard ☎ 6732–2177) carries Southeast Asian antiques and reproductions from the Qing dynasty.

Galerie Cho Lon (✉ #01–76/78, 43 Jalan Merah Saga, Holland Village ☎ 6473–7922) sells carved bookshelves from Rajasthan, four-poster beds from Ho Chi Minh City, and sheets from Jaipur, among other quirky furniture and curios. On Holland Avenue **Island & Archipelago** (✉ #02–05/21 Holland Road Shopping Centre, 211 Holland Rd., Holland Village ☎ 6463–1071) has Indonesian bowls, lamps, and fabrics. **Lim's Arts and Living** (✉ #02–01 Holland Road Shopping Centre, 211 Holland Rd., Holland Village ☎ 6467–1300) carries colonial furniture, silk cushion covers, and Asian-style houseware. For more contemporary pieces, such as one of a kind Javanese finds and Dutch colonial-inspired furniture, try the **John Erdos Gallery** (✉ 83 Kim Yam Rd., River Valley/Clarke Quay ☎ 6735–3307).

Art

Singapore is becoming an epicenter for contemporary Southeast Asian art; increasingly, the region's emerging artists are basing themselves here as they launch their international careers, and galleries continue to reserve space for local artwork. Prices for pieces by these established and up-and-coming artists can be hefty, but you'll likely be catching them before they gain international recognition.

Dealers will usually arrange for canvas artworks to be shipped home. If you choose to transport them by hand, place the work between sheets of heavy cardboard or plywood and then wrap it in the bubble wrap. Be cautious of leaving your painting in bubble wrap for extended periods of time as moisture can build up and cause damage.

WILD & WET MARKETS

ROLL UP YOUR TROUSER CUFFS and explore one of Singapore's **wet markets**. Fresh food markets are common in many cities, but wet markets are an Asian phenomenon. They're literally doused with water continually to keep the facilities clean. Most wet markets open at 4 AM and wind down around noon when the heat of the day takes its toll on the ice that keeps the produce and meats fresh.

Actually, wet markets are typically divided into two sections: the wet area (where the produce, meat, fish, and live animals are constantly hosed down) and the dry area (with sacks of herbs, spices, rice, dried noodles, dried seafood, and beans). Try to fit in one wet market visit to see the staggering range of foodstuffs that go into Singapore's multicultural dishes: eels, cow tongues, frogs, and perhaps a turtle or two. The transactions and movement of goods can make for a hectic, colorful, albeit somewhat smelly scene.

At the fascinating **Chinatown Complex** (✉ 335 Smith St.) wet market seafood and pork products are as plentiful as exotic eels. Stalls in the dry area sell such items as clothing and toys. When you're done shopping, you can stop for a cup of herbal tea at one of the traditional tea stalls.

Tekka Market (✉ 665 Buffalo Rd.), near the top of Serangoon Road, is the place to go for spices and seafood. Singaporeans flock here for dried goods, beef, mutton, curry paste, crabs, and freshwater fish. Upstairs at the **Tekka Centre** you'll find Indian clothing, brassware, linen, and some kitschy souvenirs.

At **Art Forum** (✉ 82 Carnhill Rd., Orchard ☎ 6737–3448 ⊕ www.artforum.com.sg) you can learn about Southeast Asian art. The owner will walk you through a collection with pieces from Indonesia, Malaysia, the Philippines, Vietnam, as well as from India and Australia. Call ahead—you can visit by appointment only. **Opera Gallery** (✉ #02–12 Ngee Ann City, 391 Orchard Rd., Orchard ☎ 6735–2618) showcases renowned European and Asian artists, such as Picasso, Chagall, and Chinese painter Ting Shao Kuang. At **Evolution Prehistoric Art Gallery** (✉ #02–15 Raffles Hotel Arcade, 328 North Bridge Rd., Colonial Singapore ☎ 6334–4970) you can sift through a collection of fossils and other prehistoric art. **Gajah Gallery** (✉ #01–08 MICA Bldg., 140 Hill St., Colonial Singapore ☎ 6737–4202) focuses on contemporary Southeast Asian art. The **Substation** (✉ 45 Armenian St., Colonial Singapore ☎ 6337–7535) shows three-dimensional installations and experimental pieces. **Jewel Ashley Gallery** (✉ 238 River Valley Rd., River Valley ☎ 6836–4780) adds a modern Asian twist to its furniture and home accessories such as eggshell platters, silk lantern lampshades, and hand-carved Buddha candles. **The Red Sea Gallery** (✉ 232 River Valley Rd., River Valley/Clarke Quay ☎ 6732–6711), a few shops away, sells canvases that are hand picked by its owner,

Fodor'sChoice ★

Fodor'sChoice ★

former banker Chris Churcher, who travels to meet artists before agreeing to showcase their work.

Batik

Arab Street carries genuine examples of this traditional fabric from Singapore, Malaysia, and Indonesia. Batik is hand dyed using a wax-resistant method and is typically sold in sarong lengths. Also available are machine-printed batiks with traditional designs, either by the meter or as ready-made articles.

For inexpensive batik products, particularly men's shirts and women's handbags, try the first floor of **Tang's** (⊠ 320 Orchard Rd., Orchard). More upscale is **Blue Ginger Design Centre** (⊠ #02–08 Raffles Hotel Arcade, 328 North Bridge Rd., Colonial Singapore ☎ 6334–7585), which deals in non-traditional patterns and products.

Cameras

Photo equipment may not be the bargain it once was, but the range of cameras and accessories available here is matched only by that in Hong Kong. It's especially important that you establish market prices before you start your hunt for equipment. You can go on-line or visit Lucky Plaza's department or camera stores to do your comparison shopping. Photographers frequent the **Peninsula Shopping Centre** (⊠ 3 Coleman St., Colonial Singapore) for stores that sell new and used lenses, tripods, and sundry supplies. Hold secondhand lenses to the light to check for mildew before making your purchase.

Fodor's Choice
★ For personalized service and camera repairs, try **The Camera Workshop** (⊠ #01–31, 3 Coleman St., Colonial Singapore ☎ 6336–1956), on the first floor of the Peninsula Shopping Centre. Across the street, in the **Peninsula Plaza** is the photography stalwart, **Cathay Photo Store** (⊠ #01–05, #01–07/08, and #01–11/14, 111 North Bridge Rd., Colonial Singapore ☎ 6337–4274 ⊠ #02–219 Marina Square, 6 Raffles Blvd., Colonial Singapore ☎ 6338–1746 ⊕ www.cathayphoto.com.sg).

Carpets

Afghan, Pakistani, Persian, Turkish, and Chinese carpets—both antique and new—are reasonably priced in Singapore. Most dealers are reputable, but you'll be expected to bargain, so it's a good idea to know the relative value before you begin. Bargaining for carpets can be a lengthy procedure. The seller may give you a mini history lesson about each piece that you express interest in to support its high price.

Head for Tanglin Road, between Tanglin Mall and the beginning of Orchard Road, for several carpet stores all within walking distance of each other. **Exquisite Oriental Carpets** (⊠ 123 Tanglin Rd., Orchard ☎ 6734–1035) is a huge store with thousands of carpets for all tastes and budgets. The **Orientalist Carpet Gallery** (⊠ 2 Tanglin Rd., Orchard ☎ 6235–3343) is in a large showroom opposite Tanglin Shopping Centre. You can also browse antique and rare carpets in shops along Dempsey Road. **Jehan Gallery** (⊠ #01–01/02, 26 Dempsey Rd., Orchard/Holland Village ☎ 6334–4333), run by a family with a 260-year history in the business, has magnificent collectible carpets.

Clothing

You'll recognize many labels from back home as you scout Singapore's vast selection of boutiques, many of which are around the Orchard Road area. Designer labels are concentrated at Palais Renaissance (⊠ 390 Orchard Rd.), The Paragon (⊠ 290 Orchard Rd.), and Hilton Shopping Gallery (⊠ 581 Orchard Rd.). Try Wisma Atria (⊠ 435 Orchard Rd.), The Heeren (⊠ 260 Orchard Rd.), and Centrepoint (⊠ 176 Orchard Rd.) for a good selection of mid-range lines. For cheap and cheerful clothes head to Far East Plaza (⊠ 14 Scotts Rd.) or Lucky Plaza (⊠ 304 Orchard Rd.). Sales are frequent, so bargains are easy to come by. It's important to keep in mind that Singaporean sizes run smaller than they do in the West.

For Australian swimwear, head to **Tannlines** (⊠ #03–03/04 Wisma Atria, 435 Orchard Rd., Orchard ☎ 6235–8870 ⊠ #03–49 Paragon, 290 Orchard Rd., Orchard ☎ 6235–8870). The local version of Victoria's Secret, **Blush!** (⊠ #03–09 Paragon, 290 Orchard Rd., Orchard ☎ 6235–8870 ⊠ #03–09 Scotts Shopping Centre, 6 Scotts Rd., Orchard ☎ 6235–8870), carries women's swimwear, sleepwear, and intimate apparel. **The Lingerie Shop** (⊠ #02–09A Palais Renaissance, 390 Orchard Rd., Orchard ☎ 6732–3091) has luxurious lingerie from European brands.

Visit **British India** (⊠ #02–04/06 Tanglin Mall, 163 Tanglin Rd., Orchard ☎ 6735–3466) for roomy linen apparel inspired by the British Raj. **Goddess** (⊠ #02–31 Tanglin Mall, 163 Tanglin Rd., Orchard ☎ 6333–6725) has richly colored clothing from Pakistan, as well as handmade gold and silver jewelry. You can shop for Asian ready-to-wear clothing at **icon fashion** (⊠ #01–04 Orchard Emerald, 218 Orchard Rd., Orchard ☎ 6733–1889). **Mumbai Sei** (⊠ #01–00 Palais Renaissance, 390 Orchard Rd., Orchard ☎ 6733–3188) is an upscale Indian clothing boutique.

Closet Raid (⊠ #03–08 Mandarin Shopping Arcade, 333 Orchard Rd., Orchard ☎ 6887–5081) carries evening gowns in American sizes 10–24. Several stores in the Holland Road Shopping Centre's upper levels carry Western-sized clothing for men and women. Look for **Just Wear Collections** (⊠ #02–66, 211 Holland Ave., Holland Village ☎ 6465–4569). **Export Fashion** (⊠ #02–30, 211 Holland Ave., Holland Village ☎ 6463–2972), next door, has light, loose fitting sarongs and beachwear.

SINGAPOREAN DESIGNERS The island's nascent fashion industry, which previously mimicked European designers, has developed its own ethnically influenced and urbane style. Asian designers often test the waters in Singapore before attempting to launch their lines in Australia, Europe, or the U.S. This is partly due to two annual public events aimed at developing and nurturing local talent: the Singapore Fashion Festival (usually held in March) and Singapore Fashion Week (usually held in October). If you plan to coincide your trip with these events, updates should be available on ⊕ www.visitsingapore.com.

M)phosis (✉ #B1–10 Ngee Ann City, 391 Orchard Rd., Orchard ☎ 6737–2190 ✉ #01–24 Plaza Singapura, 68 Orchard Rd., Orchard ☎ 6334–1733 ✉ #B1–28 CitiLink Mall, 1 Raffles Link, Colonial Singapore ☎ 6835–9744 ✉ #01–02 Parco Bugis Junction, 200 Victoria St., Colonial Singapore ☎ 6339–8553) specializes in outfits for the weekend. Fodor'sChoice ★ **projectshopBLOODbros** (✉ #02–33/34 Paragon, 290 Orchard Rd., Orchard ☎ 6735–0071) carries Singapore's edgiest designs. **Song & Kelly 21** (✉ #01–38 Forum The Shopping Mall, 583 Orchard Rd., Orchard ☎ 6735–3387), created by a Singaporean/British duo, is a line of simple though chic clothing. It's also available at department stores, notably Isetan in the Wisma Atria complex. **Woods & Woods** (✉ #02–23 Raffles City Shopping Center, 252 North Bridge Rd. ☎ 6338–6775) sells unconventional clothing, usually made from unusual fabrics and color combinations. Upscale department stores and boutiques carry elegant evening wear by local designers like Allan Chai, Jut Ling, Thomas Wee, and Celia Loe. **Francis Cheong** (✉ #02–18 Paragon, 390 Orchard Rd., Orchard ☎ 6734–0012) produces gowns fit for the red carpet. **Frederick Lee Bridal** (✉ 98 Tanjong Pagar Rd., Tanjong Pagar ☎ 6323–4372 🌐 www.frederickbridal.com) makes eye-catching bridal gowns and evening wear.

INTERNATIONAL DESIGNERS At the heart of Orchard Road in Takashiyama in Ngee Ann City you'll find Louis Vuitton, Shanghai Tang, Celine, and sundry elite designers. In the Paragon, across the street, are stores including Prada, Versus, and Jean-Paul Gaultier. Walking down Orchard Road, you're likely to see more brands than on a herd of cattle. This shopper's paradise has every major label covered. **The Link** (✉ #03–03 Palais Renaissance, 390 Orchard Rd., Orchard ☎ 6335–4648) boutique carries upscale brands, including Stella McCartney and Chloe. Fodor'sChoice ★ **Club 21** (✉ #01–02 Four Seasons Hotel Shopping Arcade, 190 Orchard Blvd., Orchard ☎ 6235–0753) has fashions for men and women by such designers as Helmut Lang and John Galliano. You can access this boutique from Orchard Road via the Hilton.

Jewelry

Singapore is a reliable place to buy jewelry, and there are so many jewelers that prices are competitive. Never accept the first price offered, no matter how posh the store. (All jewelers give enormous discounts, usually 30% or more, but some, especially in hotels, don't mention this until pressed.) Most will also copy designer pieces; however, this may take more than a week depending on the intricacy of the design.

All the big-name jewelers are here; there's **Cartier** (✉ #01–33 Ngee Ann City, 391 Orchard Rd., Orchard ☎ 6734–2427 ✉ Hilton Shopping Gallery, 581 Orchard Rd., Orchard ☎ 6235–0295). **Tiffany & Co.** (✉ #01/02–05 Ngee Ann City, 391 Orchard Rd., Orchard ☎ 6735–8823) has a bilevel store. One of the many small jewelers in Takashimaya is **Hour Glass** (✉ #01–02 Ngee Ann City, 391 Orchard Rd., Orchard ☎ 6734–2420), which carries dozens of designer watches. **Je T'Aime** (✉ #02–12 Ngee Ann City, 391 Orchard Rd., Orchard ☎ 6734–2275) is a reasonably priced jeweler with trendy designs. **Larry's** (✉ #02–12A Ngee Ann City, 391 Orchard Rd., Orchard ☎ 6732–3222) is a popular store with several branches in Singapore. The patient staff can tailor designs to suit many budgets and tastes. **Loang & Noi** (✉ #01–23 Paragon, 390 Orchard Rd. ☎6732–7218) carries oversize, gem-encrusted jewelry. **Tianpo Jewellery** (✉ #01–43/46 Centrepoint, 176 Orchard Rd. ☎ 6235–1889) has homemade designs at affordable prices.

Luggage & Accessories

With so many purchases, you may be forced to pick up additional luggage to bring everything home. Luggage is a bargain buy in Singapore, and every complex contains several stores that carry designer names including Etienne Aigner, Louis Vuitton, Samsonite, and Delsey. **Planet Traveler** (✉ #04–15/16 Paragon, 390 Orchard Rd., Orchard ☎ 6732–5172) has a luggage repair service. **Felt** (✉ #01–18 Capitol Bldg., 11 Stamford Rd., Colonial Singapore ☎ 6837–3393) carries wallets, suitcases, and similar items in animal prints and glossy leathers.

Pewter & Dinnerware

Pewter is an important craft item in Singapore, as neighboring Malaysia is the world's largest tin producer. Modern pewter items are heavily influenced by Scandinavian design. Jewelry, tiny figurines, ornamental plates, and traditional beer tankards are among the products. Some items are specifically aimed at tourists, such as Raffles plates and Chinese zodiac plaques.

Many tourist stores sell pewter mugs and plates engraved with such iconic images of Singapore as the mythical Merlion. Singapore's largest pewter concern, **Royal Selangor** (✉ #03–02 Centrepoint, 176 Orchard Rd., Orchard ☎ 6235–6633), has better-quality items at its showrooms in Marina Square (✉#02–127, 6 Raffles Blvd. ☎6339–3115) and Raffles City (✉ #03–32, 252 North Bridge Rd. ☎ 6339–3958).

For dinnerware, there's the popular **Christofle** (✉ #02–11/12 Hilton Shopping Gallery, 581 Orchard Rd., Orchard ☎ 6733–7257) boutique. Also try the **Waterford Wedgwood Shop** (✉ #01–01 Delfi Orchard, 402 Orchard Rd., Orchard ☎ 6734–8375) for fine tableware and crystal.

Perfume

Fodor'sChoice ★ Locals flock to **Jamal Kazura Aromatics** (✉ 728 North Bridge Rd., Arab District ☎ 6293–2350) for perfumes, essential oils, and personalized scents. Allow about 30 minutes for a consultation with Mr. Jamal, during which he'll ask questions about your life-style and favorite smells before concocting your signature scent. Call ahead to ensure he'll be there when you want to visit. Prices are comparable to those of name brands. For rare and upscale scents try **Escentials** (✉ #01–24 Raffles Hotel Arcade, 328 North Bridge Rd., Colonial Singapore ☎ 6339–7727).

Silk

Chinese and Thai silk are easy to find in Singapore. For Indian silk in sari lengths, check out the many shops in the Serangoon Road area. You pay only a fraction of what it would cost elsewhere to buy the 6 meters (6.5 yards) of silk required to make a sari, which could be the thin Kashmiri type or the heavier, embroidered Benares type. Thai silks are available by the meter along Arab Street. Tell the shopkeepers what you intend to use the silk for and they can advise you of which type would be most suitable for your needs.

Most emporiums have special departments that sell fabrics or silk clothes (ready-to-wear is standard but some places can tailor clothes for you). For the highest-quality fabrics try **Jim Thompson** (✉ #01–08 Palais Renaissance, 390 Orchard Rd., Orchard ☎ 6738–0768), which sells apparel and bedding. Its sister store, the **Siam Silk Company** (✉ #08–04 Palais Renaissance ☎ 6323–4800), carries silks in varying weights and types.

Tailoring

There are tailors and then there are tailors—what you end up with depends on how well you choose. Tailors who offer 24-hour service usually prepare items of suspect quality. Some guarantee multiple garments as part of a package at an unbelievably cheap price; these establishments often use fabric and sewing techniques that reflect their prices. Another indication of danger is not seeing a tailor on the premises. Anyone can set up shop as a tailor by filling a store with fabrics and then subcontracting the work; the results from such places are seldom gratifying. Allow 4–5 days for a good job. **Justmen** (✉ #01–36/39, 19 Tanglin Rd., Orchard ☎ 6737–3228), in the Tanglin Shopping Centre, is among the superior men's tailors. Men and women can choose from two tailors on the second floor of the Raffles Hotel Arcade. **Coloc Tailor** (✉ #02–29, 328 North Bridge Rd., Colonial Singapore ☎ 6338–9767) is one of the few tailors that can whip up a high-quality suit within 24 hours. A few doors down, **CYC Shanghai Shirt** (✉ #02–24, 328 North Bridge Rd. ☎ 6336–3556) has more than 1,000 fabrics.

UNDERSTANDING
SINGAPORE

SINGAPORE AT A GLANCE

Fast Facts

Capital: Singapore
National anthem: *Majulah Singapura* (Onward Singapore)
Type of government: Parliamentary republic
Independence: August 9, 1965 (from Malaysian Federation)
Constitution: June 3, 1959, amended in 1965 (based on preindependence constitution)
Legal system: Based on English common law
Suffrage: 21, universal and compulsory
Legislature: Unicameral 84-seat Parliament; members elected to five-year terms by popular vote; also up to nine nominated members

Population: 4.4 million
Population density: 6,375 people per square km (16,492 people per square mi)
Median age: Female: 36.6, male: 35.9
Life expectancy: Female: 84.3, male: 79.0
Infant mortality rate: 2.3 deaths per 1,000 live births
Literacy: 93%
Language: Chinese (official), Malay (official and national), Tamil (official), English (official)
Ethnic groups: Chinese 76%; Malay 14%; Indian 8%; other 2%
Religion: Buddhist (Chinese), Muslim (Malays), Christian, Hindu, Sikh, Taoist, Confucianist

Geography & Environment

Land area: 683 square km (264 square mi); almost four times the size of Washington, DC
Coastline: 193 km (120 mi)
Terrain: Lowland; undulating central plateau with water catchment area and nature preserve
Islands: Pulau Bukum, Pulau Tekong, Sentosa

Natural resources: Deep water ports, fish
Environmental issues: Pollution from industry; limited natural fresh water resources; limited land availability presents waste disposal problems; seasonal smoke/haze resulting from forest fires in Indonesia

Economy

Currency: Singapore dollar
Exchange rate: $0.60
GDP: $109.1 billion
Per capita income: $26,300
Inflation: 0.7%
Unemployment: 5%
Work force: 2 million; financial, business, and other services 49%; manufacturing 18%; other 16%; transportation and communication 11%; construction 6%
Debt: $9.1 billion

Major industries: Chemicals, electronics, entrepot trade, financial services, life sciences, oil drilling equipment, offshore platform construction, petroleum refining, processed food and beverages, rubber processing and rubber products, ship repair
Agricultural products: Copra (coconut meat), eggs, fish, fruit, orchids, ornamental fish, poultry, rubber, vegetables
Exports: $142.4 billion

Major export products: Consumer goods, chemicals, machinery and equipment (including electronics), mineral fuels
Export partners: Malaysia 17%; US 15%; Hong Kong 9%; Japan 7%; China 6%; Taiwan 5%; Thailand 5%; South Korea 4%

Imports: $121.6 billion
Major import products: Chemicals, foodstuffs, machinery and equipment, mineral fuels
Import partners: Malaysia 18%; US 14%; Japan 13%; China 8%; Thailand 5%; Taiwan 5%

Did You Know?

• After 10 years of prohibition, Singapore has relaxed its ban on chewing gum. About 20 brands are sold for "medicinal" and "dental" uses in pharmacies.

• Any dog imported into Singapore gets a 13-millimeter microchip implanted into its neck. The chip contains a number which, when scanned, will connect the pet to its owner.

• Singapore's Swissôtel The Stamford, one of the world's tallest hotels, holds an annual "Vertical Marathon," when racers sprint up its 1,336 steps. Balvinder Singh still holds the race record of six minutes and 55 seconds.

• Singapore's falling birth rate has become such a concern that the government now offers $500 or more in cash to any couple that has a second child. A local newspaper has also printed instructions for having sex in places such as the back of a car and companies have been asked to give young couples flexible work hours to encourage conception.

• With 1,683 square meters (18,117 square feet) of flying water, the Suntec City Fountain of Wealth is the world's largest fountain. It cost $6 million to build in 1997.

• A court in Singapore was recently asked to take up the question of whether a man could divorce his wife via a cell phone text message. Under Islamic law, the man can begin divorce proceedings by declaring, "I divorce you," three times to his wife. The man did so by text message. However, the court ruled that wasn't good enough.

• Hong Lim Park's Speakers Corner is the place to criticize the government, but only with its permission and by its rules. Speakers who wish to exercise Singapore's limited free speech can appear between 7 AM and 7 PM in the park, but must register in advance with police and avoid subjects such as race, language, or religion.

— Collin Campbell

THE CERTAINTY OF CHANGE

HERE'S AN AIR OF CHANGE AND NEW POSSIBILITIES ABOUT SINGAPORE TODAY, partly owing to the transfer of power to Prime Minister Lee Hsien Loong, the nation's third leader since it became fully independent. Loong, who is the son of Singapore's first prime minister, came into office in 2004 and is paying particular attention to the needs of younger citizens. Additionally, the six-day work week has been eliminated for civil servants who are no longer required to work on Saturday.

The place, however, remains crowded, competitive, and well, twitchy. With the total population of four million (including foreigners) zooming towards more than five million by 2040, and with the doors now thrown wide open post-recession to foreign professionals (especially in IT, life sciences/biotech, and the arts), there's a certain creative buzz about the place. There are also economic uncertainties as the nation competes with huge markets and lower costs of doing business in China. More Singaporeans are facing unemployment and have been forced to accept a lower standard of living.

Singaporeans are more aware than ever of the competition from foreigners for local jobs and resources, and slightly more resentful of this than in the past. The government, meanwhile, has to confront declining marriage and fertility rates, which threaten to send the local resident population plummeting to only 2.4 million by about 2050, and the available workforce with it. Add to this the familiar profile of an aging population with too few young people to support them.

How then to maintain the country's prosperity in the future without imported migrant talent? One solution: the government's "Baby Bonus Scheme" essentially pays couples to have more than one child.

Rapid change and the impermanence that goes with it, are nothing new to Singaporeans. Ever since Singapore became an independent nation in 1965, it has been a standing joke among its citizens that if you turn your back for a second, you won't be able to find your way home, you streetscape will have changed so much. Demolition, development, and renewal rotate in endless cycles on the 646-square-km (249-square-mi) tropical island, contributing to the underlying nervous tension of the place.

Singapore's history, pocked with the turbulence of the World War II Japanese Occupation and postwar communist insurgency, has left a residue of anxiety. The vulnerability many feel is heightened by the former British colony's geographical situation as a predominantly Chinese island surrounded by the more traditional and conservative Malayo-Islamic cultures of Malaysia and Indonesia. Hypersensitive to perceived danger and to criticism from without and within, Singapore's government has waged feisty battles with both the foreign press and local liberals.

A real dependence on the global economy and trading system exacerbates this strung-out feeling as the nation darts hither and thither like a nimble shrimp, deftly changing course in response to international currents. But Singapore has always insisted it's a shrimp with a sting in its tail, thanks to a well-equipped army and action-ready citizenry, schooled by compulsory military National Service for all males and regular Civil Defence drills.

This sense of insecurity has hardly been assuaged by recent and continuing turmoil in neighboring Indonesia, nor by a series of spats with prickly half-sibling Malaysia, the key supplier of Singapore's water. On top of this has come economic upheaval in the wake of the so-called

Asian Economic Crisis of 1997–2000, and the strains of globalization. Singapore acts a little humbler nowadays, conscious that it's swimming with much bigger fish.

Singaporeans have a relentless urge to develop and capitalize their limited land resources; the economy has often been primed by massive infrastructural projects, such as the construction of the world's best, most comfortable airport at Changi and also one of the world's most efficient subway systems, the MRT (Mass Rapid Transit System). In addition the government has built blocks of high-rise housing in which more than 86% of Singapore's approximately 4.2 million citizens live as home owners, thanks in part to a government-run compulsory savings fund.

Another local joke (Singaporeans do know how to laugh at themselves, notwithstanding the seemingly earnest formality of their public and official personae) has it that all the Singapore girl cares about in Mr. Right is the Five C's—Car, Condo, Cash, Credit Card, and Country Club. That's sexist—those badges of material success are pretty high on the agenda for all Singaporeans, male and female. In a country where you have to bid for the right to own a car before you even begin to buy one and where landed property sells for about S$5 million, high-rise government-built apartments for half a million, such acquisitions imply serious wealth. Or else debt: credit card debt soared to a record S$2.4 billion in 2004 compared with only S$311 million about a decade before.

Singapore always has been a social laboratory. Its citizens take pride in doing it their way, making up their own rules. Western concepts of liberal democracy, freedoms of the press, speech, and assembly, privacy of information, and the like have often been brushed aside as bothersome brakes on action by a People's Action Party (PAP) government repeatedly re-elected to overwhelming majority power since 1959. Detention without trial for both criminal elements and those deemed political internal security risks is a weapon of state inherited from the British colonial administration and still occasionally used.

There being little real prospect of electoral defeat for the PAP, a certain stability permitting efficient long-term planning has resulted. The populace is largely compliant, give or take a few intellectuals, in return for the government's guarantee of a "full rice bowl": it's an ancient, essentially Confucian, social contract.

Yet Singapore is now in one of its more liberal phases, actively encouraging the arts and even (still highly controlled) political experiments such as the "Speaker's Corner" for sidewalk orators brave enough to sip on the heady brew of free speech. The eminent former Senior Minister Lee Kuan Yew has publicly discussed the possibility that Singapore may have a subterranean gay culture in its midst. And the government says it wants its hitherto cautious citizens to dare to make mistakes, to take risks, and to innovate.

All this is largely pragmatic, as Singapore often is. The authorities are frightened that if Singapore doesn't become more of a fun city, more daring, it may lose a new generation of economic investors to more freewheeling locations such as Sydney or London. But there are always contradictions, two steps forward, one backward: the more permissive artistic environment notwithstanding, jumpy censors still forced nearly three dozen cuts in Singaporean director Royston Tan's movie *15*.

That Singapore favors tough laws—hanging for drug trafficking or mere association with firearms carried for a criminal purpose, and caning for various offenses, including immigration visa overstay and vandalism—is well known. Yet it has to be said that the streets of Singapore are among the safest in the world to walk alone at night.

There's an old saw that Singapore is "a fine city"—S$1,000 fine for littering, S$500 for smoking indoors, S$500 for not flushing the toilet; it's all part of the Singaporean penchant for order, orderliness, and Victorian-style propriety (and, sometimes, hypocrisy to match).

In pursuit of order and decorum, chewing gum is a controlled substance available only from pharmacies for prescription "therapeutic uses" (in the past, kids were jamming up MRT sliding doors and littering streets with the stuff) and not only nudity in public places but also nudity in private places visible to the public (e.g., from your own apartment window) carries a fine of S$2,000 or three months in jail. Another law holds parents liable for their minor children's delinquency, and yet another allows parents to sue grown children for financial support.

But beneath the orderly surface, tremendous social change is under way. Confronted with its limits to growth, Singapore is externalizing its economy, intentionally creating mini-Singapores abroad, notably in China and India. It's also networking with extensive expatriate and emigrant Singaporean communities in Australia, Britain, Canada, and the United States, among other locations. A general broadening of the national mind has been the inevitable result.

With the Five C's becoming ever less affordable, jobs sparser, and salaries lower than they were just a few years ago, many young Singaporeans are reassessing their culture's fabled work ethic, wondering if it's really worth striving so hard. That's a big change from their parents' attitude.

In a sense, Singapore wears a reversible costume—Western suit/Mandarin jacket—and swaps Chinese opera masks at will to reflect whatever character it wants to play at any given moment. That makes it a uniquely deceptive place, difficult to know beyond the Western gloss, hence treacherous for the unwary.

Behind the computer terminals sit people who set superstitious store in the power of numbers (unlucky 4 brings death, while lucky 8 wins prosperity) and position their homes and business premises according to the precepts of feng shui, or geomancy; in their leisure hours, some of them may be temple spirit mediums or fire-walkers.

Careful background reading, particularly of the country's history, will help you to understand these contradictions, as will study of Singapore's various languages, including that vibrant street-jive creole "Singlish," a potpourri of English, Chinese, and Malay impenetrable to the native English-speaker. (Fortunately, many Singaporeans can switch to an approximation of English, besides which the nation is permanently in the throes of an official "Speak Good English" campaign). And don't forget to talk to taxi drivers—they're very wise.

Most foreigners in Singapore (including several hundred thousand "guest workers," mostly construction laborers and maids, who do the dirtier work most Singaporeans will not do anymore) are mere birds of passage, but some have found reasons to linger. They find it hard to put their finger on what it is that has made them stay: "It's just a certain something." Some may point to an underlying gentleness bordering on innocence, a childlike enjoyment of simple, often material, pleasures, a reluctance to be openly rude, and a respect for authority and older folk that together typify the Singaporean. Others relish the vibrant multicultural street life of a tropical city. Still others cite the energy of the place, the constant sense of being busy and purposeful, of going somewhere.

As in a traditional arranged marriage, you have to *learn* to love Singapore—it's not a love-at-first-sight place. And as the old song goes, to know it is to love it. It only takes time.

— Ilsa Sharp

FROM LION CITY TO ASIAN TIGER: A BRIEF HISTORY

MODERN SINGAPORE dates its history from the early morning of January 29, 1819, when a representative of the British East India Company, Thomas Stamford Raffles, stepped ashore at the mouth of the Singapore River, beginning the process that would quickly turn a sleepy backwater into one of Asia's main commercial and financial centers. But let us go a bit farther back.

The Early Days
Though little is known of Singapore's early history, it is clear that by the 7th-century AD Malays had a settlement here known as Temasek—"sea town." According to legend, a 13th-century prince of Palembang (Sumatra) landed on the island while seeking shelter from a storm and sighted a strange animal, which he believed to be a lion but was more likely a tiger. The prince subsequently fought and defeated the ruler of the settlement and proclaimed himself king, then renamed the island Singa Pura, Sanskrit for "lion city."

The first recorded history of Singapore, from a Chinese chronicler who visited in 1330, describes a thriving Malay settlement. By the 14th century, Singa Pura had become an active trading city important and wealthy enough to build a walled fortress—and to make others covet the island. Drawn into a battle between the Java-based Majapahit empire and the Siamese kingdom for control of the Malay Peninsula, Singa Pura was destroyed and the settlement abandoned to the jungle.

In 1390 or so, Iskandar Shah (or Parameswara, as some called him), another Palembang prince, broke from the Majapahit empire and was granted asylum on the island. After killing the local chieftain, he installed himself as ruler but was driven out before long by the Javanese

and fled north into the peninsula. Singa Pura became a Thai vassal state until it was claimed by the Malacca Sultanate, which Iskandar Shah had established and brought to great prominence a few years after fleeing the island.

When, in 1511, the Portuguese seized Malacca, the Malay admiral fled to Singa Pura and established a new capital at Johor Lama. Obscurity engulfed Singa Pura in 1613, when the Portuguese reported laying waste to a small Malay settlement at the mouth of the river.

Enter Raffles
With the development of shipping routes to the West around the Cape of Good Hope and the opening of China to trade, the Malay Peninsula became strategically and commercially important to the West. To protect its shipping interests, the British secured Penang in 1786 and threw the Dutch out of Malacca in 1795. (The Dutch had thrown the Portuguese out earlier.) In 1818, to prevent any further northward expansion by the Dutch, who controlled the East Indies (now Indonesia), Lord Hastings, governor-general of India, gave tacit approval to Thomas Stamford Raffles, an employee of the British East India Company, to secure a British trading settlement and harbor on the southern part of the Malay Peninsula.

On January 29, 1819, Raffles made an exploratory visit to Singa Pura, which had come under the dominion of the Sultan of Johore and where many Malays had forged piratical alliances with Bugis seafarers, terrorizing the seas around the island. When Raffles arrived, the two sons of the previous sultan, who had died six years earlier, were in dispute over who would inherit the throne. Raffles backed the claim of the elder brother, Tunku Hussein Mohamed Shah, and proclaimed him sultan.

Offering to support the new sultanate with British military strength, Raffles persuaded the sultan to grant the British a lease allowing them to establish a trading post on the island in return for an annual rent; within a week the negotiations were concluded. (A later treaty ceded the island outright to the British in return for increased pensions and cash payments for the sultan and his island representative.)

Thus began the continual rapid changing and adapting that characterizes Singapore to this day: within three years, the small fishing village, surrounded by swamps and jungle and populated by only tigers and a few hundred Malays, besides some Chinese farmers in the interior, had become a boomtown of 10,000 immigrants, administered by 74 British employees of the East India Company. In 1826 Singapore joined Penang and Malacca in Malaya to form the British India–controlled Straits Settlements (named for the Strait of Malacca, also called the Straits—the channel between Sumatra and the Malay Peninsula that connects the Indian Ocean with the South China Sea). In 1867 the Straits Settlements broke from British-Indian control and became a crown colony in its own right.

As colonial administrators and businessmen, the British led a segregated life, maintaining the British lifestyle and shielding themselves from the local population and the climate. In the humid tropical heat, they would promenade along the Padang (cricket green), men in high-collared, buttoned-up white linen suits and women in grand ensembles complete with corsets, petticoats, and long kid gloves. In part, they believed that maintaining a distance and the appearance of invulnerability would help them win the respect and fear of the locals. Indeed, the heavily outnumbered colonials needed all the respect they could muster. But holding on to familiar ways also gave the colonials a sense of security in this foreign land where danger was never far away—in the mid-1850s, for

example, five people a week were carried off by tigers. Fevers, malaria, and dysentery were also constant threats.

As Singapore grew, the British erected splendid public buildings, churches (including St. Andrew's Cathedral, built to resemble Netley Abbey in Hampshire, England), and hotels, often using Indian convicts for labor. The Muslim, Hindu, Taoist, and Buddhist communities—swelling rapidly from the influx of fortune-seeking settlers from Malaya, India, and South China—built mosques, temples, and shrines. Magnificent houses for wealthy merchants sprang up, and the harbor became lined with *godowns* (warehouses) to hold all the goods passing through the port.

It was certainly an exotic trade that poured through Singapore. Chinese junks came loaded with tea, porcelain, silks, and artworks; Bugis (Indonesian) schooners carried in cargoes of precious spices, rare tropical hardwoods, camphor, and produce from all parts of Indonesia. These goods, and more like them from Siam (now Thailand), the Philippines, and elsewhere in the region, were traded in Singapore for manufactured textiles, coal, iron, cement, weapons, machinery, and other fruits of Europe's industrial revolution. Another major product traded here by the British was opium, grown in India and sold to the Chinese.

Meanwhile, much of the island was still covered by thick jungle. As late as the 1850s, there were dozens of tigers still to be found here. Early experiments with agriculture (spices, cotton, coffee, and the like) were soon abandoned, as almost nothing except coconuts would grow successfully in the sandy and marshy soil. (Singapore does, however, have the distinction of having introduced the rubber plant to Malaya: in 1877 the first seedlings were successfully grown here by botanist H. N. Ridley, then director of Singapore's Botanic Gardens, from plants brought out of Brazil.)

With the advent of steamships (which found Singapore's deep-water harbor ideal) and the opening of the Suez Canal in 1869, the port thrived as the "Gateway to the East." Its position at the southern end of the Straits made it a vital link in the chain of ports and coaling stations for steamers. Shipyards were established to repair the oceangoing cargo carriers and to build the ever-increasing number of barges and lighters bringing cargo ashore to the godowns. With the development of the rubber industry in Malaya starting in the 1870s, Singapore became the world's top exporter of the commodity.

The 20th Century

By the turn of the century, Singapore had become the entrepôt of the East, a mixture of adventurers and "respectable middle classes." World War I hardly touched the island, although its defenses were strengthened to support the needs of the British navy, for which Singapore was an important base. Until 1921 the Japanese and the British were allies and no need was felt to maintain a large naval presence in the region, but then the United States, anxious about Japan's growing military strength, prevailed on Britain to cancel its treaty with the Japanese, and defense of Singapore became a priority. A massive military expansion took place: barracks were created for up to 100,000 troops, the great naval base of Sembawang was built in the north, and Sentosa Island (then called "Blakang Mati" or Death Behind), was heavily fortified with huge naval guns.

As the likelihood of war in the Pacific grew, Singapore's garrison was further strengthened, and naval shipyards and airfields were constructed. The British were complacent about the impregnability of Singapore, expecting that any attack would come from the sea and assuming that they were well prepared to meet such an attack. But the Japanese landed to the north, in Malaya. The two British battleships that had been posted to Singapore

were sunk, and Japanese land forces raced through the dense jungles of the peninsula, some 18,000 of them on bicycles.

When the Japanese made their first bombing runs on Singapore, all the city's lights were on. The key to turn off the switch was in the governor's pocket, and he was at the movies. The big guns on Sentosa Island sat idle, trained vainly on the quiet sea; they were not designed to fire on land forces. In February 1942 the Japanese captured Singapore.

Huge numbers of Allied civilians and military were sent to Changi Prison; others were marched off to prison camps in Malaya or to work on Thailand's notorious "Death Railway." The 3½ years of occupation was a time of privation and fear for the civilian population; up to 100,000 deaths are estimated to have occurred during this period. The Japanese surrendered on August 21, 1945, and the Allied military forces returned to Singapore. However, the security of the British Empire was never again to be felt, and independence for British Southeast Asia was only a matter of time. The Japanese victory had dented the prestige of the former colonial masters.

Military control of Singapore ended in 1946. The former Straits Settlements crown colony was dissolved, and the island became a separate crown colony, with a partially elected legislative council representing various elements of the community. The first election was held in 1948. In the 1950s, the degree of autonomy allowed Singapore increased and various political parties were formed. One of these was the People's Action Party (PAP), established in 1954 under the leadership of a young Chinese lawyer, Lee Kuan Yew, who had recently graduated from Cambridge University in England.

In 1957 the British government agreed to the establishment of an elected 51-member legislative assembly. General elections in 1959 gave an overwhelming majority—

43 of 51 seats—to the PAP, and Lee Kuan Yew became Singapore's first prime minister. In 1963 Singapore became part of the Federation of Malaysia, along with the newly independent Malaysia, a merger opposed violently by Singapore's left-wing and communist factions.

Mainly due to the Malays' anxiety over a possible takeover by Singapore's ethnic Chinese, the merger didn't work. When it broke up two years later, Singapore became an independent sovereign state (its independence day—August 9, called National Day—is celebrated each year in grand style). In 1967 Singapore issued its own currency for the first time, and in the general election of 1968 the PAP won all 58 seats in Parliament.

In 1971 the last of the British military forces left the island. The economic future of the nation seemed unsure: how could it survive without the massive British military expenditure? But Singapore did more than survive—it boomed. The government engaged in programs for rapid modernization of the nation's infrastructure to attract foreign investment and to help its businesses compete in world markets.

The electorate stayed faithful to Lee Kuan Yew and the PAP, returning the party almost unchallenged in one election after another. It was something of a surprise when, at a by-election in 1981, a single opposition member, Indian lawyer J. B. Jeyaretnam, was elected to Parliament, followed by a second non-PAP member in the general election of 1984. The PAP's popular majority suffered more reverses over time, but recovered somewhat during the latter part of Prime Minister Goh Chok Tong's stewardship in the late 1990s. The party is still sufficiently entrenched to hold all but a few of the parliamentary seats. As acknowledged elder statesman (Minister Mentor), Lee still acts as the guiding hand behind the PAP and, hence, the government. However, recent events such as a casino project in the Southern Islands area, an idea that was anathema to Lee when he was in office, suggest that younger generations represented by his own son, Lee Hsien Loong, the current Prime Minister, may be flexing their muscles.

MODERN SINGAPOREANS are proud of their nation's multiracial heritage. In 1911 the census found 48 races speaking 54 languages, though some of these races have dwindled since then. Once 5,000 strong, the Armenian community, which built the Armenian Apostolic Church of St. Gregory in 1835, numbers fewer than 50 today. The Sephardic Jews, mostly from Iraq, Iran, and India, have moved out of Singapore to Israel, Australia, and elsewhere; just two synagogues, one on Waterloo Street and one on Oxley Rise, survive. The fortunes amassed by the cultured Arab merchants and scholars who invested energetically in real estate have passed into the hands of the few Arab families who remain, sometimes mistakenly categorized as Malays.

Still, numerous ethnic communities exist: Filipinos, Japanese, Thais, Germans, Swiss, and Italians. There are also about 20,000 Eurasians—half British, Dutch, or Portuguese; half Filipino, Chinese, Malay, Indian, Thai, Sri Lankan, or Indonesian. An overwhelming 97% of the population, however, come from among just three ethnic groups: Chinese, Malay, and Indian. The Chinese now constitute 76% of Singapore's total population. It had been Lee Kuan Yew's stated wish to make Singapore multiracial, but increasingly in his later years he has spoken of Singapore as a Sinic society and sought ethnic-Chinese immigrants from all over the world.

The Chinese

Raffles had one ambition for Singapore— to make it a thriving trading port that would secure British interests in the Orient and undermine the Dutch. To achieve these goals, he made the island a free port. Traders flocked to Singapore, and soon so did thousands of Chinese in search of work. Every year during the northeast monsoon, junks crammed to the gunnels with half-starved Chinese would ride the winds to Singapore. Many arrived intent only on saving money and then returning to their families on mainland China. However, most did not make the return journey.

These immigrants were from many different ethnic groups with different languages, different foods, different clothes, and often different religions. Each group carved out its own section of Chinatown, the part of Singapore that Raffles' master plan (drawn up with the intention of avoiding racial tensions) had allotted the Chinese, and there they lived basically separate lives.

The largest group of immigrants was the **Hokkien,** traders and merchants from southern Fukien Province, who now make up 43% of the Chinese population and still work predominantly as merchants. The early arrivals settled in Amoy Street. One of Singapore's oldest temples, the Temple of Heavenly Happiness (Thian Hock Keng), was built in 1841 by Hokkien immigrants in honor of the goddess of the sea, and here they made offerings in thanks for their safe voyage.

On Philip Street in Chinatown is the Wak Hai Cheng Bio Temple, also dedicated to a goddess of the sea. It was built by the **Teochews,** the second-largest immigrant group (constituting 22% of Singapore's Chinese), who came from the Swatow region in Guangdong Province. The temple suggests one of their chosen professions— they dominate the port and maritime labor force—but they also make a strong showing as cooks.

The **Cantonese** are the third-largest group, making up 16.5% of the Chinese population. They are often artisans and craftsmen. Their Fuk Tak Chi Temple on Telok Ayer Street is dedicated to Tua Pek Kong, who can bring prosperity and safety to a voyage. Southern neighbors of the Teochews on the mainland, the Cantonese dedicate enormous amounts of time and energy to eating. Three-fourths of all the Chinese restaurants in Singapore serve Cantonese food.

The **Hakka**—who had lived a nomadic existence in Fukien, Guangdong, and Szechuan provinces—remember old times at the Ying He Hui Guan (Hakka Clan Association Hall), just off Telok Ayer Street, which served as a sort of foster home for immigrants stepping off the junks a century ago. The **Hainanese**, many of whom work in hotel or domestic service, were employed as cooks by the colonials (you'll often see "breaded pork cutlet" on the menus at Hainanese restaurants).

By the 1920s, the number of **Straits Chinese**—those born in Singapore or in Malaya—exceeded the number of mainland-born Chinese in Singapore. Though some continued to consider themselves "overseas Chinese," an increasing number began to recognize Singapore as their home. The Straits Chinese British Association (formed at the turn of the century) served as a forum for exchanging views on Singapore's future and, unofficially, worked alongside the colonial administration in the island's development. Chinese families that had made fortunes in the 19th century began sending their children to British universities. These graduates became businessmen, politicians, and statesmen; they still wield quiet influence, although their political power was hurt because of the perception, at independence, that their community was too close to the British rulers.

One of Singapore's most interesting aspects is the more than two dozen festivals celebrated so colorfully each year, and more than half of these are Chinese, based on traditions brought over from the mainland. Even the keenest Chinese businessman doesn't discount fortune—and festivals are considered important in ensuring good fortune, by appeasing ancestral spirits during the Festival of the Hungry Ghosts, celebrating the birthday of the mischievous Monkey God, or ushering in the Chinese New Year.

The Malays

When Raffles landed on the island in 1819, there were perhaps 100 Malay houses in a small fishing village on the banks of the Singapore River. Aside from the Malays, there were about 30 *orang laut* (sea gypsies) living farther upriver in houseboats. (The orang laut, aborigines from Johore, were later decimated by an epidemic of smallpox, but there were still families living in waterborne settlements until after the Second World War. Since then they have come ashore, intermarried with Malays, and become mainstream Singaporean.)

To help develop Singapore as a free port, the East India Company encouraged Malays to migrate from the peninsula. By 1824 their numbers had grown to more than 5,000, and today Malays account for 15% of Singapore's ethnic mix.

Malays, in contrast to the Chinese, did not adapt to the freewheeling entrepreneurial spirit that engulfed Singapore. Overwhelmingly Muslim, they sought fulfillment in serving the community and winning its respect rather than in profit making. Their lives traditionally centered on the *kampong*, or village, where the family houses are built around a central compound and food is grown for communal use. Kampongs have mostly disappeared from Singapore, but you can see one on Pulau Ubin island, off Singapore's northeast coast, or in Johor state in Malaysia, across the northern Causeway. Kampongs communicate a pervasive community spirit and the warmth extends to visitors. With luck, you may even get to witness the traditional Malay sport called *sepak takraw*—similar to badminton, except that the feet, arms, and body are used instead of rackets.

The early Malays chose to be fishermen, woodcutters, or carpenters rather than capitalists, and to concentrate on the community and their relationship with Allah. The latter still matters very greatly to them. (No visitor to Singapore can fail to hear the plaintive call to prayer five times a day from the Sultan Mosque, whose gold-painted domes and minarets tower above the shophouses.) Hence, wealth and power have for the most part eluded the majority of the Malay community. However, substantial changes over the past decade or so have resulted in a growing Malay middle class and increased numbers of Malay businessmen (along with businesswomen) and professionals.

The Malay culture has infiltrated all aspects of Singapore life. Though there are four "official" languages—Malay, Mandarin, Tamil, and English—Malay is the "national language," used, for example, in the national anthem, "Majulah Singapura" (May Singapore Prosper). Many Singaporeans have incorporated Malay food into their cooking as well. Nonya (Malay for "woman" or "wife"), or Peranakan, cuisine is a blending of Chinese and Malay cultures enlivened with local spices.

The Indians

At least seven centuries before Christ, Indian merchants were crossing the Bay of Bengal to trade in Malaya. Some settled in, and their success in trade made them respected members of the community. Hindu words were absorbed into the Malay language; Singapore's name, in fact, derives from the Sanskrit *singa pura* ("lion city").

With success stories floating back to the Indian subcontinent, little encouragement was needed to entice other Indians to seek their fortunes in the new Singapore. Some, however, had no choice. Seeing a way of both ridding Calcutta of its miscreants and building an infrastructure in Singapore, the East India Company sent Indian convicts to the island in chains and put them to work draining marshes and erecting bridges, churches, and other public buildings. For themselves, the Indians built Sri Mariamman, Singapore's oldest and most important Hindu temple, in 1862 (it has since been expanded and repainted).

In fact, serving time in Singapore during the mid-19th century was not so bad. The convicts were encouraged to learn a trade, and often, after their term was served, they opted to stay. Many Tamils from South India went as indentured laborers to work Malaya's rubber plantations and, when their time was up, moved to Singapore.

The majority of Indians in Singapore are, in fact, Hindu Tamils from Tamil Nadu in South India. There are also Muslims from South India and, in smaller numbers, Bengalis, Biharis, Gujaratis, Marathis, Kashmiris, and Punjabis, from the north, west, and east of India. From Sri Lanka come other Hindu Tamils, as well as the Sinhalese (often mistaken for Indians), who are neither Hindu nor Muslim but follow the gentle teachings of Hinayana Buddhism. The Sinhalese traditionally work in jewelry and precious gems; incidentally, they are among Singapore's finest cricket players—witness their domination of the teams playing at the prestigious Singapore Cricket Club.

During the colonial period, the Indians in Singapore, much like other ethnic groups, looked to their homeland, India, and more particularly their region, as their true home. They would send money back to their families and dream of returning. When the Japanese occupied the island in World War II, some 20,000 Singaporean Indians volunteered for the Japanese Indian National Army (INA), led by Subhas Chandra Bose, which took advantage of Indian nationalism and Japanese expansionist goals in an attempt to evict the British from India. This collaboration left Singapore's Chinese and Malay communities—

both of which had suffered greatly at the hands of the Japanese—distrustful of the Indians in general. However, India, after its own independence in 1947, actively discouraged expatriates from returning "home."

Today, Indians, who account for 8% of Singapore's population, increasingly see themselves as Singaporean. Their respect for education has taken them into the influential professions of law, medicine, and government. Indians, however, remain deeply tied to their community and traditional customs. Hinduism is a powerful force—Singapore has more than 20 major temples devoted to Hindu gods—and some of the Tamil Hindu festivals (such as Thaipusam) are expressed with more feverish ritualism than in India, as often happens with communities in diaspora. Indian food, too, remains true to its roots; it has been said that one can eat better curries in Singapore than in India.

SINGAPORE'S DINING SCENE reflects the three main cultures that have settled here—Chinese, Indian, and Malay—as well as the many other influences that contribute to the island's diverse mix. Singapore's history as a port through which the products of the famed Spice Islands were traded has left its people in love with spicy food. But it's not necessarily the kind of spiciness that burns the roof of your mouth; often, spicy here means well flavored, seasoned to perfection.

Spice Traditions

Basically, there are two schools of spicy cooking, both well represented in Singaporean cuisine. The first is the Indian tradition, which uses dried spices such as cardamom, cloves, cumin, fennel, fenugreek, white and black pepper, chili peppers, powdered turmeric root, and mustard and poppy seeds. These spices are sometimes used whole but are more often ground into a powder (broadly referred to as curry powder) or made into a paste used as a base for gravies. (In Asia, gravies are thickened not with flour or cream but usually with these pastes.)

The second school is Southeast Asian, and it relies mainly on fresh roots and aromatic leaves. Typically, lemongrass, turmeric root, galangal, ginger, garlic, onions, shallots, and other roots are pounded into smooth pastes, with candlenuts and shrimp paste, to again form a base for gravies and soups. Leaves—such as turmeric, lime, coriander, several varieties of basil—add a distinctive bouquet.

The Cuisines of Many Cultures

Chinese

Chinese make up about 76% of Singapore's population, and this predominance is reflected in the wide assortment of restaurants representing their ethnic groups. The following is a sampling of the many Chinese cuisines represented in Singapore.

The best-known regional Chinese cuisine is **Cantonese,** with its fresh, delicate flavors. Vegetable oil, instead of lard, is used in the cooking, and crisp vegetables are preferred. Characteristic dishes are stir-fried beef in oyster sauce; steamed fish with slivers of ginger; and deep-fried duckling with mashed taro.

Dim sum is a particularly Cantonese style of eating, featuring a selection of bite-size steamed, baked, or deep-fried dumplings, buns, pastries, and pancakes, with a variety of savory or sweet flavorings. Popular items are the *char siew pau* (a steamed bread bun filled with diced, sweetened, barbecued pork) and *siew mai* (a steamed mixture of minced prawns, pork, and sometimes water chestnuts). The selection, which might comprise as many as 50 offerings, may also include such dishes as soups, steamed pork ribs, and stuffed green peppers. Traditionally, dim sum are served three on a plate in bamboo steamer baskets on trolleys that are pushed around the restaurant. You simply wait for the trolleys to come around, then point to whichever item you would like. The more elegant style now is to order dim sum à la carte so that they will be prepared freshly for you.

If you walk around Chinatown's fresh markets or the sidewalks of South Bridge Road towards Tanjong Pagar, you'll notice the importance of dried ingredients in Chinese cooking. The people here are **Teochew** (or Chao Zhou), mainly fisherfolk from Swatow in the eastern part of Guangdong Province. Though their cooking has been greatly influenced by the Cantonese, it is quite distinctive. Teochew chefs cook with clarity and freshness, often steaming or braising, with an emphasis on fish and vegetables. Oyster sauce and sesame oil—staples of Cantonese cooking—do not play a large role in Teochew cooking; Teochew chefs pride themselves on enhancing the natural flavors of the foods.

Characteristic Teochew dishes are *lo arp* and *lo goh* (braised duck and goose), served with a vinegary chili-and-garlic sauce; crispy liver or prawn rolls; stewed, preserved vegetables; black mushrooms with fish roe; and a unique rice porridge called *congee,* which is eaten with small dishes of salted vegetables, fried whitebait, black olives, and preserved-carrot omelets.

Szechuan food is very popular in Singapore, as the spicy-hot taste suits the local palate. This style of cooking is distinguished by the use of bean paste, chilies, and garlic, as well as nuts and poultry. The result is dishes with pungent flavors of all sorts, harmoniously blended. Simmering and smoking are common forms of preparation, and noodles and steamed bread are preferred accompaniments. Characteristic dishes to order are hot-and-sour soup, sautéed chicken or prawns with dried chilies, camphor- and tea-smoked duck, and spicy fried string beans.

Pekingese cooking originated in the imperial courts. It makes liberal use of strong-flavored roots and vegetables, such as peppers, garlic, ginger, leeks, and coriander. Dishes are usually served with noodles or dumplings and baked, steamed, or fried bread. The most famous dish is Peking duck: the skin is lacquered with aromatic honey and baked until it looks like dark mahogany and is crackly crisp. Other choices are clear winter melon soup, emperor's purses (stir-fried shredded beef with shredded red chili, served with crispy sesame bread), deep-fried minced shrimp on toast, and baked fish on a hot plate.

The greatest contribution to Singaporean cuisine made by the many arrivals from China's **Hainan** island, off the north coast of Vietnam, is "chicken rice": whole chickens are lightly poached in a broth flavored with ginger and spring onions; then rice is boiled in the liquid to fluffy perfection and eaten with chopped-up pieces of chicken, which are dipped into a sour and hot chili sauce and dark soy sauce.

Also popular here are Fukienese and Hunanese restaurants. **Fukien** (also known as Hokkien) cuisine emphasizes soups and stews with rich, meaty stocks. Garlic and dark soy sauce are often used, and seafood is prominent. Dishes to order are braised pork belly served with buns, fried oyster, and turtle soup.

Hunanese cooking is dominated by sugar and spices and tends to be more rustic. One of the most famous dishes is beggar's chicken: a whole bird is wrapped in lotus leaves and baked in a sealed covering of clay; when it's done, a mallet is used to break away the hardened clay, revealing a chicken so tender and aromatic that it is more than worthy of an emperor. Other favorites are pigeon soup in bamboo cups, fried layers of bean-curd skin, and honey ham served with bread.

Hakka food is very provincial in character and uses ingredients not normally found in other Chinese cuisines. Red-wine lees are used to great effect in dishes of fried prawns or steamed chicken, producing gravies that are delicious when eaten with rice. Stuffed bean curds and beef balls are other Hakka delicacies.

Indian

Most Indian immigrants to Singapore came from the south, from Madras (now known as Chennai) in Tamil Nadu and Kerala, so **South Indian** cultural traditions tend to predominate here. In Little India, many small and humble restaurants can be found. Race Course Road is a street of curries: at least 10 Indian restaurants, most representing this fiery-hot cooking tradition, offer snacks or meals served on banana leaves. The really adventurous should sample the Singapore Indian specialty fish-head curry (you won't find this in India!). Like all the food served here, this dish, with its hot, rich, sour gravy, is best appreciated when eaten without utensils—somehow, eating with the fingers enhances the flavor!

South Indian cuisine, generally more chili-hot than northern food, relies on strong spices like mustard seed and uses coconut milk liberally. Meals are very cheap, and eating is informal: just survey the cooked food displayed, point to whatever you fancy, then take a seat at a table. A piece of banana leaf will be placed before you, plain rice will be spooned out, and the rest of your food will be arranged around the rice and covered with curry sauce.

Vegetarian cuisine is raised to a high art by South Indian cooks. Other tempting South Indian dishes include fish *pudichi* (fish in coconut, spices, and yogurt), fried prawns and crabs, mutton or chicken *biryani* (a meat-and-rice dish), *brinjal curry* (spiced eggplant), *keema* (spicy minced meat), *vindaloo* (hot spiced meat), *dosai* (savory pancakes), *appam* (rice-flour pancakes), sour lime pickle, and *papadam* (deep-fried lentil wafers). Try a glass of *rasam* (pepper water) to aid digestion and a glass of *lassi* (yogurt drink) or beer to cool things down.

Since the 1960s, **North Indian** food has made a mark in Singapore. Generally found in the more posh restaurants, this cuisine blends aromatic spices with a subtle Persian influence. The main differences between northern and southern Indian cuisine are that northern food is less hot and more subtly spiced than southern and that cow's milk is used as a base instead of coconut milk. North Indian cuisine also uses yogurt extensively to tame the pungency of the spices and depends more on puréed tomatoes and nuts to thicken gravies.

The signature North Indian dish is Tandoori chicken (marinated in yogurt and spices and cooked in a clay urn, or *tandoor*) and fresh mint chutney, eaten with *naan, chapati,* and *paratha* (Indian breads).

Another typical dish is *rogan josh,* lamb braised gently with yogurt until the spices blend into a delicate mix of aromas and flavors. *Ghee,* a nutty clarified butter, is used—often in lavish quantities—to cook and season rice or rice-and-meat dishes (*pulaos* and *biryanis*).

In general, North Indian food is served more elegantly than is South Indian food. The prices can also be considerably higher, but increasingly there are small stalls and cafés offering modest North Indian menus that are affordable. (Beware of ordering prawns in South Indian restaurants, though—they often cost as much as S$8 apiece.)

The **Indian Muslim** tradition is represented in the Arab Street area. Opposite the Sultan Mosque, on North Bridge Road, are small, open-front restaurants serving *roti prata* (a sort of crispy, many-layered pancake eaten with curries), *murtabak* (prata filled with spiced, minced mutton and diced onions), *nasi biryani* (saffron-flavored rice with chicken or mutton), and various curries. These places are for the stouthearted only; they are cramped and not really spic-and-span.

Japanese

Japanese cuisine is a favorite among Singaporean diners. There's a large Japanese community in Singapore to support the extensive displays of Japanese goods in every local supermarket, and restaurants all over the island. Singapore now offers Japanese cuisine equal to the best served in Japan, but quick and cheap sushi meals are a popular office lunch option.

The Japanese eat with studied grace. Dishes look like still-life paintings; flavors and textures both stimulate and soothe. Waitresses quietly appear and then vanish; the cooks welcome you and chat with you.

In Singapore you can savor a modified form of the high art of *kaiseki* (the formal Japanese banquet) in popular family restaurants. It was developed by the samurai class for tea ceremonies and is influenced by Zen philosophy. The food is served on a multitude of tiny dishes and offered to guests as light refreshments. Regulations govern the types of foods that can be served: the seasoning is light, the color schemes must be harmonious, and the foods, whenever possible, must be in their natural shapes. Everything presented is intended for conscious admiration. This stylistic approach is the perfect way to mark a special occasion.

More fun for some are the forms of Japanese dining in which guests can watch the chef exercise his skills right at the table. At a sushi bar, for example, the setting and the performance of the chef as he skillfully wields the knife to create the elegant, colorful pieces of sushi (vinegared rice tinged with wasabi, or green horseradish, and topped with a slice of raw fish) make the meal special. Savor the incredibly fresh flavor and you will be hooked forever. Also watch the chef perform stylistic movements, including knife twirling, at places serving *teppanyaki:* on a large griddle around which diners are seated, fish, meat, vegetables, and rice are lightly seared, and flavored with butter and sake. Sukiyaki, too, is grilled at the table, but the meat is strictly beef and the soup is sweeter; noodles and bean curd are served at the end of the meal as fillers.

Yakitori, a Japanese *satay,* is meat and vegetables grilled to perfection and glazed with a sweet sauce. *Yakiniku* is a grill-it-yourself meal of thin slices of beef, chicken, or Japanese fish. *Shabu-shabu* is a kind of fondue: seafoods and meats are lightly swished in boiling stock, then dipped in a variety of sauces. Tempura is a sort of fritter of remarkable lightness and delicacy; the most popular kinds are made of prawns and vegetables. The dipping sauce is a mix of soy sauce and *mirin* (sweet rice wine), flavored with grated giant white radish and ginger.

Malay and Indonesian

Malay cuisine is often hot and rich. Turmeric root, lemongrass, coriander, *blacan* (prawn paste), chilies, and shallots are combined with coconut milk to create fragrant, spicy gravies. A basic method of cooking is to gently fry the *rempah* (spices, herbs, roots, chilies, and shallots ground to a paste) in oil and when the mixture is fragrant, add meat and either a tamarind liquid, to make a tart spicy-hot sauce, or coconut milk, to make a rich spicy-hot curry sauce. Dishes to look for are *gulai ikan* (a smooth, sweetish fish curry), *sambal telor* (eggs in hot sauce), *empalan* (beef boiled in coconut milk, then deep-fried), *tauhu goreng* (fried bean curd in peanut sauce), and *ikan bilis* (crispy fried anchovies).

Perhaps the best-known Malay dish is *satay*—slivers of marinated beef, chicken, or mutton threaded onto thin coconut sticks, barbecued, and served with a spicy peanut sauce. At most hawker centers, you will find at least one satay seller sitting over his charcoal fire and fanning the embers to grill sticks of satay. Tell the waiter how many of each type of meat you want, and he'll bring the still-smoking satay to your table.

Unlike the Chinese, who have a great tradition of eating out and a few classical schools of restaurant cooking, most Malay families continue to entertain at home, even when celebrating special events, such as marriages. As a consequence, there are very few stylish Malay restaurants; there are a few in the Sultan Mosque and Kampong Glam area, up Kandahar Street.

Indonesian food is very close to Malay; both are based on rice and cooked with a wide variety of spices, and both are Muslim and thus do not use pork. A meal called *nasi padang*—consisting of a number of mostly hot dishes, such as curried meat and vegetables with rice, that offer a range of tastes from sweet to salty to sour to spicy—originally comes from Padang in the Indonesian province of West Sumatra. Ready-cooked dishes are usually displayed buffet-style in glass cases from which customers make their selections.

Nonya

The first Chinese immigrants to this part of the world were the Hokkien. When they settled on the Malay Peninsula, they acquired the taste for Malay spices and soon adapted Malay foods to their cuisine. Nonya food is one manifestation of the marriage of the two cultures, which is also seen in language, music, literature, and clothing. This blended Peranakan culture was called *baba*, as were the men; the women were called *nonya,* and so was the cuisine, because cooking was considered a feminine art.

Nonya cooking combines the finesse and subtlety of Chinese cuisine with the spiciness of Malay cooking. Many Chinese ingredients are used—especially dried foods like Chinese mushrooms, fungus, anchovies, lily flowers, soybean sticks, and salted fish—along with the spices and aromatics used in Malay cooking. A favorite Chinese ingredient is pork, and pork satay is made for the Peranakan home (you won't come across Malay pork satay, since Muslims don't eat pork and find it offensive to be anywhere near it).

The ingenious Nonya cook uses *taucheo* (preserved soybeans), garlic, and shallots to form the rempah needed to make *chap chye* (a mixed-vegetable stew with soy sauce). Other typical dishes are *husit goreng* (an omelet fried with shark's fin and crabmeat) and *otak otak* (a sort of fish quenelle with fried spices and coconut milk). Nonya cooking also features sourish-hot dishes like *garam assam,* which is a fish or prawn broth made with pounded turmeric, shallots, *galangal* (a type of ginger), lemongrass, and shrimp paste. The water for the broth is mixed with preserved tamarind, a sour fruit that adds a delicious tartness.

A few years ago, Nonya cuisine appeared to be dying, like Peranakan culture itself, but since the publication of many Nonya cookbooks, there has been a resurgence of interest and of restaurants serving the food, too.

Thai

Thai cuisine, while linked with Chinese and Malay, is distinctly different in taste. Most Thai dishes are hot and filled with exciting spices and fish aromatics. On first tasting a dish, you may find it stingingly hot (tiny chilies called "chili padi" make the cuisine so fiery), but the taste of the fresh herbs will soon surface. Thai food's characteristic flavor comes from fresh mint, basil, coriander, and citrus leaves; extensive use of lemongrass, lime, vinegar, and tamarind keeps the sour-hot taste prevalent.

Thai curries—such as chicken curry with cashews, salted egg, and mango—use coconut milk and are often served with dozens of garnishes and side dishes. Various sauces are used for dipping; *nam pla,* one favorite, is a salty, fragrant amber liquid made from salted and fermented shrimp.

A popular Thai dish is *mee krob,* crispy fried noodles with shrimp. Other outstanding Thai dishes: *tom yam kung,* hot and spicy shrimp soup (few meals start without it); *gai hor bai toey,* fried chicken wrapped in pandanus leaves; *pu cha,* steamed crab with fresh coriander root and a little coconut milk; and *khao suey,* steamed white rice, which you'll need to soothe any fires that may develop in your mouth.

The larger Thai restaurants are actually seafood markets where you can pick your own swimming creature and tell the waitress how you want it cooked. For drinks, try Singha beer, brewed in Thailand, or *o-liang,* the national drink—very strong black iced coffee sweetened with palm-sugar syrup.

INDEX